REPORT WRITING

by

JOHN BALL
ASSOCIATE PROFESSOR OF ENGLISH
MIAMI UNIVERSITY

CECIL B. WILLIAMS
PROFESSOR OF ENGLISH
OKLAHOMA A. & M. COLLEGE

THE RONALD PRESS COMPANY ⟡ NEW YORK

PE
1478
B3

The English language is the most important scientific instrument at your disposal.
Learn to use it with precision.

—C. W. FOULK

Legend on the wall in the main lecture room, Chemistry Building, The Ohio State University

PREFACE

As LONG AS men make decisions based on information, there will be reports. Engineers will write them and retail buyers; they will be written by accountants, research workers, salesmen, and men and women on all levels of management.

This is a volume for today's students who tomorrow will be writing those reports. It is based on a general, functional approach to report writing. The writer of a report begins with a need for information. He has to fill that need. He seeks the needed information through direct observation, asks questions, or uses libraries, files, and magazines. He may use several of these methods. Finally he uses language and other symbols to report the information he has gathered. Our discussion of this approach to report writing, and of the ways to gather information and to use language, applies to all types of reports.

Since we believe that industrial practice does not justify the systems of classification of reports by subject matter or function found in some texts, we have omitted these groupings in ours. We have avoided also the formula approach to reports. We feel that there are no short cuts or "six easy steps" to good writing of any kind. Learning to write takes practice and time. But this book, we believe, outlines a sound approach, based on the reporter's understanding of his place in the whole information-gathering and communication situation.

Actual practice in industry and business has guided us in this volume. Throughout are many current examples of reports in a wide range of business and professional fields from the actual files of successful professionals.

Readings—articles reprinted from business magazines and other sources—are an important part of this text. In examining the principles and problems of reporting they contribute a further range that comes from having many points of view from practicing experts.

The problems at the end of each chapter and the work materials in Part IV illustrate the variety of reporting situations. These exercises deal with reports of varying sizes—long, short, and medium, and of varying degrees of formality. They include problems requiring the student to collect material from his college community as well as problems that supply material so that the student who has no access to business and industrial sources can still report on problems in industry and business.

Included are many developments of the last few years: readability and readability scales, information theory, the human relations emphasis in industry, reporting as a management-developing tool, and reporting with perspective as opposed to reporting of minutiae. We hope to encourage in the student's approach to report writing an awareness of the latest developments and a readiness for changes to come.

We owe thanks to the men we have worked with in industrial consulting, to the hundreds of students of report writing in our own classes in college and industry, and to our many friends in the American Business Writing Association. They have all helped shape our approach to report writing.

The conventions and publications of ABWA, along with the friendships and associations formed through the organization, were important in the forming of this book. It is hard to single out individuals, but special thanks go to C. R. Anderson, ABWA founder (University of Illinois); Jack Menning (University of Alabama); Ernest Hedgcock (A. & M. College of Texas); K. Baker Horning (University of Oklahoma); Richard Gerfen and Daniel Lang (Northwestern University); Frank Devlin (John Carroll University); Margaret Blickle (The Ohio State University); John Gilliam (The Vulcan Corporation); D. L. Uhling (Remington Rand, Inc.); Hilary Milton (330th Training Publications Squadron, Scott Air Force Base); Robert Bendure, James Purvis, David Thompson, and Max Allen (Armco Steel Corporation); Sybil Lee Gilmore (Standard Register Company); Ray Garrett (Champion Paper & Fibre Company); William Werner (Procter & Gamble); W. C. Gill (Douglas Aircraft Company); Fred E. Pamp (American Management Association); and James Denham, Lawrence Hynes, and John Norman (Miami University).

Through the reporting skill of these men and women and others like them industry has moved forward. Their achievement is one to be proud of, and one we hope you will share.

Oxford, Ohio   JOHN BALL
Stillwater, Oklahoma   CECIL B. WILLIAMS

January, 1955

CONTENTS

PART I

REPORTS AND REPORT WRITING

PART II

PREPARING THE REPORT

PART III

SUPPLEMENTARY READINGS AND
SPECIAL APPLICATIONS

Contents

PART I

Reports and Report Writing

Chapter 1

REPORTS: WHAT AND WHY

THE HEAD of the department asked me to send him a memo on the number of students in my class in Report Writing the first day it met this semester. I counted the students, and here is the note I put under his door:

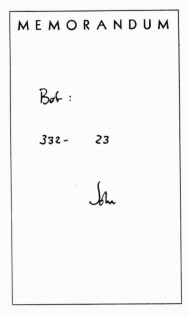

FIGURE 1. Simple Memorandum Report on Class Enrollment.

J. T. Mays sent samples of four types of glue to a General Electric Company laboratory for testing. The chemist, T. J. Maloney, tested the glue and prepared his findings for Mr. Mays:

SUBJECT: GLUE TESTS

Evendale Plant, March 16, 1954

Mr. J. T. Mays
Drafting Policy
Evendale Plant
Building 500

Samples of General Electric Glyptal, Dupont Duco, Agnus, and Barry cements were submitted by you for this laboratory to test. Samples were in good condition and were dated January, 1954. All tests were made in a room with constant temperature of 68°F.

Two stainless steel panels were cemented together with each cement and allowed to set for forty-eight hours. When adhesion was checked by pulling the panels apart, the Dupont Duco cement was found to be the best one, followed in order by General Electric Glyptal, Agnus, and Barry.

Samples of each cement were placed on watch glasses and allowed to dry for forty-eight hours. The watch glasses were then placed in a beaker of water. When checked an hour later, the Dupont Duco, Agnus, and Barry cements were no longer adhering to the watch glasses, but the General Electric Glyptal cement adhered with a hard bond.

T. J. Maloney
Chemical Unit Laboratory
Aircraft Gas Turbine
Building 200 — Ext. 257

FIGURE 2. Memorandum Report on Glue Test. (Reprinted by permission of T. J. Maloney, General Electric Co.)

John Jackson's Plymouth hit Joseph Jaske's Chevrolet at the corner of Reading Road and Northcut Avenue in Cincinnati; Field Claimsman R. A. Schneider of the Central Insurance Company investigated the accident and organized his findings this way:

TRANSMITTAL AND INSTRUCTION FORM

To: _____ W.O.R.O. _____ ☐ Reg. Claims Off.

_____ ☐ Field Claimsman

_____ Ed. Jones _____ ☐ Agent / Region

Date __Fbruary 10, 54__

On Property Fire Claims Only Indicate:

Adjustment Time _____

Copy to _____ Mileage Driven _____

Insured ____ John Jackson _____ Other Expenses _____

Adjuster's Report:

Ed:

The investigation of the auto accident involving our insured, Mr. Jackson, has been completed. The facts brought to light leave no doubt of liability.

Both our insured and claimant were negligent in the operation of the cars they were driving. No agency was developed between the claimant driver and the claimant owner. My conclusions are supported by signed statements of both drivers and the witness. A canvass of the neighboring residents developed no information that had not already been secured. The police report indicated that both drivers had a green light; that is a cynical conclusion.

I will pay Davis for his Chevrolet damage, deny Jaske's injury claim, pay Jackson's collision damage, and reimburse Mrs. Jackson for her medical expenditures.

Sub Pending ☐   Salvage Pending ☐   Risk O.K.? [X] Yes ☐ No

Open Reserves   F. ☐ T. ☐ Comp. ☐ Col. [X] P.D. [X] B.I. ☐ M.P. [X] An. Col. ☐ WC Med. ☐ WC Comp. ☐

Entire File Closed ☐   File Closed This End ☐   By ___ R. A. Schneider ___ F/C

Accident Date __1/28__   Policy No. __96-858__   Claim No. __01-6742__

☐ CLAIMS EXAMINER   ☐ CLAIMS ATTORNEY   ☐ CLAIMS SERVICES (Give Complete Details in Remarks)

Attached are: (in order)
(Auto, MA, PF, GL, BRT)

	(WC Only)
☐ Risk Report	☐ Car Ident.	☐ Employer's Report of Injury
☐ Non-Waiver	☐ Releases	☐ Settlement Agreement
☐ N/L or P/L	☐ Req. For Cash Settlement	☐ A. P. Reports
☐ Diagrams	☐ Med. Pay—Proof of Claim	☐ Statements
☐ Statements	☐ Report on a .... Claim	☐ Inj. Employee's Report
☐ Invest. Memo	☐ Photographs	☐ Adj. Initial Report
☐ Police Reports	☐ Letters	☐ Adj. Supplemental Report
☐ A.P. Reports	☐ P.D. & B.I. Report	
☐ Bills	☐ Supplemental Report	
☐ Repair Orders	☐ Draft Copies	
☐ Estimates		

Claims Services:
☐ Index (Attached I.I.M.)   ☐ See Remarks
☐ Fire and/or Theft Report   ☐ Assign Suit File Number
☐ Sale of Salvage Report
☐ Retail Credit Report
☐ Send A-4
☐ Subrogation
☐ Photostats
☐ Open ____ Reserve
☐ Reopen ____ Reserve
☐ Close ____ Reserve W/O Pay.   ☐ File
☐ Change BI Reserve   ☐ File Active
☐ Reinsurance   ☐ File Closed
☐ Excess Loss

REMARKS: (To Claims Services Only)

By _____

FIGURE 3. Insurance Claim Adjuster's Report. (By permission of R. A. Schneider.)

AUTO ACCIDENT INVESTIGATION

INSURED

John Jackson of 1514 Lincoln St., Cincinnati, Ohio,
was driving his 1951 Plymouth for the purpose of
pleasure at the time of the accident. His only pas-
senger was his wife, Mary, who was sitting in the
front right seat. Both are 36 years of age.

CLAIMANT

Joseph Jaske, age 25, of 1836 Oak St., Cincinnati,
Ohio, was driving a 1953 Chevrolet owned by Paul Davis
of 4362 Sherman Ave., Cincinnati, Ohio. Jaske had
borrowed the Chevrolet for his own purpose and pleasure and was the sole occupant at the time.

WITNESS

The sole witness is David Jaeger, age 46, of 3024 Vine
St., Cincinnati, Ohio. Jaeger was driving a 1949
Oldsmobile.

LOCATION

This accident occurred at the intersection of Reading
Rd. and Northcut Ave., Cincinnati, Ohio. The intersection is controlled by traffic lights operating
green-yellow-red and red-yellow-green. Reading Rd.
is a straight, level, four-lane highway, running
north and south at the scene. North and southbound
travel is divided by a double yellow center line.
Northcut is a straight, level, blacktop, two-lane
street, entering Reading Rd. from the east. Visi-
bility is good on all approaches to the intersection.

DATE AND TIME

January 28, 1954   10:30 P.M.

WEATHER

Clear and dry.

ACCIDENT DESCRIPTION

Jackson was proceeding west on Northcut Ave. As he
approached the intersection, the light changed to red
and he came to a proper stop. The witness, who was
also proceeding west on Northcut Ave., came to a stop
behind Jackson. While waiting for his light to return to green, Jackson put his left turn signals on.
When the light changed to yellow, Jaeger saw a northbound car in the center lane of Reading Rd. This car,
which was the Chevrolet driven by Jaske, was about 70
ft. south of the intersection and moving at approx-

imately 35 miles per hour. Jaske made no attempt to
stop. When the light changed from yellow to green for
Jackson, he instantly started forward into the intersection. Jackson had gone no more than twelve feet
when the front of his car made contact with the center
of the right side of the northbound Chevrolet. The
Chevrolet swerved to the west side of Reading Rd. and
continued north for a distance of 112 feet before
Jaske was able to regain control and stop. The forward motion of Jackson's Plymouth ceased on impact
but the front end turned clockwise as a result of the
collision. The Plymouth stopped in a position of
facing north in the center of Reading Rd. at the north
side of the intersection.

The Cincinnati police were called to the scene
by Jaeger, and a formal report was made. Mary Jackson and Joseph Jaske were removed to the General
Hospital by a police ambulance.

This description is based on Jaeger's signed
statement. Statements taken from Jackson and Jaske
tie in with Jaeger's statement with the exception that
Jaske insists his light did not change from green to
yellow until after he had entered the intersection.

INJURIES

Jaske received fractures of three left ribs and was
hospitalized for 24 hours. He is making a rapid recovery. Mary Jackson suffered the loss of two of her
upper front teeth, and a deep laceration over the
right eye. Her recovery is progressing satisfactorily.

CONCLUSIONS

Jaske was negligent for entering the intersection on a
yellow light. Jackson was negligent in that he
started into the intersection without first determining that he could do so with safety. The fact that
Jackson moved on a green light does not remove his
responsibility of showing ordinary care in entering
the intersection. Jackson stated that he did not see
the Chevrolet until the instant of impact.

SETTLEMENT

No payment will be made to Jaske for his bodily
injuries because his negligence contributed to the
accident.

We will pay Davis for the damage to his Chevrolet
since Jaske's negligence cannot be imputed to Davis,
the owner. Jackson's negligence is the basis for
payment to Davis.
We will pay for the repair of Jackson's Plymouth under
his deductible coverage. We have no right of recovery from Jaske.
Our only interest in Mrs. Jackson's injuries is to
pay her actual medical expenses under the medical
payment provisions of our policy. She will have a
good claim against Jaske for the injuries she
sustained.

Charles E. Merrill, Directing Partner, and Winthrop H. Smith, Managing Partner, had many things to say to their customers and associates in the firm of Merrill Lynch, Pierce, Fenner & Beane at the end of 1953. Some were specific: a statement of income, profit, growth. Some were more general: remarks on the capital gains tax and on the firm's and the nation's prospects for the future. Some were long-range: a review of policy since the merger which formed the present company in April, 1940, with statements on the permanent policies and philosophies of the firm's operation. In order to get these things said the company prepared a brochure, as it does every year. This year's brochure contains 14 photographs, 2 charts, 4 graphs, and a balance sheet. On pages 9-14 are six pages from the brochure, with graphs showing growth and development over a 12-year period.

The note to my department head, the memorandum on the glue tests, the insurance adjuster's review of the details of the automobile accident, and the Merrill Lynch, Pierce, Fenner, and Beane booklet are all reports. What do they all have in common? A report has a job to do, a job of carrying information—facts and ideas—to someone who needs it. He may need information as the basis for an immediate decision or as background for long-range planning; he may need a little information or a lot. The length and much of the nature of the report will depend on his needs.

The Importance of Reports. The importance of a report depends obviously on how badly the information it contains is

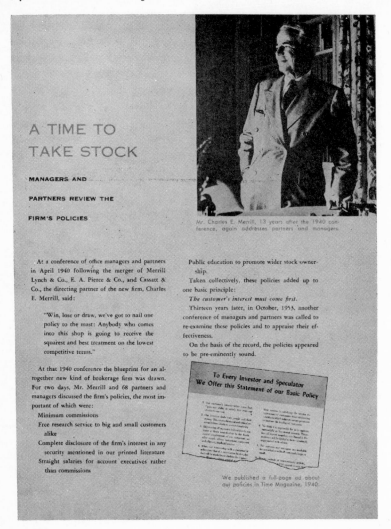

FIGURE 4. Portion of an Annual Report. (From *1953 Annual Report,* by permission of Merrill Lynch, Pierce, Fenner & Beane.)

needed. One way to test the need for information would be to declare a reporting holiday for a month, say, or a year, in any large organization: A. T. & T., General Motors, New York University, Walter Reed Hospital, the Government of the United States. We would find that without its constant incom-

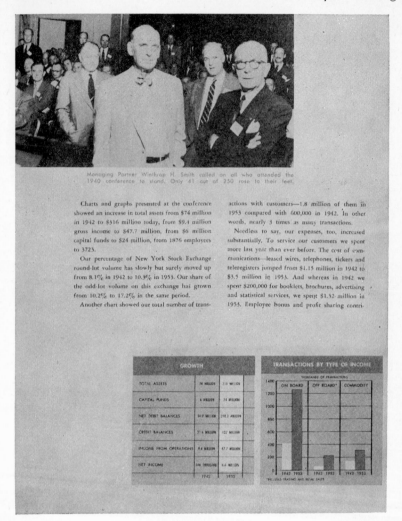

Managing Partner Winthrop H. Smith called on all who attended the 1940 conference to stand. Only 41 out of 250 rose to their feet.

Charts and graphs presented at the conference showed an increase in total assets from $74 million in 1942 to $316 million today, from $9.4 million gross income to $47.7 million, from $6 million capital funds to $24 million, from 1876 employees to 3723.

Our percentage of New York Stock Exchange round-lot volume has slowly but surely moved up from 8.1% in 1942 to 10.3% in 1953. Our share of the odd-lot volume on this exchange has grown from 10.2% to 17.2% in the same period.

Another chart showed our total number of trans-actions with customers—1.8 million of them in 1953 compared with 600,000 in 1942. In other words, nearly 3 times as many transactions.

Needless to say, our expenses, too, increased substantially. To service our customers we spent more last year than ever before. The cost of com-munications—leased wires, telephones, tickers and teleregisters jumped from $1.15 million in 1942 to $3.5 million in 1953. And whereas in 1942 we spent $200,000 for booklets, brochures, advertising and statistical services, we spent $1.32 million in 1953. Employee bonus and profit sharing contri-

FIGURE 4—*Continued.*

ing stream of information in reports the organization could not operate.

In the horse-and-buggy days of industry in America it was possible for the man in charge of a company's production to keep informed on every phase of operation by personal obser-vation; he didn't need reports because he knew what was going butions increased from $45,000 to $2.1 million in the same period.

Facts and figures showed beyond question that the firm had done well. Said Mr. Merrill, *"I firmly believe that we have achieved the position we have today because of our policies. And to the degree that we strictly adhere to them, to the extent that we put the customer's interest first, we will prosper in the future ..."*

Just how had those broad policies been translated into specific action? How had they actually been put into practice to benefit the individual customer? Here are some of the ways:

In our dealings with our customers ... We try to serve both small and large investors according to their needs. We believe success in any business is grounded on the principle of the greatest good for the greatest number. While our firm has a large clientele of wealthy individuals, we believe our business would never have reached its present proportions without the patronage of many thousands of smaller investors.

When we furnish our customers with investment information ... We try to present the facts. Our efforts to obtain the facts involve miles and miles of railway travel, hours of cross-country flight time, countless plant visits, hundreds of interviews with corporate executives and government leaders, endless treks to stockholder meetings and trade conventions, plus long hours of study over reports and analyses by our research specialists. And whether their findings are bearish or bullish, their only responsibility is to "call the shots" exactly as they see them.

Last year the Research Division answered 46,000 requests for information about securities—everything from an opinion about a single stock to an analysis of a portfolio worth millions of dollars.

Representatives from every department and 112 offices met to re-examine firm policy.

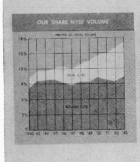

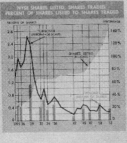

FIGURE 4—*Continued.*

on himself. The amount of personal observing a man can do is strictly limited, however, and if he calls in no help his company will have to stay small enough for him to patrol and supervise personally. Reports, then, by supplying information to supplement what the executive can observe for himself, are an extension of the executive's limited physical capacity to ob-

FIGURE 4—*Continued.*

serve, just as machines are an extension of the worker's limited bodily capacity to produce. Just as machines have made modern industrial production possible, reports have made possible modern industrial management and the management and coordinated control of all large, complex organizations. Reports

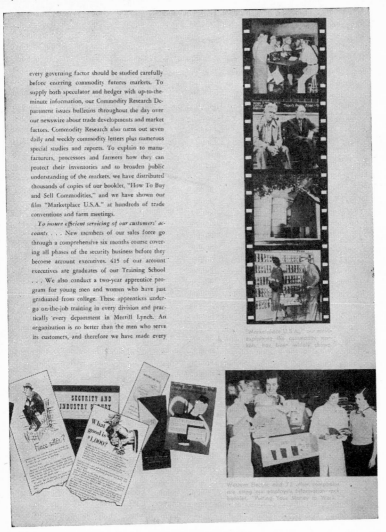

every governing factor should be studied carefully before entering commodity futures markets. To supply both speculator and hedger with up-to-the-minute information, our Commodity Research Department issues bulletins throughout the day over our newswire about trade developments and market factors. Commodity Research also turns out seven daily and weekly commodity letters plus numerous special studies and reports. To explain to manufacturers, processors and farmers how they can protect their inventories and to broaden public understanding of the markets, we have distributed thousands of copies of our booklet, "How To Buy and Sell Commodities," and we have shown our film "Marketplace U.S.A." at hundreds of trade conventions and farm meetings.

To insure efficient servicing of our customers' accounts . . . New members of our sales force go through a comprehensive six months course covering all phases of the security business before they become account executives. 415 of our account executives are graduates of our Training School . . . We also conduct a two-year apprentice program for young men and women who have just graduated from college. These apprentices undergo on-the-job training in every division and practically every department in Merrill Lynch. An organization is no better than the men who serve its customers, and therefore we have made every

FIGURE 4—*Continued.*

promise to be even more useful tools of management in the future (see pp. 311-58).

Reports Develop Future Executives. A report has a job to do, a job of transmitting information. Yet a report may carry more than its information: it may carry an impression of the

An interesting sidelight to the conference: a dinner honoring Mr. Merrill on his 68th birthday. As a present, managers and partners established a scholarship fund in his name at Amherst, his alma mater. The scholarship will be awarded annually to a son of an employee of Merrill Lynch.

effort to staff our offices with carefully selected and well trained personnel.

To avoid excessive trading for the sake of building commissions . . . We pay our sales representatives a flat salary rather than a commission. We feel our sales force deserves the security and dignity of a monthly pay-check. In our judgment this practice benefits both employees and customers, and it will continue to be one of our fundamental policies in the years ahead.

To inform our customers of our interest in any security mentioned in our literature . . . All our printed material carries a disclosure of whatever interest the firm or its general partners may have in any of the companies mentioned in the publication. We do this "so that customers may judge for themselves the possibility and extent of bias on our part in the presentation of the information set forth herein."

To educate the public about investing . . . We have steadily expanded our advertising and publishing program. Such advertisements as "What Everybody Ought To Know About This Stock and Bond Business" and such booklets as "How To

Invest" and "How To Read a Financial Report" have become classics of the business, and millions of reprints of them have been distributed to people in all walks of life. Additionally, last year our movie "Fair Exchange," which tells the story of investments in simple narrative form, was in strong demand from clubs and business and civic groups and was shown to more than seven million people.

* * *

These, then, are some of the basic policies by which this firm has operated for 15 years and by which it expects to continue operating in the future. Actually no set of policies can ever be sufficiently detailed to provide a clear-cut answer to every specific problem that arises. This is what Managing Partner Winthrop H. Smith had in mind in his final statement at the October conference of partners and managers. Said Mr. Smith, "*Whenever you have a problem that's difficult to solve, you'll usually come up with the right answer simply by asking yourself, Which decision will serve the customer's best interests?*"

That philosophy always has been and always will be the keystone of our operation.

FIGURE 4—*Concluded.*

man who wrote it, of his carefulness and accuracy, of his ability to sift out important material from unimportant, of his organizing skill and his use of language, of his knowledge and understanding of his specialization, of his ability to follow directions. And it is the nature of reports to go up instead of down; most reports are read by superior officers. Thus the report offers a rare opportunity to prove the writer's worth to the men who have the authority to advance him. As Sherman Perry says in *Let's Write Good Letters:*

> Not many opportunities come to write a report. But when the one opportunity does come, it offers the writer a wonderful chance to show the quality of his mind and the order of his method. *A terse report so clear and logical that it commands the respect of an official may be the turning point in a career.**

Not only does the report display ability, it helps develop it. The process of looking up the answers to management's questions gives practice in using the methods and tools of research, makes the report writer more familiar with his field and the organization he is working with, and builds an awareness of management's perspective—the broad view.

And so—if the boss holds out an assignment and says "Give me a report on this by Monday"—it is not so much a chore as an opportunity and a challenge.

Exercises and Problems

1. If there were suddenly to be no more reports at your college, what would break down first? What next? Trace the various functions of administration, from heating the classrooms to reporting the grades, from planning the curriculum to scheduling the major dances, to see how long each function could be carried on without reports.

2. Try the same experiment with an industry or a retail store that you are familiar with. Ask an independent businessman how many reports he writes to the government alone (include forms as reports) in the course of a year.

3. How does the function of the Merrill Lynch, Pierce, Fenner & Beane report differ from those of the other reports reproduced in Chapter 1?

4. Here is an advertisement from a magazine. Would you call it a report, or not? Discuss your reasons.

---

* Sherman Perry, *Let's Write Good Letters* (Middletown, Ohio: The American Rolling Mill Co., 1942), p. 142.

It is difficult to write a definition of the American way.
But it is easy to find good examples. Here is one:

PUZZLE:

Who got the hundred million dollars?

He walked into our office seven years ago, sat down. We knew the customer. And a wonderful credit rating he had, too.

Said he wanted airplane engines. By that time blueprints were scattered all over the place.

He was taking no chances. Not one engine would he accept without testing first, stripping apart, building up again, and testing once more Hmm!

And more. Every engine he bought would be overhauled after 15 running hours.

He didn't say so, but he must have known *we* would have ideas, too. (Lights burn all night when engineers at our place see ways to improve things we make.)

The climax was last August. The customer announced that he would allow 1,200 hours flying time from these G-E engines before an overhaul.

In other words, 80 times as many hours without overhaul as seven years ago. And today only every tenth engine is tested twice before delivery because of what has been referred to as the "perfection rate" of G-E jet engines.

Oh, yes. The hundred million dollars. With General Electric engines now giving extended service, not so many are needed. Improvements have saved the customer that much in five years.

P. S. Who's the customer? The U. S. Air Force. And what was the engine? The J-47 jet engine.

And who got the hundred million dollar saving? Who profits from more Air Force per dollar? The taxpayer, everybody. This story is one more example of what happens where research men and engineers are at work. Products gain in efficiency, do more. New products emerge, and the public is always the gainer.

You can put your confidence in —

GENERAL ⓖⓔ ELECTRIC

FIGURE 5.   An Advertisement.   (By permission of General Electric Company.)

5. Several report-writing textbooks list many types of reports—"classifications" of reports by subject matter, function, etc. Since industrial practice and textbook theory do not agree on such classifications, they have been omitted from this book (see Preface, p. v). However, you might find it interesting to talk with a report-writing professional in business, industry, or one of the professions to see what classifications of reports, if any, he distinguishes. It would be worth while to report to the class on the interview.

6. Check the periodical indexes under *reports, reporting;* read and review for your class at least two current articles.

Chapter 2

LOCATING MATERIAL

THIS INFORMATION we are asked to report, where do we find it? What facts and ideas have dollars and cents value to a firm? Let's clarify the difference between most college term papers and reports: typically, term papers have no $ and ¢ value; they are merely exercises designed to familiarize students with the facilities of libraries and to give them practice in finding and organizing material. Reports are worth what it costs to hire you for a day or a week, or you would not be assigned the job. College term papers often cause students to wonder what to write *about;* on-the-job reports never raise that question. The subject of a report is assigned; the report writer knows very well what he is to write about. His first problem is then to find the information, the facts and ideas, to put into his report—and he must be sure these facts and ideas are the real thing. They must ring true; if they are untrue or half true the decisions the executive will base on them will be poor decisions, and the report will be worse than no good—it will be an actual liability causing $ and ¢ loss to the firm.

Tom Looked at the Pump. One of my University of Cincinnati Evening College students missed the class meeting which dealt with ways of gathering material for a report. He came up before the next class meeting to explain, and to ask what he had missed. He is an engineer for a pump manufacturing company. On the night of the meeting he missed, the boss had called him and told him to take the train for Charleston, West Virginia, to investigate an emergency breakdown of a pump installation there. The engineer (let's call him Tom) hastily gathered up a set of specifications on the pump, which was a five-year-old model, threw some clothes into a suitcase, and took a cab to the 9:15.

On the way to Charleston he read over the specifications carefully to get the operational details of the pump clearly in mind. He got off the train at Charleston, took a cab to the plant where the pump was installed, and was met at the gate by the plant engineer. On the way to the pump the plant engineer told him all the pump's symptoms; Tom took a few notes and asked a few questions to pin down the length of time the pump had been behaving oddly.

When he had learned all the plant engineer knew of the difficulty, Tom went to work on the pump itself. He took it apart carefully and made notes on what he saw. He was able to make a temporary repair that had not occurred to the plant engineer; he promised that a defective part would be replaced by noon the next day and phoned back to Cincinnati to make sure the part would be put on the next train.

Then he went to his hotel, got a few hours' sleep, picked up the new part at the station, installed it, and took the train himself. On the way back to Cincinnati he wrote a three-page report of his trip, consulting his notes frequently; his main emphasis was placed on the factors that had caused the pump to fail, as well as he could determine them from what he had learned.

I told Tom he hadn't missed a thing; he had shown on his trip an excellent grasp of the methods of gathering information for a report. "I did?" said Tom. "Why, I just read about the pump, and asked questions about the pump, and looked at the pump. What's unusual about that?"

"Nothing unusual," I said, "but that's my lecture in a nutshell."

Observation. In my lecture I had called the first method of gathering material *observation*. Everything that we know from experience we have gathered by observation; we know that rocks are heavy and too much sun causes sunburn and too much of the wrong kind of food causes indigestion. A good look at a production line or an airplane or a shopping center establishes the relationship of its parts or units better than many thousands of words can do, especially if we know what to look for.

Observation requires background; if we don't know what to look for we might as well not look. I can hold up a mirror

and look at my throat when I'm hoarse and learn nothing; the
doctor who lives next door can take one glance and come up
with an accurate diagnosis. Of course, observation builds background also—it may be that if I pay close attention to what my
throat looks like when the doctor says I'm sick and what it looks
like when he says I'm not, I'll develop the ability to make a
reasonably accurate guess myself.

The answer to the question "Can we trust information
gathered by observation as much as information gathered by
interrogation or research?" can be answered only by "It depends on who's doing the looking." My observation of the
pump at Charleston, West Virginia, would be interesting to me
but useless to any firm; all I could say about the pump after
observing it would be "It doesn't work, does it?" I couldn't
even guess the reason for its trouble. Tom, the engineer from
the pump company, had the background to do far more than
make a guess—his statement was a careful analysis of observed
facts.

Interrogation or Field Research. The second method of
gathering information I had called *interrogation.* Interrogation (sometimes called field research) includes all asking of
questions, from carefully organized questionnaires and interviews to random discussion. Valuable information can be
gained from random discussion; for example, intelligence investigators in preparing reports on security risks often discuss
the person being investigated with several of his associates or
acquaintances. Knowing that direct questions often stifle the
communication process, the investigators sometimes let the person interviewed develop the interview after its direction has
been established.

Generally, however, directed discussion or planned interviews are more useful to the investigator. The plan of the interview should be informal and somewhat flexible so that the
person interviewed will not feel that he is being grilled—but
for nearly all interviews there should be a plan, somewhat as
follows:

Identify yourself, and establish the purpose of the interview briefly,
keeping in mind that an elaborate justification of your position is not
needed and that interested as you are in your subject-matter, bringing

the person interviewed up-to-date on all your research will waste his time and tend to invalidate the answers he gives you (he might give answers based on what you have just told him about your research or aimed at pleasing you by helping prove your theory).

Ask the easy questions and the background questions first, permitting some digression by the person interviewed but holding in the long run to the main points you need to cover.

Ask the hard questions (if any) very carefully. Don't force an answer if one does not come. Don't try to get the person interviewed to oversimplify a complex problem into a yes or no problem. Don't expect all the facts and figures to be at his fingertips; if he needs to do some research to answer, suggest that you call back the next day or that he send you his reply.

Give him a chance to follow up any of his answers and to ask you questions before closing the interview.

Thank him for his help; if possible, tell him you'll send him a copy of the report. It is good personal public relations for you and good public relations for your organization to make him feel well pleased with the interview and confident that he has spent his time constructively.

Go somewhere else and record your notes. Only statistics and addresses should be recorded during the interview—and when no statistics are being discussed the notebook and pencil should stay in the pocket. Be sure to record the date, name, and exact title of the person interviewed.

It is not always possible to carry on interrogation by direct questioning; sometimes the persons to be questioned live so far apart or are so numerous that it would be prohibitively expensive to talk with them personally. The questionnaire is the solution to such a problem. A carefully prepared questionnaire can gather hundreds or thousands of replies at a cost of only a few cents for each reply. In some ways the questionnaire is actually superior to the interview. It does not rely on the interviewer's memory, and it is easily tabulated and filed. It restricts the answers to the subject, and it makes sure that all answers are to the same question, phrased and asked in the same way; it is not dependent on the personality and possible bias of an interviewer. It makes repeat surveying easier. It is not influenced by the answers given by others in the hearing of the person interviewed. Henry Plexico of the Federal Bureau of Investigation reports that when information must be obtained from several persons in circumstances where some would overhear parts of interviews with others, the best method of secur-

1061 W. 35TH STREET

EXECUTIVE OFFICE   CHICAGO 9

December 1953

Dear Friend:

For many months the Spiegel catalog has been advertised on many radio
and television programs and in many magazines and newspapers.

Perhaps you have seen our catalog or heard about it on THIS IS YOUR LIFE,
TRUTH OR CONSEQUENCES, QUEEN FOR A DAY, WELCOME TRAVELLERS, PEOPLE ARE FUNNY,
HOUSE PARTY, or other programs.

We have tried to get across a few basic ideas about shopping from the big
Spiegel Home Shopping Book. Now we would like to find out how good a job we
have done in having these ideas understood.

And that's where you come in. We need your help.

The back of this letter contains a SURVEY QUESTIONNAIRE designed to give us
the information we need. It's a very simple questionnaire to answer.

It will take only a few minutes of your time to check the answers to the
questions...but it will be a big help to us. When you've finished filling out
the questionnaire place it in the self-addressed envelope enclosed and send it
back. We pay postage. No stamp needed.

We hope you will help us, and thank you in advance.

                                           Sincerely,

                                           Allen Fisher

                                           MARKET RESEARCH MANAGER

P. S. We would like to show you our appreciation for your help. Our way of
      doing this is explained at the end of the questionnaire.

ADD

                                    (OVER)

FIGURE 6. Covering Letter and Questionnaire. (By permission of Spiegel.)

SPIEGEL MARKET RESEARCH SURVEY

Market Research Department, 1061 W. 35th Street, Chicago 9, Illinois

Check YES or NO After Each Question

1. Have you bought from Spiegel within the last year?.................... Yes ☐ No ☐

2. Have you ever seen a Spiegel Store?............................... Yes ☐ No ☐
   If "Yes" what kind of Store was it?
   _____

3. Have you seen a Spiegel Catalog within the last year?................. Yes ☐ No ☐
   If "Yes" where did you see it?
   _____

4. Did you ever hear about or see the Spiegel catalog on a radio or TV show?.. Yes ☐ No ☐
   If "Yes" which program or programs was it on?
   _____
   _____

5. Do you think that catalog shopping:
   a. Is convenient .... Yes ☐ No ☐
   b. Offers good styles .... Yes ☐ No ☐
   c. Saves money.... .... Yes ☐ No ☐
   d. Gives good quality.... .... Yes ☐ No ☐
   e. Is in good taste.. Yes ☐ No ☐

6. Have you had any other mail order catalog in the past 5 years?.......... Yes ☐ No ☐
   If "Yes" which ones?
   _____

7. Use this space for additional comments:
   _____
   _____
   _____
   _____
   _____

·   ·   ·   ·   ·   ·   ·   ·   ·   ·   ·   ·

Thank you for your cooperation. To show our appreciation, I shall be glad to mail you a free catalog if you fill out the information below:

Dear Mr. Fisher:

Please send me the 480 page Spiegel Home Shopping Book for Spring and Summer, 1954. If I order from it, I may keep it, otherwise I shall return it at your request.

Name_____

| Rural | Rural | Post Office |
| Route Number_____ | Box Number_____ | Box Number_____ |

Street Address_____

City_____ State_____
(Please specify Zone if any)

FIGURE 6—*Concluded.*

ing unbiased information is to have each person fill out a questionnaire or simply write a report of what happened.*

A questionnaire can be more definitely planned than an interview; since it will be printed in quantity there is no opportunity for flexibility. Questionnaires vary greatly in length and complexity, but a good general plan would be the following:

Ask for the cooperation of your reader. Don't explain enough of what you are trying to do to affect the answers he will give, but do your best to make him feel that this project is worth while. He will fill the blanks more carefully if he wants to answer the questionnaire than if he does not want to. Be brief; your reader should get to the questionnaire proper without delay.

Explain how the mechanics of the questionnaire works. The questionnaire should be so easy to fill out that the instructions can be reduced to a sentence or two.

Ask the questions. Set up the questions with enough white space to leave them uncrowded. Make them as easy to answer as possible; proceed in easy stages with the easiest question first, avoid such difficult chores as ranking several items or factors in order of preference, and whenever possible supply alternative choices that can be marked with a check (*"Where do you do must of your shopping?* _____ In the suburban markets. _____ Downtown. _____ Don't know."*) Make the questions clear; avoid involved sentences and ambiguous words such as "kind." (*"What kind of car do you drive?"* might be answered Buick, sedan, used, British, sports.) Make the questions specific; they should ask for facts rather than motives, the particular rather than the general, points that can be known and remembered with certainty rather than hazy guesses. Avoid all questions which by their wording or their personal nature seem to call for one answer rather than the other (*"Do you use Colgate's tooth paste?"* *"Do you use alcoholic beverages to excess?"*) Avoid all questions which contain more than one main factor to be evaluated (*"Why did you buy a National prefabricated home?"* might involve the need to have a home, factors of price, the company's advertising, the arguments of the salesman, various local conditions in the building trade.)

Secure name, address, and background information such as age, occupation, income group, from the person filling out the questionnaire as an aid in evaluating the data in the study which is to be made.

The selection of the persons to whom the questionnaire will be sent is of vital importance; the validity of a questionnaire

---

* Lecture, Cincinnati Police Academy, May, 1954.

Questionnaire

How would you rate these LIFE Filmstrips according to the following plan·

A = excellent   B = good   C = fair   D = poor

	Selection of pictures	Organization of material	Educational effectiveness	Cultural value
The Atom				
Middle Ages				
Giotto				
Maya				

Using LIFE Filmstrips

Do you ever use the filmstrips without verbal commentary?_____

Do you lecture while showing them?_____ Do you find the Lecture Notes helpful?_____

Have you any suggestions as to how the Lecture Notes might be improved?_____

_____

Do you feel that the organization of the filmstrips allows you enough freedom to make your own emphases?_____

What is the approximate size of the frames as projected on your screen?_____

What is the average age of your audience?_____

What has been the general audience reaction?_____

_____

Granted that the best color reproduction is still imperfect, do you feel that LIFE Filmstrips should continue to use color?_____

Would you be interested in having study prints (black-and-white, enlarged duplicates of the frames, mounted separately) for prolonged study?_____

Would you find small posters useful in publicizing your showings of LIFE Filmstrips?_____

Which of the following subjects, now in preparation or under consideration for future release, would you find most interesting?

☐ *Renaissance Venice*   ☐ *Houses U. S. A.*   ☐ *Age of Enlightenment*   ☐ *Egypt*

☐ *The Holy Land*   ☐ *The Navajos*   ☐ *History of Theatre*   ☐ *Ancient Rome*

☐ *The History of Transportation*   ☐ *1848: Year of Revolutions*

What new subjects would you suggest for LIFE Filmstrips?_____

_____

Signed_____

Institution_____

Address_____

Figure 7. Questionnaire. (By permission of *Life*.)

study is dependent on whether the portion of a group selected (the "sample") is representative of the whole group.*

Research. The final method of gathering information, *research*, sends us to the card catalogues and reference guides of company libraries, public and college libraries, and government agencies. To the beginner in research the many files and indexes may seem like a pain in the neck, but to the professional they are the key to the world's knowledge. Anyone who begins to study a problem today is luckier than all who studied it before him—even the great pioneers in his field—because with the help of these research tools he can start where they left off.

We have only the space to supply a few hints and suggestions on research procedures and to refer you to sources of fuller information. Do not ignore the "Selected Bibliography" at the back of this book. In it we have listed index materials and major or representative sources of information in all the major fields where you will likely work. Here we will cite three useful guides, any one of which will save you countless steps and many hours of labor:

> COMAN, EDWIN T. *Sources of Business Information.* New York: Prentice-Hall, Inc., 1949. A bibliographical handbook for all the major industrial fields, with full index.
>
> DALTON, BLANCHE H. *Sources of Engineering Information.* Berkeley: University of California Press, 1948. A full classified listing of abstracts and digest services, lists of periodical articles, bibliographies, and reference books.
>
> WILLIAMS, CECIL B., and ALLAN H. STEVENSON. *A Research Manual* (2d ed.). New York: Harper & Bros., 1951. A general introductory guide to research writing. See especially Chapters ii and iii, "The Library and Its Role in Research Writing," "Library Reference Tools."

There are other valuable guides, and even your composition handbook may prove helpful. The main point is, don't go it blind; don't go stumbling around in a library for lack of consulting one or more of the available guidebooks.

---

* Good books on interviewing are Walter V. Bingham and Bruce V. Moore, *How to Interview* (New York: Harper & Bros., 1941); Anne Fenlason, *Essentials in Interviewing* (New York: Harper & Bros., 1952); and James D. Weinland and Margaret V. Gross, *Personnel Interviewing* (New York: The Ronald Press Co., 1952). An excellent discussion of the preparation and use of questionnaires appears in Lyndon O. Brown, *Marketing and Distribution Research* (3rd ed.; New York: The Ronald Press Co., 1955).

Now for a few pointers. First of all, make good use of the reference room. Here are the encyclopedias, dictionaries, handbooks, atlases, and numerous and various bibliographies and indexes. It is important at the outset to get the subject bounded, to secure general information on it. Thus you will know better what detailed source materials to look for and be able to use them more efficiently when you get them. In all reference tools, the arrangement is alphabetical; if you know the alphabet forwards and backwards, you can turn to any subject in an instant. The *Guide to Reference Books,* early editions by Isador Mudge and the current one by Constance Winchell, is the standard manual on reference room resources.

Second, learn to use a card index efficiently. Most books in a library are entered by at least three cards: author card, title card, and one or more subject cards—so if you can think of the author's last name or the first important word in the title, you can find the book easily. But if you can't think of either, then look under the most likely subject entry and other related entries if the first doesn't work. Note that subject entries are themselves *bibliographies,* that is, lists of related materials. Looking under them often supplies you with other materials to add to the title you were looking for.

Third, get acquainted with the various magazine indexes and learn to use them efficiently. An enormous amount of valuable material which never gets collected into books is published in all kinds of magazines and other periodicals. Soon after publication, it would become almost as hopelessly lost as the proverbial haystack needle if it weren't for the indexes. But with the help of the *Readers' Guide, Industrial Arts Index, Engineering Index, Public Affairs Information Service (PAIS),* and other more specialized indexes, you can get at it quickly— if your library has the magazine referred to. Winifred Gregory's *Union List of Serials* and *American Newspapers,* and Elizabeth Bowerman's *Union List of Technical Periodicals* will quickly inform you on the periodical holdings of your own and other libraries.

Fourth, learn how to make use of government publications: federal, state, and local. The U. S. Department of Commerce issues annually a *List of Selected Publications;* likewise the U. S.

Bureau of the Census, *Census Publications;* and there is the more general *United States Government Publications: Monthly Catalog*. Your reference room or document room librarian can tell you of other listings, and also acquaint you with holdings of your own college or city library.

Fifth, develop a proper working relationship with librarians. Use them as advisers and guides, not as crutches to lean on. You should know such basic things as what library classification system your library uses—Dewey Decimal or Library of Congress—and you should learn the main classifications of the system, especially if your library is of the modern open-shelf type. It is more thrilling to find things for oneself; a writer worth his salt is at home in libraries; but at the same time it is foolish to spend hours looking for something that a librarian could guide you to almost instantly. Librarians know too of such special features as loose-leaf files and clipping services and microfilm and microprint holdings.

Remember always that reports must be informative—full and accurate. They should be well written, but no writing can be good enough to atone for inadequate or undependable subject matter.

Conclusion. It all boils down to what Tom, the engineer, did about the pump:

> read
> ask
> look

The best information-getting uses more than one of these ways. Common-sense observation and experience help to check the statements in the book or the results of the questionnaire, and an interview with an experienced professional will often save time and serious errors when the report writer is working in an unfamiliar field.

Sometimes information-gathering takes time and costs money; it's worth it. The information is the whole point of the report—a decision, often a vitally important one, will be based on it. The decision requires one link of information plus another plus another plus another—and the decision is no stronger than its weakest link.

Exercises and Problems

1. What methods of gathering information would you use in writing these reports?

The current shift to the buyer's market in the shoe industry.

Advisability of establishing a roller rink in (city, state).

Current trends in automobile advertising.

A financial history of the Atlantic Coast Line Railroad.

A proposed safety program for _____ Company.

A study of wage incentive systems in operation.

An economic forecast.

Advantages of installing new pickling tank.

Plant layout of a cutting die shop.

Required protection from radiation in radioisotope laboratory.

Methods of preventing excessive drying in shipments of dehydrated alfalfa.

Early experiments and progress in public relations policy-making.

Aptitude testing methods in personnel administration.

Cost analysis of proposed installation of _____.

2. Interview someone who prepares reports (perhaps the instructor will invite an industrial executive to class so that you will have an hour to ask him questions) to find out specifically how he gets his information.

3. Take a refresher tour of the library to make sure you know where all the reference guides are. Pick one of the topics from Problem 1 above, or another topic that interests you more, and see how many references you can find on it in ten minutes. If you run into any problems, ask the librarian for help.

4. Prepare a questionnaire which could be used to gather information on some local or campus problem.

5. Discuss the questions (see p. 30) sent to alumni of Ross College to determine alumni opinion before preparing recommendations to the Board of Trustees.

Student Housing

All college campuses face the mutual problem of temporary, inadequate housing. At Ross College, the normal housing capacity for men and women is 1214. The normal capacities of many rooms are expanded by placing another person or two in each of them. Through these expanded facilities, Ross College can house 1585 students. The enrollment this year totals 2720. Approximately 350 students are living in fraternity houses and annexes. The rest are living in private homes in Camden and vicinity, as well as in "The Barracks," University operated temporary housing.

A handbook entitled "Rules and Regulations Governing Student Activities and Student Organizations" reflects an official opinion of the standards of this temporary housing:

"Sophomores who desire to live in College Housing facilities are assigned to the Barracks unless they have lived in them during the greater part of their freshman year for emergency reasons.

"It is planned that sophomores and transfer students assigned to The Barracks shall live there no longer than for two semesters. Experience has indicated, however, that it is not always possible to move men eligible for halls to such halls at the end of two semesters because of lack of hall spaces. Men remaining will always be moved as soon as possible in order of numbers drawn at drawings."

Living conditions in town are often far below standard, and room rents are more often far in excess of College rates and the students' pocketbooks. In many cases sanitary facilities are extremely inadequate. There are fire hazards, overcrowding, and lack of proper study facilities.

1. Should Ross College exercise control over all student housing in town?

   _____

2. Should all Ross men, as well as women, be required to live in College-approved residences? _____

   _____

3. Should student room rents in town be controlled, and be based on reasonable, minimum requirements set by the College for student housing? _____

   _____

4. Should Ross College set a time by which it hopes to abolish The Barracks—and also bring back the pre-war standard of two students

per room in all Residence Halls—and then work toward that time goal? _____

_____

Freshmen women in College Residence Halls are guided by a house chairman, who is a junior woman, and counselors selected from the sophomore class, as well as the Housemother especially selected for her job by the College. The women students serving in the afore-mentioned positions receive no pay for these services, and are rewarded only with possible election to some service honorary in the last two years.

Freshmen men living in College Residence Halls are guided by upperclassmen, also known as counselors, who receive **free room accommodations** in return for their counseling services.

5. Do you believe that your Long Range Committee should recommend a change in this policy to provide for equality in the recognition of student counselor services? _____

_____

In connection with student housing, the question of sorority houses has again arisen. At present, most sororities are allotted a suite (living room and kitchenette) in the women's Residence Halls.

6. Do you think the sorority house question should be reviewed again?

_____

7. In your opinion, should Ross have sorority houses built and owned by the College?_____

_____

_____

Chapter 3

ORGANIZING FACTS AND IDEAS

Protect Yourself from Your Material. The more investigating you do, the more material you find; and the more books, articles, surveys, charts, tables, and statistical summaries you accumulate on and around your desk, the harder it is to start writing. One of the strangest paradoxes of the writing game is that the person who takes most cheerfully to research for writing and who is most industrious in the accumulation of the raw materials for manuscript production is often the one who achieves the fewest books, articles, and reports. A friend of mine has been working twenty years on a biography of an English writer and publisher; he has gathered so much information in tangible form that he can barely find room to sit in his study. He doesn't sit in his study much, however, because the bulk of material facing him scares him away; he is now further from writing his book than he has ever been. He spends his time gathering more material so that he won't have to sort the stuff in his study. Unless the study burns down he'll never write the book.

There are two ways I know of to protect yourself from your material—don't gather so much, and don't gather it in tangible form so that it stacks up.

The first way has its points—many research men don't know when to quit researching and start reporting. You don't have to read all the books going back to the seventeenth century on road building to prepare a report on the best road construction method for the loading, delivery, parking, and traffic circulation area of an industrial site. Neither do you have to become an expert on cosmetology to lay out the floor plan for the cosmetics department of a shopping center branch of a department store. An important part of the research plan is the setting of a kind of practical limit to the research—a limit based on time available, budget, geography (distance from major research centers and libraries), but, most of all, on the needs which motivated the research project in the first place.

The second way to protect yourself from your material is to gather it in your mind instead of in bulk—to learn it instead of to accumulate it. It is just as easy, once you have got into the habit, to read something so as to *know* it, as to read it to know where it is. If you read to know you will take few notes, and the ones you do take will be the shortest possible notes that will recall to your mind the situation or statistic that you encountered in your reading. These brief notes, called *minimal cue notes*, will be discussed in the next few pages. If you read to know you will be able to write your report out of your mind, directly and freely, rather than haltingly by looking up and combing material from several sources spread out on the desk or on the desk and the floor around your chair. Professor W. S. Campbell, Director of Professional Writing at the University of Oklahoma, reporting on his experiences as a Rhodes Scholar at Oxford University, said that the most valuable part of his training was the writing of source papers purely from memory— with no recourse to books or notes. Reports written from the resources of your mind after you have completed your research differ basically from reports written by combining source materials through the direct cutting and pasting or paraphrasing methods of the hack writer. Rudolf Flesch describes the difference in his book *How To Make Sense:*

... To write and speak well—to make sense—you have to live fully in both worlds, the outer and the inner. You have to have experiences first, as much experience as possible, facts, pictures, events that fill your mind. Then, after you have done your work in taking notes or at least observing and learning, you ought to *forget* all that you have learned. Let it sink down into your unconscious, it's the only place where it will do you any good. And then, when the moment of communication is here—to an audience or at least to yourself—pour it out without thinking, pull it up again from your unconscious by the act of writing and speaking, and you will have something that you can communicate successfully. Otherwise— if you collect material and then laboriously reproduce that material for your listeners or readers—you haven't contributed anything in the process: you are just a parrot or a phonograph. There won't be any life in what you say or write, because you haven't *given* it any life. You were afraid:

you didn't have the courage to let it go, drop it into your unconscious and get it up again when you needed it. You didn't trust your own powers before an audience or before a blank sheet of paper. So you stutter and stumble; you hesitate; you erase; you correct; you qualify; you shrink back from revealing what is really on your mind. The result is failure.°

Minimal Cue Notes. Notes are memory aids. They make it possible and practical for you to write from the resources of your mind. Let's say you find some statistics that you want to use in your report: something like the total U. S. imports from Latin America in 1953 ($3,442,600,000). It is not necessary to memorize such figures, even if your memory is reliable enough to be trusted with them; you may write yourself a note about them instead. Most writers of reports remember what they can—all the general information and most of the specific—and use notes to call the rest to their minds, like this:

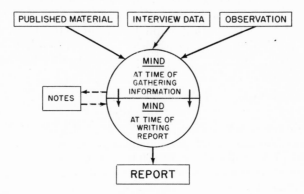

Minimal cue notes are not intended for the record; they will be valueless after the report is written. In college, students take full notes, are proud of them, go back and study them before each test, file them sometimes for years. In industry the report writer may take notes if his memory needs help with the facts and ideas he is gathering; he will keep these notes only until the report has been written and will then throw them away.

There is no required number of notes for a report, and no required form. Both will be determined by the help your

---

° Rudolf Flesch, *How To Make Sense* (New York: Harper & Bros., 1954), pp. 165-66.

memory needs with the project under way. It is convenient to make all your notes on the same size card or sheet of paper, and it is wise to list with each note (at the bottom of the card or on the back) the sources of its information. If the source is printed, include the full accurate bibliographical entry in case you need it, and note the page number:

301-152
N554

NIELANDER, WILLIAM A
AND RAYMOND, W. MILLER

PUBLIC RELATIONS

New York : The Ronald Press
Company, 1951

p-211

If your source is an interview, list the date, place, person talked with, and his title or position. Sometimes your identification data for a note will be quite a bit longer than the note itself.

About the note itself, and that phrase *minimal cue:* the less you need to put down, the better. If your Great Dane is about to sink his teeth in the ankle of your best girl's father, you don't waste words ("Hamlet, it is not the thing to do to bite my guests, especially the relative of my best girl"; "Please take your teeth away from that ankle, old boy"; "Now, Hamlet, you know better than that; stop it at once")—the minimal cue is "NO!" or "HAM—: NO!" If you are taking notes on a talk made at your college by William Whyte, Jr., of *Fortune,* you would not need to waste words like this:

Mr. Whyte said that he had interviewed a large number of men in top management jobs—presidents and vice-presidents—and an equal number of personnel directors. He had been trying to find out whether they would rather hire and advance to executive work (1) men who are good administrators and good at getting along with people, managing people, or (2) men who are imaginative, vigorous, creative—even brilliant—

leaders, though they may not contribute so well to the harmony of the group. He said that in his survey he found the vote 1 to 1, or even, among the presidents and vice-presidents, and 3 to 1 in favor of the "good administrator type" among the personnel directors. His conclusion was that high up in a company, on a policy-making level, there is likely to be recognition of the importance of imagination, ideas, the courage to strike out against majority opinion, the creative urge to reach out into the unknown and knock the lid off previously accepted limitations; while in middle management, in the personnel office, there is likely to be a glorification of "adjustment to the group" and a de-emphasis of the value of individuality and imagination.

That is the substance of what Mr. Whyte said, yes; but you don't need to put half that much down on paper to recall the talk to your mind. In fact, if you put that much down on paper you'll be writing so fast (unless you know shorthand *) that you'll miss many points in the talk.

As we said at the beginning of the chapter, gather most of the material for your report *in your mind*, not on paper.

I heard Mr. Whyte give this talk, called "Suburbia and the New Illiteracy," at the Corning Glass Center, Corning, New York, in October, 1953. Here is an exact copy of my own notes on the part of his talk summarized earlier:

CORNING GLASS CENTER
CORNING · NEW YORK

Administrator vs imaginative and vigorous leader

1-1 among top mgt

3-1 among personnel directors

---

* And if you know shorthand, and write down everything said, what do you have? It is like "reading" an article by making a copy of it, word for word. Morris Bishop wrote a delightful satire called "The Reading Machine" (printed March 8, 1947, *The New Yorker*) in which Prof. Entwhistle suggests such a method of "reading"—instead of reading an article to find out what is in it, to *know* it, the student merely puts the article in the machine, which "reads" it very rapidly and turns out a neat, typewritten copy of what it has "read"—a typescript suspiciously similar in appearance to a term paper.

My notes are not special in any way; they are just adequate. They serve to bring the results of Bill Whyte's interviews back to my mind, and to keep the figures straight. My notes would mean very little to anyone but me—but they are not supposed to. They are *minimal cue* notes—the *least* notes that would be

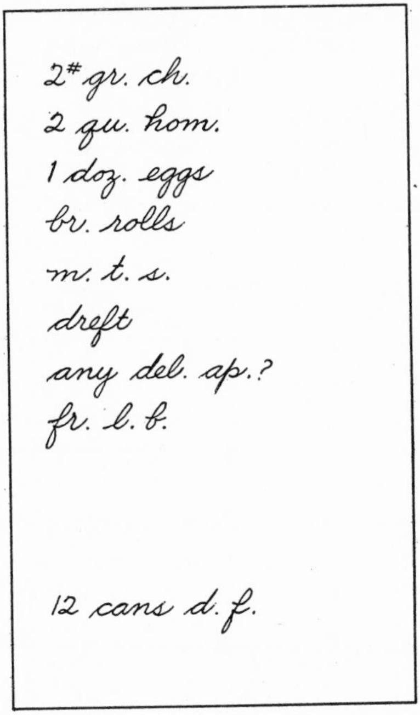

FIGURE 8. Recognize this most common of minimal cue notes? It is a grocery shopping list—and it is perfectly clear to its writer.

helpful to my memory in re-creating the part of this particular lecture I want to remember. As you can see, my minimal cue notes use abbreviations, and I use indention to indicate main points and subtopics. These are not rules for your minimal cue notes—there are no rules. You are the one who has to read them and understand them.

Most of your notes, then, for report writing should be minimal cue notes. The better your memory is—or the better you can train it to become—the briefer they can be. However, you will need to take a *few* fuller notes. Especially, if you want to quote something to emphasize or lend authority to a point, you will need to write out the *quotation note* fully and accurately, to the last capital letter and comma. And for all notes on points that will require documentation (discussed in Chapter 10), you must be sure to include in every note the exact source—author, title, facts of publication, and page or pages.

Organizing Information. By the time you have reached the point of shaping up your report, you have your topic well in mind. Without looking up a single point you could give an easy, relaxed, extemporaneous summary of your report-to-be.

So why worry about organizing? Try giving that summary, to a friend or in your own mind, and see if the organization doesn't pretty much take care of itself. Does it tell the reader what he needs to know in the order that makes the most sense? If so, go ahead and make your outline, and then start writing. If not, see how you can best juggle it around so that it will.*

Card System of Organizing. You may wish to experiment with another excellent method of organizing, the card system. I don't use it myself, but those who do swear by it.

The quickest way to put a shuffled poker deck in order is to lay the cards face up on the table in suits, putting each card about where you think it belongs and leaving space for the others (see Fig. 9). You keep on dealing until the cards are all on the table, and then you pick them up in order. The card system of organizing works much the same way. You have written all the possible topics you may cover on separate cards, and you lay each one down where you think it will fit in the finished report, leaving spaces for the others: Again, you keep on spreading out cards until all are down. If you don't like the completed plan, it is easy to shift the cards until the pattern suits you.

---

* Rhetoric books and composition handbooks give several kinds of order and methods of development, in the whole composition or in paragraphs of it; all college students have gone through them at least once. If you feel that you need further study in planning and achieving clear organization, consult a good text, such as (1) for paragraphs, Porter Perrin, *Writer's Guide and Index to English* (Chicago: Scott, Foresman & Co., 1950), pp. 170-82; (2) for the whole composition, Donald Davidson, *American Composition and Rhetoric* (New York: Charles Scribner's Sons, 1953) chap. ii; Norman Foerster, J. M. Steadman, and James B. McMillan, *Writing and Thinking* (Boston: Houghton Mifflin Co., 1952), pp. 50-63; or Cecil B. Williams and Allan H. Stevenson, *A Research Manual* (New York: Harper & Bros., 1951), chap. v.

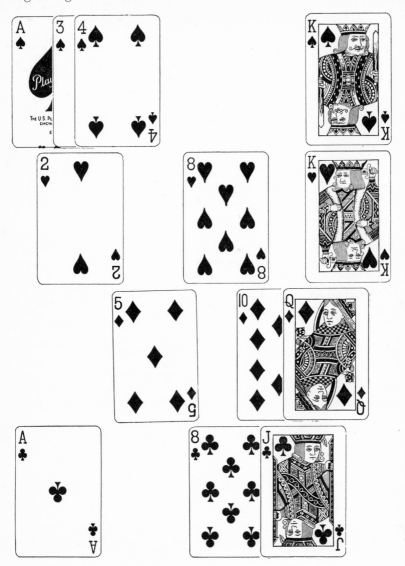

FIGURE 9. "Organizing" a Deck of Cards.

The card system works. The requirement of a system of organizing data is that it should work; with practice you can make any of several ways work extremely well.

(Topic: Shopping centers as locations for sporting goods stores)

Outlines. A report outline is the skeletal representation of the report's organization; if you have used the card system of organizing, your outline is a tabular copy of the topics and subtopics shown on your cards, arranged in their final order.

This is a *formal* outline:

    I.
    II.
            A.
            B.
                    1.
                    2.
            C.
    III.
            A.
            B.
    IV.

This is a *decimal* outline:

    1.
            1.1
            1.2
                    1.21
                    1.22
                            1.221
    2.
            2.1
            2.2

3.

    3.1

    3.2

    3.3

        3.31

        3.32

4.

This is a *tabular* outline, or *informal* outline:

All these systems of outlining work. The *formal* system is still generally used for show, when anyone except the writer is likely to see it; college courses and textbooks generally recommend it. The *informal* or *tabular* system is very widely used because of its simplicity and convenience; sometimes it is modified by the use of Arabic numbers for main headings only. Though there has been no widespread study made to give actual evidence, my opinion is that most outlines in actual reporting situations use the informal system. The *decimal* system is the most accurate and foolproof of the three, once it has been learned. It is gaining ground steadily at the expense of the formal outline; it has been used in many recent articles and books, including the major work on information theory, *The Mathematical Theory of Communication*, by Claude E. Shannon and Warren Weaver (Urbana: The University of Illinois Press, 1949).

Since the headings and subheadings (see pp. 143-46) of the completed report will probably come directly from the outline topics and subtopics, you should phrase your outline so that the topics and subtopics are roughly parallel in structure.*

---

* See Porter Perrin, *Writer's Guide and Index to English*, pp. 670-75. Parallel structure means the same kind of grammatical structure for each topic. Do not mix sentences with topics (phrase and name headings and subheadings). Since it is more graphic and more economical of space, the topical outline is preferable to the sentence outline for reports.

Knowing that the backbone of the outline will show in the headings and subheadings of the report should also make you choose your outline topics carefully; the outline becomes actually a part of the report, and thus its importance becomes dramatically clear.

Exercises and Problems

1. Attend a meeting, lecture, play, concert, or game; write a simple account of what happened from your own memory. Then, when the newspaper accounts of the same event are published, write the story again, this time using only material paraphrased from the papers. Use the two versions as a basis for class comment and discussion.

2. Be on the lookout for "hack writing"—cut-and-paste authorship—in various kinds of publications you read. Collect examples if you can. How can such writing be recognized? Possibly your school's news bureau can show you a recent press release and a dozen "different" stories based on it by different papers.

3. Read Chapter 8 in *How To Make Sense* by Rudolf Flesch (New York: Harper & Bros., 1954) and report to the class.

4. Look up "minimal cues" and "mnemonics" in a psychology text; report to the class on their application to note-taking as an aid to memory.

5. Go through several pages of your class notes for any one of your courses and make minimal cue notes out of them. Hand in a sheet of the notes "Before" and "After" to your instructor.

6. Make an informal study, by interview, of methods of outlining in actual use. Find out why each user prefers the form he uses; report to the class on your findings.

Chapter 4

WRITING AND REVISING

"YOU WERE TALKING about putting the information in your own words, but I can't do it. I can get the information all right, and I can get it into an outline that seems to make sense, but then I put a blank sheet of paper in the typewriter and just stare at it. I can't get even the first line down in my own words."

That's his story; his report was late. "Who won the game last night?" I asked him. "We did, 97-87," he said. "I missed it. Tell me how it went," I said. He told me the story of the game without a pause. "Now, that's what I mean," I said. "That's telling me in your own words, just what I've been talking about. Why can't you do it on paper?" "That's different," he said. "Why, I was *at* the game. I was there." Pause. "I guess you're wondering where I was when I was getting stuff together for this report," he said. "I guess I was *there*, too." Longer pause. "I guess I'd better just go back to the house and start writing it down." "Fine," I said. "No time like the present."

Getting Under Way. A lot of writers seem to come without built-in self-starters. Actually, it doesn't matter where in a report you begin to write—the beginning; the middle; where you have the most interest or the most material; or (as I often do) where you have the least interest and the greatest wish to get it over with. The important thing is to start—and the best place to start is what seems to you the easiest place.

Take any of the topics or subtopics in your outline and write it in pencil at the top of a sheet of paper—notebook paper or any kind of paper you have handy. Start to tell about it. Suppose I asked you to tell me, orally, the answer to the question,

43

"What are you going to tell the reader about this topic?" What would you say? Write it down. Allow plenty of space between lines and in the margins to make changes; write on every other line or every third line. Keep writing. If you can't think of a word you want to use, skip it and leave the space blank, or put in a substitute in parentheses. Remember: it doesn't have to be perfect. It doesn't even have to be right. This is the rough draft, the first draft. You will go back over it and catch everything—but later, not now. On this first draft, anything goes—no one will see it but you. Therefore there is nothing to worry about, nothing to be self-conscious about. Grammar, spelling, punctuation need not get in your way and hold you back. If you come to a place for a footnote, don't worry about numbering it; just draw a line across (or part way across) the page right under the line where the reference occurs, write the footnote in, draw another line under it, and keep writing:

*the distinction between report writing and hack writing.**

**Cecil B. Williams and John Ball, Effective Business Writing* (New York: The Ronald Press Company, 1953), pp. 443-45.*

The real purpose of research writing is

When you have finished with one topic or subtopic from your outline, pick another and start a fresh page.

Headings and Subheadings in the Rough Draft. When your rough draft has taken shape you will for the first time be able to decide how well your outline stacks up against the needs of the reporting job. Each of the topics of your outline was potentially a heading for your report, and each of your subtopics a subheading. Your actual writing, however, may well show that some of the topics are really subtopics, that some of the subtopics deserve to be separate main topics, that some of the subtopics just did not develop and should be scratched, or that there are subtopics or even topics showing up that you hadn't thought of at all when you made your outline. There may be a need to shift the order of topics, or even the whole approach of the report. From the way your rough draft shapes up you can make a new outline, this one a tentative table of contents, with headings and subheadings phrased to be consistent with each other, as you will want them to be in the final draft. Then you can go through your rough draft rephrasing headings and subheadings, if necessary, to make them fit the tentative table of contents. Underline main headings three times to show that they are to be put in full capitals in the final draft, and underline subheadings once to show that they will be underlined in final draft.*

Working with the Rough Draft. With the skeleton or framework of your report now clearly defined by the headings and subheadings, you can turn back to the order and organization within the topics, within the subtopics, and finally within the paragraphs and sentences. What you want is clarity, conciseness—you don't want to be a report-writing Fancy Dan. Building suspense or emotional tension is outside your province as a writer of reports; the questions you will ask of each section of your rough draft are:

Is it clear?
Can I make it clearer?
Are these ideas in the right order? Can I find a better order?
Would an example or a case study help?
Would a table or a graph help?
Is it concise?
Have I wasted words?
Suppose I cut this, or this, or this—what would happen?
Is it coherent?
Does it stick together? (Did you ever try making popcorn balls and have them fail to stick together? Sometimes pieces of paragraphs are just as uncooperative as pieces of popcorn.)
Does it seem to flow along smoothly from one idea to another? (Try reading it aloud.)

When you find something to change, draw a line through your first draft version and change it. If the change is major, rewrite the section, using margins, spaces between the lines, or stapled-on slips of paper. I use 8½ × 11 gummed sheets of plain white paper for major changes; I cut off the right size

* Actually there are several alternative ways to set up headings and subheadings; we will not rule out use of other methods.

piece with my paper-cutter and stick it right on top of the obsolete wording.

Second Draft. Some report writers type their final copy from their corrected rough pencil draft; some compose their rough draft on the typewriter, correct it in pencil, and retype

The Baldwin Locomotive Works was founded in 1831 *in Philadelphia, Pa.,* by Mathias W. Baldwin. The company *operated under* ~~has various~~ names, *during the 19th century* and at the turn of the 20th century was a general partnership under the name of Burnham, Williams, and Company. On June 8, 1909, the Baldwin Locomotive Works was incorporated at Harrisburg, Pennsylvania, with the provision that the stockholders, who were the partners at the time of incorporation, would be the Board of Directors and officers *of the corporation.* The firm had $20,000,000 of $100 par capital stock outstanding of which $10,800,000 was preferred stock entitled to one vote for each of two shares. The remaining stock was *no par* common stock with full voting power. The preferred stock ~~was~~ entitled to 6% per annum cumulative dividends and ~~were~~ preferred both as to dividends and liquidation of principal assets. The main plant was located in Philadelphia with a large branch at Eddystone, Pennsylvania Baldwin also owned the Standard Steel Works, Burnham, Pennsylvania.

~~1910~~ On May 1, 1910, Baldwin issued $10,000,000 first mortgage 5% 30 years sinking fund gold bonds with the provision for a 2% sinking fund to begin in 1915 for which the bonds ~~could~~ be purchased at the stated price of 107½ and interest This issue was secured by all real estate, buildings, */and* machinery, amounting to $14,500,000, and capital stock of the Standard Steel Works ~~at~~ $3,500,000. Bonds to the amount of $5,000,000 ~~were~~ reserved for additions and improvements *On condition that they* ~~not greater~~ *supplied* than 75% of the cost of such *additions and improvements* It was noted that earnings applicable to interest have in the last 10 years been approximately $2,800,000 per year. The net assets after application of ~~present~~ proceeds and deducting bills and accounts payable ~~are~~ *were* greater than $30,000,000. The entire bond issue was sold at 99½.

FIGURE 10. Page of a Second Draft from a Report by Nancy Kiehborth, a Miami University Junior.

it to get their final draft. But many experienced report writers use a method I strongly recommend to all beginners: they type a second draft from the corrected rough pencil draft, check it carefully, and type their final copy from the second draft.

The best place to catch spelling errors, nonstandard English usage, and editorially unsatisfactory punctuation is in the second draft; if no second draft is used, of course all these faults must be corrected on the rough draft. The second draft gives the writer a chance to read his report rapidly in type, just as his reader will read it, and to give its content and organization a further evaluation. Often the report reads better in type than it did in longhand; if it reads worse there is still time to fix it.

At every reading the writer will find some improvement to make in his phrasing: some balky construction will clear up or some cliché will suddenly seem unnecessary. The best of the professionals will keep tinkering with their wording; as newspaper desk men sometimes say, "There is no good writing; there is only good rewriting."

Footnotes are inserted where they belong in the second draft, and are numbered consecutively. When it is certain that there will be no further major change, pages are numbered tentatively; and page references to other parts of the report or to the appendix are tentatively filled in.

Typing the Final Draft.

This label is the key to good final drafts. All the work should have gone into the rough draft and the second draft; nothing is left but a typing job to complete the final copy. Neatness, good fresh ribbon, good bond paper, and above all *carefulness* are essential.

Illustrations, diagrams, and graphs should be drawn in ink, although colored pencil may be used for coloring bars or segments in graphs.

Proofreading. (Also see pp. 225-30.) Amateur and professional writers alike must read proof—and they are never happy about it, either. Reading proof is hard; it means concentrating word after word, sentence after sentence, on each detail of printer's proof or a final draft of a report.

> Is this the way I had it?
> Is this the way I mean it?
> Does this make sense?
> Did I copy this figure right? (Better check my notes.)
> Is this 100% right?

One thing that makes reading proof hard is the way we get caught up in the meaning as we read along. We will be reading proof carefully,

> The . . best . . style . . for . . reports . . uses . . language . . as . .
> a . . perfectly . . transparent . . medium. . . . Clear, . . clean . . glass, . .
> though not as beautiful as stained glass, . . lets . . in . . more . .
> light; . . in the same way a plain, . . clear . . style . . does . . not . .
> call attention to itself . . but . . does . . pass along the facts with
> maximum efficiency.*

and in spite of all we can do we see phrases and groups of logically connected words as units of meaning. "In the same way," "call attention to itself," and "pass along the facts" normally group themselves in our minds for efficient reading, and generally that is a valuable aid to us—but when we are reading proof it is our greatest handicap.

A related difficulty in the form of a mental quirk is the fact that a proofreader of his own writing is likely to pass up typographical errors because he tends to read not what is there but what he intended to put there. The thing is correct and clear in his mind, and so, going merrily along reading manuscript that is generally satisfactory, he fails to catch little slips like *there* for *their*, or even larger deviations and failures to make a point crystal clear. Often a very careful proofreading will show you that the point you thought you had made was only partly expressed—must be rephrased if the reader is to get it. You

---

* Cecil B. Williams and John Ball, *Effective Business Writing* (New York: The Ronald Press Co., 1953), p. 445.

must communicate continuously with your reader; you can't afford either to lose his respect through errors or to baffle him through lack of clarity.

Effective proofreading, then, must find some way to break the normal reading patterns we use. Reading each page backward, one word at a time beginning with the last, is one good way to break the pattern—though with this system there is no way to recognize words that are spelled right from the dictionary's point of view but that are not the right words for the context: *to* instead of *too*, or *principal* instead of *principle*. My suggestion is that you develop the habit of bringing each word into focus separately, as though a small magnifier were being passed slowly across the page:

After the basic **theory** of radioactive disintegration

One of my students actually brought a magnifier with him to his final examination to proofread his paper; it seemed to work, for he found all but one small error. (However, results are not guaranteed.)

Along with the one-word-at-a-time proofreading, you should of course read the report once or twice for meaning. If this seems like a lot of bother, let's agree that it is and take time for yet one more check of the report. Are its pages in the right order? Are any paragraphs left out? Sure those figures aren't ten or a hundred or a million off? From the digging-for-information stage through the rough draft to this stage, the report has been work—it's worth some trouble to make this final draft *right*.

Exercises and Problems

1. On the next page is a paragraph of very rough first draft; work it over. Type up a second draft and hand it in to your instructor.

④ The Diference Between Pleasing and Distracting sounds
   There is no deffinate "nice" sound What is ~~nice~~ pleasing to
one person, may be extreemly irrating to some one else
In general though, sounds which consist of fairly
~~and~~ uniform vibrations tend to be ~~~~ pleasant
to the ear, while those of non-uniform vibrations, ~~of~~ or
of ~~thereby~~ high intensity are unpleasnt, or comonly
called noise. The good accoustics engineer will
reduce so called noise trying to leave the pleasant
sounds.

2. Prepare a final draft from your second draft; proofread it carefully and hand it in.

3. Here is a paragraph of second draft that needs some work. Revise it.

> During President Thompson's administration(1852-1874)
> the road almost reached its present geographical limits. By
> means of finamcial loans, stock and bond purchase and guaran-
> teed bonds, the Pennsylvania acquired an interest in most of
> the impostant roads in Ohio and Indiana. The main reason for
> such financial assistance was to help itself through the
> interchange of freight and passengers. A few of those roads
> so assisted included the Ohio and Pennsylvania, Ohio and
> Indiana, Ft. Wayne and Chicag, Marietta and Cincinnati,
> Steubenville and Indiana, and the Philadelphia and Erie. At
> the same time they were also building up strong branch-line
> network in these states. The same expansion took place to
> the east and southeast of Pittsburgh. At the end of 1862 the
> investment in other roads amounted to only $2,777,000 but by
> 1673 it was in excess of $70,000,000 and today it is
> $660,000,000.

4. This paragraph of copy was submitted as final copy even though it contains several typographical errors. Copy the paragraph and mark the errors with the appropriate proofreaders' marks (see p. 228).

We will first consider river transportation. Each
barge has a capacity of 900 tons. The transportation rate
from Pomeroy to Cincinati is 65¢ per net ton. The riverfront
facilities at Cincinnati are located on the north bank of the
Ohio River, near the Louisville and Nashv lle bridge. The
Riverfront Transpostation Company owns the Fulton Coal
Tipple, also accessible to the Motor Carriers. The elevation costs includes the handling of the coal from the barges
to the wharf at the rate of 35¢ per netton. The Riverfront
Company has facilities to stockpile 30.000 tons for storage.
The storage rate is 25¢ per net ton for a period of six
months. There is an additional charge of 25¢ pernet ton for
elevating the coal at the time it removed from riverside
storage. The two ways of transp orting the coal from the
wharf at the riverfront to our plant are via Motor Truck or
Railroad.

5. Explain the use of *stet.*, ¶, ⸖, l. c., ⌒.

6. Write a rough draft paragraph summarizing a talk or lecture.

7. Write the second draft of your paragraph.

8. Prepare an accurate final copy, and submit all three drafts
to your instructor, along with your notes on the talk.

Chapter 5

LANGUAGE

A WORD can carry a lot of freight. Take "Hi."

Jack had been working for years to be mayor. This had been his *big chance*. Nominated by the dominant party in town politics, supported by all the councilmen but one: how could he lose? His opponent had been Pete—much younger, still working on his law degree, not even supported fully by his own minority party. Pete had run a reckless campaign, recruiting school kids to ring doorbells, going in to talk where he hadn't been invited; Jack had called it "undignified." The morning after the election Jack met Pete at the drugstore. "Hi, Mayor," Jack said.

Another fellow named Jack in the same town was a professor at the college. Don, one of his students, had done the work of ten men to promote a concert at the college by the George Lewis Jazz Band of New Orleans, last of the great authentic bands. The band had come, excited by their first trip North since they'd gone to New York with Bunk Johnson in 1945. The band had never played so well: "Careless Love," "Corrine Corrina," "Ice Cream," "Burgundy Street Blues," "The Saints." An overflow crowd of students had given them a standing ovation. After the concert, at the party at Jack's home, George Lewis had told Jack and Don that this had been the happiest day of his life, that it had made him feel that his music was worth all the trouble it had been to build the band and keep it going. Jack and Don were short on sleep the next morning when they met at the door of their 8 o'clock. "Hi, Don," Jack said.

"Hi" meant different things to the two men named Jack—and it sounded different when they said it. The greeting was more than just the word—it was the way the voice made the word: slow, fast; high, low; loud, soft; harsh, gentle. It was the tim-

52

ing—the hesitation or eagerness. It was the facial expression, the gesture.

What *did* "Hi" mean? Take "Hi, Mayor"—did that mean "How are you, Mayor?" No, I imagine it meant something like this: "I know you know how much I wanted to be mayor, and I imagine you wonder how I'm going to take it that you've won. Well, a man has got to live in the present, not in the past, and I'm going to take it without complaint if you'll let me. Without committing myself any more than I can help, I can imply that if you want to be friendly, I'm willing—I'll listen to the way your voice sounds and figure out from that whether our relationship in the future will be closer or farther apart."

Language Is Words Plus. The process of using language to communicate is more complex than a few terms and rules in a book (or more simple, if you happen to think that life is simpler than a stack of textbooks). Language is part of our life. What we put into communication is an awareness and understanding of human relationships, of human behavior, and of symptoms of human attitudes that it has taken our lifetime to develop. We have acquired a kind of radar (sometimes called *perceptiveness*) that warns us when our communication is getting off the track or approaching danger zones. We put our bodies into communication—our hands, our faces, and most expressive of all, our voices. During our lifetime we have learned to play the musical instrument which is the voice so that it can make *Yes* out of *No* and *No* out of *Yes*. Intonation, pitch, intensity, voice rate: these are technical terms, but without knowing what one of them means a 10-year-old is master of them all.

Another thing we put into communication is words.

Words Are Symbols. A word is a symbol that stands for something else. We would use the something else instead of its symbol except that as Swift implied in the third book of *Gulliver's Travels* it is often impractical to carry around with us all the somethings we might want to use in conversation. If we are not near enough to Mt. Everest to point, we have to refer to it by using symbols:

The symbol *M* plus the symbol *t* plus the symbol . plus the symbols *E, v, e, r, e, s,* and *t* make two *words*—symbols standing for the big hunk of windswept rock over in Asia.

As the example shows, there can be symbols within symbols, symbols standing for symbols. Here are some more symbols; see if you can identify them:

1. π 6. ¶

2. □   7. 卐

3.   8. £

4. ð   9. 山

5. - - - - - - -   10. O

The answers are at the bottom of the page.*

Men have been using symbols for so long and have become so accustomed to having them convey meaning that they take them for granted; they often fail to apply to them the scientific objectivity of approach they use in their work. Two of the commonest errors of approach to symbols are a confusion of the symbol with the thing symbolized and a tendency to talk and define in symbols that are too abstract (or remote from the thing symbolized) to pin down meaning exactly.**

The Word Is Not the Thing. In primitive magic a name was often considered to carry with it some of the characteristics it described; to make a child swift of foot a parent might call him

* 1. Pi, a Greek letter and common mathematical term.
  2. Map symbol for county seat.
  3. Borzoi, the colophon of Alfred A. Knopf, New York publisher.
  4. Eth, an Anglo-Saxon letter of the alphabet, pronounced *th*.
  5. Another map symbol: road proposed or under construction. Failure to properly identify this one stranded me on top of a Virginia mountain once.
  6. Proofreaders' symbol: start a new paragraph here.
  7. Swastika, symbol of Hitler's Germany.
  8. British monetary symbol: pound sterling.
  9. Chinese word meaning *mountains*.
  10. Stands for zero, or for the fifteenth letter of the alphabet.

** Other errors in man's approach to symbols are discussed in any thorough work on semantics, such as S. I. Hayakawa's *Language in Thought and Action* (New York: Harcourt, Brace & Co., Inc., 1949).

Fleet-as-a-Deer. Even today we personify names and other symbols. We love or hate flags and emblems depending on our previous experience with them or what we have been told about them; we react to the label "red" as if the label itself were something to become emotionally disturbed about. The word or symbol cannot be the thing, any more than money can be the goods it buys; treating the symbol as if it were the thing leads to fuzzy thinking and fuzzier writing. The general semanticists say it leads to un-sanity. An example: at the beginning of World War I the inhabitants of a small midwestern town turned in fury on a *word*, taking out on it, defenseless as it was, their indignation at a *thing* out of their reach. They changed the name of their village from *Germantown* to *Liberty*, and burned all evidence that the awful word had ever been connected with them.

Abstraction. All symbols are two stages removed from life itself. To abstract means *to remove*, to move away from the specific or concrete. We can best show the process of abstraction through a chart (Fig. 11).

There is nothing wrong with the symbols at the top levels of abstraction—they are perfectly good symbols. Our error in using them comes from the fact that it is easy to get into the habit of defining or explaining in terms that are farther from the process and experience levels than the symbol we are defining. If someone asks "What is a mosquito?" we automatically say "An insect." We should, if we want to define sharply, say "Go out on the porch on a summer night and sit near an electric bulb. That buzzing sound that seems to power-dive at your ear is made by a mosquito. You'd better get it before it gets you."

The semanticists call a definition that points toward the process and experience levels an *operational definition*. The value of the operational definition is shown when dissenting groups try to agree on the application of higher-level abstractions like "right." What does "right" mean in "Right to strike"? Try defining it the traditional way (term, genus, differentiae) first, then the operational way. If disputing parties can get down to examples and cases they can always find specific areas of agreement—and from small agreements large agreements grow.

ABSTRACTION CHART *

SHOWING LEVELS GROWING MORE AND MORE ABSTRACT FROM BOTTOM TO TOP

The vertical bar, as it changes from black to lighter and lighter gray, reflects the LEAVING OUT of characteristics in the process of abstraction.

Living
  organism

Human being

Man

Graduate
  student

Bruce Buckley

SYMBOLIC LEVELS

This level and all those above it are symbolic levels which grow more and more abstract, LEAVE OUT more and more of the characteristics of Bruce Buckley; they spread out more and more and pin down less. Korzybski called these second-order symbolic levels INFERENTIAL LEVELS.

Korzybski called this first-order symbolic level the DESCRIPTIVE LEVEL; it refers as directly as symbols can refer to the things or events pointed to beneath the symbolic barrier at the experience or process levels. Yet even at this level symbols LEAVE OUT all individual differences and changes in process—changes in Bruce Buckley, say, from 12:01 to 12:02, from July to November, from 1955 to 1965.

QadcR42bztheg$(kmz&JopW$.,q-z;½$RBEaliwWbplq.zo-3& . . . This is the theoretical SYMBOLIC BARRIER which keeps us from dealing directly with things and events . . .).a-½¢2nRbT7a'(qmnRga¢23BTYeaTbqp9U62ma&ma62-½¢a/2WdqbaHTP

EXPERIENCE LEVEL

This level LEAVES OUT all that our senses cannot perceive, unaided or with the help of such equipment as lenses or electronic devices. Put another way, it ABSTRACTS from the process level only those characteristics which our senses can perceive. Bruce Buckley can be seen, heard, recognized through the senses; the concept at this level includes the man as we know him—how he looks, sounds, walks, etc.

PROCESS LEVEL

The level at which all things function and all events occur: photosynthesis, cell division and growth, erosion and decay, seeing and thinking. Most of the qualities of things and beings at the process level are unknown or imperfectly known. A man is so complex and multidimensional on the process level that the concept staggers our symbol-bound imaginations. The concept includes everything about the man—chemical, physical, psychological—at one moment of time, everything known and everything unknown. As the symbol at the extreme left implies, nothing is LEFT OUT, even at the atomic level.

FIGURE 11. Chart Showing Process of Abstraction.

* A clear adaptation of Alfred Korzybski's Structural Differential on which this chart is based in part, is found in Irving Lee, *Language Habits in Human Affairs* (New York: Harper & Bros., 1941), pp. 264 ff.

The Way We Get Meaning. The writer strings symbols along in a row; he puts his meaning into them. His language is the language of speech, less the dynamics of speech and (too generally) the idiom of speech. Since the writer cannot rely on the raised eyebrow or the raised voice, he must be more explicit than the speaker; his language must be somewhat more rigid, less fluid. He can indicate some difference in pauses and emphasis by punctuation, spacing, typography. When he gets done, though, the writer has crowded his meaning into a few symbols, for better or worse: a few one-dimensional symbols lined up in a row.

The reader starts at the beginning of the row; his objective is to get the meaning out of the symbols, to see what the writer has to say.

How We Get Meaning as We Read

A "A." Well, so far we know that the next word is likely to be the name of something.

s
t Now we have a good notion of what the whole sentence is about.
o Unless the word is used figuratively (and we'll stay on the alert
r for such a usage) we are going to learn about storms or a par-
m ticular storm. Next word—very likely an action word, a verb.

o We were right—a verb. And it is storms in general and not some
c particular storm that we will read about. I'd say we are going to
c find out what makes a storm (part of which we probably know
u already from the television weather men) or possibly something
r about how often storms occur in some particular place or places.
s

w Yes, I'll bet 98 to 2 it's going to be about what makes a storm. We
h are going to read about cold fronts and warm fronts hitting each
e other and kicking up a ruckus. Next word: "a."
n

a What did I tell you? From here on we can read groups of words.
It's easy.

FIGURE 12. Chart Showing Process of Gaining Meaning from Writing.

This process of developing meaning is indebted to information theory (see pp. 158 ff.) and to structural linguistics. For a good linguistics bibliography see John B. Carroll, *The Study of Language* (Cambridge: Harvard University Press, 1953).

m
a
s — Flip a coin: it will be "mass of cold air" or "mass of warm air" next.
s

o
f

w
a — Now we know the next seven words: ". . . air and a mass of cold air."
r — After that it will say "come together" or "meet."
m

a
i
r

a
n
d

a

m
a
s — This is a little like free-wheeling or coasting.
s

o
f

c
o
l
d

a
i
r

m
e — "Meet" was right. We aren't going to learn anything more—this
e — sentence can quit anytime.
t

a
n
d

FIGURE 12—*Continued.*

a
t
t
e   Next word: "to."
m
p
t

t

o

d

i

s

p   "Each other"—and *that* will finish the sentence; it could have stopped
l   long ago.
a

c

e

e

a

c

h

o

t

h   We know, we know.

e

r

     Good—a period. Now we can see if the next sentence tells us some-
     thing we don't know already.

FIGURE 12—*Concluded.*

The reader brings to the job of seeking meaning a wide range of experience with symbols and with the life they relate to; he brings also a willingness, even an eagerness, to learn from each symbol, even from each punctuation mark, how to interpret the meaning of the whole.

To show how the process works, I have set a row of symbols vertically down the page in Fig. 12, with a running commentary on the rapidly developing body of meaning gathered by the reader.

Now, in the sentences which follow, try observing the way you get meaning; read the words in capital letters, stop, and see if you can fill in the rest of each sentence by guessing.

SOME SENTENCES KEEP YOU HUNTING MEANING
right down to the end.

OTHERS GIVE YOU 95%
of the meaning in the first few words.

A PERSON WITH READING KNOWHOW DOES NOT
waste time with a sentence after he has found its meaning; he scans it quickly and goes to the next one.

The Futility of Classifying. What does all this about storms and warm air masses and meaning in Fig. 12 prove?

We build meaning as we read.

By the time we finish a sentence we have its meaning—or we never will have. Generally we don't even need the last words of a sentence to get the sentence's meaning.

In other words, analysis, or tearing apart a completed sentence and naming the pieces, is *not* the way we get meaning, and is unrelated to the process of getting meaning.

Neither does tearing apart a completed sentence and naming the pieces supply the kind of background it takes to *write* good sentences. Write for me, now, a proper noun followed by a transitive verb, past tense, followed by an infinitive phrase, the object of the verb, made up of the subject of the infinitive, the infinitive of an irregular, intransitive verb, and a first person pronoun in the same case as the subject of the infinitive. Want a clue? The situation is one of mistaken identity, and the subject is *Jack*. Go ahead—write it.* It's easy—unless you have lived a normal life so far and learned to use your language more or less in spite of the formal rules of grammar.

What is basic about written language is the way symbols carry meaning—the way meaning goes into a sentence, the way it comes out, the ways it may get lost in between, and the ways to keep it from getting lost. We learn these things not by learning dead rules but by working with the living language.

* One answer—not the only one—is "Jack thought him to be me."

Grammar is abstract; it is full of symbols for symbols, names for names. Once these abstractions get put into a book they remain static, an unchanging record of the way language was once. Language itself is constantly changing, however, and the only way to keep up with that change is to learn from the living language. Change is good, it is healthy, it is inevitable; no one book or thousand books can build a dike against it. The split infinitive, the sentence ending in a preposition, and the contraction were once out of the question in most college English classes; now they're becoming OK. The distinction between *shall* and *will* and the whole use of the subjunctive mood are on their way out of the language.

Don't let what we have just said shake your confiden⌄e; everyone who can read this book has learned a lot about his language, and should have confidence in his ability to use it. What we are saying is that grammar and our language are not the same thing; you can use the language skilfully and not know one rule of grammar, or you may know the grammar book by heart and be unable to explain why you were late to class. If you have learned grammar till it is coming out your ears, your study has helped build your concept of good usage, and you won't have to unlearn your rules unless the changing language makes them obsolete.

Whether you know grammar or not, most of what you know about language is not grammar. You learned to talk English without knowing a single rule—you learned to talk by imitating the talk of others, unself-consciously and freely. And you have learned about writing by observing and imitating effective writing—or you should have. You have developed the radar of language perceptiveness we mentioned earlier. You have developed your own style, your own taste and judgment in language, and your own stock of symbols. You can use these resources without referring to the rules of grammar—just as a man can walk without telling his gastrocnemius to get busy and operate his tendo calcaneus.

The Ways We Lose Meaning. The process of using language is made easier and surer if the writer sees precisely what it is that he is doing. Let's take an idea in the mind of the

writer and see what happens to it as we put it in the symbols
we call words.

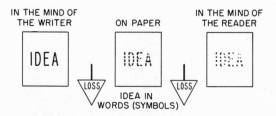

First, we may be making too big an assumption when we say
that the idea is *clear* in the mind of the writer—but let's make
that assumption anyway. When the idea is put into symbolic
language (English words in this case) it suffers a loss, or what
we might call a *leakage* if we visualize our idea as traveling in
a fluid state—a loss or leakage of meaning (the idea becomes
through this loss less like its original, and may end up as no
idea, or a part of an idea, or even some other idea altogether).
The idea loses meaning between the writer's mind and the
symbols on the paper

1. Through the inadequacy of the language, of *any* symbols,
   to carry the whole meaning of any idea (symbols cannot
   reach the process level or the experience level).
2. Through the carelessness of the writer.
3. Through the lack of language skill of the writer.

Very little can be done about the first; the second and third are
more or less in the writer's own control. The only thing it takes
to conquer carelessness is determination. The writer's language
skill can be built up through practice, imitation of good writing,
breaking down of self-consciousness, more practice, more imitation of good writing, more practice.

Most college composition courses stop worrying about the
ideas after they have been put on paper; as a result most of us
fail to remember that the most important factor in the communications process has not yet been mentioned. *After* the
idea has been translated into the symbols on the paper it has to
be translated back into idea again, and the man who will do
that vital job is the reader. The man at whom any writing job
is aimed is the reader; it is only what reaches his mind that

counts. Between the page of symbols and the mind of the reader leakage can occur

1. Through the reader's lack of language skill.
2. Through the reader's carelessness.
3. Through the reader's overt or subconscious resistance (to something new to him, something strange, something which seems to threaten his way of doing things, something which will cost him money, something which will require thought and attention to figure out, etc.)

Though all these seem to involve only the reader, not the writer, the writer can nevertheless compensate for all of them to some extent.

The Counterattack: Ways to Combat Loss of Meaning. The writer can write so *accurately,* so *concisely,* and so *clearly* that the reader's carelessness is unlikely to cause loss of meaning.

Give each of these report sections about 15 seconds of your divided attention (you'll be looking at your watch too) and see which one gets most of its meaning through to you:

The next item to report is the movement of coded merchandise. About the middle of last month a communication was received from the merchandise manager regarding procedures for handling obsolescing merchandise. The communication stressed the necessity for culling from the stock all merchandise coded X6 within a few weeks. The directive was administered except for about one-twelfth of the obsolescing stock that same month, and by the ninth of this month the final fulfillment of the directive's purpose was achieved.

X6 coded merchandise

On April 18 Mr. Solway wrote that all our X6 stock had to be moved out of the warehouse by June 1.

On April 18 we had 726 cases coded X6; on May 1 we had 61; and on May 9 we shipped out the last X6 case.

The writer can *adapt his language* to his reader to overcome the handicap of the reader's possible lack of language skill.

In the examples which follow, not only the language but the whole approach has been adapted to the differing audience of the reports. It is safe to assume that most stockholders of a manufacturing company are familiar with the specialized language of finance and that most employees in the plant are not (though some firms, particularly those whose employees hold

considerable stock, eliminate the language of finance from stockholder reports and send the one report to both stockholders and
employees).

Excerpt from Champion Paper & Fibre
Co. 1953 Annual Report to Stockholders:

As to the outlook for the coming year,
demand for most of our products is
currently strong, and—barring a major
change in general business conditions—
it appears likely that our sales volume
will be maintained at a satisfactory
level. The increased costs we experienced last year will undoubtedly continue to be a factor affecting our
earning power. Also, at present writing there is no assurance as to how
much, if any, relief we may get from
the heavy and inequitable burden of
the so-called "excess profits" tax.

We believe, however, that our investments in natural resources and productive facilities, and our progress in
developing new and improved products, have substantially strengthened
our competitive position; and that we
can rely on the continuing enthusiasm
and cooperation of the people who
make up the Champion "team." We
feel, therefore, that there is reason for
confidence in the ability of our enterprise to meet successfully the chal-
lenges that may lie ahead.

Excerpt from Champion Paper
& Fibre Co. 1953 Annual Report
to Employees:

Now a brief look at the future.
The next fiscal year will be another in which we spend heavily
for the tools of production.

We have laid out an even
heavier budget for plant expansion, but our purchase of forest
lands will be reduced somewhat.
In addition, we're due to make
substantial repayments of money
we borrowed to buy tools. We
expect that all of this money
will come out of our earnings
and depreciation, as dollars
"plowed back" into the business.

Thus, we are continually improving our ability to make
more and better paper at a
lower cost per ton. The industry is growing steadily more
competitive and our individual
skills, our teamwork, and the
quality of our machines will be
put to the test. I am confident
that we will continue to make
progress worthy of the history
of our company.

The writer can sometimes *motivate* the reader to partially
overcome carelessness or resistance; he can make it seem worth
the reader's time and trouble to get meaning by making clear
the report's relationship to the reader's own interests.

Another excerpt from the Champion Paper & Fibre Co. 1953
Annual Report to Employees shows this principle in action:

At the end of the year, gross earnings of the average hourly
worker were about 6% above the corresponding period a year ago.
This was due to increases in the cooperative earnings bonus, the
cost-of-living bonus, and the average number of hours worked
each week. Furthermore, the 25% increase in our Retirement
Income Plan, financed entirely by the company, required an initial
payment of $700,000.

A notable accomplishment in the field of industrial relations is the fact that our safety record was the best in the company's history During the year our lost-time injuries numbered 1.88 per million man hours of work, as compared with 14.30 for the pulp and paper industry. This is a splendid showing, and much credit is due our supervisors as well as all other Champion men and women.

The writer can *establish relationships* for the reader. Understanding is a process of establishing relationships; if I encounter a new concept, I try to find its internal relationship (the way it hangs together) and to find something I already understand that it can be related to. If I can't establish such relationships for the new concept I just won't understand it at all. What do I mean, relationships? Well, a brother and sister are related, and so are two events that happened the same time or place, two ideas based on the same premises, two answers to the same question, two books by the same author, two ways of doing the same job. Causes are related to effects: the muddy track is related to the thunderstorm. Heat is related to friction. Physical laws are related to each other, and to some laws that haven't been codified yet. What we know is always related to something we don't know, and with luck what we don't know is related to something we already have in our experience.

If the reader has to figure out the relationship of the ideas in a sentence he may take too long or even miss them altogether; if the writer can, he should make the relationships clear as he constructs the sentence. In order to help the reader relate a concept to something in his experience, the writer may use examples or suggest applications to the reader's experience. A good concrete example actually becomes a part of the reader's experience when he reads it and then offers a kind of anchor to tie relationships to.

In order to show the reader the relationship existing among the ideas within a sentence or paragraph, the writer can arrange his row of symbols so that the relationship among the symbols is sharply defined; from the relationship among the symbols the reader can see the relationship among the ideas. Manipulating the symbols to help the reader get meaning from them brings in some of the basic principles of rhetoric: *

* See the textbooks by Perrin and by Foerster, *et al.*, cited on p. 38 n.

= *Coordination* means giving two ideas of the same importance
the same sentence structure. What kinds of structure are available to give the ideas? In order of decreasing importance,

> independent clause
> dependent (subordinate) clause
> phrase
> single word modifiers.

If the reader sees two independent clauses connected by a
coordinating conjunction ("and," "or," "nor," "for," "but") he
knows that according to the writer's judgment both the ideas
expressed are important and the two are of roughly the same
importance. "Karl accepted the change of status, but Paul
decided to resign" shows how two men reacted to the same
dilemma. If the reader sees two modifiers given the same sentence structure, "Our employment curve for next year will show
a *slow and steady* uptrend," he will recognize that both are
qualities of the same uptrend, and that the writer weights them
about equal in their influence on that uptrend. The equals
sign (=) is the sign of coordination.

\# *Parallelism* also shows equality of relationship by giving ideas
not only equal but identical sentence structure. The underlined parts of the sentence you are now reading are an example
of coordination and at the same time of parallelism. My sign
for parallelism adds two parallel vertical lines to the sign for
coordination: (\#).

> *Subordination* means giving inferior sentence structure to part of
an idea to show its lesser importance, or giving a cause-and-
effect relationship to ideas. "Our big picnic will be held on
the Fourth of July, *which falls on a Tuesday this year*" shows
the reader the lesser importance of the "which" clause. "We
lost $97,000 in orders *as a result of the strike*" shows the reader
a cause-and-effect relationship. Subordination can be indicated
by the mathematical symbol "is more than" (>).

! *Emphasis* shows the reader what the writer considers most important. Mechanical emphasis uses underlining, exclamation
points, full capitals, color, or some other typographical atten-
tion-getting device. Logical emphasis uses sentence structure

to point to the important idea; suspense (better not try it in a report); facts listed 1, 2, 3, building to a strong conclusion; contrast (use of very short or otherwise unusual sentences or paragraphs); and many other means. The exclamation point is the sign of emphasis (!).

Transition means showing the relationship between the ideas from one sentence or paragraph to the next so that the thought will flow smoothly and the reader will not fall into any such traps as this: "He was always broke, and he had no ambition. His classmates voted him 'most likely to succeed.'" "Huh?" you say, as the contradiction hits you, and you go back and read it again to make sure. Mechanical transition uses special transitional words and phrases (such as *therefore, thus, on the other hand, consequently, then, however*) to serve as road signs and warnings to the reader. *However* means

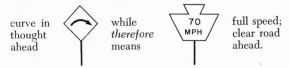

curve in thought ahead   while *therefore* means   full speed; clear road ahead.

Logical transition repeats a key word, phrase, or idea to show how the stream of thought flows. The repeated key phrase in this sentence is *repeated key phrase,* a paraphrase of the definition of logical transition; the paraphrase shows the reader what part of the first sentence is going to be taken up further in the second. My sign for transition is the symbol for drawing together or bridging the gap (◯).

The Writer's Language Responsibility. Does it begin to seem that the writer has a very considerable language responsibility to his reader—a responsibility very similar to that of a quarterback on a pass play? The quarterback has to throw the ball where the receiver is, or the pass is not good. The quarterback can't catch the ball for the end, of course, or *make* him catch it—but he can put it in the end's hands. After that it is up to the end.

How does the quarterback put the ball in the end's hands? Skill, knowhow, practice: it's not an accident. How does the writer prepare to do his full share of the communication job—

to put the idea clear across through the symbols into the reader's mind, to make his language carry its weight? Again, skill, practice, knowhow.

For anyone not satisfied with his language skill and knowhow, we have some recommendations:

Practice   Write whether anyone reads your writing or not. Write your letters, your term papers, all your written work more fully and more carefully than you would need to. Write in your own good language, without self-consciousness. Afraid someone will find fault with your writing? Relax. It happens to everybody.

Read and listen   Observe the use of language by others whose use of language you admire. The more skillful language-use you encounter the more will stick with you. Also, as you read and listen, look for evidence of language change; keep close to the living language. In 1970 you should use the language of 1970, not this year's language.

*Collect symbols   When you read, build your stock of useful symbols as
as a hobby*   you go; master the new words you run into. There's nothing magical about a big vocabulary; and an artificially acquired one (say where you just start to learn A, Aardvark, etc., or to study a vocabulary list) is nothing, period. On the other hand, adding new words from day to day as you encounter them is education, no less, and a good language-skill builder.

*Know the "plus"   Don't let your thinking about language become too
in "Language is   academic. Remember that language is a human trait,
words plus"*   best studied in a human situation. If you listen, you can learn how to use language effectively at the garage or the bowling alley, at the sales conference or the political rally. Language shows how people feel as well as what they have to say; even what is not said can sometimes tell a great deal. Language is far more complex, individual, human, than it seems when its words line up in neat rows according to neat rules; research will tell us much more in the future about the nature, function, and far-reaching influence of language.

*Develop a
semantic
orientation*

Keep your symbols separate in your mind from what they stand for; beware of talking in circles of abstractions. Keep up with semantics to see what new light it can throw on language.

*Study leakage of
meaning, and
learn to plug
the holes*

A valuable part of your language knowhow will be your awareness of the way meaning is put into symbols and taken out, and of the ways meaning may get lost in the process. Every situation where communication breaks down should be considered an opportunity to study this problem directly. Such study will teach you not only specific pitfalls to avoid, but also the full responsibilities of the writer to the reader, and the importance of establishing relationships as you write.

Exercises and Problems

1. Read and report on one of these books:

CHASE, STUART. *Power of Words.* New York: Harcourt, Brace & Co., Inc., 1954.

FLESCH, RUDOLF. *How To Make Sense.* New York: Harper & Bros., 1954.

HAYAKAWA, S. I. *Language in Thought and Action.* New York: Harcourt, Brace & Co., Inc., 1949.

2. Read the *Fortune* article on the Information Theory (December, 1953, page 136 and following). Report on its application to the way we get meaning; discuss its possible implications for communications and reporting. Check the periodical indexes for current articles on the same topic.

3. Discuss the inadequacy of language as a carrier of meaning. Is there any chance of using technology to eliminate some of the loopholes in language? Would a new, consistent, "perfect" language solve the problem?

4. Make a list of 10 more symbols from various fields to supplement the list on p. 54.

5. Make operational definitions for

green
thunderstorm
traffic jam
bum
stuffed shirt
butterflies in the stomach

6. Make a list of ten symbols (words this time) that you encounter in your reading, and trace each one down to the process
level, thus:

> boy
> John D. Doe
> what we can see, hear, sense on the experience level
> the process level: the whole functioning human mechanism

Of course the more abstract the word you begin with, the more
levels you will have to trace.

7. Current English usage: material from an article by Norman
Lewis, "How Correct Must Correct English Be?" *Harper's Magazine*, March, 1949. Mr. Lewis circulated this questionnaire to
authors, editors, English teachers, and others who work with
language; he received 468 replies. Before you read about his
results, take the test yourself, and try it on at least three others whose
use of language you respect. Then get the March, 1949, *Harper's*
from the library and see how your results compare with his. Use
the problem as a basis for class discussion.

Current English Usage

Directions: Here are nineteen expressions about which there is today
a good deal of controversy, and we'd like your opinion, as an educated adult, of their acceptability in everyday speech.

Do not be influenced by whether these usages do or do not violate
formal grammatical rules. Rather, indicate by an affirmative vote,
that you would be willing to use the expression listed or that you
believe such an expression has become sufficiently current in educated American speech to be labeled acceptable usage; by a negative
vote, that the expression, as used, is unacceptable in educated circles.

YES   NO

_____ _____ 1. His attitude makes me *mad*. (*Mad* as synonym for
               angry)
_____ _____ 2. I *will* pay your bill if you accept my check.
_____ _____ 3. The reason I'm worried is *because* I think she's ill.
_____ _____ 4. His work is different *than* mine.
_____ _____ 5. We had a *nice* time at the party.
_____ _____ 6. *Can* I have another helping of dessert, please?
_____ _____ 7. I encountered *less* difficulties than I had expected.
_____ _____ 8. Everyone put on *their coats* and went home.

YES   NO

____ ____   9. How much money have you *got*?

____ ____ 10. *Due to* the storm, all trains are late.

____ ____ 11. She has an *awful* headache.

____ ____ 12. We *only* have five left. (Position of *only*)

____ ____ 13. Let's not walk any *further* right now.

____ ____ 14. We must remember *to accurately check* each answer.

____ ____ 15. He's one person I simply won't do business *with*.

____ ____ 16. Go *slow*.

____ ____ 17. It is *me*.

____ ____ 18. She acts as if she *was* my wife.

____ ____ 19. *Who* did you meet?

8. Rewrite this report so that it will conform to good usage in every way:

March 2, 1955

Mr. K. L. Meyer
Northrup Fabricating Co.
Seattle, Washington

Dear Mr. Meyer

Following is the report you requested on the overtime situation at this plant.

Checking with the personnel manager, he said the instrument mechanics were where the most of the compaints were coming from, I interviewed the 40 men employed in that trade.

I also interviewed all of the foreman throught the plant after which I can say with a certanity that this report covers the entire plant as to the felling of the men employeed.

Sincerly

Casper Amburgy

The insturment mechanics have worked a total of 2045 hrs overtime in the mos. of Jan. and Feb., this total was divided so unevenly as to have given one man 480 hrs and another man only 8 hrs.

This not only make employer-employees relation bad and the men discontended but it has started hard feelings amoung the men themselves.

Some of the men have got an I dont give a darn
attitude. Many jobs now take a full eight hrs to do
where before it might have only took two hrs. Some
have to be done over 3 or 4 times before it is completed correct.

I believe this should be remied immediatly.

Of the many recomendations I have had a chance
to have heard from the men and foreman the most
pratical one is;

    (1). Post a list of the employees names in
        the various trades. Give each overtime
        as their name come up on the list.

    (2)- If a man not care to work when their
        name come up he should be credit with
        the time on the list irregardless.
        When everyone have been credit with
        overtime start over.

I beleive this system will keep the overtime even
and the employees contended.

9. A good way to get experience in establishing relationships
for the reader is to synthesize sentences from fragments of ideas.
Find a current article containing descriptive sentences, explanatory
sentences, or whatever kind of sentences you would like to use for
practice. Have a friend break each sentence up into as many pieces
as possible and put each piece in a sentence or fragmentary sentence
of its own; then see how well you can arrange the pieces and put
them together. Of course there are many ways to put each set of
fragmentary ideas together, and the original sentence may not be
the best way. Here are some samples to practice on; when you
have finished putting them together, check the footnote to see how
their original author, Jerome Namias, wrote them.

First sentence: The forecaster is a long-range forecaster. He works
with one kind of data. He hardly ever uses any other kind. The
kind he uses is about the upper air. He uses the character of the
weather flow. Also he uses the movements of the weather flow.
That is, the weather flow in the upper air.

Second sentence: He takes this information. And he tries to deduce
something. He hopes to figure out the weather conditions. The

ones that will prevail over large areas. This is in the United States. These are not specific conditions he is after, but general conditions. He wonders whether it will be wetter than normal. Or drier. He is wondering about the weather a month ahead. He wonders whether it will be colder. Or it might be warmer.

Third sentence: His forecast is called the extended forecast. There are some things it does not take in. An example would be, things like individual storms.*

---

* Original form of sentences given above:

The long-range forecaster works almost entirely with data about the character and movements of the weather flow in the upper air. With this information, he tries to deduce the *general* weather conditions that may prevail over large areas of the United States—whether, a month ahead, it will be wetter or drier than normal, or colder or warmer. The extended forecast does *not* take in things like individual storms.

From *The New York Times,* June 6, 1954, Magazine Section, p. 34, "The Weatherman Explains the Weather," by Jerome Namias.

Chapter 6

STYLE

YOUR LANGUAGE has a personality all its own. If I were to read a dozen letters or papers or reports you had written, it is very likely I would be able to recognize that personality, and say "I know who wrote this," if I saw a sample of your prose without your name on it. This special, individual personality of language is *style*.

Style in spoken language is like style in written language, except that it is expressed in more ways—by tone of voice (gentleness, firmness, sharpness, harshness), by pitch (high, medium, low), by intensity (softness, loudness), by speaking rate (rapidity, slowness, use of pauses), and by many other means (including gestures and facial expressions). A good example of the importance of these stylistic aids to speech is the story about Mark Twain—he had been shaving and his wife (who disapproved of swearing) had overheard his vivid language. She repeated a string of his best epithets to rebuke him; he replied, "You've got the words right, Livy, but you don't know the tune." *

The writer of prose has no tune; he places words on paper one after the other, and the only way he has of raising his voice or pausing for emphasis is through the imagination of his reader or a few inadequate mechanical devices (underlining, exclamation points, dashes, three or four dots).

It is amazing, considering the handicaps of the written word in comparison with speech, that prose is able to develop much style at all. The style it has depends mostly on the reader's wide previous experience with language and his resultant ability to catch individual differences in the use of symbols to

* Albert Bigelow Paine, *Mark Twain, a Biography* (New York: Harper & Bros., 1912), Vol. 1, p. 559.

express and to imply meanings. The reader uses his imagination to supply intonation and other speech dynamics as he reads; if he reads "Moider de umpire" he knows that the sound of the words in his mind should be different from the sound of "To determine the hypotenuse, take the square root of the sum of the squares of the other two sides." The writer's tools are merely choice of words, order of words, and punctuation, but given a perceptive and experienced reader he can get a lot of personality across with them.

It is interesting that the first stylistic experiments in writing by a grade-school pupil tend to overwork the mechanical devices; carried away by the possibilities of "raising her voice" by underlining words, the fifth-grader underlines practically everything; excited by the potentialities of exclamation points, he (or she) uses them in bunches; a particularly startling bit of gossip about a schoolmate may deserve as many as ! ! ! ! ! Often the language used by adults seems so limiting in its ability to assert personality or to attract attention that the child or youth adds to it, inventing a language of his own. Sometimes aspects of the unusual, over-elaborate style of youth will persist (like a weakness for lavender ink) into adulthood.

A highly individualized style may be an asset and not merely an idiosyncrasy in adulthood. TV comedians, syndicated columnists, writers of personal essays or humorous articles, politicians, and salesmen are among the many who make style pay. Stylist Red Barber's odd ways of saying things are so well known that stylist James Thurber was able to base a successful short story on them: "The Catbird Seat." *Personality* sells cars and oil stock and vacuum sweepers and haircuts; it gets jobs and wins elections. And style is not merely an expression of personality: it is *part* of personality.

Style in Reports. Style is a highly controversial matter in reports.

Some books and teachers say that No style, NO individuality can go into a report. A report deals with facts, they say; it should have no more personality than a statistical table has. Style belongs properly to language used to persuade or to please —to sales letters, advertising copy, short stories, essays—but not to the language used to report. The report writer should suppress his individuality completely; he should translate fact into symbol without intruding himself into the process in any way. His language should not be the language he uses to buy cigarettes or to make a business appointment, for that language has personality; his language should be instead "the language of science" or "the language of economic forecasting" or the language of whatever is being reported.

There is strong criticism of using a special "language of science" from those who feel that style cannot be separated from reports. There is no language of science, they say; there is just language. What is often called the language of science is a stylistic variation of ordinary language—for being precise, objective, impersonal, addicted to scientific jargon, and a little dull adds up to a kind of style. And this style of science—far from making science clearer and easier to understand—actually has been shown by test to be less readable than ordinary language to scientist and layman alike. Also, they ask, how can all personality be removed from language? If it were theoretically possible to take all the personality out of a paragraph, then that paragraph would have the very distinctive style or personality of being without personality. If a man's face, say, were perfectly blank—no features at all—no eyes, nose, mouth— wouldn't he be distinctive and even striking in appearance? You wouldn't say he had "no appearance"—on the contrary.

Fortunately it is not possible to remove all personality from language—and fortunately the trend is away from trying to. Tradition is not enough of a reason to use a stilted, artificial style for reports; if we'd let tradition have its way we'd still be writing all our important documents in Latin. Not that reports should sound like William Faulkner or W. Somerset Maugham; not that report writers should inject personality for its own sake the way some direct mail and advertising men do. Just plain English will do—good, clear, living language, neither spiked with a little old and rare personality to give it a kick nor treated so that 98 per cent of the human elements are removed.

Fig. 13 shows an example that I like—a report Max Allen made

cc: M.E. Carruthers
    A.L. Feild
    B.C. Huselton
    P.E. Ramseyer
    Wm. Rupp, Jr.

                                    November 15, 1951

TO: Mr. R.P. Hindman, Works Metallurgist
                        Butler Division

FROM: P.M. Allen

SUBJECT: Pickling of Bright Annealed 2 Mil 18-10 Ti

When Bill Rupp returned to Butler this week he took two
samples to be given to you of 2 mil, bright annealed 18-10 Ti.
The history of these samples follows:

    Sample #1

    Bright annealed at Butler
    Pickled - 5 feet/minute at 170°F.
    Acid bath proportions -

                    60 gallons water
                    20 gallons nitric acid

    Tank length - 12 feet

    Sample #2

    Bright annealed at Butler

As you can readily see, there has been very little dulling of
the bright surface of the pickled sample. This pickled
surface is much brighter than has been desired by Thompson
in the past.

The end of this same coil had a light scale on it. This scale
was not completely removed during pickling under the above
conditions.

In order to produce a #1 finish on the rest of the bright
annealed coils, it was necessary to scale the surface with a

FIGURE 13. Memorandum Report Showing Unaffected Use of Language in
Technical Writing. (Used by permission.)

regular annealing treatment followed by a pickle. The metal
surface was slightly darker on the bright annealed coils
than on the hard rolled coils which were scale annealed and
pickled. However, the darkening should not be objection-
able.

                                    P.M. Allen
                                    Junior Research Engineer
                                    Research Laboratories

Figure 13—*Concluded.*

What would the lover of stilted scientific language do with
that? Possibly he'd begin the third paragraph "It was noted
that before being subjected to the pickling process Sample #1
showed a slight scaling on its surface near one of its extremities."

What would he lose? Readability, certainly, and some of his
reader's time. What would he gain? Respect? I think not.
Industry does not evaluate words by weight or specific gravity.
Some professional associations may (but judging from some of
the sprightly and readable scientific papers I've encountered
lately I'm inclined to doubt it); business and industry certainly
do not. I'll bet my money on Max's way for the future.

Jargon. The most obvious thing about the style of poorly
written reports is their use of jargon. Jargon is a facet of style;
report-writing jargon, like any other kind, is a symptom of careless use of language.

In the first place, jargon probably comes from sterility of
language, from inability of the writer to focus or concentrate
his attention on his writing, or from the desire to make an impression. The writer knows he talked to four salesmen to find
out why their orders for Model Y had fallen off sharply. He
wants his report to sound impressive from the very beginning;
he feels sure it would not do to say simply and directly what he
did. The "blah's" in the following passage will be filled with
jargon as he writes.

> In order to blah, find out why Model Y isn't selling, blah, blah.
> I, that is the writer, blah, talked, blah, with four salesmen, who
> ought to know, blah, blah. Blah, blah, I, that is the writer, blah,
> am going to put down, blah, blah, what they told me, blah, blah.

Now let's try it with the jargon, using the stilted phrase and the cliché wherever there seems to be a likely opening:

> In order to pin-point the nature of the reason for the progressive declination in the market curve for our Model Y, the writer spent some time in discussing this matter with a number of our most capable sales representatives, men who are in a position to keep an experienced eye on the fluctuations and variations in the broad market pattern. In the pages which follow the material presented is their interpretation of the market situation as these facts became known to the writer in pursuance of investigation of the problem at hand.

We may have overdone it a little, but you get the idea. Jargon is a kind of double-talk. It says things the long way 'round, on the general theory that it doesn't pay to use three little words when eleven big ones will do as well. It runs to clichés and overworked expressions; it prefers the vague to the specific and the fuzzy to the incisive every time. It is a kind of substitute for plain English used by those who feel that plain English is either too plain or too much trouble to write or both. But it isn't effective, for the simple reason that it offends the "listening ear" of the reader. You know how it is with you when you listen to a dull, windy speech—pretty soon you are just hearing blahs and getting nothing whatever from them except noise, plus perhaps annoyance or resentment.

If we are to be quite fair we must admit that many men who respect plain English and are fully capable of writing it are addicted to jargon as a kind of narcotic habit. They picked it up quite innocently by reading reports by other people, and many of them have no idea how strong a hold the habit has on them.

The best way to get rid of jargon is simply to write plain English, and to eliminate all language from a report that you wouldn't use in a careful but extemporaneous oral report. There is no need to refer to a glossary of report jargon—ask yourself if you would *say* it, and if you wouldn't say, don't *write* it. All but the most common clichés will be caught by this test—and if a cliché is a commonplace in careful spoken English it is probably firmly enough entrenched in the language to pass as plain English.

This is probably the place to say that we recognize the big difference between speaking and writing. We don't suggest "writing like you talk" with all the "uh's" and "ah's" and back-trackings and repetitions. We know the language of the bowl-ing alley and the clubhouse is inappropriate for reports. But the careful language of the oral report *is* appropriate for written reports after we screen out the special signals and the structural peculiarities of speech.

Subjectivity and Objectivity. If a report is to be used as the basis for executive decision it must be objective. However, reports may be one thing and seem another. A report may be

(1) Based on objective research and written in objective style.
(2) Based on subjective material and written in objective style.
(3) Based on objective research and written in subjective style.
(4) Based on subjective material and written in subjective style.

Though strict interpretation would allow only (1) and (3) to qualify as reports at all, the order of believability and ap-parent authority of the group would be (1) and (2) equal, fol-lowed by (3) and (4) equal; (2), which is not to be trusted, is far more likely to be trusted than (3), which has a sound basis.

In other words, with nothing to go by but the report in his hands the reader's judgment of subjectivity and objectivity is determined by the style—the way it is said—although the writ-er's approach to getting his material may be misrepresented by that style.

It seems obvious that the report writer needs to develop an objective style. But objective style isn't achieved by use of third person ("the writer") instead of "I." Somehow this avoid-ance of "I" has become confused with the whole idea of objec-tivity in some academic courses in reporting. Objectivity means something else entirely, something far more important; it would save a lot of our time if the avoidance of one word would achieve it. There is nothing wrong with avoiding "I," by the way—if we said there was we'd be buried under a mountain of brickbats. The controversy stirred up by that one little word, particularly in engineering reporting and engineering reports teaching, is hard to believe. Technical reports traditionally avoid any hint of personal opinion or any use of the first person, and some firms and schools make the prohibition of "I" a rigid rule. Times are changing, and we see more and more good technical reports that use "I"; someday the prohibition will have to be lifted. If you can get away with using "I," go ahead —though use it with judgment; if the rule where you write is NO, don't let the use of "the writer" become a habit that you can't break when the rule is lifted. Using "I" with judgment would mean rephrasing "I saw that there were several changes I would have to make in my equipment before I could start carrying out my plan for the experiments," perhaps to "The plan for the experiments made several changes in equipment necessary." However, "Mr. King asked the writer several questions" should be "Mr. King asked me several questions."

The objective style reports; it does not make inferences or judgments (see pp. 259-64, Semantics). The objective style does not exaggerate or seem to exaggerate; it does not make large, loose statements that no one could prove or disprove. The objective style is concrete; it gives examples and refers to experiments, controlled studies, or tables of figures to support its statements. The objective style stays clear of any hint of personal bias or of the writer's holding a preconceived opinion. The objective style is wary of connotations, accidental or on purpose. And of course the objective style is most convincing when it is honest—when it is based on objective research. The objective approach may be put like this: reporting the facts shown on the indicators of his laboratory instruments, the report writer should become himself a laboratory instrument —a camera taking a word-photograph of the instrument readings.

Exercises and Problems

1. Make a specialized collection of individual or unusual ways of saying things under one of these headings:

  Style in sports writing
  Style in James Thurber's stories
  Style in teen-age conversation
  Style in advertising copy
  Style in sales letters
  Style in the *New Yorker*

2. Make a collection of jargon peculiar to some special field (sports, engineering, economics, teaching, letter-writing).

3. Make a collection of jargon generally shared by all fields (clichés and stock phrases such as "in the case of," "in due course").

4. Discuss the case for and against jargon. Isn't it true that many usages once considered jargon are now standard English?

5. Discuss the case for and against personality in reports.

6. "No one can be 100 per cent objective; he is a human being, seeing, hearing, feeling with a human's senses, thinking with a human's brain—and all these human factors bring the subjective element in." Discuss.

7. Collect opinions on the use of the first person in reports from science teachers, business writing teachers, and business teachers; industrial executives who use, assign, or write reports; and textbooks and reference sources (including the *ABWA Bulletin*). Make these opinions the basis for a class discussion of the question.

Chapter 7

VISUAL AIDS

The Use of Graphic Devices. Some reports use graphic devices to supplement the text; some don't. Tables, charts, and graphs are worth while if they make information more meaningful to the reader or if they make information meaningful more quickly. Their use depends on the reader, then, and on the nature and level of difficulty of the subject. They should not be used for their own sake, or from force of habit; James Lillis of Burroughs (at the Wayne University Business Communications Conference, 1950) singled out "the willy-nilly preparation of graphs by amateurs" as one of the major pitfalls of reporting. If the report content is clearest and most readily understood in prose, we use prose. If the report contains information that seems logically to fit into orderly columns, a table will best show the interrelationship of such information and will probably increase readability. If the report contains information that can be visualized better in space, through charts or graphs, than in prose, we use charts or graphs. Often we use all three.

Lists and Tables. The simplest kind of graphic device is the list. It makes items in a series stand out, either by the use of numbers or letters in parentheses running along in the text or by using separate lines and indention, with or without numbers or letters, for each item. Lists are used a good deal in reports, likewise in texts. For examples see pp. 127, 182-83, and many other places in this book.

Tables can also be quite simple, but some, as the following pages show, are designed to carry out several functions at once. They are extremely useful in presenting a variety of material for easy comparison.

There is no one right way to make a table; the use of lines, dots, or other mechanical dividers to separate the lines or columns varies greatly, though the tendency is toward simplicity. Here is a brief, uncomplicated table from *The Aluminum Data Book,* a technical publication of the Reynolds Aluminum Company. The table occurs as part of the text.

Aluminum Alloy	Maximum Forging Temperatures
32S	800 F
18S	820 F
14S, 17S, R317	840 F
25S	860 F
A51S, 61S	880 F

Figures 14, 15, and 16 show a group of more complex tables from the same source. These tables demonstrate some of the range of use that tables can have.

STANDARD TOLERANCES
ROLLED AND EXTRUDED STRUCTURAL SHAPES

Table 47. CROSS-SECTIONAL TOLERANCES

SHAPE	DIMENSIONS			TOLERANCE Inches or Percent of Nominal Dimension ALLOWABLE DEVIATION FROM NOMINAL DIMENSION
ANGLES up thru 6 x 6 inches		t	thickness	±2½%, ±.010 min.
		b	flange width	±2½%, ±1/16 min.
ZEES up thru 6 x 6 inches		t	thickness	±2½%, ±.010 min.
		b	flange width	±2½%, ±1/16 min.
		d	depth	±2½%, ±1/16 min.
CHANNELS up thru 10 inches		t	thickness	±2½%, ±.010 min.
		b	flange width	±4%
		d	depth	+3/32, −1/16

FIGURE 14. Table from *The Aluminum Data Book,* Published by the Reynolds Metals Company. (By permission.)

Table 113. 180-DEGREE COLD BENDING—METAL TO METAL

KEY TO SYMBOLS	TEMPER	GAGE	ALLOY
Alloy Alloy A—2S F—61S B—3S G—R301 C—C50S H—24S D—52S J—75S E—4S	O	.016" .032" .064" ⅛" ³⁄₁₆" ¼"	ABCDEFGH ABCDEFGH ABCDEF ABCD ABC ABC
	H-12 and H-32	.016" .032" .064" ⅛" ³⁄₁₆" ¼"	ABCDE ABCD ABC ABC AB AB
NOTE GAGES NOT TABU- LATED HAVE EQUAL WORKABILITY IF WITHIN THE MAXIMUM LIMITS INDICATED.	H-14 and H-34	.016" .032" .064" ⅛" ³⁄₁₆" ¼"	ABCD ABC ABC AB A A
	H-16 and H-36	.016S	A

FIGURE 15. Table from *The Aluminum Data Book,* Published by the Reynolds Metals Company. (By permission.)

Graphs and Maps. Graphs, which may be thought of as including map graphs or even maps, are the form of visual aid most widely used in report writing.[*] One of the two most popular graph forms is the line graph. Fig. 17 from the Champion Paper & Fibre Company shows caption (at left), vertical scales on both right and left for the reader's convenience, horizontal scale along the bottom below the base line or zero line, and two lines, both labeled, one broken and one solid, across the grid. The other most popular graph form is the bar graph. Fig. 18, an example from the same company, shows the caption at top left, the key below the caption (the key explains the meaning of the different colors or shadings used for the bars), and the bars running vertically from the base line. Each pair of bars is dated, and each bar is labeled with its value.

A third kind of graph also considerably used is the pie graph, as in Fig. 19. As you can see, it is the best device for segmentation—for making clear how something is sliced up into parts.

[*] For standard engineering practice in using and preparing graphs, refer to American Standards Association Z 15.3, *Engineering and Scientific Graphs for Publications* (New York: American Society of Mechanical Engineers, 1947).

Table 115. FINISHES FOR ALUMINUM PRODUCTS

Type of Finish	Name of Finish(1)	Principal Purpose of Finish	General Description of Treatment
MECHANICAL	Grinding	To remove surface imperfections	Bonded abrasive wheel, 25 to 50 grit. Speed 8000 rpm. Grind dry or use tallow or lard oil.
	Polishing	To remove surface imperfections and to achieve decorative finish	Steps include (1) roughing (50-100 grit), (2) greasing or oiling with soft felt wheel faced with 100-200 grit aluminum oxide and lubricant, (3) buffing, and (4) coloring, to obtain high gloss and lustre, using soft abrasives embedded in grease, muslin disks and light wheel pressure. Speeds 6000 to 8000 rpm.
	Scratch Brushing	To obtain coarse or smooth lined texture	Rotary wire brush, using stainless steel or nickel wires of 0.010″ diameter. Speed 2000 rpm.
	Satin Finish	To obtain soft smooth sheen	Modification of scratch brushing. Minute parallel lines are scratched on aluminum surface. Wire diameter 0.005. Speed 2000 rpm.
	Burnishing	To impart fine finish to large number of small parts	Also called tumbling. Use rotating barrel (30 rpm), containing abrasive balls and soap solution. Time 1½ hours for medium finish, 3 hours for fine finish.
	Sandblasting	To produce uniform matte surface	Use silica sand of desired particle size. Generally, lower pressure and finer sand must be used than for heavy metals. Finish is rough and should be protected by oxide treatment or painting.
CHEMICAL	Caustic Etch	Decorative "frosted" finish	1 minute dip in 8% caustic soda at 160°F, followed by 4 minute dip in 40% nitric acid at 70°F.
	Alrok(1)	Paint base	20 minute dip in 2% sodium carbonate—0.1% potassium dichromate at 150°F, followed by 8 minute dip in 5% potassium dichromate at 150°F.
	Bonderite(1)	Paint base	4 minute dip in 7% Bonderite 170—1% boric acid—1.5% sodium bifluoride, at 190°F, followed by one minute rinse in 0.1% Parcolene at 175°F.
	Alodine(1)	Paint base	2 minute dip in Alodine bath at 115°F, followed by ½ minute dip in Deoxylyte bath at 110°F.
	Chemical Polishing	Bright finish or base for anodizing	½ to 1 minute in nitric-phosphoric acid mixture (proprietary composition) at 240°F, usually followed by sulfuric acid dip to remove smut or discoloration.

Type of Finish	Name of Finish[1]	Principal Purpose of Finish	General Description of Treatment
CHEMICAL	Phosphatizing	Paint base	5 minute dip in 8% phosphoric acid at 70°F.
	Zincate	Base for electroplating	Vapor degrease; alkali clean. Zincate bath 55% caustic soda—10% Zinc oxide, 3 minute 70°F.
ELECTROLYTIC OXIDE	Alumilite[1] (Sulfuric Acid Anodize)	Hard, corrosion-resistant oxide film	Alkali clean, Anodize 25 min. in 20% sulfuric acid, 70°F, 18 volts, 13 amps/sq ft. Hot water seal 25 min. 190°F. If dyed coating desired: 20 min. dye bath 160°F. Seal in 1% nickel acetate, 20 min. 190°F.
	Chromic Acid Anodize	Hard, corrosion-resistant oxide film	Alkali clean. Anodize 35 min. in 8% chromic acid, 95°F, 38 volts, 2 amps/sq ft. Hot water seal and dyeing treatment same as above.
	Alzak[1] (Electropolishing)	High light reflectivity	Alkali clean. Anodize 8 min. in 2.5% fluoboric acid, 85°F, 30 volts, 15 amps/sq ft. Final oxidation 15 min. in 7% sulfuric acid, 70°F, 20 volts, 12 amps/sq ft.
ELECTRO-PLATING	Chrome Plate	Abrasion-resistant and decorative finish.	Prepare surface by zincating and copper plating. Chrome plate: 53 oz. chromic acid, 0.5 oz. sulfuric acid per gal. of water, 4 min., 7 volts, 210 amps/sq ft, 125°F.
PAINTING			Paints, lacquers, and enamels adhere tenaciously to aluminum providing the following steps precede the final coating. (1) Clean aluminum surface by either vapor degreasing, solvent washing, or by use of acid or alkaline solution. (2) Phosphatize the surface by use of phosphoric-acid type solution. (3) Apply a zinc chromate type primer.

Notes: (1) The Alrok, Alumilite and Alzak treatments for aluminum are patented to Aluminum Company of America. Alodine is patented to American Chemical Paint Co. Bonderite is patented to Parker Rustproof Co.

(2) See Reynolds Process Manual, "Finishes For Aluminum" for detailed recommendations.

FIGURE 16. Table from *The Aluminum Data Book*, Published by the Reynolds Metals Company. (By permission.)

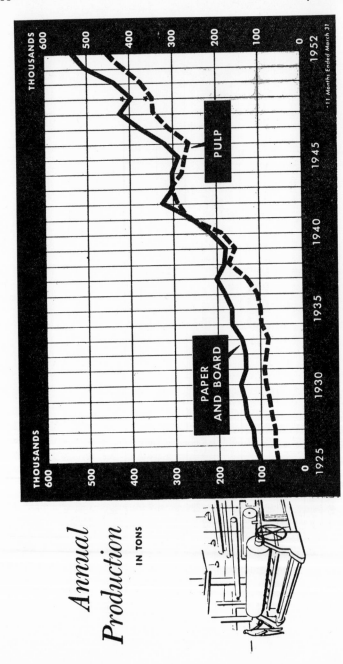

FIGURE 17. Line Graph from 1952 Annual Report of the Champion Paper & Fibre Company. (By permission.)

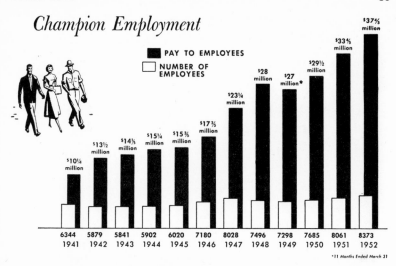

Champion Employment

FIGURE 18. Bar Graph from 1952 Annual Report of the Champion Paper & Fibre Company. (By permission.)

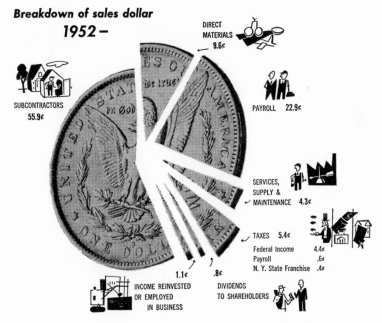

FIGURE 19. Pie Graph from the 1952 Annual Report of Republic Aviation Corporation. (By permission.)

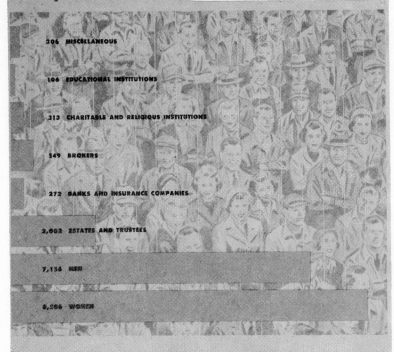

OUR **19,110** SHAREHOLDERS

206 MISCELLANEOUS

106 EDUCATIONAL INSTITUTIONS

313 CHARITABLE AND RELIGIOUS INSTITUTIONS

549 BROKERS

272 BANKS AND INSURANCE COMPANIES

2,002 ESTATES AND TRUSTEES

7,156 MEN

8,506 WOMEN

The total number of shareholders, both common and preferred, rose to a new high of 19,110 in 1952. This is an increase of nearly 800 as compared with 1951. The above chart portrays the number of shareholders by classes. Individuals, men and women, represent a total of 15,662.

Of the total there are 16,906 common and 2,204 preferred stockholders. Nearly one-third live in Ohio and 19 per cent in our service area. Others reside in every state and several foreign lands.

Participation in the Employees' Stock Plan has been steadily increasing. An original block of 50,000 common shares set aside with the stockholders' approval for employees in 1950 was exhausted and another 50,000 shares added in 1952. At the end of 1952 there were 586 employees owning 83,986 shares of common stock of which 51,024 shares were purchased under the Employees' Stock Plan.

FIGURE 20. Picture Graph from 1952 Annual Report of The Dayton Power and Light Company. (By permission.)

The term picture graph is also used, but actually the picture graph is just a development of one of the other kinds. The pie graph just given has pictures with it. Fig. 20 is a bar graph with pictures of faces added to humanize the presentation.

Maps are commonly thought of as belonging in atlases, histories, and geographies, but certain kinds of maps, such as the

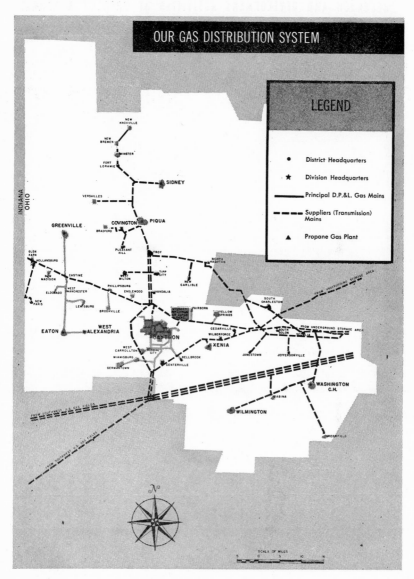

FIGURE 21. Map Graph from 1952 Annual Report of The Dayton Power and Light Company. (By permission.)

RESEARCH AND DEVELOPMENT ACTIVITIES AT PROCTER & GAMBLE

Research and development activities are carried out by a number of different units in the Company. The integration of these units in the Company organization is shown in the chart below.

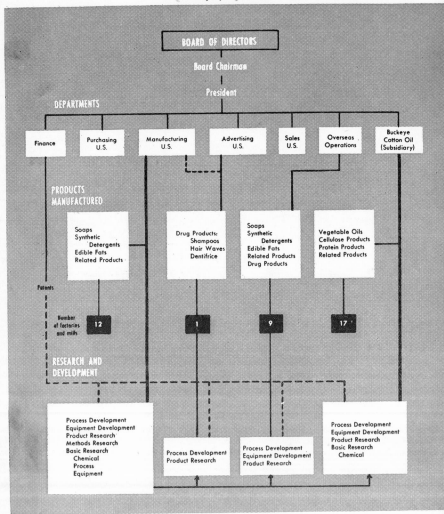

FIGURE 22. Organization chart, from "Research and Development," a pamphlet published by The Procter & Gamble Company on the occasion of the dedication of the Miami Valley Laboratories at Venice, Ohio, September 12, 1952. (By permission.)

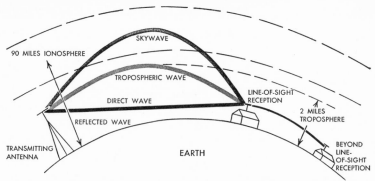

FIGURE 23. Diagram Showing TV Wave Paths. (By permission, from *General Electric Review*, July, 1954, p. 14.)

one in Fig. 21, have their reporting uses too. Sometimes such maps are called map graphs.

Charts, Diagrams, and Flowsheets. Charts are so closely related to graphs that they are sometimes included under graphs. However, we prefer to classify the chart as a visual represen-

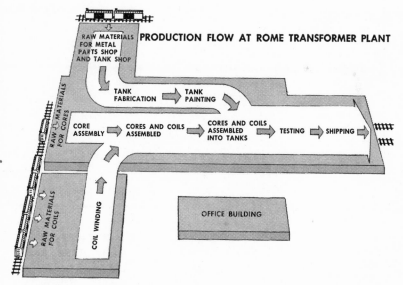

FIGURE 24. Simplified Flowsheet Showing Production Flow at Transformer Plant. (By permission, from *General Electric Review*, July, 1954, p. 23.)

tation between the graph and the diagram, especially the kind used to show organizational interrelationships, as in Fig. 22.

Diagrams are the kind of visual representation used to show the parts of and working relationships in machines, electrical circuits, factories, and the like. (See Fig. 23.) If the diagram shows step-by-step procedures, as from the beginning to the end of a chemical experiment, or the progress from raw material to finished product, as in Fig. 24, it is called a flow diagram or flowsheet.

FIGURE 25. Conveyor Roller on Boom Control Mechanism. (An illustration from the report quoted on pp. 140 ff. By permission.)

Photographs and Drawings. Sometimes the most suitable way to transmit information in a report is by using actual photographs. These may be taken by the person preparing the report, but they are more likely to be borrowed, with proper acknowledgments. Fig. 25 is an illustration from the report on pp. 140-47, "Current Sales Outlook of the Strip Mining In-

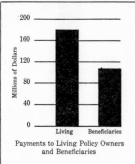

Payments to Living Policy Owners
and Beneficiaries

1953 in Review

For New York Life 1953 was a very good year in terms of increased benefit payments, record sales, higher investment earnings, an improved product and a strengthened organization for better service to our policy owners.

Payments

During 1953 your Company paid out well over a quarter of a billion dollars to policy owners and to the beneficiaries of New York Life policies. Significantly, the larger proportion of these payments went to the policy owners themselves. This is not to deny that the basic function of life insurance is protection for the family in case of death. The fact that New York Life paid out more than $100 million to the beneficiaries of about 24,000 policy owners in 1953 is evidence enough of this continuing need and service. But there has been a growing volume of payments to policy owners and this indicates that our product, the policy contract, is performing an additional role in society.

	1953	1952
Payments to Policy Owners and Beneficiaries	$293,088,561	$267,914,637
In Death Benefits	109,124,229	103,900,538
To Policy Owners	183,964,332	164,014,099
Dividends	76,428,304	64,603,732
Matured Endowments	25,992,002	25,690,878
Annuity Benefits	19,748,398	20,266,612
Accident and Sickness Benefits	24,519,054	19,042,954
Surrender Benefits	37,276,574	34,409,923

In the past year, payments to policy owners included some $25 million under matured endowments. Before these policies matured and made funds available for such purposes as the college education of children or the financing of a new

FIGURE 26. Graphs in Context—Variations in Placement of Visual Aids and Text. (By permission, from 1953 Annual Report of New York Life Insurance Company.)

1952–A BRIEF REVIEW

SALES:

Commissions earned on the purchase and sale of listed securities in 1952, as in the past, constituted the largest segment of the firm's income, accounting for 50%. Off-board trading, retail sales, and underwriting contributed 16%. Commissions on commodities amounted to 18%, and interest and miscellaneous income was 16%.

The firm completed 1,383,242 separate security transactions, on which income averaged $19.67 per transaction.

The average price per share of security transactions made by our customers on the New York Stock Exchange in round lots was $27.39, while in odd lots it was $40.43.

During 1952 our customers bought and sold through us almost three billion dollars worth of securities. Purchases exceeded sales by over $300 million.

Our Municipal Department almost doubled the business it handled in 1951. We participated in 163 municipal underwriting deals in which our commitments totaled over $44 million.

COMMODITIES:

The volume of trading on all commodity futures exchanges in 1952 was 12% higher than during the previous year. Our own volume was 28% higher. More than half of the contracts we executed were for trade accounts. Last year we executed 374,590 transactions at an average commission of $20.92. Our cash commodity revenue was up from $394,554 to $562,841.

Our Commodity Division maintains a staff of 100 experienced people to properly service our growing business in both spot and futures markets. Our specialists in six major groupings of commodities are in direct contact with trade accounts and are available for consultation at any time.

The firm participated in the retail sale of 213 common stock issues and in 43 issues of preferred stock. Including corporate bonds, we participated in the sale of 354 security issues with aggregate sales of $125,600,000, exceeding 1951 sales by over $17 million. Sales in various issues of municipal bonds amounted to over $86 million.

UNDERWRITING:

Last year Merrill Lynch was seventh among all houses in corporate security underwritings. Our total underwritings surpassed all previous records. During 1952, we participated as underwriter in 153 corporate issues with an aggregate commitment of over $130 million. During the year we managed either solely or jointly 35 corporate issues which amounted to over $300 million. As in the past, we were active in the private placement field.

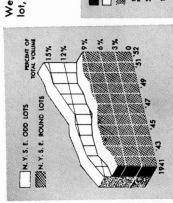

We handled 16% of NYSE odd-lot, 9.4% of round-lot trading.

More shares are listed on the N. Y. Stock Exchange than ever before.

FIGURE 27. Graphs and Modern Captions. (By permission, from 1952 Annual Report of Merrill Lynch, Pierce, Fenner, & Beane.)

dustry of Southern Indiana, Southern Illinois, and Eastern Missouri," by Juvenal C. Schnorbus, Jr.

Modern Trends in Graphic Devices. Figs. 26 and 27 show some possible variation in the combination of visual aids with text. Fig. 27 shows two modern three-dimensional or structural line graphs, and also illustrates the trend toward use of captions which say something about the information contained in the graph. Instead of "An Analysis of Market Changes in Middle-Priced Models, 1945-55" the modern graph says "Middle-priced models double market from 1945 to 1955." The old-style caption might as well say "I am a graph showing something about market changes in middle-priced models. Can you figure out what it is that I show about them?" The modern caption cuts the time required to analyze the graph.

Adaptation in Visual Aids. The graph should be appropriate to its reader and to its subject-matter. If the audience for the report has technical training, a graph may not be needed at all; the less technical background the reader has, the more useful graphs are, and the more pictorial and easy-to-read each graph should be. Graphs prepared for stockholders or non-technical employees may use unusual colors, photomontages, or other devices adapted from advertising to hold the interest of readers while meaning is being conveyed. There is no rule to keep graphs prepared for technically trained men from trying some variety, for that matter—though tradition has so far prevented scientific reports from blossoming out as reports to stockholders have done. The attractive covers, pictorial inserts (often in full color), and varied typography of stockholder reports have nonetheless had some influence on all reporting.

Exercises and Problems

1. Make a collection of visual aids used in reports and technical publications. Bring them to class for analysis. What percentage use color? Are bar or line graphs more popular? Are captions modern or old-style? How many use pictures as part of the graph?

2. Study the visual aids (tables, charts, graphs) used as part of advertisements in an issue or two of *Fortune* or *Dun's Review*.

How do they differ from the visual aids used in reports and technical publications?

3. What types of graph could be used to show the number of minutes you study for all your classes each day for seven days?

4. How could you construct a graph to show how many minutes of each hour of the 24 you spent in study on each of the seven days?

5. Would it be possible to compare your hour-by-hour study pattern with that of a classmate on the same graph? How?

6. What ways can be used to distort information by using a graph? Do you have examples of such distortion of information?

7. Can all tables be represented graphically? Defend your answer.

PART II

Preparing the Report

Chapter 8

FORMS, PUNCHED CARDS, MEMORANDA

So FAR WE have considered reports as custom-built or individually prepared means of carrying information in writing. We have considered *full reports,* all written out in prose, as contrasted with fill-in-the-blanks reports, memoranda, or punched-card reporting systems.

The Full Report, from Two Points of View. Paul Wilgus, industrial salesman, visited nine customers yesterday. Some bought; some didn't. Two had questions for the home office; one had a complaint. One asked for an extension of time on a bill. At the end of the afternoon Paul went to the Drake Hotel for dinner and then in his hotel room wrote nine reports, one on each of the calls he made during the day. The reports were very much alike, but each had to be placed on a separate sheet of paper and given what Paul's boss calls "the full treatment." Paul has often heard the boss say it: "When I want a report on those calls, I want a report, now, none of those six-word notes. I want to know when you got there, what you talked about, when you left—everything, mind you; give it the full treatment."

From Paul's point of view, the full treatment is a nuisance and worse—a rankling sore point—the thing he likes least about his company. It means a late start on an evening that won't be much anyway, an intrusion of the company into Paul's private time. It means also—and this Paul can't forgive—that the boss doesn't trust him to pay his calls. The reports are "full" to prove to the boss that Paul saw the customers and talked with them, Paul feels. He has never known the boss to make any other use of the details in his reports.

From the boss's point of view, the full treatment is a daily reminder to his salesmen that the calls they make are more

SALESMAN'S DAILY REPORT

City or Cities_____ State_____ Date_____

| CUSTOMER No. 1 | DATE | CALL BACK DATE | RECORDS ☐ ADD ☐ REMOVE | MAILING LIST ☐ ADD ☐ REMOVE |

Company _____
Street Address_____
City and State_____
Mr._____Title_____
Mr._____Title_____
Mr._____Title_____
Called with Mr._____

SIZE OF PLANT
☐ Large ☐ Medium ☐ Small

REASON FOR CALL
☐ Follow Up ☐ Service
☐ Inquiry ☐ Goodwill
☐ New Call ☐ Coverage

RESULTS
☐ Order ☐ Lost Order
☐ Inquiry ☐ General
☐ Must Quote ☐ Trouble
For other remarks see letter
Dated_____

| CUSTOMER No. 2 | DATE | CALL BACK DATE | RECORDS ☐ ADD ☐ REMOVE | MAILING LIST ☐ ADD ☐ REMOVE |

Company _____
Street Address_____
City and State_____
Mr._____Title_____
Mr._____Title_____
Mr._____Title_____
Called with Mr.

SIZE OF PLANT
☐ Large ☐ Medium ☐ Small

REASON FOR CALL
☐ Follow Up ☐ Service
☐ Inquiry ☐ Goodwill
☐ New Call ☐ Coverage

RESULTS
☐ Order ☐ Lost Order
☐ Inquiry ☐ General
☐ Must Quote ☐ Trouble
For other remarks see letter
Dated_____

| CUSTOMER No. 3 | DATE | CALL BACK DATE | RECORDS ☐ ADD ☐ REMOVE | MAILING LIST ☐ ADD ☐ REMOVE |

Company _____
Street Address_____
City and State_____
Mr._____Title_____
Mr._____Title_____
Mr._____Title_____
Called with Mr._____

SIZE OF PLANT
☐ Large ☐ Medium ☐ Small

REASON FOR CALL
☐ Follow Up ☐ Service
☐ Inquiry ☐ Goodwill
☐ New Call ☐ Coverage

RESULTS
☐ Order ☐ Lost Order
☐ Inquiry ☐ General
☐ Must Quote ☐ Trouble
For other remarks see letter
Dated_____

Lunch With

| CUSTOMER No. 4 | DATE | CALL BACK DATE | RECORDS ☐ ADD ☐ REMOVE | MAILING LIST ☐ ADD ☐ REMOVE |

Company _____
Street Address_____
City and State_____
Mr._____Title_____
Mr._____Title_____
Mr._____Title_____
Called with Mr._____

SIZE OF PLANT
☐ Large ☐ Medium ☐ Small

REASON FOR CALL
☐ Follow Up ☐ Service
☐ Inquiry ☐ Goodwill
☐ New Call ☐ Coverage

RESULTS
☐ Order ☐ Lost Order
☐ Inquiry ☐ General
☐ Must Quote ☐ Trouble
For other remarks see letter
Dated_____

| CUSTOMER No. 5 | DATE | CALL BACK DATE | RECORDS ☐ ADD ☐ REMOVE | MAILING LIST ☐ ADD ☐ REMOVE |

Company _____
Street Address_____
City and State_____
Mr._____Title_____
Mr._____Title_____
Mr._____Title_____
Called with Mr._____

SIZE OF PLANT
☐ Large ☐ Medium ☐ Small

REASON FOR CALL
☐ Follow Up ☐ Service
☐ Inquiry ☐ Goodwill
☐ New Call ☐ Coverage

RESULTS
☐ Order ☐ Lost Order
☐ Inquiry ☐ General
☐ Must Quote ☐ Trouble
For other remarks see letter
Dated_____

| CUSTOMER No. 6 | DATE | CALL BACK DATE | RECORDS ☐ ADD ☐ REMOVE | MAILING LIST ☐ ADD ☐ REMOVE |

Company _____
Street Address_____
City and State_____
Mr._____Title_____
Mr._____Title_____
Mr._____Title_____
Called with Mr._____

SIZE OF PLANT
☐ Large ☐ Medium ☐ Small

REASON FOR CALL
☐ Follow Up ☐ Service
☐ Inquiry ☐ Goodwill
☐ New Call ☐ Coverage

RESULTS
☐ Order ☐ Lost Order
☐ Inquiry ☐ General
☐ Must Quote ☐ Trouble
For other remarks see letter
Dated_____

Dinner With

Reason if no calls   Miles Driven Today

Planning for Tomorrow_____

FIGURE 28. Form Sales Report. (By permission of Monarch Machine Tool Company.)

than a matter of cut-and-dried routine. The boss knows that some firms use fill-in-the-blanks forms; in fact, he tried them once himself. He says he can't bear to think of a salesman paying a call on old Ed Grubb at Lewiston Mining Co. with that form in his hand. "Mr. Grubb, I'm with Sandler Gear. It says here, how do you like the gears you bought from us? OK? Good. It says here, do you need any replacements, and if so, how many? No? Well, it says here, will you be needing any new gears, and if so, how many, and when? No? That's too bad. Well, I guess that's all I'm supposed to ask you, Mr. Grubb. Goodbye." There is some merit in knowing what the conversation was really about, the boss says; it is a good thing to be able to check up on a salesman from time to time to see that he isn't going stale. Helps in breaking in new men, too.

Paul and the boss both have some good arguments in their favor. There are some arguments against the boss's point of view that Paul didn't know about, however—the full reports are more expensive, harder to file, more affected by variations among salesmen and therefore harder to use as a source of comparative data. In spite of these points, some companies continue to use the full reports for sales, though in most companies their place has been taken by punched-card systems (see p. 109) or by forms like the one illustrated as Fig. 28.

In general, when the full report is used in a reporting situation of any kind it is because that situation calls for evaluation, interpretation, analysis, or reorganization of the straight facts for some specific purpose. In many specialized fields there are other reasons for using the full report: Paul's boss, for example, used it to help break in new salesmen. By studying the approach they used as it was reflected in their reports, he learned what advice to give them. If neither the general reasons nor special reasons exist, there is no point in using the full report; it can profitably be replaced by a simpler reporting method.

Forms. It is obviously foolish to have a report writer repeat information on report after report; the parts which would be repeated can be printed to save him the trouble. The Daily Service Report used by the Monarch Machine Tool Company (Fig. 29) is typical of thousands of time-saving and money-saving forms in use. This form does not do away with the need for the writer to use prose, though it does eliminate the need for the writer to plan the report and organize his material.

Mr. Clifford Fening of the Personnel Division of Baldwin-Lima-Hamilton Corporation changed over to forms for his department's personnel analysis reports in 1954; he explains that

DAILY SERVICE REPORT

THE MONARCH MACHINE TOOL CO.
Sidney, Ohio

Date_____ By_____

Dealer_____ Customer_____

Interviewed_____ Interviewed_____

Machine: Size_____ Model_____ Serial No._____ Date Shipped_____

SERVICE REPORTS SHOULD BE WRITTEN DAILY

Headstock ☐	Taper Attachment ☐	Rapid Traverse ☐	Alignments ☐	End Gearing ☐
Gear Box ☐	Tailstock ☐	Form Turning ☐	Keller ☐	Electrical ☐
Apron ☐	Relieving Attachment ☐	T. A. Variator ☐	Bed Type Turret ☐	Special Parts ☐
Carriage ☐	Sub-Headstock ☐	Auto. Sizing ☐	Ram Type Turret ☐	Operator ☐
EE Electrical ☐	Keller Electrical ☐	Auto. Sizing Elec. ☐	Magna-Matic Elec. ☐	Regular Elec. ☐

Complaint_____

_____

_____

_____

Cause_____

_____

_____

_____

Correction_____

_____

_____

_____

_____

_____

_____

_____

_____

_____

Production data form on reverse side of this sheet.

Remarks:_____

_____

_____

_____

Approved by_____ Has call been completed? Yes_____ No_____

FIGURE 29. Daily Service Report. (By permission of the Monarch Machine Tool Company.)

forms make it possible for a clerk or secretary to prepare the reports while otherwise executive time would be wasted in their preparation.

The form illustrated as Fig. 30 is one of a series prepared weekly; similar reports are made for each of the shops, for the

FOUNDRY   PERSONNEL

Month of_____19___

Classification	Begin Month Totals	Transfers		Put Ons	Pay Offs	End Month Totals
		Add	Deduct			
Brass Foundry						
4 Molder Helpers						
5 Brass Molders						
6 Clerk						
7 Casting Shippers						
8 Core Makers						
Iron Foundry						
9 Apprentice Molders						
1 Iron Molders						
2 Core Makers						
3 Apprecntice Core Makers						
11 Molder Helpers						
12 Casting Chippers						
13 Sand Blasters						
14 Yard Laborers						
15 Core Room Laborers						
16 Foundry Laborers						
17 Millwrights						
19 Clerks						
21 Night Crane Operators						
20 Crane Operators						
22 Night Laborers						
25 Pattern Storage						
10 Cupola						
23 Niles Pattern Shop						
24 H.O.R. Pattern Shop						
TOTAL						

FIGURE 30. Foundry Personnel Report Form. (By permission of Baldwin-Lima-Hamilton Corporation.)

toolroom, for the powerhouse, and for the office personnel throughout the company. These reports are then used in the preparation of the weekly personnel analysis report, which makes it possible to control the balance of productive and non-productive employees and to keep an exact check on the whole

BALDWIN-LIMA-HAMILTON CORPORATION
HAMILTON PLANT
PERSONNEL ANALYSIS

NON-PRODUCTIVE EMPLOYEES

TOTAL EMPLOYEES

INCREASE OR (DECREASE)

Description

Machine Shop:
10 Niles Shop
20 H.O.R. #1 Shop
27 H.O.R. #2 Shop
30 Diesel "A" Shop
36 Diesel "B" Shop
39 Diesel "B" Tool Room
40 Machine Shop-Others
44 Shop Engineering
45 Process Engineering
48 Power House-Heating
49 Power House-Others
50 Iron Foundry
57 Brass Foundry
58 Pattern Shop
59 Pattern Storage
60 General Shop-Others
61 Packing & Shipping
62 Gen. Shop-Inventory
63 "   " -Employ. & Welfare
64 "   " -Purchasing
65 "   " -Watchmen
66 "   " -Traffic
67 "   " -Safety
68 "   " -Planning & Control
69 "   " -Blue Print
70 Eng. General
71 "   Machine Tool
72 "   Diesel Engine
73 "   Can Machinery
74 "   Other Products
75 "   Laboratory
79 "   Detroit
80 Selling - Hamilton
83 "   - Detroit
84 "   - Chicago
85 "   - New York
86 "   - Pittsburg
87 "   - Washington
88 "   - Estimating
89 "   - Export
90 G. & A.-Others
96 G. & A.-Tabulating
97 G. & A.-Payroll
98 G. & A.-Cost
99 G. & A.-Mailing & Messenger

TOTALS

PRODUCTIVE EMPLOYEES

Machine Shop:
10 Niles
20 H.O.R. #1 Shop
27 H.O.R. #2 Shop
30 Diesel "A" Shop
36 Diesel "B" Shop
50 Iron Foundry
57 Brass Foundry

TOTALS

TOTAL EMPLOYEES

FIGURE 31. Personnel Analysis Report Form. (By permission of Baldwin-Lima-Hamilton Corporation.)

108

personnel pattern of the company. The new personnel analysis form is shown as Fig. 31. The three columns under "Total Employees" are for a control week's figures (say 2-6-54), last week's figures (5-8-54), and this week's figures (5-15-54). The three columns under "increase or (decrease)" are for the change from control week to last week (2-6-54 to 5-8-54), the change from last week to this week (5-8-54 to 5-15-54) and the change from control week to this week (2-6-54 to 5-15-54). The parentheses around "(decrease)" mean that figures entered in the columns showing change are entered in parentheses if they show a decrease.

If it were not for the stronger trend to punched-card systems, it would be safe to say that there is a definite trend toward the use of forms wherever they are appropriate. As it is, the trend pattern is complex, though it is definitely toward the simpler systems.

Punched-Card Systems. It may be misleading to call punched-card systems "simple"—the machines that make them possible are anything but simple. The simplification comes in classifying, filing, and using the information the cards contain.

Basically, a punched-card system includes a punching machine which punches the information into the cards in a pattern of rectangular or round holes, and a machine or series of machines to read the information by mechanical, electrical, or electronic contact through the holes. The machines which read the information use it to perform a wide range of functions, from simple alphabetizing or sorting to tabulating and computing. Frequently the TV program *Dragnet* shows the Los Angeles Police Department punched-card system at work; the operator supplies the collating machine with a witness' description of an unidentified criminal wanted by the department —his approximate age, height, color of hair, and the type of crime committed—and then runs thousands of cards on known criminals through the machine. The machine sorts out all the cards which fit the information it has received, piling them in a neat stack, and Sergeant Friday and Officer Smith then start to question the men named on the cards.

Information is put on the cards in the first place from several possible sources: reports, forms, printed material. Often the cards themselves contain blanks—miniature forms—which are filled out at the source of the information, in the plant or out in the sales territory; the cards are then sent in to the punch operator who punches into the cards the information they already contain in longhand. The information itself is not changed or improved by being placed on the card; what is gained is phenomenal ease of access to the information and greatly increased accuracy and efficiency of use of the information.

Punched-card systems are used in accounting, sales, personnel, industrial management, market research, banking, the armed services, the F.B.I., the U.S. Treasury Department and many other governmental agencies; in university administration, hotel and hospital management, research laboratory information control—in fact, in nearly every kind of work where the handling of information is complex and extensive. Not nearly all the billions of punched cards used each year are used in reporting, of course; nearly every organization which used the cards makes several kinds of use of them. Some uses of punched cards help compile information for major reports; other uses replace former hand-written reports or typed reports; many uses have no direct connection with reporting. A study of the influence of punched cards on one sales organization's reporting system appears on pp. 311-15.

An analysis of the effect of punched cards on reporting at several different levels of industrial size might be helpful. If you go to work for a "giant" such as GM or GE you will probably find that punched cards have taken over the place, replacing nearly all the routine reports; most of the reporting is done in technical fields of research or near the top in management. The "giants" have punched-card or tape-operated computers which can store complicated instructions or vast quantities of background information in their "memories" for use at lightning speed; with such machines a complete sales and production analysis of one day's work can be completed before the next day, and shifts in demand can be recognized and can affect production in a matter of hours. Such machines obviously revolutionize reporting.

In a large firm employing several thousand men and women there is less likelihood that the revolution will have come.

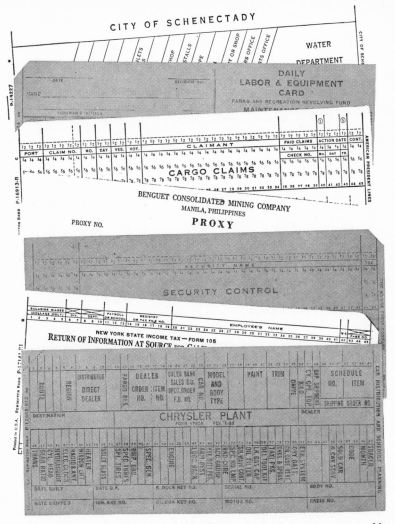

FIGURE 32. Punched cards used to make reported information more readily accessible in a wide range of applications. (By permission of Remington Rand, Incorporated.)

There will almost certainly be considerable use of punched cards as an aid to reporting and in replacement of routine reports, though it is likely that the punched cards will have more use in some divisions than in others. The smaller the size of the firm, the less likely it is to make full use of punched cards.

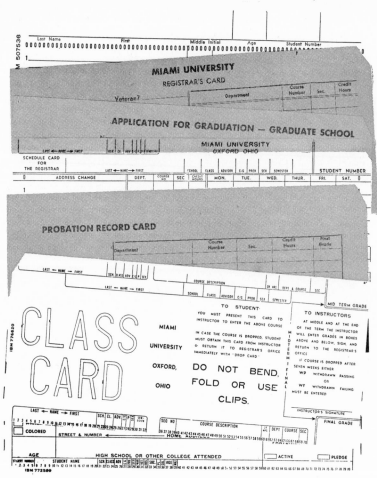

FIGURE 33. Punched cards used to make reported information more readily accessible—a range of uses within one university. (By permission of International Business Machines Corporation.)

Some firms employing one or two thousand men and women are just beginning to shift from the old-style "full reports" to time-saving and money-saving fill-in-the-blank forms for their routine reporting jobs. As these firms grow and as the price of card systems falls they will shift again, this time to punched cards. In a small firm, employing about 100 or 200, it will probably be a long time before punched cards can be used because of their cost—unless a large part of the firm's business is statistical or involves the correlation of information. A market research organization of twelve employees might find punched cards a good investment.

The smaller the firm, the less well organized the reporting is likely to be—and of course when one man runs the whole show and has his accounts and sales and production all under his direct surveillance, he doesn't need reports at all.

In twenty years the information-handling machines may well have changed reporting policy and practice much further, and in other ways—and the cards or tapes which feed them information may look very different from those shown in Figures 32 and 33. No field today is moving ahead faster; what is produced today is often obsolete tomorrow.

Memoranda. A memorandum is a simplified kind of letter report—a note carrying information. What is the least possible identification that will make a report meaningful?

> Whom it is to.
> Whom it is from (a name, and if the name is not known to the reader, something more—title, company).
> When it was sent.
> Possibly, what it is about.

The memorandum provides for that least possible identification: To, From, Date, Subject. Dozens of attractive memorandum forms are available, custom-built to the individual needs of the firm or department; one such form is illustrated above.

In a trend toward simplification, the memorandum report comes into its own—it saves time and yet is fully adequate for

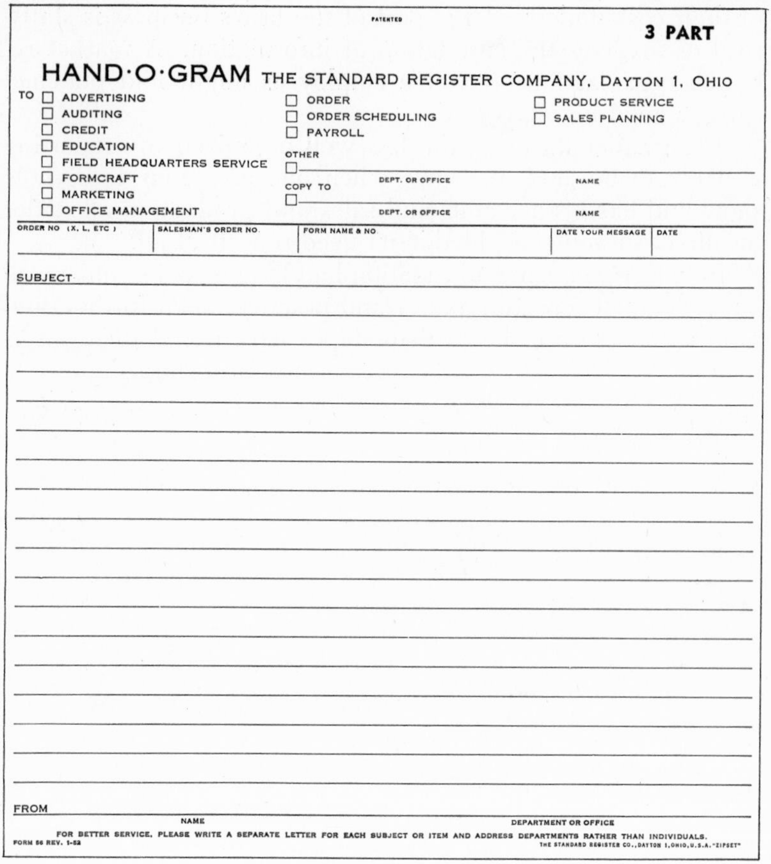

PATENTED

3 PART

HAND·O·GRAM THE STANDARD REGISTER COMPANY, DAYTON 1, OHIO

TO
☐ ADVERTISING
☐ AUDITING
☐ CREDIT
☐ EDUCATION
☐ FIELD HEADQUARTERS SERVICE
☐ FORMCRAFT
☐ MARKETING
☐ OFFICE MANAGEMENT
☐ ORDER
☐ ORDER SCHEDULING
☐ PAYROLL
OTHER
☐ DEPT. OR OFFICE NAME
COPY TO
☐ DEPT. OR OFFICE NAME
☐ PRODUCT SERVICE
☐ SALES PLANNING

ORDER NO (X, L, ETC)	SALESMAN'S ORDER NO.	FORM NAME & NO.	DATE YOUR MESSAGE	DATE

SUBJECT

FROM
NAME DEPARTMENT OR OFFICE

FOR BETTER SERVICE, PLEASE WRITE A SEPARATE LETTER FOR EACH SUBJECT OR ITEM AND ADDRESS DEPARTMENTS RATHER THAN INDIVIDUALS.

FORM 56 REV. 1-52

THE STANDARD REGISTER CO., DAYTON 1, OHIO, U.S.A. "ZIPSET"

FIGURE 34. Form prepared by Standard Register Company for hand-written memoranda—a time-saving and cost-saving device for use when typed letters or reports are not considered necessary. Two second sheets and two sheets of carbon paper are pre-inserted in this patented "Zipset." (By permission.)

all but the most lengthy and involved reporting jobs. Memorandum reports are appropriate

If the report is short. (I have seen very few memorandum reports over four pages long; they are nearly always one or two pages long.)

If there are few or no tables and graphs.

If there is little or no need for documentation.

If the prestige factor is absent (that is, if the reporting situation calls for efficiency and informality rather than dignity and impressiveness).

Actually most memorandum reports are written to someone in the same organization (intra-company or *internal* reports), though there is a tendency for the convenient memorandum form to be used more and more for other reports (inter-company or *external* or *outside* reports).

Psychology is on the side of the memorandum report. The writer of reports and letters often puts off a job that must be given the full, formal treatment—but a memo is different. The approach to a memo is simple and direct, not studied and stilted. You just put down the information you have. It seems less like work; it raises no self-consciousness in the writer. The emphasis is obviously on the information, not on the way it is said. Of course this should be the emphasis in all reporting—but it is especially clear to the writer using the memo form.

From the reader's viewpoint, also, the psychology of the memo report is good. The informality of the memo makes it sound more personal. A hand-written memo, for that matter, is still more personal—and besides is a quick and inexpensive way to transmit information. It is a saying in some firms that the higher up the ladder the executive is, the more hand-written memos he writes. The Standard Register Company uses the Hand-O-Gram form on p. 114 for many of its brief reports within the company. "Why not?" they ask.

Don't carry this line of reasoning too far and decide that anything goes in the memorandum report. There remains the need for clarity, for sticking to the subject, for putting the facts and ideas in a reasonable order, in other words, for using language intelligently. "Informal" doesn't mean "sloppy."

Fig. 35 illustrates a carefully prepared memorandum report on a technical subject. (See also pp. 3, 4, 77.)

In some firms the memorandum report is very widely used; 95 per cent or more of all reports in the organization may be set up in that way. Mr. Gerald F. Propst of the Industrial Relations Division of Republic Steel Corporation reported to the 1954 Midwest Regional Meeting of the American Business Writing Association that a great many of his firm's reports at

December 5, 1950

TO: Mr. R. H. Heyer, Supervising Metallurgist
                Research Laboratories

FROM: James C. Wilkins

SUBJECT: A Method for Measuring Grain Size:
                Report on Trip to Butler to Demonstrate
                This Method

On November 22 and 24, 1950, the Metallurgical Laboratories
at the Butler Plant were visited for the purpose of showing
the Metallurgical personnel the method of grain size
determinations used by the Research Laboratories.

The standard grain size charts for low carbon steel,
austenitic stainless steel, wheel steel, and stabilized
steel were shown to the Laboratory personnel. The grain
size measuring instrument was demonstrated on both the
Bausch & Lomb ILS metallograph in the General Metallurgy
Laboratory and the B&L research metallograph in the Wheel
Works Laboratory. No changes would have to be made in the
present design of the grain size measuring instrument for
use with the ILS metallograph. The only problem would be
the darkening of the room in the area of the metallograph by
a sliding curtain or by some other means. Mr. Hindman indicated that this problem would be worked out in some way.

The Wheel Works Laboratory has the metallograph located in a
room which can be darkened. It was found that it is a very
simple matter to remove the binocular eyepiece from the B&L
research metallograph and to insert the single tube eyepiece
with the projection prism attached to it. However, the
bracket for holding the disks would have to be somewhat different from the present instrument used in the Research Laboratories. It would be a very simple operation to adapt the
grain size measuring instrument to this model metallograph.

The General Metallurgical Laboratory at Butler has a projection prism, but the Wheel Works Laboratory does not (B&L
catalogue No. 42-65-51 - cost approximately $15).

FIGURE 35. Memorandum Report. (By permission of Armco Steel Corporation.)

Mr. R. H. Heyer
Page 2
December 5, 1950

Considerable interest was expressed by the Butler personnel in adopting this method of grain size measurement. At the present time they are measuring grain size by observing their micros through the eyepiece and using the A.S.T.M. Standards as a comparison. This method is far from being as accurate and convenient as the projection method using Armco materials as a standard. The metallographic section of the Research Laboratories has found this method to be very satisfactory. Therefore, it is believed that this method should be made available to Armco Metallurgical Laboratories.

James C. Wilkins

James C. Wilkins
Metallographer
Research Laboratories

LPW
cc: R. S. Burns
R. P. Hindman

FIGURE 35—*Concluded.*

supervisory levels are one or two pages long, and that two major problems with new employees are that their reports are

Too long and wordy, running 10 or 12 pages instead of 1 or 2.
Too short to do their job, a paragraph instead of a page.

Two other major problems are (1) important points missed entirely, report containing nothing but subsidiary material; and (2) important points present but smothered in detail.

From Mr. Propst and about thirty other personnel men in a dozen states I gather the impression that the report-writing skills my students will find most in demand when they look for jobs are these:

Clarity.

Conciseness.

Ability to organize facts and ideas.

Ability to write brief (one- or two-page) memorandum-style
reports.

Exercises and Problems

1. Discuss the *pro's* and *con's* of the use of the full report in the
sales division of Sandler Gear. If you were sales manager, how
would you set up the reporting policy?

2. Discuss the advantages of punched-card systems with an
I.B.M. or Remington Rand salesman or user; report to the class.
What reporting functions do you find punched-card machines used
for in your area?

3. Read about the newest computers and electronic brains in
Fortune and other business magazines (the periodical indexes will
help you find current articles). Report to the class on new uses
related to reporting.

4. Collect some forms (any kinds of forms used to transmit information) from local firms and from your college. Discuss their
makeup: are some better *as forms*—better planned, better for their
purpose—than others? In each case, why is a form (rather than
some other method of getting or transmitting information) used by
the organization? (If you aren't sure, ask.)

5. What do you think of hand-written memos in business?
What do business executives in your town think?

6. Write a memorandum in answer to one of these requests:

(from a professor)   *a*) Please let me have your class schedule.
                     b) Give me a memo to remind me that this absence was
                          excused.
                     c) Please hand in a list of the English courses you have
                          taken in college.
                     d) Jot down for me the main reasons you are taking this
                          course.

(from a prospective   *e*) Give me a brief résumé of your work experience.
    employer)   *f*) Please send me the names of three references who
                          have known you for some time.

7. Write a memorandum report on one of these topics or on one assigned by your instructor:

(for your hometown
  or college town)   *a*) Growth since 1900 census.

(for your college)   *b*) Enrollment trends over a five-year period.
                     c) Where our students come from.
                     d) Where our students go.
                     e) Occupational range and distribution of our graduates in the last five classes.

(for your professor
  about a longer
  report you have
  been assigned)   *f*) Potential sources of information for my report.
                     g) Progress to date on my report.

Chapter 9

THE INFORMAL REPORT

THIS IS A hard chapter to name. The chapter just before it is "Forms, Punched Cards, Memoranda"; the chapter which comes after it is "The Formal Report." The most accurate title for this chapter would be "Everything Else."

Even such loose and informal distinctions are misleading. I stopped in to see a friend of mine who is public relations director of one of Ohio's largest firms. "Ray," I said, "I'd like a couple of reports to use as models in a textbook: a short report and a long report."

"How long and how short?" Ray asked.

"Oh, you know, a long formal report and a short informal report."

"I'm afraid I don't know," he said. "Your terms bother me. As you know, we use hundreds of reports from book length down to a few lines and the only distinction we make in terminology is that some are confidential and some are not. I imagine you have to break them down some way to handle them in class; to us, they're all just reports."

"Sure," I said, "I look at them that way too. But I need an informal report four or five pages long and a formal report, oh, say, twenty pages long."

"I'll see what I can do," he said. "But you tell those students we've got short formal reports and long informal reports and middle-sized reports and some I bet a quarter you couldn't tell what to call them."

Informal report doesn't seem to be quite the term we need, but for lack of a better, we'll use it. You should keep in mind, however, that we are here dealing with the main body of reports used in the business and scientific world; that is, practical reports assigned for specific purposes and typically prepared

120

quickly and submitted promptly. They are more elaborate than the report *forms* just discussed and less elaborate and philosophic but more utilitarian than the formal reports to be discussed in the next chapter.

Plan of the Informal Report. Short, middle-sized or long, the informal report adheres to no rigid pattern. What it includes is based on the needs of the reader. It may conform in certain ways to the organization's written or unwritten reporting standards: its title page, for example, or its letter of transmittal may follow company policy rather than the needs of the reader. But with few exceptions the plan of the informal report is based on the questions

What does the reader need to know?
How can the writer best give it to him?

Here are some typical plans actually used in business, industrial, and professional reporting:

Report introduced only by *To, From, Subject, Date* at top of page (this is the memorandum report discussed on p. 113).
Memorandum letter of transmittal; report.
Cover; letter of transmittal; report.
Title page; letter of transmittal; report.
Cover; title page; letter of transmittal; report.
Title page; letter of transmittal; table of contents; report.
Title page; letter of transmittal; report; appendix.
Title page; letter of transmittal; introductory summary; report.
Title page; letter of transmittal; report; conclusions and recommendations.

The possible combinations seem unlimited.

The Report from the Reader's Point of View. Since the plan of the report depends on the reader's needs we shall look at the ways various parts of a report help the reader at his end of the two-way street which is communication.

Cover. The cover protects the report against smudging, tearing, loss of pages. It is easier for the reader to file, to handle, to carry. The organization's own prepared cover should be used, though sometimes covers are made from paper or light flexible cardboard if the report is to be stapled instead of bound. Attractive covers for college reports can be purchased at the book store. If company policy permits, the cover should show the title of the report and possibly the name of the author.

TITLE PAGE. The title page gives the reader at a glance the subject of the report, the name of its author, and the date it was written. With this information he can decide whether to read it and when to read it without being placed in the paradoxical position of having to read it to find out. The title page gives the reader's secretary all the information she needs for quick, accurate filing of the report and for adequate identification of it when she must go to the files to find it. In order to serve this function the title must be specific, even at the sacrifice of conciseness. Various ways to set up title pages are shown on pp. 140, 160, and in Figures 36 and 37.

LETTER OF TRANSMITTAL. The reader may expect the letter of transmittal to inform him of the writer's opinion of the report project, its limitations, and his method, to record what the writer has learned outside the narrow range of his topic while conducting his research, and to fit the report into proper perspective by relating it to its purpose and to its possible application. It is true that in some firms the letter of transmittal seems to be merely a routine form with no function whatsoever; even in such firms, however, there is no rule against making the letter of transmittal meaningful and functional.*

TABLE OF CONTENTS. The table of contents offers to the reader an advance outline of the content of the report which he can use to make a preliminary evaluation of the report and to plan his use of it. Since page numbers are shown for the items in the outline, the reader can, if he wishes, skip material that is familiar or irrelevant and turn directly to the pages on which he wishes to concentrate. The table of contents is also useful in helping the reader locate specific material in the report in re-reading or review (very few reports have indexes; the table of contents is assumed to do the index's job).

* For full treatment of the letter of transmittal see Chapter 11.

```
                              FORD MOTOR COMPANY
                              AUTOMATIC TRANSMISSION DIVISION
                              AIRCRAFT ENGINE DIVISION
                              CINCINNATI, OHIO




                    BITUMINOUS COAL REPORT

              FOR STOCKPILING    1951 - 1952














     Prepared By:  E. S. Novatny
                   Traffic Manager
```

FIGURE 36. Title Page. (By permission of Ford Motor Company.)

There is no one right way to set up a table of contents. Practice varies, as the examples on pp. viii and 162 indicate.

TABLE OF FIGURES. The table of figures gives the reader a preview of what diagrams, graphs, tables, and illustrations he may expect to find in the report; it also helps him locate any

REPORT ON

THE

PROPOSED ARRANGEMENT

OF THE

DISTRICT TRAFFIC OFFICE

OF THE

AMERICAN TELEPHONE AND TELEGRAPH COMPANY
ROOM 909, 209 WEST SEVENTH STREET
CINCINNATI 2, OHIO

MISS CATHERINE LYKINS
FEBRUARY 28, 1950

FIGURE 37. Title Page. (By permission of American Telephone and Telegraph Company.)

of them for review or reference. Examples of tables of figures appear on pp. 147 and 163.

INTRODUCTORY SUMMARY. The introductory summary (précis or abstract) offers the reader the essence of the report in a few words. "Here is what the whole report says, stripped of discussion and proof," the writer seems to say here. "If you want to take my word for it, and if the bare facts are all you need, you can quit right here. If you aren't interested in what my report says, you can quit right here. Otherwise, keep reading, and I'll start at the beginning and show you how I got this result." Many busy executives read only the introductory summary of nine-tenths of the reports they receive.

There can be no rule for the length of an introductory summary, though its function is certainly handicapped if it takes up more than five per cent of the text of the report. An extremely long report should not have more than a page or two of summary for a hundred pages of text; many short reports which could be read completely in two or three minutes have no introductory summary at all. A typical introductory summary appears on p. 333.

INTRODUCTION. The introduction fills in for the reader the background information that he will need in order to read and understand the report. The introduction may include

Historical material

> A résumé of previous experiments or studies of the problem.
> Investigation of direct or indirect causes of a situation which the report will analyze.
> A simple chronological account of the growth and development of the project or organization that is the subject of the report.

Technical background material

> Information the reader needs before he is prepared to read and understand the technical part of the report.

Orientation to the point of view of the report

> Introduction to the philosophy of the report or the philosophy of approach of the report (especially important if the approach is new or unorthodox).

BODY OF THE REPORT. The body of the report contains the information which the reader wanted in the first place when he assigned the report. This information is clearly, carefully, and fully set down with the reader's needs foremost in mind. The use of headings and subheadings makes it easy for the reader to see how each part of the information is related to the whole. Sources of information are pointed out in text or footnotes so that the reader can see where each unit of information came from. Knowing the sources of the information, the reader can better evaluate its validity and can better follow up facts and ideas he would like to trace and investigate further.

CONCLUSIONS AND RECOMMENDATIONS. Many organizations use a report outline which includes at the end a heading "Conclusions and Recommendations." This section, in effect, says to the reader "In view of the facts and evidence presented I find the situation to be thus and so. My recommendations for what to do about it are these: 1, 2, 3." This conclusions and recommendations formula leaves much to be desired in most reports. The conclusions and recommendations section is quite acceptable when it is appropriate; the trouble comes when it is used as a routine formula in all reports. Since most reporting assignments do not ask for conclusions and recommendations we do not recommend its use unless it is specifically assigned or unless it has become a tradition in your organization.

CONCLUDING SUMMARY. If no recommendations are called for in the original report assignment and if enough points have been made in the report to justify drawing them together in review at the end, the logical way to close a report is with a concluding summary. Such a summary offers the reader a concise restatement of the main points of the report. It differs from the introductory summary in that it may refer to examples, cases, or experiments given in the report; the introductory summary may not, for the examples and cases obviously are not part of the reader's experience before he reads the report. Compare the concluding summary ("Conclusion") of Robert T. Hamlett's article, p. 358, with the same article's introductory summary.

BIBLIOGRAPHY. If books, magazines, encyclopedias, company publications, or other printed sources were used in preparing the report, a list of them should be included.* Such a listing shows the reader how thoroughly the writer did his research and how up-to-date his material is; it also gives the reader a good start on where to go if he wants to carry the research further himself. Occasionally a report uses an *annotated bibliography*, one which makes helpful comments for the reader on each of the sources listed.

APPENDIX. An appendix is the place to put things that go with the report but not in it. Here are some of the things that might be found in an appendix:

    balance sheet
    photographs
    diagrams
    case studies
    sample forms
    sample questionnaires
    market research work sheet or tally sheet
    full experimental data
    graphs
    blueprints
    specifications
    flow charts
    architect's drawings
    planned layout drawings (before and after proposed changes)
    statistical tables
    ten-year financial history
    excerpts from testimony
    excerpts from source material on which report is based

The advantage of the appendix to the reader is that he may read the report straight through without getting bogged down in exhibits and statistics; then if there is anything he wants to check, he knows exactly where to find it at the end of the report.

There is no one right way to set up an appendix; however, generally it is preceded by a page marked "Appendix," and each separate section is numbered and accompanied by a self-explanatory caption.

* See Chapter 10, pp. 154-57.

GLOSSARY. If the report uses technical terms unfamiliar to the reader they are usually explained in context with footnotes; if there are a great many such terms, however, or if the writer is not sure whether the reader understands the terms, a glossary may be used. The glossary lists the terms in alphabetical order, giving a clear, brief, practical definition or explanation of each one, using diagrams when necessary. Following is an example of a short glossary.*

BREAK: a brief ensemble pause by a jazz band so that one player can extemporize a solo for a few measures.

JAM SESSION: a musical get-together in which all the playing is collectively improvised.

LEAD: melody, instrument that plays the melody in a band, solo chair of a section in a band.

TAILGATE: New Orleans style of trombone playing.

WALKING BASS: a bass part that moves up and down the chords.

INDEX. Not one report in 10,000 is indexed, since the table of contents is nearly always adequate to do the work of the index. In a book-length report full of closely packed information, the usefulness of the index to the reader is obvious.**

The Report Fits the Reader's Needs. Fortunately no informal report will ever need all or nearly all of the report sections discussed in this chapter. There is no formula or rule to use in deciding what to include in your report. Plan your report, considering your reader and the reporting situation. What is needed? Include just that. Use as long a report and as many sections or parts as it takes to do the reporting job.

Summary of New Developments and Trends in Industrial Reporting. The last few pages have described and discussed the parts that go together to make up a report—many more parts than any one report would be likely to use. The tendency in reporting in industry has been to use fewer and fewer parts, eliminating all those which were generally used because

---

* From Milton Mezzrow and Bernard Wolfe, *Really the Blues* (New York: Random House, Inc., 1946).

** If you need to prepare such an index, you will find helpful material in Part One, *Indexes and Indexing* (pp. 21-72) by Robert L. Collison (New York: John de Graff, Inc., 1953).

of custom or tradition and retaining in a specific report only those which fill a need in the specific reporting situation. The main long-range trend in industrial reporting in the twentieth century is a trend toward simplification: simplification in plan and structure, simplification of discussion of complex trends or analyses through use of visual aids (and simplification of the visual aids themselves), simplification in use of language, simplification in handling the completed report and making use of the information contained in it.

Simplification as we have used the word here does not mean translating reports to the primer level, or "talking down" to the reader on the assumption that he has a twelve-year-old mind. It does mean starting all over with the concept of reporting, disregarding custom and building a report around what is needed. Which of the possible parts of a report will help carry facts and ideas to the reader in this specific reporting situation? What diagrams, pictures, graphs (if any) would best help carry the facts and ideas? How can these particular facts and ideas best be handled, filed, used (shall the information be typed on white paper, recorded on magnetic tape, photographed on microfilm, punched in cards)? And what of the language? Is the reader familiar with our technical terms, or should we substitute common terms for them? How can we use our language knowhow to help him establish the relationships we want him to establish?

All these questions involve the reader, the reader's need for the facts and ideas in the report, and the facts and ideas themselves.

The process of building a report around what is needed may be compared to Frank Lloyd Wright's concept of functional architecture, once considered impossible to put into practice but now basic in our modern society. We start not with the outside of a house—a house like, say, the one across the street—building a framework according to tradition or fashion and chopping up the interior into boxes which the buyer must adapt his life to, since he has no choice; we start with what the homeowner plans to do with his life at home, and build around it. If we could visualize an open area, say a giant theater set, with large flat spaces and some levels higher and lower, we could have our homeowner-to-be put his chairs and books and

M. P. REPORT NO. 1364A

THE CHAMPION PAPER AND FIBRE COMPANY

RESEARCH DEPARTMENT

Project No. 42002   Date Written: 11/7/50
                                                     Date Typed: 11/8/50

Title: Lab. Service to Process Sales

Author: W. Brenton

Period Covered: October 31 to November 3, 1950

Work Done By: L. Hopkins, H. Brashear, Bob Willer

Reference: Letter from Percy Paetz to Ralph H. Rogers Jr.
            dated October 17, 1950.

Summary

          Percy Paetz submitted a small sample termed Czechoslovakian
clay for testing purposes. We reported this clay as being suitable for
machine coating in M. P. Report No. 1345, July 14, 1950. In a
discussion Mr. Paetz had at Frohnleiton, it came out that the sample
of clay was most probably Austrian clay and was marked Czechoslovakian
clay by mistake. Consequently, Mr. Paetz requested them to send us
a sample of the best Austrian coating clay for further tests. This
clay was identified as Austrian coating clay K.60.

          The K.60 clay showed 33.9% of the particles above 5 microns
on check tests. Although the five micron fraction is above 20% it
probably would be worthwhile to make a trial on this grade.

FIGURE 38. Research Report. (By permission of Champion Paper & Fibre
Company.)

beds and stoves and bathing facilities wherever they worked in
most conveniently, moving them about as use taught him their
best arrangement, screening off those parts of the developing
"house" that seemed to demand privacy and leaving the rest
open. Once the interior of the "house" was fitted to the user's

-2-

The K.60 clay sample was in the form of large lumps. For the high speed agitator type dispersion it would be necessary to have the clay delivered in a pulverized form. The K.60 clay dispersed at 55% solids with .2% - .4% T.S.P.P. had the same viscosity as spray dried HT clay at 60% solids.

The K.60 clay showed 6 points lower gloss, 1.3 points lower brightness after coating and calendering and a little lower printing quality than HT clay.

PARTICLE SIZE TESTS

	Austrian Clay	Czech Clay	Spray Dried HT Clay 6-19-50	HT Clay 6-14-48
5 Microns & Above	33.9-33.9	24.7	12.7	20.7
2 Microns & Above	61.8-60.5	50.6	37.2	42.8
.5 Microns & Above	88.9-88.4	82.7	86.2	81.9
Below .5 Micron	11.1-11.6	17.3	13.8	18.1
Block Brightness	81.1	81.8	84.1	83

Assuming the Austrian and Czechoslovakian clays are from the same source the difference in particle size reported may be due to variations in the clay, sampling or in the test itself. Unfortunately, the Czech clay sample was so small we didn't have enough left to run a check particle size test.

With the exception of the particle size test other tests indicate the two clays are the same or very similar. The block brightness of the two clays checked and they gave the same slurry viscosity when dispersed with T.S.P.P. both being heavier than spray dried HT clay at the same solids. A sheet coated with Czech clay, but uncalendered, saved from the July test was calendered and printed along with the Austrian clay sheets. Both clays gave the same gloss - 60 against 66 for HT clay - and the prints were little below HT clay in quality.

s/ Walter Brenton

8c
mjb-1p

FIGURE 38—*Concluded.*

needs, he could frame it in with exterior walls if, and in whatever way, shelter and safety made exterior walls desirable.

Of the many tendencies toward simplification of industrial writing, perhaps the most publicized has been the "readability" movement. The Rudolf Flesch formula for measuring reading ease caught on just right somehow, to the surprise even of its

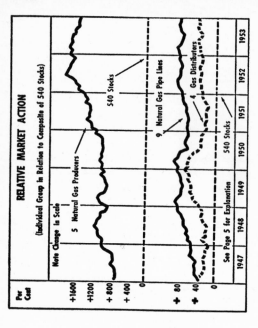

RELATIVE MARKET ACTION

(Individual Group in Relation to Composite of 540 Stocks)

NATURAL GAS

MARKET PROSPECTS: (See Inside Front Cover)

Integrated—Pipe Line Companies..............Average

Distributors ....Average

Producers ....Average

Recurrence of the *unseasonably mild weather* experienced in the last quarter of 1952 and the first quarter of 1953 *could serve as a deterrent to any material price improvement* for natural gas equities as earnings reports may be somewhat disappointing. Should any pronounced weakness develop in the market as a whole, stocks of natural gas companies could be expected to follow the general trend.

TRADE APPRAISAL:

Legal developments have over-shadowed earnings and other factors in the natural gas industry in recent months. It is probable that **important long range effects** will be the outgrowth of these developments. Among the more important legal rulings have been 1: U. S. Supreme Court upholding a Circuit Court of Appeals ruling that the Federal Power Commission had regulatory authority over producing companies; 2: U. S. Supreme Court sustaining the FPC in denying the use of state-fixed minimum prices as a proper expense charge by a pipe line company for gas produced from its own wells and 3: Circuit Court decision that the FPC erred in fixing a 5½% rate of return for Northern Natural Gas.

Even with these developments, however, the **regulatory atmosphere** has very definitely **taken a turn for the better.** Despite this fact the impact of earlier FPC rate rulings still was reflected in earnings for natural gas companies generally.

Although many rate increases had been granted, they were insufficient to permit full reflection of improved revenues by net income. In the 12 months ended October 31, 1953 gross revenues of natural gas companies (exclusive of producers) rose by 20.1% over the corresponding period of the previous year. This was considerably offset by higher gas purchased costs and other increased expenses so that net income for the period was only 7.8% above the earlier period. The trend was emphasized in the figures for the month of October alone when the anticipated rise in the profitable space-heating load failed to fully develop. Gross revenues in October were up 10.9% but net income declined 13.8% as compared with October 1952.

	Fiscal Year Ends	Earnings—$ per Share 1952	1951	Interim Period	Interim 1953	Interim 1952	Consec. Years Div. Paid	Divs.—$ per Share Paid 1953	Paid or Decl. Last 12 Mos.	Price Range 1943-52 High	1943-52 Low	1953-54 High	1953-54 Low	Approximate Price 1-20-54	Yield %
Investment Type															
*Amer. Nat. Gas (Integ.)	Dec.	2.34	2.58	12 mo. 9-30	3.55	2.16	51	1.90	2.00c	35½	13	42	31¼	42	4.8c
Cons. Nat. Gas (Integ.)	Dec.	4.19	5.67	12 mo. 9-30	4.02	4.67	11	2.50	2.50	64¼	24	58	48½	56	4.5
P'ples. Gas Lt. & Coke (Gas Dist.)	Dec.	8.26	9.16	12 mo. 9-30	9.44	9.44	18	6.00	6.00	145	46¾	148½	127	139	4.3
Liberal Income															
B'klyn Union Gas (Dist.)	Dec.	1.79	2.22a	12 mo. 9-30	1.65	2.13	6	1.50	1.50	27½a	4⅝a	27⅞	22½	27	5.6
Equitable Gas (Integ.)	Dec.	1.83	1.83	12 mo. 9-30	1.88	1.82	4	1.32½	1.40c	24¼	18¾	24⅞	20⅜	24	5.8c‡
Natl. Fuel Gas (Integ.)	Dec.	1.38	1.19	12 mo. 9-30	1.28	1.28	52	0.95	1.00c	17¼	18⅜	17	13⅞	17	5.9c
Good Quality: Wider Price Movement															
Columbia Gas (Integ.)	Dec.	0.83	1.06	12 mo. 9-30	0.72	0.87	12	0.90	0.90h	16⅜	1⅞	15	12½	13	6.9h‡
North. Nat. Gas (Pipe)	Dec.	1.48	1.76	12 mo. 9-30	2.40	2.72	19	1.80	1.80	47¼	11¾a	46¾	34½	41	4.4‡
Oklahoma Nat. Gas. (Integ.)	Aug.	1.39a	1.46a	12 mo. 11-30	0.89	1.68a	16	1.15a	1.20	20¼a	4¾a	21⅞a	18	20	6.0‡
Panh. East. P. L. (Pipe)	Dec.	4.99	3.03	12 mo. 9-30	4.89	4.14	17	2.50	2.50	83½	8⅛a	88¾	64½	74	3.4
South'n. Nat. Gas (Pipe)	Dec.	2.35	2.24a	12 mo. 9-30	2.19	2.13a	18	1.40k	1.40k	30½a	5⅜a	33¾	23	30	4.7k‡
*United Gas Corp. (Integ.)	Dec.	1.56	1.56	12 mo. 9-30	1.93	1.40	10	1.25	1.25	29⅛g	8⅞g	30	23½	29	4.3‡
Speculative															
*El Paso Nat. Gas (Pipe)	Dec.	2.93	3.04	12 mo. 11-30	3.01	2.97	18	1.60f	1.60f	38⅜	7¾a	37⅜	30	37	4.3f‡
Shamr. Oil & Gas (Prod.)	Nov.	3.31a	3.51a	9 mo. 8-31	2.80	2.48a	11	2.10m	2.40c	37⅞a	2⅛a	44½	35⅝	44	5.5c
Tenn. Gas Trans. (Pipe)	Dec.	1.86	1.39a	12 mo. 9-30	1.62	1.60	7	1.40	1.40	26⅛n	4⅝n	25⅞§	21§	24	5.8‡
*Tex. East. Trans. (Pipe)	Dec.	1.11	1.75	12 mo. 9-30	1.00	0.90	4	1.00	1.00	21¼§	8½§	20½§	15§	20	5.0

*—Relatively most attractive (see inside front cover). ‡—Offering of new issue based on data contained in Prospectus, available upon request. §—Approximate Off-Board prices. a—Adjusted. c—Indicated or current annual rate. f—Current indicated annual rate excluding $0.4167 value of Western Natural Gas common g—Range since recapitalization in 1944. h—Indicated or current annual rate, including extras. k—Current annual rate; also paid 0.25306 sh. of Alabama Gas common in 1953. m—Plus 10% in stock. n—Range since offering in 1946; adjusted.

FIGURE 39. Trade Appraisal Report on Natural Gas Industry, February, 1954. (By permission of Merrill Lynch, Pierce, Fenner, & Beane.)

The Champion Paper and Fibre Company
COMPANY CORRESPONDENCE

TO: .Dwight J. Thomson, Vice-President   DATE   June 23, 1954

                                                  COPIES TO:
FROM: Cal Skillman, Public Relations

SUBJECT: Movie Attendance Report
          By States

        You may be interested in the attached tabulation of movie
        attendance listed according to our individual movies--
        "Good Business," "Deep Roots," and "Paper Work"--and each
        of the 48 states.

        I can point out nothing in this tabulation which is
        particularly outstanding unless it might be that through-
        out the entire United States all three of the movies are
        drawing at the maximum rate possible according to the
        number of prints that we have made available in that area.

        Even in states in which we have never conducted an all-out
        sales campaign, the movies are drawing by virtue of Modern
        Talking Pictures' publicity.

        CS:ch
        Enc.

FIGURE 40. Public Relations Report. (By permission of Champion Paper &
Fibre Company.)

author, who disclaims in *How To Make Sense* * much of what
his followers claim for the Flesch method. Based on sound
logic and good sense, the earlier Flesch books (particularly
The Art of Plain Talk and *The Art of Readable Writing*) ad-
vocated unpretentious and functional use of language and spent

* New York: Harcourt, Brace & Co., Inc., 1954.

SHOWING AND ATTENDANCE RECORD

to March 31, 1954 by State

State	"GOOD BUSINESS"		"DEEP ROOTS"		"PAPER WORK"		TOTAL	
	Show-ings	Attend-ance	Show-ings	Attend-ance	Show-ings	Attend-ance	Show-ings	Attend-ance
Alabama	35	2,763	46	3,644	20	1,606	101	8,013
Arizona	12	488	9	661	7	325	28	1,474
Arkansas	20	653	42	2,569	15	1,070	77	4,292
California	130	23,351	278	19,196	162	10,002	570	52,549
Colorado	40	2,366	77	5,610	54	4,262	171	12,238
Connecticut	20	794	16	1,003	28	948	64	2,745
Delaware	4	244	20	1,042	11	787	35	2,073
Dis. of Col.	22	1,153	27	1,489	15	841	64	3,483
Florida	18	1,585	61	3,503	35	3,288	114	8,376
Georgia	38	1,794	33	2,304	41	2,249	112	6,347
Idaho	15	861	16	1,275	29	1,518	60	3,654
Illinois	183	9,443	356	20,631	260	20,383	799	50,457
Indiana	113	4,935	260	16,309·	163	8,359	536	29,603
Iowa	87	3,921	129	6,858	92	5,690	308	16,469
Kansas	70	3,128	136	4,963	69	3,774	275	11,865
Kentucky	52	3,452	87	5,626	53	2,951	192	12,029
Louisiana	22	940	26	1,889	18	685	66	3,514
Maine	13	821	36	2,333	35	1,844	84	4,998
Maryland	29	1,823	71	3,868	51	3,746	151	9,437
Mass.	58	4,009	105	8,711	69	4,840	232	17,560
Michigan	96	7,203	179	9,924	115	6,075	390	23,202
Minnesota	89	3,403	140	8,540	122	7,108	351	19,051
Mississippi	27	1,620	34	2,773	30	2,001	91	6,394

FIGURE 40—*Continued.*

comparatively little time on the measurement of readability. Flesch's reasoning was clear: plain talk is the most functional kind. Do you, his reader, use plain talk? Let's measure your use of language and see . . . No, your readability index is too high. Now what can you do about it? And the main part of the book, the real meat, follows. In spite of the emphasis placed on it and the publicity it received, the readability for-

Report Writing

Page 2

State	"GOOD BUSINESS"		"DEEP ROOTS"		"PAPER WORK"		TOTAL	
	Show-ings	Attend-ance	Snow-ings	Attend-ance	Show-ings	Attend-ance	Show-ings	Attend-ance
Missouri	80	4,000	134	8,585	110	6,109	324	18,694
Montana	16	623	18	1,352	12	1,329	46	3,304
Nebraska	44	1,803	74	3,052	61	2,846	179	7,701
Nevada	4	192	5	214	5	234	14	640
New Hamp.	11	606	15	838	14	956	40	2,400
New Jersey	67	3,407	100	5,797	88	3,993	255	13,197
New Mexico	9	510	25	2,419	19	1,361	53	4,290
N. Carolina	58	4,905	82	7,382	72	5,466	212	17,753
New York	171	8,619	295	24,214	204	15,346	670	48,179
N. Dakota	22	1,291	22	1,807	17	1,115	61	4,213
Ohio	203	9,850	397	27,392	300	17,685	900	54,927
Oklahoma	42	4,451	52	3,882	40	2,308	134	10,641
Oregon	30	1,150	31	1,410	29	1,969	90	4,529
Pennsylvania	222	14,877	415	36,528	322	20,760	959	72,165
Rhode Island	2	120	4	633	7	1,032	13	1,785
S. Carolina	33	2,150	34	2,372	44	3,305	111	7,827
S. Dakota	30	1,459	42	2,058	32	2,034	104	5,551
Tennessee	38	3,925	73	6,052	51	4,788	162	14,765
Texas	155	7,616	183	10,302	151	14,272	489	32,190
Utah	22	1,374	33	1,300	34	2,122	89	4,796
Vermont	9	305	22	1,139	7	725	38	2,169
Virginia	46	1,971	67	2,970	35	1,732	148	6,673
Washington	36	1,397	61	2,480	49	2,106	146	5,983
W. Virginia	35	2,287	44	2,828	36	1,605	115	6,720

FIGURE 40—*Continued.*

mula itself is of no more value than a thermometer is in heating
a cold room. Its publicity helped direct a great deal of thought
and attention toward language use: probably a desirable by-
product of the readability craze. And those who read beyond

	Page 3							

State	"GOOD BUSINESS"		"DEEP ROOTS"		"PAPER WORK"		TOTAL	
	Show-ings	Attend-ance	Show-ings	Attend-ance	Show-ings	Attend-ance	Show-ings	Attend-ance
Wisconsin	76	4,278	165	9,528	127	7,480	368	21,286
Wyoming	3	51	7	190	3	43	13	284
Modern Total	2,657	163,967	4,584	301,445	3,363	217,073	10,604	682,485
Carolina Off.	33	4,059	85	8,732	48	6,186	166	18,977
Ohio Office	38	4,775	33	3,976	25	3,856	96	12,607
Texas Office	35	4,137	32	5,252	34	2,783	101	12,172
General Office	128	12,598	139	9,563	143	9,443	410	31,604
Accumulative Total	2,891	189,536	4,873	328,968	3,613	239,341	11,377	757,845

FIGURE 40—*Concluded.*

the formulas, and who have also read *How To Make Sense,* have certainly learned a lot that is worth while from Flesch. Robert Gunning, Norman G. Shidle, and others have helped build the readability movement.

Along with the major tendency toward simplification of reporting, industry shows a tendency to eliminate routine, factual, or statistical reports through automation. I once lived in an apartment building where the temperature in the rooms was controlled by reports: if it got too hot or too cold we would phone the custodian and report to him and he would try to do something about it. Such routine transmission of temperature information is generally handled nowadays by electrical circuits connecting thermostats and relays which control temperature with accuracy to a fraction of a degree. If we think of the electrical impulse which controls the furnace as *information*, as it is, of course, it is clear how many other transmissions of information which once would have required reporting are now handled by automation. Compare the oral reports of the Mississippi sounder, lowering his lead line and shouting, "Quarter past twain," with the radar and control panel of a modern jet plane. Compare the stockman's report that we are low on top-grain leather for our chair factory with modern automatic inventory control. At the same time automation is eliminating routine reports, however, it is making possible plant expansion which increases the need for reports at a higher level—reports on which decisions of long-run rather than short-run nature will be based. Although we can't speak for the distant future, at the present reports are growing more numerous and more significant near the top and are being superseded by machines near the bottom of the industrial structure. In ten years or in twenty, there will still probably be a need in industry for reports like those illustrated as Figs. 38, 39, 40, and 41. There will be new needs for types of reports probably not now known, and there will certainly be more machines to handle the collection and transmission of information, so that some of the reports we now consider indispensable will be superseded and forgotten.

If we hold a functional concept of reporting, rather than a traditional concept, we will be ready for any information problems this new electronic age confronts us with.

March 12, 1954

From—Juvenal C. Schnorbus, Jr.

To—Charles Burt, Vice-President In Charge of Sales

Subject—Report on the strip mining industry of Southern Indiana, Southern Illinois, and Eastern Missouri, based upon my recent visit to that area.

Attached is my report on the current sales outlook for our company concerning the above mentioned area. This report is based on actual data gathered in the field, through interviews with the personnel of the customers concerned, and from the records of our sales department.

When assigning this report to me, you suggested that I write a summary of the situation, including in it any ideas I might have regarding our steadily and rapidly declining sales in this area. This summary is included in my report.

Knowing your interest in photographs of our products in actual use, I have included several in this report. Three of them are excellent examples of the terrific abrasive conditions so prominent and characteristic of this region. The photography is my own; so if the detail is of questionable quality, you may put the blame on an ardent, but woefully amateur photographer.

This report would not have been made available without the co-operation of the personnel at the plants visited, and I am deeply indebted to Ed Brady, of our local sales force, and to the Markham Engineering Service, our agents in St. Louis, for their kind attention to me while I visited companies in their districts. I offer these gentlemen my deepest thanks and appreciation.

FIGURE 41. Sales Engineering Report. (By permission of J. C. Schnorbus, Jr.) Company names have been changed; in actual use this report was instrumental in changing company production policy.

CURRENT SALES OUTLOOK OF THE STRIP MINING INDUSTRY OF SOUTHERN

INDIANA, SOUTHERN ILLINOIS, AND EASTERN MISSOURI

By Juvenal C. Schnorbus, Jr.

Sales Department

FIGURE 41–*Continued.*

2

SUMMARY

For many years, Sandler products were the only good heat-treated and car-burized products to be found in the strip mining industry. It is true that we always had competition from the original manufacturers of the shovel equipment, such as Marion and Bucyrus, but their replacement parts were of a rather poor quality steel, and their deliveries were as long as ours. In those days, we could cram our twenty, thirty, and even forty week deliveries down our customer's throats and make them like it.

But that situation no longer exists. Marion and Bucyrus both manufacture their replacement parts out of AISI-E 4140 steel and heat treat to a good Brinell hardness range; also they stock 77 to 95% of their replacement parts for immediate delivery. Derwent is our newest and most feared competitor. They use an excellent AISI 4340 steel for all their material. (We were not able to obtain this steel since the start of the Korean War in June, 1950. The 3 - 3-1/2 nickel it contains made it a very critical material and we could not get a priority to use it. But Derwent managed to get a priority.)

Besides using a better steel than ours, Derwent boasts that they can offer any replacement part at a maximum nine weeks delivery, and they have been backing this boast by actual performance. They also guarantee their products the same way we guarantee ours, which puts them on an equal basis, and maybe even a little above our gearing. And further, a guarantee of products in the shovel industry is unusual. Other than the original manufacturers, we were the only company who would guarantee their product until Derwent came along.

To sum up, there is one thing we must give our salesmen and representatives to work with — better deliveries. And I think we can do it. We can stock more castings and forged blanks, and we can add more semi-finished items to our stock. It is not a choice of what we would like to do; we must decrease our delivery times or eliminate ourselves from the once very lucrative shovel gearing field.

Juvenal C. Schnorbus, Jr.

Sales Department

Note - See comparative delivery chart, next page.

FIGURE 41—*Continued.*

COMPARATIVE DELIVERY

3

To further illustrate the difficulties we are encountering in regards to extremely long deliveries, I have prepared the comparative delivery chart below. The parts were chosen at random from the various manufacturer's catalogs, and they are parts which we have furnished many times to a variety of customers.

Catalog No.	Part Description	Original Mfg. Delivery	Derwent Delivery	Our Own Delivery
Marion 17794	Shipper Shaft	Marion - 5 wks	4 - 6 wks	29 - 32 wks
Marion 17482	Gear, 46 Teeth, 1 CP, 8 Face	Marion - 1 wk	1 wk	16 - 20 wks
Marion 17103	Bevel Gear, Split 82 - 1 DP - 11	Marion - 4 wks	7 - 8 wks	34 - 35 wks
Marion 14488	Crawler Shaft	Marion - 6 wks	3 wks	10 - 14 wks
Marion 14397	Gear, Bevel Hypoid 44 - 3-1/2 - 6	Marion - immediate	immediate	6 wks[1]
Marion 19907	Pinion, 16 - 1 - 8	Marion - immediate	immediate	6 wks[1]
Bucyrus 10002	Pinion, 15 - 1 - 4	Bucyrus - immediate	immediate	4 wks[2]
Bucyrus 10043	Gear, Bevel Hypoid 67 - 2-1/2 - 5-1/2	Bucyrus - immediate	immediate	17 - 19 wks
Bucyrus 10902	Shipper Shaft	Bucyrus - immediate	immediate	8 wks[3]
Bucyrus 14000	Pinion & Shaft	Bucyrus - immediate	immediate	18 wks
Bucyrus 15083	Pinion & Shaft	Bucyrus - immediate	5 wks	18 wks
Bucyrus 14400	Sheave Wheel	Bucyrus - 3 wks	6 wks	1 wk[4]
Northern 8450	Gear, 45 - 2 - 6	Northern - 2 wks	7 wks	44 - 46 wks[5]
Northern 8002	Gear, 57 - 3 - 4-1/2	Northern - 2 wks	7 wks	44 - 46 wks[5]
P & H 631	Pinion, 26 - 6 - 3	P & H - 1 wk	4 wks	4 wks[2]
P & H 486	Pinion, 24 - 2 - 5	P & H - 2 wks	6 wks	4 wks[2]
P & H 307	Gear, 100 - 3 - 6	P & H - 2 wks	9 wks	4 wks[2]
P & H 558	Shaft	P & H - 4 wks	8 wks	29 - 32 wks
P & H 504	Sheave Wheel	P & H - 2 wks	9 wks	1 wk[4]

[1] Material in semi-finished stock. Heat treat, finish turn and finish cut.

[2] Finished stock, re-bore and re-ketseat.

[3] Raw material on hand, this delivery if order put on emergency list.

[4] Delivery based on receipt of raw material from Delta Steel Castings, Lockland, Ohio. Heat treatment, finish turn, and cable groove buffing are only necessary operations. A few of these castings on hand in our raw material warehouse.

[5] Included in this delivery is the 18 weeks required by Northern to cut their special tooth shape.

Note - Above deliveries from Schedule A - 54, issued 2 - 8 - 54.

FIGURE 41—*Continued.*

4

HAMPTON COLLIERIES

Location.- Terre Haute, Indiana

Our Sales Representative - Edward Brady, Cincinnati Office

Ownership & Personnel Data
        Owned by - Hampton Collieries, Incorporated
        Chief Engineer - Paul Carvel
        Maintenance Engineer - John Dickson
        Purchasing Agent - Miss Helen Campbell

Major Equipment Inventory
        4 Marion 240-B Shovels
        1 Bucyrus 100¼ Shovel
        3 Northern Engineering Shovels, Miscellaneous Models
        Approximately 1-1/2 miles Conveyor Chain, gudgeon and bushing link type.
        Note - Originally made by Link-Belt, our replacements used.

Sales History
        First order received - May, 1935
        Most recent order - Gearing, July 1950. Order now underway for 600 gudgeons.
        Inventory of parts sold - 284 gears and pinions, 12 track wheels, 2 brake wheels,
           402 miscellaneous, 3890 gudgeon and bushing parts.

Miscellaneous Data
        Above plant operating at 70% normal capacity. Marion Manufacturing Company and
        Derwent replacement parts used on all above shovels. Chief Engineer likes our
        gearing, but the other personnel prefer to order parts from Derwent, which
        offers immediate delivery on all parts, prices about 10% lower than ours, and
        a guarantee similar to the one we offer.

        Our gudgeon and bushing parts are also losing favor with this company, and the
        order for 600 now underway in our shop is to be their last until they complete
        a test to determine if our gudgeons are so superior to our competitors as to
        warrant the much higher price we demand. Link-Belt Company, manufacturer of the
        original belting, offers replacements at a third of our price, made of better
      • steel and their deliveries seldom run more than two weeks, as compared to our
        present delivery of 18 weeks.

Future Outlook This Customer
        Very poor. Looks as if our company is entirely out of the picture as far as the
        shovel gearing is concerned, and we are rapidly losing ground in the gudgeon and
        bushing field. Our only solution is better steel, immediate or very short deliv-
        ery, and lower prices. Chief Engineer is sold on our product but he cannot order
        our material. He must deal with Derwent because his superiors like their delivery
        and steels and price better than ours.

FIGURE 41—*Continued.*

5

NORTON COLLIERIES

Location - Brazil, Indiana

Our Sales Representative - Edward Brady, Cincinnati Office

Ownership & Personnel Data
        Owned By - United States Steel Corporation
        Chief Engineer - Burton Fink
        Maintenance Engineer - Daniel Collins
        Purchasing Agent - John King

Major Equipment Inventory
        12 Marion 414-8C Shovels
        16 Bucyrus 1004 Shovels
         2 Bucyrus 880-B Drag Line Crawler Shovels
         4 Alliance Cranes, Various Models

Sales History
        First order received - June, 1939.
        Most recent order - Gearing, June, 1950. No order since this time.
        Inventory of parts sold - 1005 gears and pinions, 1009 miscellaneous.

Miscellaneous Data
        Above plant operating at full capacity. Terrific abrasive conditions in this
        area. All replacement gearing furnished by original manufacturers of the shovels
        and by Derwent Company. This company kept records which definitely proved our
        material superior to competition, but not superior enough to warrant our higher
        prices and longer delivery.

Future Outlook This Customer
        This customer has long term contracts with the original builder of their shovel
        equipment to furnish replacement parts at a discount and with a maximum deliv-
        ery of six weeks. Any other gearing needs are referred to Derwent. Track and
        brake wheels are machined here, using forged blanks supplied by USS. Terrific
        abrasive conditions prevailing here are ripping their shovel gearing to pieces,
        and a month in service is considered excellent. Chief Engineer thinks our gearing
        would be best, as a few pieces of our bevel gearing, sheave wheels and shaft pin-
        ions are still in use. If abrasive conditions prevail, and gearing suppliers are
        not able to cope with them, there is a chance they will ask to be relieved from
        their present contracts rather than replace the defective material. Derwent has
        had to replace or adjust some six thousand dollars worth of material over the
        past three months, while Bucyrus and Marion have run even higher. If this does
        happen, it would be a perfect opening for us, and I think a gift of several items
        of gearing, made of our Thermold J steel would be most welcome. The future
        outlook on sales to this company cannot be any worse. It has been al-
        most four years since their last order. Ed Brady has said he will continue to
        call on this customer in the hope something will break for us, and if it does,
        the Chief Engineer will probably give us his full support.

FIGURE 41—*Continued.*

COMARGO QUARRIES

Location - Hannibal, Missouri

Our Sales Representative - Markham Engineering Service, St. Louis, Missouri

Ownership & Personnel Data
    Owned By - Lone Star Cement Company, Incorporated
    Chief Engineer - Glen Cannon
    Maintenance Engineer - Dennis Johnson
    Purchasing Agent - Ed Landreth

Major Equipment Inventory
    1 Erie 811 Dray Shovel
    1 Bucyrus 44-C Drag Line Shovel
    7 Northern Engineering Shovels, Miscellaneous Models
    2 Simonds Crushing Machines

Sales History
    First order received - June, 1950
    Most recent order - Gearing, July, 1952. Order for abrasive cones underway.
    Inventory of parts sold - 70 gears and pinions, 106 cones and other parts for
       their Simonds Crushers, 109 other miscellaneous parts.

Miscellaneous Data
    Above plant operating at full capacity. All of their gearing replacements now
    being supplied by Derwent, who in addition to their immediate delivery
    can also furnish that special tooth shape necessary in the Northern shovels.
    Their big Erie Dray shovel and their Bucyrus Drag Line are still using a few of
    our bevel gears, purchased in June of 1950. Our shipper shafts used in the
    crawler part of the drag line are wearing well, and have outlasted all their
    competition thus far, and I was told we are in solid as far as our shafting
    goes, but that our delivery on other parts in general is just too long. Our
    abrasive cones are wearing well in their crushers, but they are currently run-
    ning a test of cones purchased from Paulson Manufacturing Company, of West
    Allis, Wisconsin. These cones are 45% cheaper than ours and are delivered
    with two weeks notice; our delivery is 24 to 28 weeks.

Future Outlook This Customer
    Shovel gearing very poor. Derwent has this business pretty well sewed up,
    because of delivery and the fact they can cut that odd cycloidal-type tooth
    used by Northern Engineering. The outlook for our shovel shafting is excellent.
    No real competition at this time. Our cones and other crusher parts are per-
    forming well, but our long delivery is killing the business. If their test on
    those Paulson cones is successful, they are to try some of their other parts,
    and their quick delivery could well be our downfall.

FIGURE 41—*Continued.*

ILLINITE COLLIERIES

Location - Granite City, Illinois

Our Sales Representative - Markham Engineering Service, St. Louis, Missouri

Ownership & Personnel Data
       Owned By - Louis Koehler & Associates
       Chief Engineer - David O'Brien
       Maintenance Engineer - James Sullivan
       Purchasing Agent - Rachel Newman

Major Equipment Inventory
       1 Bucyrus 880-B Drag Line Crawler Shovel
       2 Bucyrus 440-C Drag Line Crawler Shovels
       1 Marion 42 Shovel
       2 Northern Engineering 1005 Shovels
       4 Northern Engineering 1007 Shovels
       4 Pratt & Harnischfeger Shovels, Miscellaneous Models
       2 Morgan Engineering Cranes, 15 and 30 Tons
       1 Whiting Corporation Crane, 25 Ton

Sales History
       First order received - May, 1934
       Most recent order - Gearing, November, 1953. Crane wheels, order underway.
       Inventory of parts sold - 468 gears and pinions, 108 track wheels, 24 brake
         wheels, 880 miscellaneous parts.

Miscellaneous Data
       Above plant operating at full capacity. Products include everything from rock
       and cement to coal and granite. Their order for gearing, received by us in No-
       vember of last year, and still underway in our shop, is their last order of
       gearing from us. I was told by everyone at this plant that they liked all of
       our products very much, but that they could not tolerate our ridiculous de-
       livery and high prices, when Derwent offered immediate delivery and a fine
       quality of finished product at a lower price. The only thing they will continue
       to order from us, will be our track wheels, which we offer at an 8 to 10 weeks
       delivery. Our wheels so outlast our competition that they are willing to wait
       and pay more for ours.

Future Outlook This Customer
       In general, the outlook is poor. Up until June of 1952, this customer was one
       of our best in the strip mining area. Derwent entered the picture at that
       time, and since then our sales have declined steadily and rapidly. This customer
       has said they like our material, but will not tolerate our higher price and
       elongated delivery when they can get almost the same quality goods, guaranteed,
       and with almost immediate delivery, from our competition. It would seem we
       can expect their track wheel business to continue, but in this respect, our
       wheels last such a long time that we can expect only an occasional order. Our
       shipper shafts are used in all their drag line shovels, but their warehouse is
       full of Derwent replacement shafts. Derwent gave them six shafts to run in
       competition with ours, and they performed well, so Illinite bought more, and
       will replace ours with these shafts as needed. This customer has just bought
       the four Pratt & Harnischfeger shovels listed above, and this may well be our
       ray of hope with this company. P & H prefers that, next to their own, our gear-
       ing be used in their equipment, and they maintain a large stock of our gearing
       to give their customers immediate delivery if they request our material. The
       people at Illinite said that they would order replacements from P & H, specifying
       our material, if they could get immediate delivery and still be covered by our
       guarantee. I assured them they would be covered by our guarantee.

FIGURE 41—*Continued.*

8

TABLE OF ILLUSTRATIONS

PLATE 1 - Bucyrus 880-B Drag Line Crawler, Illinite Collieries

PLATE 2 - Sandler Gearing In Operation Since 1950, Despite Terrific Abrasive Conditions. Norton Collieries.

PLATE 3 - Cast Tooth Shrouded Pinions In Operation On Old Erie Dray Shovel. On Right Is Our Pinion, On Left Is One By Derwent. Camargo Quarries.

PLATE 4 - Cast Tooth Sprockets & Gear In Operation On Crawler Mechanism of Bucyrus 880-B Shovel. Gear Is Ours. Two Smaller Sprockets Are By Boston Gear Company, While The Large Sprocket Is Made By Derwent. Picture Taken At Norton Collieries.

PLATE 5 - Conveyor Rollers On Boom Control Mechanism. Bucyrus 440-C Drag Line Crawler Shovel. Illinite Collieries.

PLATE 6 - Sandler Sheaves In Action On Marion 240-B Shovel, At Hampton Collieries.
Note - These sheaves have been in constant use since July, of 1947. A performance record for this company.

PLATE 7 - Sandler Screw Used On Conveying Equipment At Hampton Collieries. In Actual Service Since 1943. Has Never Been Reconditioned. Note Small Spalls And Case Fractures.
Note - Performance record for this company.

PLATE 8 - Sales Engineer Ed Brady Investigates The Extremely Rich Coal Deposits of The Big Bend Collieries.

Photographic Data
Camera - Automatic Rolleiflex, with Tessar f3.5 lens
Film - Eastman Kodak Super XX

FIGURE 41—*Concluded.*

Exercises and Problems

1. What is the difference between an informal report and a memorandum report?

2. What is the difference between an introductory summary and a concluding summary?

3. What is the difference between an introductory summary and an introduction?

4. Assume you are writing a report on the reforestation of a specific tract of land. Where would you put the following material?

> A map of the area.
> History of tract before reforestation was begun.
> An acknowledgment of helpful advice from an official of the U.S. Department of the Interior.
> The titles of four books on reforestation which you studied but did not quote directly.
> The title of a book from which you quoted a paragraph.
> A photograph of a portion of the reforested area.
> A step-by-step account of the reforestation process in this particular tract.
> A list of the headings and subheadings used within the report itself.
> The date the report was submitted.
> An explanation of the writer's inability to gain access to certain material.

5. Write an informal report suggested by one of the following topics:

> Sales presentation: men's dacron suits.
> Export sales organization of the John Deere Co.
> Current employment trends in the Carbondale area.
> Proposed recreation program for Beech-Nut Packing Co.
> Analysis of baked-goods market in the Aurora, Nebraska, area.
> A high-fidelity sound system for distribution through retail record stores.
> Talent scouting report submitted to the Cleveland Browns.
> The effects of changes in relative humidity on the removal of stretch and the tensile strength of X crepe paper.
> Laboratory control of the manufacturing processes: Schenley Distillers, Inc.

Comparative analysis of four varieties of deck faucets.

Why Geo. Eustis and Co. should have an office manual for stenographers.

Load test of shakeproof plastic shelf support #204–290500–00.

Shall Mullane's Tearoom and Gift Shoppe add a line of greeting cards?

Report on three-day time lapse between production operations.

Report on 16-in. plain gap lathe made to suit 1955 design.

Suggested improvements in automobile motor tune-up procedure to cut mechanics' time.

Appraisal report on property located at 7320 Hardy Boulevard.

Comparative production costs, January, 1954–January, 1955.

Report on proposed Park Avenue business site for Atlas Ribbon and Carbon Co.

Need for a personnel department at *The Cincinnati Post*.

Shall the Eden Dairy change to the paper milk bottle?

Need for a receptionist at Ajax Distributing Corp.

The advisability of extending the O.K. Trucking Company's services to St. Louis, Missouri.

The advisability of using automatic pencils in place of wooden lead pencils in order to decrease administrative expense.

Fruit spoilage before and after the purchase of a J. S. Schmidt refrigerated display case.

The work required in preparing material for shipment to our Venezuela Gulf Refining Co.

Life test of National lock mechanism L–16040.

Noise reduction in the production planning office.

How illustrations can be used to increase the average readership of food and grocery advertisements in newspapers.

Proposed method of handling perpetual inventory information at Will Winnes Co., Inc.

6. Write an informal report suggested by one of the topics on pp. 385-89.

7. Write an informal report based on a comparative study of:

Bond prices (figures taken from several issues of a newspaper).

Degrees and academic rank at your university (college catalog).

Enrollment in various divisions of your university (university directory).

Growth in population of various cities in your area (census figures).

Services available in two cities (yellow pages of phone books).

Industrial growth in two cities (Chamber of Commerce figures).

Opportunities in engineering for graduates of your college over several years (placement-office figures).

Job opportunities in your area (want-ad section of newspapers).

Real estate turnover in your city (real-estate section of newspapers).

Depreciation in automobiles (used-car advertising and auto dealers' blue book figures on original cost).

Chapter 10

THE FORMAL REPORT

As we saw in the last chapter, the informal report grows out of and adapts to a specific assignment: "Give me a report on this by Tuesday." It has a job to do; it discharges a function in industry or technology; it makes a contribution to the world's work.

Where the informal report is based on need, the formal report is based on tradition. To be sure, the formal report may fill needs too; however, it does not adapt to those needs in its presentation, but follows the rigid pattern it inherits from the past. It grows out of independent research, class practice, or habits formed in independent research or class practice; its motivation is typically philosophical or scholarly. Often independent research is undertaken just for its results, with no specific audience in mind and no tangible needs to adapt to. The written account of such research seems as a matter of course to fall into the pattern of the formal report. If you have ever studied the documented research paper or "term paper" you have a good start on formal reports.

Reporting and Research. Research which has no ax to grind —which is seeking not a short cut or a quick buck but knowledge—is often called *pure* research. *Applied* research is similar in means but different in goal; it aims to put the knowledge gained through pure research to work in a practical way. It is the kind of research used in preparing informal, utilitarian reports. The stronghold of pure research is the university, where men work part-time teaching the methods of research to others while they themselves are carrying on their attempts to move forward the frontiers of knowledge. About eight per cent of company-financed research is also pure research: "research

151

which has as its primary objective the development of basic information." *

Nearly everyone seems to have the natural curiosity that pure research requires; what small child has not wanted to take the clock apart to see what makes it tick? A main job of the university is to encourage and stimulate that kind of curiosity, to give access to books and equipment which will help the student solve the problems his curiosity sets up, and to develop a sound research method.

Perhaps the formal report is more a part of that research method than we have thought all these years. The academic trappings of the formal report are in a sense a kind of *language of research;* according to the metalinguists ** language shapes thought directly, since we think in language and can think only in terms of concepts and patterns of thought present in our language. It may be, then, that the research itself is shaped in part by its eventual method of presentation.

Research materials and methodology for formal, scholarly reports do not differ sharply from those used for informal, practical reports. Both types of reports utilize materials from observation, interrogation, and library investigation; however, the library typically figures more centrally in research for formal reports. For information on research materials and techniques, review Chapter 2 and consult the "Selected Bibliography" on pp. 393-401.

Origin and History of the Formal Report. Where does the formal report come from? Apparently it has been so long taken for granted that we seldom find the question raised. The pattern is obviously that of the scholarly dissertation: the long paper or book written by Ph.D. candidates and adapted elsewhere in academic work for masters' theses and seminar reports. There have been reports since the beginning of time (a classic favorite for completeness and conciseness is Caesar's

---

* Howard S. Turner, "How Much Should a Company Spend on Research?" *Harvard Business Review,* May-June, 1954, p. 108. Mr. Turner concludes, "Research has become a main function in industry's existence and a dominant factor in its future." (P. 111.)

** An article by Stuart Chase, "How Language Shapes Our Thoughts," *Harper's Magazine,* April, 1954, pp. 76-82, reviews some of the main points of the metalinguists and cites several authors who have written fuller studies in the field.

"Veni, vidi, vici") but only in the last 100-150 years has there been anything like the scholarly report in full dissertation form.

The German universities seem to have invented the dissertation. American graduate schools, which emulated Germanic scholarship, liked and kept the long formal papers. They are now used at all levels of research, inside the university and outside—passed along directly in teaching and indirectly in reporting.

How Formal Reports Are Written. As our title for it suggests, the formal report is more formal in style than the informal, utilitarian ones. Typically it is written for rather well-educated readers, who may either be a general interest group of the public at large (as for a biography or a new book on semantics), or a specialized interest group (such as the subscribers to the *Publications of the Modern Language Association,* the *Journal of Applied Physics,* or the *Harvard Business Review*). However, it should not be too "stiff"; that is, the vocabulary should not be pedantic or ostentatious, and the organization should be clear as a whole and in all parts so that the reader will not waste time and energy in finding the information which he is seeking in the report.

Research and writing procedures for formal reports include principally (1) industrious and skilful use of libraries, (2) outlining for clear organization, (3) note-taking for completeness and accuracy, (4) documentation to guarantee authenticity, (5) clear writing, and (6) neat presentation.

You have received instruction on library usage in Chapter 2, and you will find the "Selected Bibliography" very useful. A great many form manuals have been prepared to show the exact tradition of scientific and scholarly writing; some of the best of these are included in the first section of the Bibliography. Skilful library usage is largely a matter of using research tools efficiently. If a short cut has been prepared in the form of a bibliography, handbook, or manual, by all means use it; there is no merit in doing things the hard way. Also utilize what you have learned about efficient reading. The research writer is not a pedestrian sauntering through the woods, but an eager hunter, hot in pursuit of game.

The working outline is important. You will need to determine early in your research both the dominating idea (thesis)
of your problem and the major divisions into which it naturally
falls; that is, the main topics of the outline. Your outline is the
tangible form of your working plan, and should follow such a
scheme of organization as chronological, comparative, enumera-
tive, group relationship, or cause and effect.

Note-taking is not a haphazard matter, either. Successful
library research is especially dependent on a good system of
note-taking. As you read your various source materials, you
will be constantly on the alert for choice bits for quotation,
significant facts or data which will support points you will want
to make, or pertinent theories, ideas, or conclusions which will
fit into your own discussion material. A good system of note-
taking includes (1) use of a suitable unit (probably a 4×6-
inch card or slip will prove best) for each and every note,
(2) accurate reproduction of material; that is, exact quotation
or faithful summary, (3) exact identification of sources, including page reference.

Documentation, a rather small matter usually in informal
reports, is comparatively important in the formal report. Formal reports are essentially derivative. They depend on source
materials in such a way that the writer must give credit: (1) in
a general way by grouping his various sources in a bibliography, and (2) more specifically through supplying footnotes
wherever he owes acknowledgment to a source or needs to explain something not fully clear in his text.

A bibliography is a source-materials list, arranged according
to some established form or scheme, usually a simple alphabetical listing. For a report, it comprises all the books, magazine articles, and other items that have been utilized, including
not only those cited in footnotes but also any others which
were in some way useful. These materials must be arranged
alphabetically by authors' last names, or in the absence of an
author, by the first important word (excluding articles) of the
title. The bibliography reproduced as part of the specimen
report in this chapter shows our recommended form for varied
entries in a bibliography. It is a variation of the documentary
system sometimes called the Chicago system, employed by The
University of Chicago Press *Manual of Style*, The University of

Chicago *Manual for Writers of Dissertations,* and the Williams-Stevenson *Research Manual.* Other manuals, especially those for scientific and "education" writing, recommend slightly different forms, the differences being mainly in punctuation. There is no clear superiority of one system over another, although the Chicago system seems to be gaining on the others. The system doesn't matter so much as careful consistency in whatever system is used. If your instructor prefers a system different from ours, follow his preference cheerfully—and consistently.

Footnotes are the second important aspect of documentation. A footnote is a device for giving credit where credit is due or supplying needed definitions or explanations without cluttering the text with distracting material. The majority of footnotes are citation footnotes; that is, they give the source of a quotation, fact, or idea. A citation footnote supplies, in compact form, as much information as a reader of the report would likely be interested in. For the first citation of any given source, your reader would want to know at least the name of the author, the title of the book or magazine article, and the page or pages being cited. Since formal reports have bibliographies, there seems to be no point in including the publisher's name in a footnote, but your reader might want to know what city the book was published in or what magazine carried the article, and he quite likely would want the date. Primary, or first, footnotes for any given source therefore supply author, title, city or magazine, date, and page. When the same source is cited further on, the reader will not need all the information repeated; so shorter (secondary) forms have been adopted.

The primary form for any given footnote is used only for the first citation of that source in a short report, or the first citation in a chapter of a long report. After that use *ibid.* for an immediately following footnote to the same source, or the author-title-page or author-page form where footnotes for other sources intervene. Number footnotes consecutively through short reports and through chapters of long reports. Note that the footnotes in the body of this text include the publisher. This is standard practice where the published work does not include a formal bibliography of source materials. For further information on footnote form and usage, observe the footnotes in the specimen report (Fig. 42) at the end of this chapter and consult the Williams-Stevenson *Research Manual* or some other manual recommended by your instructor.

Closely related to note-taking and documentation is the handling of illustrative material, discussed above in Chapter 6. Pictorial material is used less in formal reports than in informal, technical reports, but both kinds employ it. If you need only a few graphs, maps, photostats, etc., you can introduce them by casual text reference and document them just as for footnotes. Where much illustrative material is used, however, it is better to use text references of Fig. 1, Fig. 2, etc., and document each illustration separately by including the source in the descriptive note immediately beneath it. Wide tables or graphs may be placed the long way of the page, with the heading on the binding side and the credit line beneath.

That the formal report should be clearly written and neatly presented could almost go without saying. The manuscript should be typed, double-spaced. Quotations longer than three lines should be single-spaced; single-spacing takes the place of quotation marks. Margins should be about one inch at top, bottom, and sides, which means about a half inch extra on the left side for binding. Indent five spaces at the beginning of each paragraph and footnote, but indent the beginning of a single-spaced quotation only when there was indention in the source. If you use as your backing sheet a piece of paper or thin cardboard about half an inch wider than typing paper, you can easily scale the lower part of it to enable you to stop at the right place, with or without footnotes. Number prefatory material with small Roman numerals at the bottom of the page and text material in Arabic numerals in the upper right-hand corner. Any necessary erasures should be made so neatly they will not show; otherwise the page should be retyped.

The final organization of a formal report as evidenced in its table of contents, is somewhat flexible, but a typical listing is the following:

Preface

Table of Contents

List of Figures (or Illustrations)

Chapters

    I.   (Include chapter title here.)

    II.

    III.

    IV.

    V.

    VI.

Bibliography

Appendix or Appendixes

Index (found only in some long reports)

For the shorter reports not employing chapter divisions, the word "Body" replaces the chapter entry.

The final step in preparing the completed report for handing in is to prepare an appropriate title page and bind the whole neatly and attractively, with a name-date-title label on the front cover. We will not try to tell you exactly what sort of binder to use, as your choice will be influenced by instructor preference and bookstore supply. In the final stages of report preparation, the key word is neatness. A good report deserves an attractive dress.

Specimen Documentary Forms.

Bibliographical entry for a book:

> ALFORD, LEON P. Principles of Industrial Management. New York: Ronald Press Company, 1951.

Bibliographical entry for a magazine article:

> CHASE, STUART. "Korzybski and Semantics," The Saturday Review, XXXVII (June 19, 1954), 11-12; 46-48.

Or CHASE, STUART. "Korzybski and Semantics," The Saturday Review, June 19, 1954, pp. 11-12; 46-48.

Primary footnote for a book:

> [1] Leon P. Alford, Principles of Industrial Management (New York, 1951), p. 134.

Secondary footnote for a book:

> [2] Alford, Principles of Industrial Management, p. 163.

Or   [3] Alford, p. 163.

Or   [4] *Ibid.*, p. 179.

Primary footnote for a magazine article:

>   [1] Stuart Chase, "Korzybski and Semantics," The Saturday Review,
>   XXXVII (June 19, 1954), 47.

Or   [2] Stuart Chase, "Korzybski and Semantics," The Saturday Review,
June 19, 1954, p. 47.

Secondary footnote for a magazine article:

>   [3] Chase, "Korzybski and Semantics," p. 46.

Or   [4] Chase, p. 46.

Or   [5] *Ibid.*, p. 48.

Primary footnote form for book in report not containing a
bibliography:

>   [1] Leon P. Alford, Principles of Industrial Management (New
>   York: The Ronald Press Co., 1951), p. 134.

Exercises and Problems

1. Cecil B. Williams and Allan H. Stevenson in *A Research
Manual* state that examples of research writing at all levels can be
found in the library: "advanced apprentice (Master's theses);
journeyman (many Ph.D. dissertations, some of the articles in
scholarly journals); and master or expert (polished scholarly articles, standard biographies, and books by accomplished authorities
in all fields)." In your college library find at least one example of
each level of research writing. Read enough of each to compare
it with the others; report to your class.

2. As a specific project, investigate the origins of formal reporting
or dissertation writing. (There is less information than might be
expected on this interesting subject.)

3. Make a study of several formal reports written by students
(perhaps your professor can put some on reserve or arrange a visit
to his files). What flaws or weaknesses are most common? What
serious flaws do you find? Write a brief memorandum report on the
flaws you find in student formal reports.

4. What changes would be necessary in the model report on p. 140 or in the one on p. 343 to make an acceptable formal report of it?

5. Prepare a rating chart for formal reports, listing the qualities you think a formal report should be graded or rated on, and weighting each quality with a number (% of 100) showing its relative importance.

6. Write a formal report based on one of the case studies in Section IV, pp. 361 ff.

7. Write a formal report on a topic suggested by one of the actual report topics listed on pp. 390-92.

8. Write a formal report exploring some new concept or changing body of knowledge in your own field. Read some current magazines to discover what the new developments are: *Fortune, Scientific Monthly, Iron Age,* etc.

9. Write a formal report suggested by one of the following actual report topics:

Plan for a sporting goods store in a suburban shopping center.
Top management organization of Thompson Products Corp.
Legislation affecting the retail liquor dealer.
Profit sharing and wage incentive plans.
Wage incentive plans by merit rating.
A wage incentive plan for Selden Fabricating Corp.
An analysis of the results of United Nations action, 1953.
Survey: reader preferences on pictures in advertising.
The roller skating rink business in 1955.
A public relations program for the secretaries of General Electric Corp.
Survey: night opening in downtown department stores.
Survey of department store managers: how a store in the suburbs can attract customers.
Promotion methods for a pizza company.
Two-year business forecast: Hubble Cural Tonic Co.
Proposed change to make the Peaseway Home plan more flexible.
Prospective locations for the Auto-Stoker Co.
Merchandising of appliances in a buyer's market.
Personnel counseling in four selected industrial firms.
Future applications of machine accounting.

THE MEASUREMENT OF INFORMATION
by
John Dark

The University of Cincinnati
January 12, 1955

FIGURE 42. A Brief Formal Report on the Information Theory.

11

PREFACE

In preparing to write my report I have had the rare privilege of standing at the border of a vast, nearly unexplored body of knowledge and feeling the magnetic pull of new frontiers. Though my report attempts only to explain in simple language the basic terms of information theory and to describe with examples the method of measuring information, I have become a victim of the infectious enthusiasm for their subject of the authors of my source books; I know I won't be able to stop with this report. Perhaps I can use other aspects of information theory for further research projects; otherwise I'll continue on my own.

The measurement of information makes possible the evaluation of the effectiveness of communication--and from the evaluation it is but a short step to scientifically-controlled improvement of communication, not only over wires or wave lengths but in letters and reports. Thus a field of knowledge which has always operated on intuition and hope comes under the method of science.

I should mention one obstacle which has handicapped me in the preparation of this report: I have not had enough mathematics to understand all Mr. Shannon's formulas in The Mathematical Theory of Communication. I hope this handicap will not be serious with the limited goal I have set for this report.

FIGURE 42—*Continued*.

CONTENTS

FIGURE 42—*Continued.*

ILLUSTRATIONS

FIGURE 42—*Continued*.

1

INTRODUCTION

The Information Theory has a very brief history: it has
grown up since the beginning of World War II. Norbert
Wiener, author of Cybernetics, an M. I. T. mathematician,
was one of the theory's discoverers; Claude Shannon, a
Bell Laboratories engineer, was the other. Cybernetics and
Shannon's A Mathematical Theory of Communication were both
published in 1948. Warren Weaver, Research Director of the
Rockefeller Foundation, contributed certain related theories
of his own on the implications of the new discoveries, along
with his interpretation of some of Dr. Shannon's technical
papers, to the same 1948 volume which contained Shannon's
major explanation of his theory. Since 1948 a number of
articles on Information Theory have appeared; a selected
bibliography in Etc., A Review of General Semantics, Summer
1953, pp. 316-317, shows 36 entries.

Francis Bello, writing in Fortune, evaluates the Information
Theory:

Great scientific theories, like great symphonies and great
novels, are among man's proudest -- and rarest -- creations. What
sets the scientific theory apart from and, in a sense, above the
other creations is that it may profoundly and rapidly alter man's
view of his world.
In this century man's views, not to say his life, have
already been deeply altered by such scientific insights as relativity

FIGURE 42—*Continued.*

2

theory and quantum theory. Within the last five years a new
theory has appeared that seems to bear some of the same
hallmarks of greatness. The new theory, still almost unknown
to the general public, goes under either of two names:
communication theory or information theory. Whether or not
it will ultimately rank with the enduring great is a question
now being resolved in a score of major laboratories here
and abroad.

The central teachings of the theory are directed at
electrical engineers. It gives them, for the first time, a
comprehensive understanding of their trade. It tells them
how to measure the commodity they are called upon to transmit --
the commodity called "information" -- and how to measure the
efficiency of their machinery for transmitting it. Thus the
theory applies directly to telegraph, telephone, radio,
television, and radar systems; to electronic computers and to
automatic controls for factories as well as for weapons.

It may be no exaggeration to say that man's progress in
peace, and security in war, depend more on fruitful application
of information theory than on physical demonstrations, either
in bombs or in power plants, that Einstein's famous equation
works.[1]

INFORMATION

The aspect of Information Theory which this report will

discuss is the method of measuring the amount of information

in a message, a method developed through the theory and made

possible only by it. Although this method is but an aspect of

the theory as a whole, it is the aspect which is arousing the

most interest among specialists in a number of fields,

particularly mathematical biology and semantics.[2] It is also

the aspect of the theory which is likely to have the greatest

effect on reporting theory and practice.

---

[1] Francis Bello, "The Information Theory," *Fortune*, XLVIII
(December, 1953), 136.

[2] Anatol Rapoport, "What Is Information?" *Etc.*, X (Summer,
1953), 248.

FIGURE 42—*Continued.*

3

Information as we will discuss it in its meaning in
Information Theory has nothing to do with meaning. A message
may be coded or uncoded, plain language or nonsense; its
information content can be measured as well one way as the
other. As Warren Weaver puts it, "...this word information
in communication theory relates not so much to what you do
say, as to what you could say. That is, information is a
measure of one's freedom of choice when one selects a message."[1]
If there is no freedom of choice, there is no information. A
message without freedom of choice is entirely predictable:
for example, these series --

    A B C D E F G H I J K L M N O P Q R S T U V W X Y Z

    1 2 3 4 5 6 7 8 9 10 11 12 13 14 15 16 17 18 19 20

    1 11 111 1111 11111 111111 1111111 11111111 111111111

    2 4 8 16 32 64 128 256 512 1024 2048 4096 8192 16384

Once the pattern of the message is clear to the reader, the
transmission of the message becomes redundant or unnecessary.
The more pattern or predictability the message has, the more
redundancy and the less information is being transmitted.
The less pattern or predictability, conversely, the more
information. The maximum flow of information comes when the
signals in the message are arranged quite at random and occur
at about the same frequency. Fig. 1 shows the flow of
information in three sample messages.

---

[1] Warren Weaver, "Recent Contributions to the Mathematical
Theory of Communication," in Claude E. Shannon and Warren
Weaver, The Mathematical Theory of Communication (Urbana: The
University of Illinois Press, 1949), p. 100.

FIGURE 42—*Continued.*

4

A GRAPHIC REPRESENTATION OF THE FLOW OF INFORMATION

Message 1: K K K K K K K Y K K K K Y K K Y K K K K Y K Y K K

In transmission, K receives no pulse and Y receives one pulse
of electricity. Only when a Y is sent is there a flow of
information. 5 units of information are sent in Message 1.

Message 2: 82 81 81 80 78 76 74 72 73 72 70 73 73 70 72 74 75

In transmission, all temperatures over 70 receive no pulse and
all temperatures 70 or below receive one pulse of electricity.
One pulse of electricity turns on the automatic oil furnace.
2 units of information are sent in Message 2.

Message 3: NO YES NO NO NO YES NO YES NO NO YES YES NO YES YES

In transmission, all artillery shells that are on the target
receive no pulse and all artillery shells that are not on the
target receive one pulse of electricity. One pulse of
electricity records a "miss" on the firing record. 8 units of
information are sent in Message 3.

Fig. 1.

FIGURE 42—*Continued.*

5

THE UNIT OF INFORMATION

Weiner and Shannon define the <u>unit of information</u> as
<u>that which makes a decision between two equally probable
events</u>.[1] The unit was named the <u>bit</u> at the suggestion of
John W. Tukey; <u>bit</u> stands for <u>binary digits</u>,[2] the simplest
possible symbols to use in coding information for transmission.
The messages in Fig. 1 are the simplest possible kind of
messages, involving only two possibilities: yes or no,
on or off, pulse or no pulse. Such messages can be coded
by bindary code groups only one bit long -- 0 can stand
for no pulse and 1 can stand for pulse, so that Message 2
would read 00000000001001000.

To handle messages involving more than two possibilities,
binary code groups two or more bits long are required. The
code group two bits long offers four possible alternatives,
00, 01, 10, 11 -- and these four can stand for A, B, C, D;
yes, no, maybe, no answer; 5, 6, 7, 8; or any other group
of four possible components of a message.

The binary code group three bits long offers eight
possible alternatives, 000, 001, 010, 011, 100, 101, 110, and 111.
These eight can stand for any eight possible components of
a message. In order to encode the alphabet (26 possible
alternatives) binary numbers five bits long are required.
Fig. 2 shows the alphabet encoded in binary numbers.

---

[1] Bello, "The Information Theory," p. 140.

[2] <u>Binary</u> means two digits, 0 and 1. We are more accustomed
to the decimal system; <u>decimal</u> means ten digits, 0, 1, 2, 3, 4, 5,
6, 7, 8, and 9. The first ten numbers in binary notation are 0, 1,
10, 11, 100, 101, 110, 111, 1000, 1001.

FIGURE 42—*Continued.*

6.

THE ALPHABET ENCODED IN BINARY NUMBERS

A	00000		N	10000
B	00001		O	10001
C	00010		P	10010
D	00011		Q	10100
E	00100		R	10101
F	00110		S	10110
G	00111		T	11000
H	01000		U	11001
I	01010		V	11010
J	01011		W	11100
K	01100		X	11101
L	01110		Y	11110
M	01111		Z	11111

Fig. 2.

Figure 42—*Continued.*

7

Actually not all the binary code groups five bits long
are required to encode the alphabet; 32 are available and
only 26 are used. The average number of bits required per
letter, therefore, is about 4.7.

In summary,

a decision between two equally
probable events requires   1 bit of information

while a decision among 26
equally probable events requires   4.7 bits of information

Each additional bit of information doubles the number of
possibilities; if the game of Twenty Questions were assumed to
supply one bit of information for each question, the 20 bits
should identify 2^{20} possible objects: over a million. [1]

Though the measurement of information required to permit
a decision among events of unequal probability grows extremely
complex and is outside the strict scope of this report, one
of Dr. Shannon's experimental studies on the amount of
information contained in ordinary English sentences (which of
course involve unequal probability of letters and words) is
described briefly in the Appendix because of its startling
implications for reporting and other communications.

---

[1] Ibid., p. 149 n.

FIGURE 42—*Continued.*

8

BIBLIOGRAPHY

Bello, Francis. "The Information Theory." Fortune, XLVIII
    (December, 1953), 136-158.

Berkeley, Edmund C. Giant Brains. New York: John Wiley &
    Sons, Inc., 1949.

King, Gilbert W. "Information." Scientific American, CLXXXVII
    (September, 1952), 132-148.

Rapoport, Anatol. "What Is Information?" Etc.: A Review of
    General Semantics, X (Summer 1953), 247-260.

Shannon, Claude E., and Warren Weaver. The Mathematical
    Theory of Communication. Urbana: The University of Illinois
    Press, 1949.

FIGURE 42—*Continued.*

9

APPENDIX

THE GUESSING GAME: AN APPLICATION OF INFORMATION THEORY
TO THE MEASUREMENT OF INFORMATION IN PLAIN ENGLISH SENTENCES

    Theoretically, 4.7 bits of information are required to

encode each letter of the alphabet. In order to test plain

English sentences to see how many bits of information are

required to make correct decisions about the messages they

contain, Dr. Shannon devised an experiment:

    In one game he would pick a passage at random, from a book,
and ask someone to guess the letters, one by one. He would tell
the subject only if he were wrong, and the subject would continue
until he finally guessed the right letter (or space). Shannon
quickly discovered that the average person requires substantially
fewer than 3.3 guesses to identify the correct letter in ordinary
text. The relation between guesses and bits of information
should become clearer in what follows.
    One of Shannon's favorite passages for this type of game
was "There is no reverse on a motorcycle a friend of mine found this
out rather dramatically the other day." In this passage there are
102 letters and spaces, including a final space after "day." Going
through the passage letter by letter, one of Shannon's subjects
guessed right on his first guess 79 times, and correctly identified
all 102 letters and spaces with only 198 guesses, or less than two
guesses per letter or space.
    After mathematical analysis of many such experiments Shannon
concluded that in ordinary literary English the long-range
statistical effects reduce the information content to about
one bit per letter. That is to say, if one sees the first 50
or 100 letters of a message, he can be reasonably certain, on the
average, that the next following letter (which he hasn't seen)
will be one of only two equally probable letters. To remove this
much uncertainty requires, by definition, only one bit of information....
    Shannon's calculation...has this surprising implication. It
says that with proper encoding it should be possible to translate
any page of ordinary English into a succession of binary digits, 0
and 1, so that there are no more digits than there were letters
in the original text. In other words, twenty-four of the twenty-six
letters of the alphabet are superfluous. So far as printed English
is concerned, this is the goal that information theory establishes
for the communication engineer. [1]

---

[1] Francis Bello, "The Information Theory," *Fortune*, XLVIII
(December, 1953), p. 149.

FIGURE 42—*Concluded.*

Chapter 11

LETTER OF TRANSMITTAL

IT'S A GOOD FEELING to finish a report. You've gathered the material, put it together, set it up in report form, proofread it to make sure it's in good shape. It's *your* report, and you have some opinions about it and the work it came out of and possibly the work that may grow out of it. You can't put these opinions in the report; it is supposed to stick directly to the assigned subject. But if you were to go into the boss' office to hand in your report, you wouldn't just lay it on his desk, give a hand salute and leave. You would stop a minute and say, "On this report, Tom, there are a couple of things that bother me and I want you to know about. I wouldn't want you to depend too much on the last part of the report, the one about the market shift. Just this morning I ran into some figures that seem to point in the other direction; since the report is due now, I couldn't do it over. Another thing—I wouldn't want to take credit for that big chart at the end; Jim Donovan drew that for me on his own time. I guess that's all, unless you have something else you want me to do on this."

Whatever comments you have to make about your report, whether you will have a chance to speak to the boss about it or not, should go into your letter of transmittal or preface.

Functions of the Letter of Transmittal. The first function of a letter of transmittal is to make a record. The subject of the report, the date it was submitted, and all your comments on it will, through the miracle of carbon paper, go into both your file and the file of the person to whom you submit the report. To make full use of this function, the report-writer should think of what is needed in the record to accompany his report.

173

Inter Office Correspondence
THE HUNNEWELL SOAP CO.

Date: March 1, 1949

From: Brion C. Sawyer

To: Leslie Webb

Subject: Material Handling Improvement

       I am submitting this report as you requested last Monday, February 28.

       I made the changes embodied in this report with due respect to labor, time, and monetary savings.

       When I decided to make the change I took into consideration the slope and condition of the floors, also cost to realign and plate them with 1/4" sheet steel of a suitable safety design. The expenditure for such a program would have been prohibitive.

       Therefore I installed the monorail system, a vast improvement over the old system, for transporting material from the initial carrier to storage points in the factory.

FIGURE 43. Letter of Transmittal to Accompany a Report. (By permission of The Hunnewell Soap Co.)

FEDERAL RESERVE BANK

OF CLEVELAND

OFFICE CORRESPONDENCE

TO: Mr. C. Harrell, Assistant Cashier
Cincinnati Branch

DATE: March 1, 1949

FROM: R. P. Oettinger, Assistant Manager of
Building, Cincinnati Branch

SUBJECT: Report on the
Proposed File
System for the
General Archives

The following report containing the results of a
survey of the present and proposed systems in the
General Archives is submitted for your approval.

The facts presented, regarding the present system,
were obtained by an actual count and inspection of
each storage unit. Mr. Molique, Manager of the
Check Collection Department, was consulted as to
the future requirements for additional storage units,
to accommodate the increased volume of I.B.M. tapes,
following the installation of 41 new proof machines.

Should the recommended system be adopted, it will
be necessary to purchase 827 legal size Safe-T-Stak
Files for immediate use. The acquisition of this
equipment will result in a more efficient and adequate method of retaining records in the General
Archives.

R.P. Oettinger

Assistant Manager of Building

FIGURE 44. Letter of Transmittal to Accompany a Report. (By permission
of Federal Reserve Bank of Cleveland.)

CCCOMMUNICATIONS CONSULTING · PUBLIC RELATIONS
JOHN BALL · OXFORD · OHIO

MEMORANDUM TO   Police Chief Stanley R. Schrotel
City of Cincinnati

1 May 1954

PUBLIC RELATIONS AND COMMUNICATIONS
IN THE CINCINNATI POLICE DEPARTMENT

This report was made possible through the helpfulness
and cooperation of Colonel Schrotel, Captain Sandman,
Captain Clift, Sergeant Reis, and officers and patrol-
men throughout the department.

I did not begin with the idea in mind of presenting
a detailed analysis of all phases of the department's
public relations; I planned to make a general survey,
find the trouble spots if any, and concentrate on
them for the main substance of my report. I have
carried out that plan.

I am available at the department's pleasure to discuss
my report or to assist with any public relations
problems which may come up in the future.

John Ball

John Ball

FIGURE 45.   Letter of Transmittal to Accompany an Independent Consultant's
Report.

To:
THE BRITISH IRON AND STEEL FEDERATION
THE IRON AND STEEL TRADES CONFEDERATION
THE NATIONAL UNION OF BLASTFURNACEMEN, ORE MINERS, COKE
WORKERS AND KINDRED TRADES

Gentlemen: We, the members of the British Iron and Steel Productivity team, present our unanimous Report arising out of
the visit we made to the United States of America in May and
June, 1951, under the auspices of the Anglo-American Council
on Productivity and the Technical Assistance Program of
E. C. A.

In preparing this Report we have been conscious of the
many difficulties, not the least being that of generalising
about a country where "the only safe generalisation is that
it is a land of contrasts". In the time available only a
small part of America's enormous iron and steel industry
could be visited and studied. When we were in the United
States industrial activity, stimulated by the defence programme, was at a high level. Nevertheless, we feel that much
of what we have to say is valid as a true impression of
longer-term conditions there. Furthermore, quite apart from
the knowledge which we gained of the American industry, the
visit has enabled us to look at and analyse our own steel
industry from a new viewpoint.

For us it has been a very stimulating and valuable experience, partly because of the friendly welcome given to us by
our colleagues in America, and partly because we tasted some
of the enthusiasm of that pioneer people as they go on building an even greater and richer country. In view of the close
links which have existed for so many years between our re-
spective iron and steel industries we did not expect any
major surprises, at least in the technical field. At the
same time no comprehensive analysis of relative productivi-
ties in the two industries had previously been attempted,
and, as was to be hoped, the visit revealed many interesting

FIGURE 46. Letter of Transmittal Prepared and Signed by Sixteen British
Iron and Steel Trades Executives and Engineers Who Visited the United States
to Study American Steel-Production Methods.

This letter is printed here to show the essential similarity of reporting problems on an international scale; except for minor differences in form and the
British spellings (generalisation, programme, analyse) this letter of transmittal
is quite similar to ours in America.

points of difference in methods of production and
organisation.

We have drawn freely on the views and advice of many
friends, but are alone responsible for the contents of our
Report. Its object is simple and clear: to help the British
iron and steel industry and the people who serve in it to
raise productivity, and to enable them to play an even larger
and stronger part in the national economy. This cannot be
done without self-criticism, stated or implied, but we trust
that no one will mis-use such criticism, which should be
considered as a stimulus to further achievement.

[*Sixteen signatures followed here*]

Figure 46—*Concluded.*

Another function of the letter of transmittal is the encouragement of the transmission of useful comments, suggestions, and
proposals for future research projects. When a company puts
an intelligent and perceptive man to work on a specialized
project, it is surprising if he does not learn something outside
the range of that project while he is working on it. The existence of the letter of transmittal as an informal communication
channel encourages the passing along of useful information and
ideas to the company even though they are not related enough
to the topic to be included in the report. It would have been
a pity, for example, if on the day the mixer ran too long at
Procter and Gamble no one had reported that the "spoiled"
batch of soap would float.

An important function of the letter of transmittal, as of any
letter, is its public relations function.* A friendly, thorough,
helpful letter is good for personal public relations as well as for
company public relations; the fact that most reports go to
someone within the same company should not cause the report
writer to produce a careless or routine letter of transmittal.
A cooperative attitude and a good long-range perspective and
understanding of his job, shown in the letter of transmittal of
a report reaching top management, can do the report-writer

* See Cecil B. Williams and John Ball, *Effective Business Writing* (2d ed.;
New York: The Ronald Press Co., 1953), chap. x.

March 2, 1954

To: Mr. George Goller, Supervising Metallurgist
          Research Laboratories, Rustless Division

From: P. E. Ramseyer, Development Engineer

Subject: Central Steel & Wire Co.   FOR TIME STAMP
          Chicago 80, Illinois

          Type 440A Stainless Steel

Attached is a letter we received from Mr. L. T. Johnston, Jr.
through our Chicago Office requesting information concerning
Type 440A stainless.

Will you please review this letter and let us have your comments to the questions outlined. We would appreciate your
comments as soon as possible so that we can determine whether
Type 440A might be suitable for the application.

PER:cs
Attach.

FIGURE 47. Letter of Authorization. (By permission of Armco Steel Corporation.)

The letter of authorization for a report, assigning the project and often laying
out the method of approach, was once as a matter of custom submitted with the
report. This practice is now nearly extinct; if a letter of authorization is received
its suggestions are followed, of course (such a letter may be a valuable aid to
the report-writer in clarifying what is wanted), but the letter itself is then
filed in the report-writer's files rather than sent back to the person making the
assignment. To check the frequency of use of the letter of authorization as a
part of the completed report, we studied over 3000 reports and found only
one which included a letter of authorization.

more good in a practical way than dozens of letters sent outside the company. Even if company policy requires a formal third-person report, there is no conceivable justification for writing a formal third-person letter of transmittal. Your letter should sound like you, should have the "you attitude," * and should avoid the stilted jargon of the nineteenth century.

Memorandum, Letter, or Preface. The form of the letter of transmittal depends on the needs of the communication situation: what the reader needs to know, how much the writer has to say, the length and nature of the report the letter is to accompany. A brief memorandum report needs no separate letter of transmittal; it may incorporate prefatory material in its opening lines. However, some writers prefer to make a separate letter of transmittal, even on very short reports, particularly if the reports are primarily statistical (I once saw a two-page letter of transmittal used, with complete justification, to accompany a half-page statistical report). Very long reports —book length or thesis length—generally use a preface to accomplish the purpose of the letter of transmittal. Between the very short and the very long fall the great majority of reports. Of these, the ones going outside the company generally use standard letter forms for the letter of transmittal and the ones going to another part of the company use interoffice correspondence or memorandum forms.

Memorandum Form. There are a wide variety of memorandum forms, but all include much the same information. Typical forms are shown on pp. 113-17. Type your memorandum with good wide margins, single-space within paragraphs, and double-space between paragraphs. Sign your memorandum in ink. A signature identification is not needed since the writer's name is typed after "From" at the top of the report. Don't clutter up your memorandum with such unnecessary features as "Dear Sir" and "Sincerely yours"; the great advantage of the memorandum form is its simplicity, its easy convenience.

Interoffice Correspondence Forms. A few firms distinguish between memorandum and interoffice correspondence

---

* "You attitude": an approach to letter writing which is based on what the reader needs to know and which tries to look at every problem from the reader's perspective. See Williams and Ball, *Effective Business Writing*, pp. 65 ff.

forms; the interoffice form is sometimes rather complex with a number of blanks keyed to the special requirements of the company's filing system. The simplicity of the memorandum is lost; in fact, some interoffice forms are much more difficult to prepare than ordinary letters and require special attention in the company's training program. If your company has such forms you will be trained to use them; there is no need to discuss them further here.

LETTER FORMS. In the language of the trade, letters which go from one company to another company, to a customer, or to other individuals are *outside* letters. Though a report going outside the company may be accompanied by a memorandum letter of transmittal, a firm often prefers to use its standard company letterhead and letter form. The letter should be single-spaced, with wide margins, and should be just about centered on the page. If an individual is addressed, the salutation should be singular (Dear Mr. Jones: or Dear Ralph, or rather rarely these days, Dear Sir:); if a company is addressed, the salutation should be plural (Gentlemen:). *Sincerely yours,* and *Cordially yours,* have gained ground in the past five years over *Yours very truly,* and *Very truly yours.* Most of the conventions of letter form are based on a combination of custom and convenience, and since opinions on both differ, there are two or more "right" ways to set up almost every part of the letter, from the date (1 March 1955 or March 1, 1955) to the postscript (P.S. or p.s.). The gradual simplification of letter form over the past fifty years seems destined to bring into full favor in the future a form like the NOMA simplified letter on p. 223.*

PREFACE. A preface is a kind of letter of transmittal bound into a mass-produced report or into a long report destined to be read by more than one reader.** The preface is similar in content to the letter of transmittal (though, as I have indicated, it is generally directed to a somewhat larger audience), except

---

* For a detailed analysis of letter form see Williams and Ball, *Effective Business Writing,* chap. ii.

** For an example see the preface at the beginning of this textbook. To simplify the subject, the standard content of a preface is often said to come under these three headings: (1) the "author's excuse for his book," (2) materials and methodology, (3) acknowledgments.

that its form is much modified. It is introduced only by its head-ing—*Preface* or words with similar meaning such as *A Note to the Reader*—and it closes with the typed or printed name or initials of the writer (at the right) and usually the date (at the left). The function of the preface should be clearly distin-guished from that of the introduction; the preface does not contain background material on the content of the report but only the type of information described in the following para-graphs.

Content. The letter of transmittal or preface may contain any of these items or several (but not all) of them:

> *Identification of the assignment or authorization for the report.*
> *Explanation of the purpose of the report.*
> *Explanation of the limits originally set for the study.*
> *Pointing out of your bias* or personal prejudice if there is a chance that it would have affected the report.
> *Discussion of your philosophy* of science (or whatever field is being reported on) if it would help in the understanding of your method and your results.
> *Pointing out of a significant point or trend* that might otherwise be missed, of a key chart or graph (especially if it is buried in the appendix), or of related reading in journals or peri-odicals.
> *Explanation of peculiarities,* seeming contradictions, or possibly ambiguous sections of the report. (Are you sure you can't fix them instead of just talking about them?)
> *Explanation of the method of research used in getting material.*
> *Explanation of changes in method of research* from those as-signed.
> *Discussion of the limitations that showed up while the study was in progress.* The last-named is an extremely important point, for it vitally affects the validity of decisions the reader of the report will make. If the unknown, the unavailable, the incomplete, or the doubtful necessarily enter into your report, show how, clearly and frankly.
> *Mention of unexpected difficulty in obtaining information* through lack of cooperation within the organization or out-side it.
> *Evaluation of method of research that you used.*

Explanation of method of organization.

Acknowledgment of helpfulness and actual contributions to the report by others.

Listing of persons who expressed interest in the report and wished to be kept informed of its progress.

Discussion and evaluation of comments on the report by persons to whom the writer has shown the report before submitting it in final form.

Your own evaluation of the report project itself if you think its importance or unimportance is particularly worth mentioning.

Your own conclusions and recommendations if you wish to make them and if they were not specifically requested in the report. (Depends on the boss; some would welcome unsolicited suggestions more than others.)

Your attempt to fit your report into the big picture, the long-range perspective.

Suggestions for application in practice of material in the report.

Suggestions for further projects for your own research.

Mention of new material encountered during research, unrelated to your project but in your opinion worthy of investigation.

Answers to questions raised in the letter of authorization, if any. (See Fig. 47.)

Importance. You can see, then, that in a sense your letter of transmittal or preface does a selling job on your report. It sets forth, either directly or by implication, your qualifications for writing it; it shows what you were trying to do and how well you think you succeeded; it shows who helped you and how; and it highlights the significance of the project. You phrase it as an informed person, with all the research and investment in writing your report behind you. You are now an authority on your subject, hence in a position to introduce your report in such a way that it will be of maximum interest and value to the reader. Any report is only as good as it is effective—and your letter of transmittal can be important in achieving your report's effectiveness.

Also, your letter of transmittal is an opportunity to communicate with your reader on another level than that of the report—a level in a way informal and off the record, even if the letter of transmittal is filed and kept by the reader. We communicate on two levels at once all the time in speaking: in so many words, we may say "Don't think a thing of it, Jack; I was about to get a new pen anyway" while by our tone of voice or look (the second level) we may make it clear that we hold it against Jack for losing the pen, and that we don't plan to forgive him. The letter of transmittal gives you a chance to show your reader that you feel a sense of urgency, that you consider the information vital, or, more important to the reader's decision-making, that you feel somewhat apologetic because of incomplete information or lack of complete confidence in your results. Thus you can submit your report and comment on it at the same time.

Exercises and Problems

1. In writing a memorandum or letter to accompany a report, is it permissible to insert personal news, use nicknames, or refer to golf scores if the person to whom you are writing it is a close friend? There is no answer in the back of the book; we're just interested in what you think.

2. Discuss the simplified letter form with several businessmen. What do they think of it and of its chance for general adoption? What do you think?

3. You've gone through a lot of texts and reference books in your lifetime; how many of their prefaces have you read? Go through the texts you now use and read the prefaces; compare their content, approach, style, usefulness. Use the project for a class discussion.

4. Set up the following brief letter of transmittal in memorandum form to hand in.

(for Mr. T. R. Bell, Executive Assistant to General Manager, T., C., and St. L. Railway, from L. E. Buell, Transportation Dept.)

Here is the report that you asked me to give you, showing the Transportation Department safety performance during November, 1954.

As disappointing as this performance is, there is a 5.7 per cent decrease in ratio as compared with November, 1953.

Although only 4 of the injuries were sustained as a r
snow and ice, the high Yard Service ratio, I believe,
indicates that the weather could have been a major f
our unfavorable performance. This ratio shows a 46.3
cent increase as compared with the Yard Service ratio for
November, 1953.

5. Write a memorandum letter of transmittal to accompany the
annual report of the college librarian to the president of Markham
College, Markham, California. Here are selected excerpts from the
report which you, as librarian, may want to mention:

Statistics for Comparison	1945	1954	1955
Total circulation	101,473	207,884	200,405
Books lost by theft	412	270	31
Book purchase budget	$75,000	$75,000	$75,000
New acquisitions, number of volumes	15,304	10,205	8,427
Budget for student assistants	$4,000	$4,500	$4,500
Hourly wage rate paid student assistants ..	$.50	$.60	$.65

6. Revise the letter of transmittal on p. 184—this time paying
especial attention to its content.

7. Submit a draft of the letter of transmittal to accompany your
long report assignment.

8. Discuss the three letters of transmittal which follow. How
well do they perform the function of a letter of transmittal? What
revisions would you suggest? Rewrite whichever letter your instructor assigns.

INTER-OFFICE CORRESPONDENCE
Johnson Advertising, Inc.
Office Atlanta

Date 2/28/55

From T. O. Munns
Attention B. R. Sutton   Order No.

Per your request of February 13, 1955
you will find attached the complete
procedure of the contract department.

The report is divided under headings
in the order of their importance.

At your request a revised report can
be written at a later date to bring
in any future changes.

Inter-Office Correspondence
UTAH CHEMICAL CORPORATION
Finishes Division

DATE February 24, 1955

FROM Robert Beckman
TO   Donald Liming, Vice President, Finishes Division
ATTENTION OF
        SUBJECT: Labor Turnover - 1954

During the year 1954, labor turnover became an
important factor in our overall costs, not only from the
standpoint of the Finishes Division, Salt Lake Plant, but
from within the organization, namely, our Personnel
Department.

With the emphasis being placed on reduced costs,
we believe our Personnel Department could contribute considerably to the overall reduction you are striving to
accomplish. To this end, we have completed a comprehensive
survey, bringing forth the unadulterated facts as to the
many reasons for our terminations, both voluntary and
company releases. We feel certain the information will
produce sufficient reasons for consideration in a change of
our present rate structure, and a general improvement in
working conditions; not to mention the increase in
production that would be realized.

                                        Robert Beckman

Encl:
      Report
      Exhibit A
      Exhibit B

Inedible Process Division
Delta Company
Cincinnati, Ohio
March 2, 1949

Mr. P. S. Jones, Superintendent
Inedible Process Division
Delta Company
Cincinnati, Ohio

Dear Mr. Jones:

Attached is my special report project for the month of March. It is a written procedure on the necessary safety measures to be taken in the preparation of solvent tanks for welding and repairs.

The procedure has been checked by the operating and mechanical supervision. Several very good suggestions were made by them, and these suggestions are now incorporated in the report attached.

You will notice that we recommend that the procedure be incorporated in Maintenance Standards. It is the opinion of all supervision that the damage possible to the department by neglecting the safety rules mentioned in the report warrants an inclusion in Maintenance Standards. Since our department is the only one of its type in the company, a fire or explosion could hamper the production of company products at every factory location. Any assistance that you may give in our campaign to include safety measures in the actual Maintenance Standards will be greatly appreciated by all members of Inedible Process Division.

A copy of this report has also been sent to Mr. Clifford Smythe, Process Safety Engineer.

I have tentatively selected a procedure for rapidly determining the percent propylene glycol in alcohol for my special report project for the month of April. If this meets with your approval, I shall begin work on this project immediately.

                    Respectfully submitted,

                              Thomas C. Perry

PART III

*Supplementary Readings
and Special Applications*

Chapter 12

GENERAL READINGS

Writing a Report *

Most of us find ourselves at some time up against the job of writing a report. It may be a business report or the report of a meeting; it may be our report as secretary of an organization, or an analysis of a situation in a factory.

Writing a report need not be the ordeal so many of us fear it to be, and sometimes find it. Like so many other things, it is not particularly difficult if we break it down into small jobs. The purpose of this Monthly Letter is to show, step-by-step, how to write a report. All the suggestions will not be appropriate to every report, but the principles will be generally useful.

We should try to make reports constructive. Instead of threshing old straw, or moving in a pedestrian way through an account of some convention or meeting, it is much more interesting to offer vigorous and thought-provoking interpretations and ideas of our own.

To prepare a good report we need to cultivate dependability, resourcefulness and patience, and do some hard work. Dr. Ewen Cameron says in *What Is Life?* that Mme Curie combined the intellect of a first-rate scientist with the skill of a first-rate craftsman and the patience of a first-rate charwoman. That is the recipe for holding the interest of listeners and readers; it is the only way in which we can discover or rediscover great truths.

There are, broadly, two kinds of business reports: the information report and the research report.

The information report is to keep an executive up to date with events, developments, and projects. The research report is the outcome of your investigation of phenomena. This may be in any

* Reprinted from *The Royal Bank of Canada Monthly Letter*, February, 1952. By permission of the Royal Bank of Canada.

branch of human activity, from politics to labour relations, from some crank's idea about taking electricity out of the air to a plan for extending customer use of the power already developed.

Any report upon which action may be based, or which may influence executives in this or that direction, is an important piece of work, and deserves our earnest attention. There is no more engrossing job than that of exploring in search of material for such a report.

Before Beginning. Your work starts long before you make a motion toward your pen. You must be properly briefed, and that is a joint responsibility of you and your boss. You must know exactly what is wanted and why it is wanted. Requests for reports should refer to definite and limited problems.

This simple working chart will be of help: (1) comprehend what you are required to report on; (2) ascertain all possible sources of information; (3) decide upon what sources to draw; (4) gather information and explanations; (5) sift the evidence; (6) synthesize the acceptable evidence; (7) abstract what is to the point and discard the rest; (8) throw what is left into report form; (9) summarize your findings.

There are at least four limitations upon research for a report; time, staff, money and data. It is important that the report writer should do his best within these limitations, and his report should note any shortcoming because of them. If the report is taken from the files years hence, it should provide evidence of the difficulties the research man encountered, so as to give a realistic starting point for following up or modernizing the report.

Economy of effort will be possible to the report writer if he keeps a clearly defined purpose in mind, and refuses to allow himself to be drawn away by other things, however attractive they may be.

Aesop Glim, known to advertising men through his articles in *Printers' Ink*, advises that, the problem being stated, the person preparing a report should sit down with time to make notes of all he knows about the subject. "Don't try to skimp and save words," he advises. "Go into detail. Enjoy yourself to your heart's content in writing sentence after sentence. Tell everything you know—explain the problem fully."

The Objective. In planning the report, serious thought should be given to the need and temperament of the person for whom it is being prepared. Some persons want great detail, others will be content with deductions; some will want tables and graphs, while others will run a mile from a statistic. "What," the report writer should ask himself, "is to be done with what data by whom?"

The kind of report we are considering now—one that gives information on the basis of which an executive may take action—is a sort of diagnosis. It tells what is right and what is wrong, and gives an interpretation which serves as the executive's guide to the remedy, should one be needed.

There are two occasions when recommendations by the report writer are in order: when they are requested, and when the writer believes that because of his knowledge, experience, and other qualities, his voice is worth listening to.

All recommendations are touched with the personality of the writer of the report. The wise man will make a distinction between his conclusions, based upon the facts he has uncovered, and his suggestions, based upon these conclusions. The former are actualities, the latter are tinged with the colour of his opinions.

If recommendations are made, they should be clear and definite. They should tell what to do, who is to do it, where it should be done, at what time, and why this is recommended.

Form of the Report. Writing a report will be much easier if you work out a form, or skeleton.

A good plan for the inexperienced report writer is to start with a statement in one sentence, setting forth the objective of the study which is being reported upon. This will focus attention upon the primary purpose. Then follow with main and subheadings, growing out of the sentence and leading toward the conclusion.

It is surprising how greatly this plan helps to eliminate vagueness, fill in gaps in information and reasoning, and keep the writer on the track of competent thinking.

Although it does not hold true in every case, the success of many reports may be attributed to a well-written introduction or synopsis. If attention of the reader is seized at this point, he is likely to proceed into the body of the report with an expectant mind. Even when one is sure the report will be read, as when the topic is one of particular interest to an executive, it still is good practice to provide a summary telling what the report is about and what point it makes. It should be sharp in its diction, sparing of words, and careful to promise no more than is in the report.

When you come to your preliminary outline, it should be drafted so as to give you a fairly clear idea of the road ahead, enable you to judge what you should stress, and provide you with a test of the adequacy of your research.

The sheet which accompanies this Monthly Letter gives an idea of an adaptable outline as it is applied to this article. It may be used by anyone for a business or institutional or philosophical report, merely by using appropriate headings and subheadings.

It is not necessary, in this short mention of the form of the report, to go into detail about the appendix, the table of contents, the index, and suchlike. These are features which are required only in exhaustive and lengthy reports, and they fall into place quite naturally when their use is indicated.

Chronological Reports and Research. The person who writes a report which records happenings in the order of their time sequence must bear in mind that events sometimes follow one another in successive points of time without tending toward an end. He needs to look out for cause-and-effect relationship. His report should tell origin, history, and development. It should bring out what is the focal point, the turning point, the key event that marks a change or indicates the need for a change.

Many a chronological report is only a collection of episodes; only the starting place for research. Nothing much that is useful will flow from our work until we start asking questions and finding answers.

This leads us into consideration of the analytical report, which starts off with the idea that there is a problem to be solved, and marches toward definite conclusions. It is not a mere collection of data; it gathers facts for and against the proposal being studied, and then goes on to assess them by comparison and testing.

The person embarking upon preparation of such a report has need of an open mind. His is a quest for truth, unbiased, unprejudiced and clear-headed. He will not suspend his researches until they have reached the point where the returns from the investigation have ceased to be really important. He will modify his thesis as he goes along, if necessary, to fit the new thoughts born of his study.

There can be no more illustrious purpose than that of the research man: "To find the truth no matter how obscure; to recognize it no matter in what strange form it may present itself; to formulate it honestly; to state it unmistakably; and to reason from it remorselessly and without regard to prejudice."

Business research is of many kinds. It may be designed to solve a merchandising or production or distribution problem; it may be called upon to find ways of effecting economies; it may be done in response to management's desire to anticipate trade developments within the industry, shifts in the economy of the country, or progress in technology.

Its leading questions are: what is true? what is best? what is necessary? how do we do it? A good test question, to be used when the others have been answered, is: if I do that, then what happens?

The writer of a report can be sure he has done a good job if he is confident that he has analysed more profoundly than others the problem put before him; that he has achieved an original focus of facts toward a desired purpose; that he has supplied, in his report, alternative courses of action, the foreseeable consequences of which he has fully thought out; and that he provides not only a well-written report but a solid block of knowledge on which to build.

Not much need be said about the various kinds of analytic reports except just to name them. The case study, while incomplete in itself because no conclusions can be drawn from one case, is useful as part of a larger project. It can be enlightening, and because of the narrowness of its field, it can be thorough. The genetic study traces the development of its subject, stressing the causal sequence of events. The comparative method involves bringing together significant facts. Its chief impediment seems to lie in the danger of bias attending selection of the facts to be compared, and the perplexity of discriminating wisely.

Much of abiding value may be learned by report writers and research men who study military "appreciations." These follow logical sequence:

    I. The object to be attained
   II. Factors which affect attainment of the object
  III. Courses open to
        A—our own side
        B—the enemy
  IV. The plan.

Instruction in preparation of appreciations is given in *Field Service Pocket Book, Part 1, Pamphlet No. 4,* issued by the War Office, London. The factors relevant to a military situation do not all apply in industrial or social life, but the thorough analysis of the problem demanded by the military people is suggestive for all who write reports.

Sources of Information. Collecting information is the foundation of all good reporting. Thomas Edison gave this advice: "The first thing is to find out everything everybody else knows, and then begin where they left off."

While every problem will have its peculiar requirements, certain sources of data are common to nearly all: observation, experimentation, books, questionnaires, interviews, workshop and accounting records. The successful writer will be resourceful in his research activities, thinking of new approaches and seeking data overlooked hitherto.

Data may be primary or secondary. Just as in law the evidence of an eye-witness is more valuable than that of a person who testifies at second-hand, so in business and other reports the fruits of observation and experimentation rate high marks. He is a wise report writer who applies, whenever possible, observation and experimentation to check the findings of others; he is likely to remain unremarkable for his work if he merely echoes the opinions of others, believes things because others believe them, and uses only books and papers with which he is in complete accord.

Secondary sources depend for their value upon their accuracy, their acuteness of valuation, the validity of their reasoning, and the applicability of their conclusions to the case being studied.

No statement is more reliable than its source. The report writer must spend long hours in gathering facts, arranging them, interpreting them—and then as much time again in checking the accuracy and worthwhileness of what he has in his hand. It is useless to quote a writer unless he is known to be competent in his field. It is dangerous to give the opinion of a man unless he is recognized as being unbiased, up-to-date and in all respects reliable.

Writing the Report. Having gathered the facts and laid them out in order, we must compose our report.

This is a time when a writer wishes to be alone. John Ruskin had circulars which he used to head off visitors, invitations and letters. They read like this: "Mr. J. Ruskin is about to begin a work of great importance and therefore begs that in reference to calls and correspondence you will consider him dead for the next two months."

Literary skill, in whatever field it is exercised, means ability to present a subject as accurately and as vividly as possible. We should at least write our reports as if we were interested in what we are trying to write, and when we do so we have gone a long way toward giving our reports significance.

The report writer needs to analyse, and group, and marshal his facts into order. He must classify and conquer the elements of the chaos around him before he can hope to appeal with any force to the intelligence of other people. In this process of viewing the whole situation and at the same time seeing its components, the writer will detect incongruities to avoid and discern a path to follow.

These are skills which come only, so far as we know, with practice, but there are some hints about the process of writing which apply in all circumstances.

THE REPORT MUST BE PRACTICAL. We have a loose way of thinking of a realist as one who not only sees things as they are materially, but acquiesces in them: let us rather, as report writers, consider ourselves as being realists in the sense that we understand things as we have found them, not as we would find it convenient to believe them.

THE REPORT MUST BE COMPLETE. We must have walked all around the matter about which we are reporting, seeing the good and the bad, the perfect and the imperfect, the desirable and the undesirable. We must have provided adequate proof for our favourable and our unfavourable findings. Do not be content with one opinion: it may be the wrong one. As Cicero once pointed out, nothing is so absurd that someone has not called it profound; nothing so profound that someone has not called it absurd.

THE REPORT MUST BE CONCISE. It may be as long as a roller towel, or as short as the message on a post card: length is not the criterion. Conciseness does not consist in using few words, but in covering the subject in the fewest possible words that will express what is in the writer's mind.

Here is the story of the Odyssey in 79 words: "A certain man is away from home for a number of years, being closely watched by Poseidon and stripped of all his companions, while his affairs at home are in such shape that his money is being squandered by wooers of his wife, and his son is being plotted against. After being shipwrecked by a storm, he arrives home, makes himself known to some, and attacks the wooers, with the result that he is saved and his enemies destroyed." In giving us this gem of condensation in his *Poetics*, Aristotle remarks: "That is the real story of the *Odyssey*. The rest is episodes."

We recall Prime Minister Winston Churchill's wartime memoranda, demanding that his cabinet ministers confine their reports on the most momentous matters to a single page. "It is," he told the Secretary of State for Foreign Affairs, "sheer laziness not compressing thought into a reasonable space."

THE REPORT MUST BE CLEAR. Only the careful organization of facts and interpretation will enable the reader to follow what is to the writer a clear-cut line of reasoning. The art of good prose resides not so much in the swing and balance of the language as in the marshalling of argument, the orderly procession of ideas, the disposition of parts so that each finds its proper place. The writer misses his target if the idea in his mind is not received with understanding. As Alice said after reading *Jabberwocky:* "Somehow it seems to fill my head with ideas—only I don't exactly know what they are."

Use of trite expressions shows that the writer is in a rut. If he has no imagination in his language is it likely, the executive will ask, that he exercised any imagination in his analysis of this problem?

There is no place in good writing for proverbs, saws, and tinkling aphorisms.

Foggy language detracts from the force of writing, and use of words loosely may well vitiate all usefulness that might have been incorporated in a report. We say nothing against trade, occupational or professional jargon so long as the report is solely for people who are on speaking terms with it. That sort of talk is not infrequently the only kind in which a writer can convey the true meaning of his thought to a particular audience. But jargon has no place in reports which may be read by the uninitiated.

THE REPORT MUST BE INTELLECTUALLY HONEST. The facts must be scrupulously weighed and properly evaluated, and the writer must sincerely attempt to present something that has a judicial quality. He will draw a distinct line between what he has found to be fact, what is his opinion, and what he sets up as hypothesis.

THE REPORT MUST BE READABLE. We cannot afford to assume that our report will be read because the boss is interested in the subject. We should try to add to the clarity of our presentation something that will lift it above the ordinary.

There may be an ivory-tower disposition toward decorum, leading us to think that research requires a depersonalized manner of writing. The truth is that nothing written is useful unless it is attractive enough to be read. We are entitled to be as brilliant and interesting as we can be, so long as we observe the requirements of correctness, relevance and the objective.

And Having Written. Having written it, the writer would be well advised to forget about his report for as long as time permits. If he tries to make corrections and improvements as soon as he has finished the writing, his memory of what he meant to write may be so strong that he will overlook the shortcomings of what he actually wrote.

Here are some questions to ask at the time of revision: is my report fair, broad-minded and dignified? Have I used enough imagination in presenting the facts? Have I answered all the pertinent questions likely to arise in the reader's mind? Does my report read as if a human being wrote it?

It is well to read the report aloud: if it is easy to read you may bank upon its being easy to understand. If you hesitate over a word, a phrase or a sentence, take a second look.

Finally, don't allow yourself to be lulled into feeling that writing a report is an easy thing to do.

The writer who achieves distinction of expression, conciseness, directness—and, if the nature of his work permits it, dramatic quality, beauty of rhythm, and some adventurousness of phrase and idea— has not done something miraculous. He has worked hard and intelligently.

Included with *The Royal Bank of Canada Monthly Letter* issue of February, 1952, containing "Writing a Report," was a blue card containing three sample report outlines:

WRITING A REPORT

Here are three sample outlines, adaptable to many kinds of reports.

The first is the outline used in preparing this Monthly Letter; the second is an imaginary outline for a report on electrical development, and the third is the very concise type of outline used in the Army.

(1) Writing a Report

There are four steps in writing a report:

    I. Define your Objective
        A. Information
        B. Policy Making
            1. With diagnosis of conditions
            2. With recommendations for action
   II. Determine the Form
        A. Narrative
            1. Chronological . . . (causes, origin, successive stage of development, results, conclusions from the study)
            2. Episodic . . . (in story form)
        B. Analysis (research)
            1. Case Study
            2. Genetic
            3. Comparative
            4. Appreciation
        C. Compilation
  III. Search your Sources
        A. Kinds of Sources
            1. Primary
                a. Observation
                b. Experimentation
            2. Secondary
                a. Documents
                b. Comments by critics
        B. Reliability of Sources
            1. Informed Observation
            2. Written Information
                a. The Writer
                b. The Work

IV. Do the Writing
    A. Completeness
    B. Conciseness
    C. Clarity
       1. Semantic clearness
       2. Intellectual honesty
    D. Readability
       1. Simple
       2. Short paragraphs and sentences
       3. Etc.

(2) A "Progressive" Outline

I. Canada's resources in electric energy are adequate, for
    A. The present source of supply shows that
       1. The hinterland storage areas are plentiful, and
       2. Artificial catchment areas provide alternative storage.
    B. The sites available for power development are in excess of presently foreseen needs.
    C. Water power may be expected to furnish a supply, for
       1. Precipitation is fairly constant
       2. The flow is regular, or
          a. may be regulated by afforestation
          b. or by storage dams

II. Therefore no alternative kinds of power would be useful, for
    A. They would be uneconomical
       1. in cost
       2. by duplication of existing facilities
    B. Canada's potential industrial development is limited
       1. by the nature of its land
       2. by market inaccessibility
       3. by competition

(3) An Army Appreciation

I. The object to be attained
II. Factors which affect attainment of the object
III. Courses open to
    A. our own side
    B. the enemy
IV. The plan

Report Writing *

by A. S. DONNELLY

Some of us may still recall our introduction to reports—those dread days of reckoning when, hoping for the best but fearing the worst, we saw our parents read our school reports. With school days behind us we gradually saw that business executives as well as headmasters, write and read reports. Perhaps we began to realise that modern business could not function properly without reports—reports prepared by various people for various purposes.

So you can see that knowing how to write effective reports is a question of importance to almost everyone in business. Yet little attention is given to this subject in business education. In practical training it is often overlooked. Public libraries have several texts on reports for the engineer, chemist, and other technical men, but practically nothing on the business report.

These things arise, I think, from a mistaken belief that report writing is not worthy of separate study—a belief that writing a report is merely a routine matter involving no special skill. Hence there are some who say that little can be gained by a study of this subject.

Merely to write a report may not require much specialised skill. But to write an *effective* report certainly does. And remember that a report is not effective unless it conveys clearly *to the reader what is in the mind of the writer*. This involves a systematic approach, careful organisation, the use of good English and a style of writing most likely to be effective.

If you have to write a report your work consists basically of two major tasks. Firstly you must organise the material for the report. Then you must write the report.

Organisation. Just how you should approach the task of organising a report depends on such things as the type of report, the person for whom it is being prepared, the relative importance of the subject matter, and the facilities available. There may be other specific factors to be taken into account. The time available for the job is

* Reprinted from *The ABWA Bulletin*, January, 1954, pp. 5-12, by permission of the author and The American Business Writing Association. This article was originally an address delivered to the members of the Brisbane, Australia, Junior Chamber of Commerce. Mr. Donnelly is the editor of *Brighter Business*, Brisbane, Australia.

important. Sometimes it may be better to produce a report quickly with investigation of major issues only, rather than to spend time on a more detailed investigation.

Know What Is Required. You must have clearly in your mind just what is required by the report. Perhaps an examination will reveal that the time is not ripe or that there are not sufficient details available. If this is so, then you should promptly contact your client, principal, or the executive responsible and tell him what you have found. He may defer the report or perhaps cancel the instructions altogether.

A little thought along these lines would probably save the Government printer a great deal of work. Some Ministers have an obsession for calling for reports which are seldom used. Indeed their enthusiasm in calling for reports is matched only by their consistency in failing to take action on the reports which have been prepared.

Sources of Information. When you have a clear picture of the real purpose of the report and know what is required, the next step is to decide on these things:

What sources of information are available?
How intensive must the examination be?

For some reports you may need only to refer to a few files or interview a few people. Others may involve a great deal of research work. This work may be done as part of normal routine. For example, the reports of auditors are based on notes made during the course of the audit.

You may have to refer to sources outside of your own organisation. A report on sales promotion may be more effective if it includes reference to the trend of total sales in the industry. Statistics such as the Survey of Retail Establishments conducted by the Commonwealth Statistician are helpful. The person who has much to do with writing reports—or in directing others to write reports—should make it his business to know what relevant information is available. Trade associations, professional institutes and public libraries are possible sources of information.

Gathering Information. Thus far you have clearly fixed in your mind what is required by the report. You have decided what sources of information are available and the extent of the investigation necessary. Next step is to gather this information. Here the habit of notetaking is invaluable. Work always on the idea that some accident may befall you and somebody else may have to take over the task. If you do this you are more likely to write an effective report.

Gathering information for a report is likely to be useful in other directions as well. Sometimes the gathering of information may be almost as fruitful as the presentation of the report. . . .

Where reports are presented at regular intervals, some time may be saved by a degree of standardisation. Standard working papers may lessen the chance of items being overlooked. Standardisation of routine is wise, but standardised reports may or may not be a good thing. It is essential for the report writer to keep an open mind. Disregard of this maxim is likely to make the report almost valueless. In practically every office you will find reports that are never read—or if they are read given scant attention—because they are stereotyped and fail to arouse interest. I am afraid that public accountants are among the greatest offenders in this regard.

Sorting the Information. It is unwise to attempt to sort the information until you have completed the examination. To do otherwise is like betting on a card hand before you have bought cards. The two cards you buy may turn three of a kind into a full hand. Something revealed at the end of the examination may have a far reaching effect on the rest of your investigation. Trying to knock the report into shape before you complete the gathering of information is likely to make you jump to conclusions. The report writer must strive to be objective. Jumping to conclusions during the investigation is likely to make the report too subjective. This need to be objective is important in all reports; in reports prepared by independent experts it is vital.

First stage in sorting the information is to read through it—or glance through it—to determine what information is of secondary importance only. This information may be eliminated. Or it may be better to exclude it from the report, but convey the information personally or by letter to interested parties.

After this primary sorting, you will have left information which either:

1. Is to go into the report; or
2. Has a bearing on what is to go into the report.

Perhaps some of it is documentation for statements which you will make in the report. This is important. You need chapter and verse to support any statements that may be challenged.

Tentative Conclusions. At this stage the pattern of your investigation will begin to take shape. From the summarized facts you can see what conclusions and recommendations (if there are to be any) are likely to appear in the final report. This is the appropriate place to follow up any queries.

If you have to make an adverse report on a Department or Section, it is usually better to ask for the comments of the responsible person on the point. There may be a simple explanation. If there is, you would look rather foolish if this explanation were made to the person for whom the report was prepared *after* the report has been completed. It would tend to lessen the confidence of the reader in the rest of your report. There may, of course, be special circumstances where this course is inadvisable; e.g., a case of suspected theft.

The conclusions you have reached and the recommendations you propose to make should be listed. Then you should think over them and check them to see that they are

> Logical.
> Appropriate.
> Not beyond the terms of your authority or the scope of the report.

If you are drawing conclusions from statistics be careful to check them. Most important, apply the good old test of common sense to them. A statistically perfect deduction that is at variance with common sense should not be accepted—at least not without further investigation.

If it is practicable—particularly for the relatively inexperienced —consult a colleague or refer to case histories, files, or copies of similar reports in the past. This final check before listing your conclusions and recommendations is a safeguard against presenting a misleading report.

Try to plan things so that there is some time for thinking over the conclusions before writing the report (that is, in the case of an important and lengthy report). Sleep on your tentative conclusions if you can. In practice this may not always be possible, but careful planning may ensure that this important phase of the task is not rushed.

Importance of Organisation. This now brings us to the stage of commencing the actual writing of the report. Perhaps some of you may be inclined to say "it's about time." You may be able to recall really good reports which you or others have written without going through all the "fuss and bother" already outlined. This would probably be due to the fact that all the information was at your fingertips or readily available without much research. Perhaps you were so familiar with the subject matter that you were able to commence writing the report with practically no planning.

What I have described are the main principles of organising a report. The application of these principles would vary a great deal depending on the type of report and the knowledge of essential facts which is possessed by the report writer. The principles may be applied subconsciously by the expert. But remember that the organising work is the "bones" of the report and the writing is the "clothes" in which the fact finding is wrapped. Though it is said that clothes make the man, lack of character in a man will eventually be revealed no matter how attractive his clothes may be.

So with reports. A good writer may be able to partly conceal the lack of fact finding, or to gloss over the imperfections. But anything more than a casual glance at the report will reveal its shortcomings.

Length of Report. From what you have learned in the course of your examination, and what you know of the person for whom the report is being prepared, you must decide on the approximate length. That does not mean that you must try to set in advance a length and then stick to it when you write the report. To do that would probably mar the report. But by nature some reports are more comprehensive than others.

Mostly the people for whom reports are prepared are extremely busy men. They don't want to spend any more time than necessary on reading reports. So anything you can do to shorten the report without leaving out essentials is a good thing. Here the sorting which you did in the organisation stage will be helpful.

Incidentally, shortening a report saves typing time and filing space and reduces paper costs. By and large it can mean a considerable saving where many reports are written.

That's why brevity should be one of the main goals of the report writer. There is a common but incorrect belief that a brief report must necessarily be less comprehensive. But this is not so. I have seen many very long reports that were far from comprehensive; they have been mainly words and more words with little substance.

You can write brief but complete reports by being selective. Give attention in your report to major items. Either eliminate or mention only briefly those facts which are of minor importance.

It may be better to place tables of figures separately after the end of the report—as a sort of appendix—rather than clutter up the report with them. A lot of figures interrupts the even flow of reading and makes it harder to digest the report. If you use an appendix you need refer only briefly to the most important items in the text.

Mostly it is better to eliminate shillings and pence from the report as they have little significance and tend to confuse (particularly if the report is to be read at a meeting). Indeed it is often advisable to refer to the nearest hundred or thousand. Remember that in the report it is only with the major items that you are concerned. A reader interested in details can refer to the table in the appendix.

If possible use words rather than figures. For instance, suppose you were commenting on sales which this year were 748,123/17/9 compared with 688,876/3/4 last year. Why not say this:

> Sales (in thousands of pounds) amounted to a little over seven hundred and forty-eight compared with just under six hundred and eighty-nine last year. This is an increase of almost nine per cent.

Style. To write brief and effective reports you must give some thought to the matter of style. This does not mean that you need a grand literary style. Nor does "Style" in this sense have the same meaning as it has when we describe a flashily dressed person as a "ball of style."

In fact the essence of a good style is sincerity and simplicity. But as businessmen we have a bad habit of using a rather over formal style of writing. We tend to use passive words rather than active terms. Our sentences are long, and their complexity greatly reduces the reader appeal. If we want to arouse the interest of those who read our reports, we must make an effort—and it is an effort because old habits die hard—to be more dynamic, less formal and more interesting in what we write.

If we don't do this, the value of all the work we did in organising the report may be wasted. In reading, as in other things, first impressions tend to be lasting. The reader of the report does not want to burrow through a mass of verbiage, hackneyed phrases and passive words.

Here are a few rules or guides to an interesting effective style of writing. Many of them apply as well to letters. (Attention to letter writing is excellent practice for report writing.)

> *First.* Use a short word in preference to a long one. Don't say "communication" when you mean "letter"; "acknowledge" when "receive" is just as good; "anticipate" when "expect" means the same.
>
> *Second.* Use an active or concrete word in preference to an abstract or passive one.
>
> *Third.* Avoid technical terms unless the report is destined to be read by technical people or unless there is no other word *just right* for what you wish to say. An accountant is more likely to be understood if he uses the term "amounts owing to the firm" or "Accounts receivable" rather than "Sundry Debtors."
>
> *Fourth.* Avoid hackneyed phrases which have little real meaning. "Thanking you in anticipation"—"Assuring you of our best services at all times"—"Enclosed please find" are examples of phrases which should be omitted or replaced by a better phrase.
>
> *Fifth.* Avoid long sentences. An average sentence length of about twenty words is desirable. But it is wise to vary sentence length somewhat to avoid monotony.

There are a few simple devices which you can use to create emphasis and to prevent the report from appearing tedious. The chief of these are:

> 1. *The use of punctuation*—particularly the dash and colon where you wish to highlight a few words.
> 2. *The use of what is known as the rhetorical question.* This arouses the interest of the reader and tends to emphasise what follows. For example, after setting out reasons for action, or describing difficulties, one of the following questions may be suitable:
>
>> Is there any alternative?
>> Can anything be done now?
>
> followed by "Yes, we can start to reorganise immediately" or something along these lines.

   3. A small sentence containing a few words; e.g., "But this is not all" or "The benefits go even further."
   4. A judicious use of tabulation; e.g., setting out advantages or reasons one under the other draws attention to them.
   5. Inverting the usual order of the sentence. For example, you may say "That the system was weak is proved by these facts."

Now here is a paragraph showing how some of these devices can be used:

> To regard punctuation as a necessary evil in writing is to overlook its real purpose. It can be a help—and a valuable one—towards a free pleasant style. And that is not all. The use of dashes can help to emphasise points—provided you don't overdo it. Remember this fact: to emphasise everything is to emphasise nothing!

You will see how the inverted sentence, the dash, the very small sentence, the colon and the exclamation mark have been used. . . .

Human Interest. What has been said will help you, I hope, to write reports that are easy to read. But a report will be even more effective if you can "bring it to life." To do this you need to use personal pronouns such as "he," "she," "I," "you," "we" and proper names wherever you can.

In many reports—mainly those of important experts—this may not be possible. But it should be done wherever it can.

Naturally you should not use the term "I" too much. It may create an impression of egotism. But occasionally it can be used. "I submit" or "I suggest" or "may I suggest" is more interesting and more lifelike than "It is suggested."

Illustration. A Chinese proverb says that one picture is worth a hundred words. Remember this when you write reports.

A simple diagram may illustrate an idea very clearly. Most—but not all—people can understand financial results better when they are shown in graphical form rather than in long rows of figures.

There are however some traps for the unwary in graphical presentation; care is necessary in choosing the form to be used. . . .

Appearance. If you have a good product to sell you don't spoil its chances by unattractive packaging. So don't spoil your report by a poor layout.

The modern company report shows what can be done with a good layout to attract interest. Even in the shorter typed report the appearance can be improved by such things as double spacing, sectional headings, tabulation, the use of an attractive cover, etc.

Conclusion. Earlier I said that there is an art in report writing. A few acquire the art easily. But for most of us it is a matter of hard work. We must constantly strive to improve our ability in this subject by constant practice.

This can best be done by applying the principles wherever possible. Many of them can be applied in letter writing and public speaking. Whether you have written one report or a thousand you should not miss any chance of improving your skill by practice.

To sum up: An article recently published by the Royal Bank of Canada set out the marks of a good report as:

> Practical
> Complete
> Concise
> Clear
>
> Trite expressions should be avoided.
> It must be intrinsically honest.
> It must be readable.

If you want to write good reports use those items as a check list. This will help you a great deal. It will help the organisation with which you are connected.

And in the field of public relations it will do more than that. Good readable company reports . . . will dispel a lot of myths fostered by the enemies of society.

Finally, such reports will demonstrate the truth of what your creed sets out, namely "That economic Justice can best be won by free men through free enterprise."

Report of the 1953 ABWA Reports Committee *
by

VERNON EDWARDS, Mississippi State
DOROTHY GREENWALD, University of Michigan
JOHN HISLOP, Riverside College (California)
H. B. KNOLL, Purdue University

* The "Report of the 1953 ABWA Reports Committee" is used by permission of the committee chairman, Professor E. D. Hedgcock, Professor of English, Agricultural and Mechanical College of Texas. Professor Hedgcock made a general compilation of the company comments and has supplied the data on ob-

Stephen B. Miles, Jr., Lockheed Aircraft Corporation
Robert L. Shurter, Case Institute
Norman Sigband, De Paul University
Cecil B. Williams, Oklahoma A. & M. College
Ernest Hedgcock (Chairman), A. & M. College of Texas

For the benefit of the American Business Writing Association membership the 1953 Reports Committee set out to collect specimen reports and also to get comments by business executives concerning the use and preparation of reports. A display of the returns was made at the national convention in Cincinnati, December 28-30, 1953.

Requests for such matter were sent to approximately 150 nationally known companies in all parts of the country. Seventy-nine of the 150 contributed their ideas about reports; 14 sent 25 reports which they wrote or were using; 11 of the reports were in the "long" category, 14 "short."

Following is a summary of the findings of the committee:

1. Actual business or professional reports are hard to get. (Two members of the committee, members with excellent business contacts, got none at all. And they tried.)
2. Opinions about reports are comparatively easy to secure.
3. There is universal agreement that ability to prepare a report is of great importance, perhaps of equal importance with having information to convey. (Note: One executive thinks that entirely too many reports are written.)
4. Ability to prepare a good report practically insures the writer's advancement and even in slack times his steady employment.
5. Aside from the obvious aim to convey requested information, the primary concern of the writer of a report is to save the reader's time. (Neither the time nor the feelings of the writer are of consequence, and the higher the reader's rank the greater is the need for brevity and clarity.)
6. Formalities are important, but they vary with the needs and whims of the reader. They are therefore of little importance in a college course as compared with sound language principles and practices.
7. Almost never is a person just out of college able to prepare a satisfactory report because (*a*) he lacks the ability to analyze a problem, get the facts about the issues involved, classify the facts or data, and organize them logically; (*b*) he cannot write clearly and concisely;

---

jectives and results of the survey and the summary of findings. He informs us that Professor John Hislop, Riverside College, contributed a great many of the company comments. The selecting of comments from Professor Hedgcock's compilation and arranging them under headings was done by Cecil B. Williams. The committee's questionnaire stressed intra-company reports.

or (*c*) he lacks either the realization of the difficulty of preparing a good report or the nerve to undergo the ordeal.

Importance of Business Reports.

First National Bank of Boston. The importance of the ability to write worthwhile reports cannot be over-emphasized. We have many employees who know their work thoroughly and yet are not reaching the top-level jobs, principally because they cannot write brief, well-constructed, and understandable reports.

First National Bank of Minneapolis. I concur with your emphasis on the importance of training students along these lines, and it is one of the fields in which considerable progress could be made. It seems to me that the ability to express oneself in written form is one of the most important fields of training which a man should secure for business. Perhaps it is second only to ability to express oneself orally and before groups.

Glenn L. Martin Company. We are in full accord with your objective of developing, by means of actual examples and otherwise, an ability on the part of students of business administration to write good intra-company reports. In our opinion, it cannot be impressed too strongly upon potential administrative personnel that their value to their employers, and hence their possibility of advancement, are contingent to a most important extent upon the effectiveness with which they can convey their thoughts in writing. This is true whether they intend to be engaged in the sales, financial, public relations, engineering, production, or virtually any other function of the business, and this facility tends to increase in importance with the size of the firm.

North America Companies. Why are reports prepared? So far as I can see, a report is prepared to give to someone else the experiences undergone by the report-makers. This broadly worded phrase is intended to include such events as minutes of meetings, attendance at conventions, and studies made to discover answers to more or less specific questions. It is important, I think, to realize that they are a means of making economical use of time—the person to whom the report is made has not had the opportunity as a rule to attend the meeting or the convention or to investigate the problem personally. Instead, he wants a report made to him by someone who was there for that specific purpose. To my way of thinking this fundamental must never be forgotten when the preparation of a report is undertaken.

Peoples Gas Light and Coke Company. Your subject is indeed one that needs attention; the only opportunity many young executives have of presenting their views and becoming known to their superior officers is through their reports; therefore, they must be good.

Requirements of Good Reports.

Burroughs Adding Machine Company. The principal comments we would have about reports are that they should be as short, as much to the point, as logically organized, and in as simple, narrative language as possible.

Columbia Broadcasting System. Although many of us have had formalized instruction in report writing at schools of business administration and, in numerous cases, exposure to the "staff study" techniques of the military establishments, we agree that, for our particular purposes, correct reference to organizational principles and human relationships is of greater value than reference to rules regarding report structure. We assume, of course, literacy and general intellectual standards sufficient to allow for written expression of thought with reasonable facility.

Douglas Aircraft Company. More consideration should be given to demands on executive time. Reports often are written with the view of showing off the intellect of the writer. Top executives have mountains of reading to do, and consideration should be given to this fact since a long, dry report, even though important, may not "get through" to the executive as well as a simple résumé, backed up by research.

Massachusetts Mutual Life Insurance Company. In all the training with our supervisory staff, we rather urge them to make their reports brief, yet complete enough to give all of the necessary data. We also encourage them to refrain, as much as possible, from generalities and to make the contents of their reports specific, using figures and well-defined units as frequently as possible.

Mississippi Power & Light Company. We have tried to simplify our reports by using non-technical language and express our views in words of one syllable and not more than five letters. I have always felt that short, concise sentences phrased in ordinary day-today conversation are much better than a display of rhetoric and the use of words which the reader must refer to a dictionary to understand.

Motorola, Inc. I think there are five important ingredients in any report that is made, particularly from a junior executive: (1) Imagination—to thoroughly understand and analyze the assignment which has been given or to think up a matter on which a report is required; (2) Research—complete, thorough scientific research into the matter; (3) Be sure of the facts; (4) Exercise best judgment available—weigh both the tangible and intangible; (5) Finally, an ingredient which is left out of far too many reports—make a definite recommendation.

National Rubber Machinery Company. Like everyone else, in reading reports we appreciate clarity of thought and conciseness of presentation. So many papers come across one's desk that brief, precise reports are essential. Our experience would indicate that involved sentence structure, redundant phraseology, and indefinite reference are common faults of report writing today. A vague understanding of the mechanics of punctuation is also evident.

Techniques in Report Writing.

American Bosch Corporation. I have a feeling that it is very difficult to standardize the form or style of intra-company reports. Assuming that the report writer has all the necessary facts and information for the report, the writer's objective is to produce a report in the form and style which pleases his particular supervisor. My point is that a report writer must not only have some knowledge as to what constitutes a good report, but must in addition determine and take into consideration what his supervisor *thinks* constitutes a good report. I find that there is a great variation of opinion on this subject among successful supervisors.

American Surety Company. It would seem that the type of report to be rendered depends to a large extent upon what level of management is to be reached. At the lower level, reports will usually be quite detailed and lengthy. As the same report is considered by higher authority it is reduced to bare essentials. As it reaches top management it will contain only a fraction of its original material. In our opinion a good rule for reports of any kind is that they be accurate, concise and free from ambiguity or contradictions.

Armour and Company. I think that a business report should be written so that an executive can absorb the essence of it in a hurry. At the same time the report should contain sufficient detail so that the statements of the person making the report are fully supported by facts. There are two ways to do this. One is to set the report up with captions and subcaptions which tell the story in very much the same manner as newspaper headlines tell the essence of the news. The other method is to write a complete report and then attach a summary of the contents. . . . The report . . . should tell what is wrong with the operation, the data supporting this conclusion and the investigator's recommendations for correction. After that, if the investigator wants to make some favorable comment in justice to the persons involved, that is all right. We also see reports in which the subordinate submits a lot of data and says, in effect, "Here is what I found out and maybe we should do this or maybe we should do that." Usually the executive does nothing about a report of this nature, and the work put in on the entire project is wasted. Young people, particularly, have a weakness for putting inconclusive, half-developed ideas on paper. If the report is worth writing, it should contain a concrete proposal that the person addressed can say yes or no to. It should call for definite action to reach a definite objective. The first thing a person should decide in writing a report is what he thinks the boss wants to know . . . and what he thinks the boss ought to do about it. Once these decisions are made, writing the report should be comparatively easy.

Fairchild Engine and Airplane Corporation. As for the actual technique of writing the report, I think it is probably wiser to start with an outline and, if possible, to summarize the contents at the beginning with a few brief paragraphs, for the executives who will not read beyond a paragraph or two regardless of the report.

Home Life Insurance Company. Consultation with several department heads who deal directly with new trainees has yielded the following deficiencies: (1) Failure to properly analyze the problem by eliminating extraneous material and correctly weighting the important aspects; (2) Failure to organize and integrate the material in logical sequence of presentation from the salient facts to conclusions drawn. In this respect it is important not to lose sight of the over-all objective of the report; (3) Simply accepting other people's verbiage instead of couching the ideas in the writer's own terms. Too often the trainees' departmental reports are simply a replay of the phraseology employed by the department head; (4) Failure to be impersonal or objective, particularly when discussing actual work and activities where personalities are involved. This seems to be a common failing which most men correct after they have been in business for a while. Conversely, the opposites of these deficiencies would seem to represent the most important qualities of good reports.

Monsanto Chemical Company. Business executives are confronted with the necessity of reading too many lengthy reports. It is our firm conviction that the objective and scope of the report, along with a summary of conclusions and recommendations, should be condensed to one page. Detailed and supporting evidence should be indexed and follow after this summary sheet. Too many intra-company reports are of the "For your information" type. Even young employees should be encouraged to *make recommendations as well as arrive at conclusions.* This one requirement will do much to mature their business thinking.

Mutual Life of New York. [Suggests organization in terms of five-part outline.]

I. *Facts* (Introduction, Scope, etc.). This division should contain a statement of the material to be covered or the project undertaken, and summarize briefly the subject covered. It should contain the elemental facts in possession of the writer which are essential to the subject matter.

II. *Discussion.* This division should contain discussions, explanations, ideas, opinions, and comments, bearing on the contents of the first section.

III. *Conclusions.* This division should state definitely what conclusions the writer has reached in consideration of the foregoing facts and discussion.

IV. *Recommendations.*

V. *Appendix.*

What the Colleges Can Do.

Citizens National Trust & Savings Bank. It is my experience as lawyer, trade association executive, and bank officer, that there is a great need in the business world for people who can express themselves in written form in simple, direct, and easily understood words. . . . If the schools would concentrate on training young men and women to put these principles into effect they would be making an important contribution. Neither the subject matter of the report nor its form is as important as simple, straightforward exposition. If this is combined with a logical organization of material and a clear analysis of the problem, the report will indeed command attention.

Consolidated Edison Company of New York. It seems to me that there is no substitute for years of experience in high school and college in the study of English and writing themes.

E. I. Du Pont de Nemours & Company. It is our opinion that if students are taught the fundamentals of good letter and report writing, such as clarity of expression in simple language, conciseness and accuracy, they will have but little difficulty in meeting the requirements of business.

First National Bank of Boston. In discussing your project with several of my associates, I have gathered that the following points would fairly represent our collective judgment as to what business-writing teachers should stress: (1) Organization—greater facility in arranging material in an order that fits the subject and the purpose of the report; (2) Word-sense—resourcefulness of vocabulary, to avoid vague, "cover-all," or stereotyped terms; (3) Sentence structure—solid grounding in mechanics, especially subordination, transitions, and connectives.

Hewitt-Robins, Inc. It is my personal feeling that the ability to express oneself orally or in writing, concisely and clearly, is one of the most valuable to the young college man and is one which is frequently lacking. A great deal has been said about the necessity for brevity: I would rather see brevity sacrificed in the interest of clarity.... The use of outlines or outline forms also leads to better understanding in reports. A good secretary-stenographer is also considerably helpful.... On the whole ... successful report writing is like successful public speaking in that it requires a thorough knowledge of the subject matter as the prime criterion. I find the average college man, after five years in industry, very frequently fails to get the correct story, the whole story or the background, before he sits down to present his oral or written report. Invariably he flounders as a result.

Hudson Motor Car Company. If schools and colleges will only train students in spelling, grammar, the composition of a simple

and straightforward sentence, and in the art of expressing themselves clearly and directly, the students will have no difficulty in
writing proper memoranda and reports, no matter what business
they may enter. There is nothing special about "intra-company reports." Instructions, comments and reports should obviously be written in clear, concise English sentences and that is all that is required,
regardless of the subject matter. There is an appalling lack of basic
preparation in recent college graduates almost regardless of the
school which they attended. This is particularly true of those having Bachelor of Arts degrees. The scientific schools are perforce
required to give their students more basic training and as a result
the technical graduates are successfully invading fields in business
other than those for which they were trained.

Masonite Corporation. My main criticism of college graduates
and other personnel who should qualify for executive and supervisory positions deals with their lack of training in the fundamentals of analysis. Many seem unable to discover the important
questions in a problem which should be answered. I believe more
failures take place in this respect than in reporting as such.

Standard Oil Company (Ohio). In our opinion, the most valuable things to teach students who are later to enter business life
are ability to think and ability to write good and precise English.
If these basics are provided, it is a simple matter to train them in
the special requirements of report writing for our particular business operations.

United States Steel Corporation. Use laboratory type technique
in teaching composition. Don't merely grade papers submitted but
personally advise each student how to improve on what he has submitted and then have him apply these suggestions by completely
rewriting his manuscript. This should be followed by another period
of personal advice and consultation.

What Business Firms Can Do.

Baltimore and Ohio Railroad Company. On the B & O, we want
reports to be clear and concise, so that the reader can quickly
digest the information given him. Proper organization of material
and the use of plain language help a man to write an accurate and
complete report. Of course, a knowledge and facility in basic grammar is of first importance in any type of writing. We are not interested in the development of "style" as such. Our executives will

not become disinterested if business reports are not "catchy" or full of human interest. They will, however, become annoyed if the report is lengthy, or if the language is involved and the sentence structure complex. At present our company is sponsoring Readability Clinics for key employees all over the system. These readability clinics are designed to improve the writing ability of our employees. This is proof of our interest in getting better intracompany reports.

Corning Glass Works. While we have never conducted any formal courses in report writing, we do try to keep all reports to a minimum. Reports are an important tool to the operation of any business, but they can quickly dull through unnecessary or indiscriminate use. Hence we urge our people to: (1) Make sure the report is necessary; (2) Write simply and concisely, using easy-to-understand words and putting the "who, what, where, when and why" of the subject in the fewest possible sentences; (3) Confine distribution of report to people who have an immediate interest in it.

I am afraid that I haven't been very helpful and that my observations might sound like those of a crank, but as one who receives entirely too many reports on every conceivable subject and from every conceivable kind of company, I can't help feeling that a lot of wasted money would be saved and wasted effort channeled to productive ends if the present large volume of unnecessary reports were eliminated.

Dow Chemical Company. I tell our men that the reason they do not write better research reports is that report writing is the hardest work they are called upon to do. It requires real thinking to do a good job. I have yet to find an easy out.

Ensco Derrick & Equipment Company. As a matter of interest, we encourage our various field representatives and sales representatives to write quite detailed reports and to express themselves as they see fit. Quite frequently these reports have to be edited for general distribution; however, we feel that this policy aids us in developing the full thoughts and ideas being expressed by those whose responsibility it is to present them for consideration.

First National Bank of Boston. As an indication of the importance we attach to good report writing, we recently conducted a seminar on this subject. A member of our Personnel Department . . . served as discussion leader. . . . Members of the group studied and discussed examples of their own work and used the Flesch formula as an index of readability.

Mutual Life Insurance Company of New York. We have given the subject of report-writing a good deal of attention in recent years because of the increasing importance of business reports. In one of our training courses, we stress the need for clearly written, readable reports, not only from the viewpoint of stimulating action, but also from the viewpoint of the impression which the reader receives of the writer of the report.

You Can't Afford to Write a Poor Letter *

A comparison of the chief physical characteristics of the Simplified Letter with those of the most popular "standard" letter will show how you can profit by a change.

The Conventional Letter   **The Simplified Letter**

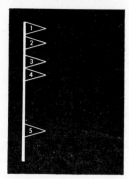

1. The date is at the far right. Why?
2. The address shifts to the far left. All's well.
3. The meaningless salutation stays

1. The date is at the left—you're starting where the typewriter starts.
2. The full address is at the left—ready for a window envelope and

* The Simplified Letter has caused much comment, most of it favorable, since its introduction by the National Office Management Association in the late 1940's. It reflects a trend toward simplification that has been increasing in momentum since the first World War, but it has a considerable barrier of tradition to overcome. Though many firms use the Simplified Letter now, or something very similar, it is unlikely that it will find complete acceptance before the 1970's.

The accompanying discussion of the Simplified Letter, reprinted by permission from a National Office Management Association leaflet, is required reading for any report-writer who wants to write letters that look to the future rather than to the past.

put but is waste since it's not you, but form that dictates it.

4. To be fancy, the paragraphs are indented five spaces. This job is multiplied by the number of paragraphs.
5. Back to the left margin for the body of the letter.
6. Zoom! Over to the right again for the "complimentary" close.
7. The company name picks another spot—why use it when it's shown in the letterhead?
8. A final zig to the left to put in the dictator's initials (why?) and the typist's to the right.

as permanent reference on the letter itself. Think of the keystrokes saved by not having to retype the address on the envelope.
3. Next the subject—at the left. A provocative opening and filing clue.
4. No indentation—paragraph starts without tabular delay.
5. The typewritten signature again at the left. No matter how weirdly the letter is signed the reader still knows who wrote it.

Every feature of this letter is on a flagpole. In a pile of papers, by lifting the left edge of the covering page a little, *all* the reference information springs into view. Try that with a conventional form!

It's Costly in Time, Money, and Good Will. A comparison such as this may seem to be based on unsupported opinion but here are the cold facts: A basic motion unit analysis of the typing alone on a 96-word letter proves a saving with the Simplified Letter of over 10.7%. A saving like that can't be ignored.

Here's our challenge: you and your secretary try the SL for 30 days. Elect her letter-writing queen. Find out what she says after the tryout. Compare it with what you've found out.

If you're a one-finger specialist, try it on your typewriter. We won't guarantee to promote you to two fingers but we'll bet you'll find the job easier and less nerve-racking.

To what does all this add?

1. Reduction in keystrokes—more production.
2. Reduction in motion for positioning typewriter—more production.
3. Improvement in typist's morale—more production.

The dull routine of many styles in use is removed. The typewriter follows its simplest mechanical course with minimum use of space bar, tabulator set key, tabulator bar. The letter looks as the typewriter was made to make it look.

All set? Mechanically, perhaps. But what's in your letter? There's a good reason for the slogan: "There's more to a truly Simplified Letter than simply dropping 'dear' and 'yours truly.'" The form is important but most important is the improvement in the content of the business letters you write.

Remember to whom you're writing. Everyone who writes a letter, a report, a memorandum—giving, asking, or exchanging information—is faced with a creative problem of first degree. The mere adoption of the Simplified Letter won't end the thinking required in good letter writing, but the philosophy behind the Simplified Letter formula seeks to reduce slow starting and the often stodgy results of production line letter writing.

With the Simplified Letter philosophy, you can stray the least from a normal, friendly, relaxed type of attitude you'd use in a successful conversation. Instead of remembering a string of dusty clichés to link your thoughts together you can seek the fresh, orderly flow of a clear mind, informed on the subject—really pointed "To whom you are writing."

At the start, instead of fumbling around, trying to decide whether to begin "Dear Sir, Dear Mr X, Dear Bob, or Esteemed Sir," you forget it altogether.

Then comes the subject. Usually, this matter never comes up until you've consumed several paragraphs—state the problem or the point of the letter at the outset.

Then your first sentence—all important in getting your reader to read. The first line of your letter—like the first handshake—is your introduction to your reader. Make it firm and convincing. Make it different—not stereotyped. Make it pertinent.

It makes sense to plan your letters. Organize your facts in logical order. Follow your logic. When you've spoken your piece, break it off—not by a fatuous "Yours truly," but by a little reminder that *you're you*.

Hold to firm principles of conciseness, clarity, and courteousness. Usually, the fewer the paragraphs the better. It may be good sense to use a cliché that still has meaning to the writer—as long as it's still lively. Like big words, don't avoid them when they spice or amplify your writing. Whatever tone you achieve will be the sound of your own thinking.

And please be friendly. Warmth and friendliness—when dispensed with an intelligent and courteous touch—can make up other letter deficiencies. Adjust your faucet to the reader. Don't scald him. But don't give him goose pimples.

Go as far as you can in putting a soft collar on your business correspondence—never write a letter without being fair to yourself

NATIONAL OFFICE MANAGEMENT ASSOCIATION
132 WEST CHELTEN AVENUE
PHILADELPHIA 44, PA.

this is a
SIMPLIFIED
letter

Dated Today

Ms. Office Secretary
Better Business Letters, Inc.
1 Main Street
Busytown, U.S.A.

HAD YOU HEARD?

There's a new movement under way to take some of the monotony
out of letters given you to type. The movement is symbolized
by the Simplified Letter being sponsored by NOMA.

What is it? You're reading a sample.

Notice the left block format and the general positioning of
the letter. We didn't write "Dear Miss ----," nor will we
write "Yours truly" or "Sincerely yours." Are they really
important? We feel just as friendly toward you without them.

Notice the following points:

1.   Date location
2.   The address
3.   The subject
4.   The name of the writer

Now take a look at the Suggestions prepared for you. Talk
them over with your boss. But don't form a final opinion
until you've really tried out The Letter. That's what our
secretary did. As a matter of fact, she finally wrote most
of the Suggestions herself.

She says she's sold -- and hopes you'll have good luck with
better (Simplified) letters.

Arthur H. Gager

there is more to a truly
SIMPLIFIED LETTER
than simply dropping
dear and yours truly

ARTHUR H. GAGER - STAFF DIRECTOR, TECHNICAL DIVISION

cc: R. P. Brecht, W. H. Evans, H. F. Grebe

FIGURE 48. The Simplified Letter.

and to your reader. Simplified Letters make sense—try sensible simplification today.

Letters Simplified—for Secretaries. Every time you shift a type-writer carriage, make a keystroke or space for positioning, you con-sume working seconds. Every time you do one of these things needlessly, you reduce your production and add to fatigue. The Simplified Letter stresses real economy of motion for you. Its use results in better looking letters with less effort. It will give you the pride of producing more effective letters. After a fair trial—talk it over with your boss!

Suggestions for Typing.
1. Use block format.
2. Place date in top position on left-hand margin.
3. Type name and address in block style at least three spaces below date (for use in window envelope). Use abbreviation Ms. if not sure whether to use Mrs. or Miss. This modern style solves an age-old problem.
4. Omit the formal salutation.
5. Subject should be typed in capitals at least three spaces below address.
6. Use a double space between paragraphs.
7. Indent questions, listings or like items in the body of letter five spaces from left-hand margin, except when preceded by a number or letter.
8. Omit the complimentary close.
9. Type name of dictator in capitals at left-hand margin at least five spaces below end of letter.
10. Align initials of typist at left below the signature, if used.
11. List, on the left-hand margin below signature, names of individuals who should receive carbon copies. Precede by "cc:".

A Proofreader's Nightmare

They write the same language

KETTLE-DRUMMERS and contraltos, crooners and composers, Paderewski and your little sister who is just starting to learn piano — all of them read the same notes. For the system of musical annotation is just as much a language to all people of music as English is to the people of America.

So it is with the proofreaders' code of symbols. This code is the common language of all men and women who write and prepare the written matter we read. Editors, authors, playwrights, poets, copywriters, typographers, printers, proof-readers, newspapermen, publishers, advertising managers — all know this language of proof-marks.

It is a language that has been used by the trade even as far back as Caxton and Gutenberg. It has evolved just as the English language has: it has its own slang — or corruptions of the regular form . . . it has its own modernisms . . . its own local variations. But a typographer in far-off Australia would instantly comprehend the carets, "stets," and "deles" of a Brooklyn proof-reader.

VISUAL EDUCATIONAL MANUAL
CLUETT, PEABODY & CO., Inc.
10 East 40th Street
New York 16, N. Y.

FIGURE 49. Exercise Sheet for Proofreading. Used by permission of Cluett, Peabody & Co., Inc.

My friend, Joe Holmes, is now a horse

JOE ALWAYS SAID when he died he'd like to become a horse.

Lne day; Joe died:

Early this May I saw a horse that looked like Joe drawing a milk wagon?

I sneaked up to him and whisdered: ;;Is it you, Joe:"

He said; "Yes; ind am I hap py "

I said, "why?"

He said, "I am now wearing a comfortable collar for the firts time in my life: My shirt collars always used to shrink and murder me, In fact; one choked ma to death: That is why I died "

"Goodness, Joe," I exclaimed; "Why did t you *tell* me about yor shirts sooner? I would have told you about Arrow shirts: *They never shrink* out *of perfect fit*: Not éven the oxfrods:"

"G'wan;"said Joe: "Oxford's the worst shrinker of all "

Maybe," I replied, "but not *Gordon*, the Arrow oxford: I know. I,m wearing one, It's Sanforized.labeled –can't shrink even 1% Besides, it has Arrow's unique Mit Oga tailored fit! And," I sadir eaching a crescendo; "Gordon comes with plain or button-down collar!"

"Swell;"said Joe. "My needs boss a shirt like that: I'll teli him about Gordon: Maybe hee'll me give an extra quart fo oats. And, gosh, do I love oats "

If it hasn't an Arrow Label, it isn't an Arrow Shirt

ARROW SHIRTS

Sanforized-Labeled—a new shirt free if one shrinks out of fit

Made by Cluett, Peabody & Co., Inc.

FIGURE 49—*Continued.*

Exercise Sheet for Proofreading *

This ad [Fig. 49 on opposite page] contains 60 typographical errors (more or less). Can you spot them?

Obviously this ad would never be released even from the most amateurish typographer's shop. If it were, it would be his last. We have incorporated practically all the errors in the book in this setting merely to provide you with pied (disarranged) copy, so that you can try your hand in specifying corrections by using the proofreader's symbols.

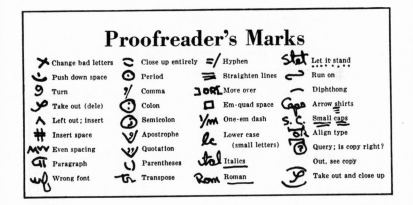

Proofreader's Marks

✗ Change bad letters	⌒ Close up entirely	=/ Hyphen	Let it stand
Push down space	⊙ Period	Straighten lines	Run on
9 Turn	⅋/ Comma	Move over	Diphthong
Take out (dele)	⊙ Colon	Em-quad space	Arrow shirts
∧ Left out; insert	⅋ Semicolon	One-em dash	Small caps
⌗ Insert space	Apostrophe	Lower case (small letters)	Align type
Even spacing	Quotation		Query; is copy right?
Paragraph	Parentheses	Italics	Out, see copy
Wrong font	Transpose	Roman	Take out and close up

* Cluett, Peabody & Co., Inc., prepared the accompanying Exercise Sheet for Proofreading and the explanatory pages following it so that apprentice proofreaders or anyone interested in learning how proofreading works could get some practice looking for errors, marking them, and checking their work against the corrected copy. How many of the 60 errors can you find?

General Explanation

THE ORIGINAL TEXT or copy of an advertisement is submitted to the client in typewritten form with the layout. The client's copy changes are cleared with the agency copywriter and, if approved, are incorporated in the text. The copy is then turned over to the production man together with the layout. He then has the type specialist "specify" type. The copy is sent to the typographer for the original setting. First proofs are read in the agency for typographical and grammatical errors, marked up and returned to the typographer for revision. Revised proofs are re-read by the agency and, if satisfactory, submitted to the client for his final approval.

Proofreader's Marks

✗ Change bad letters	⌒ Close up entirely	=/ Hyphen
⊥ Push down space	⊙ Period	≡ Straighten lines
⊘ Turn	⅋ Comma	]ᴏʀ[Move over
ℐ Take out (*dele*)	⊙ Colon	▯ Em-quad space
∧ Left out; insert	⊙ Semicolon	⅟ₘ One-em dash
# Insert space	ⱽ Apostrophe	*lc.* Lower case
∧∧ⱽⱽ Even spacing	ⱽⱽ Quotation	(small letters)
¶ Paragraph	( ) Parentheses	*ital.* Italics
wf Wrong font	*tr* Transpose	*Rom.* Roman
Stet Let it stand	*Caps* Arrow shirts	⟨?⟩ Query; is copy right?
⟿ Run on	S.C. Small caps	Out, see copy
⌒ Diphthong	⊔ₒᵣ Align type	ℐ Take out and close up

These are the symbols used by the proofreader to indicate corrections to be made in the type setting. These marks are standard for *all* writers of books, newspapers, magazines, legal documents, advertising, or what have you.

FIGURE 49—*Continued.*

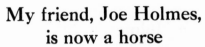

My friend, Joe Holmes, is now a horse

JOE ALWAYS SAID when he died he'd like to become a horse.

One day, Joe died.

Early this May I saw a horse that looked like Joe drawing a milk wagon. I sneaked up to him and whispered "Is it you, Joe?"

He said: "Yes, and am I happy!"

I said, "Why?"

He said, "I am now wearing a comfortable collar for the first time in my life; My shirt collars always used to shrink and murder me, In fact; one choked me to death; That is why I died."

"Goodness, Joe," I exclaimed; "Why didn't you tell me about your shirts sooner? I would have told you about Arrow shirts; They never shrink out of perfect fit; Not even the oxfords;"

"G'wan," said Joe: "Oxford's the worst shrinker of all,"!

"Maybe," I replied, "but not Gordon, the Arrow oxford? I know. I am wearing one, It's Sanforized-labeled—can't shrink even 1% Besides, it has Arrow's unique Mitoga tailored fit! And," I said reaching a crescendo "Gordon comes with plain or button-down collar!"

"Swell," said Joe. "My boss needs a shirt like that; I'll tell him about Gordon! Maybe he'll give me an extra quart of oats. And, gosh, do I love oats."

ARROW
SANFORIZED

*If it hasn't an Arrow Label,
it isn't an Arrow Shirt*

ARROW SHIRTS
Sanforized-Labeled—a new shirt free if one shrinks out of fit

Made by Cluett, Peabody & Co., Inc.

Obviously this ad would never be released even from the most amateurish typographer's shop. If it were, it would be his last. We have incorporated practically all the errors in the book in this setting merely to show how they are designated. Incidentally there are four or five typographical errors which are not indicated—*can you spot them?*

FIGURE 49—*Continued.*

My friend, Joe Holmes, is now a horse

JOE ALWAYS SAID when he died he'd like to become a horse.

One day Joe died.

Early this May I saw a horse that looked like Joe drawing a milk wagon.

I sneaked up to him and whispered, "Is it you, Joe?"

He said, "Yes, and am I happy!"

I said, "Why?"

He said, "I am now wearing a comfortable collar for the first time in my life. My shirt collars always used to shrink and murder me. In fact, one choked me to death. That is why I died!"

"Goodness, Joe," I exclaimed, "Why didn't you tell me about your shirts sooner? I would have told you about Arrow shirts. *They never shrink out of perfect fit.* Not even the oxfords."

"G'wan," said Joe. "Oxford's the worst shrinker of all!"

"Maybe," I replied, "but not *Gordon*, the Arrow oxford. I know. I'm wearing one. It's Sanforized-labeled—can't shrink even 1%! Besides, it has Arrow's unique Mitoga tailored fit! And," I said reaching a crescendo, "Gordon comes with plain or button-down collar!"

"Swell," said Joe. "My boss needs a shirt like that. I'll tell him about Gordon. Maybe he'll give me an extra quart of oats. And, gosh, do I love oats!"

ARROW ►►► SANFORIZED

If it isn't an Arrow Label, it isn't an Arrow Shirt

ARROW SHIRTS

Sanforized Labeled—a new shirt free if one shrinks out of fit

Made by Cluett, Peabody & Co., Inc.

This is the way the ad looks after the corrections have been made and plates are ready for the publications.

Litho in U. S. A.

FIGURE 49—*Concluded.*

Chapter 13

ORGANIZING FACTS AND IDEAS—READINGS

Make a Map to Guide Your Writing *
by HILARY H. MILTON
Editor, 3300th Training Publications Squadron
St. Louis, Missouri

"This piece of training literature reminds me of the cowboy who got on his horse and rode off in all directions!"

Did you ever have such a thought while you were reading a training project outline or a training manual? Further, did you try to understand *why* the writing left that impression?

Maybe you have and maybe you haven't. But chances are that if you had examined the text closely, you'd have noticed the absence of good organization.

In discussing writing improvement, many of us have talked about such things as direct style, active verbs, simple sentences, familiar words, and the like. But all too often we distort the problem because we fail to consider the basis of any good written piece: *Organization.*

Very few things can mean as much to the success of a good manual or Training Project Outline (TPO) (Student study guide) as the way it is organized. In fact, nothing else has as much to do

---

* Quoted by permission from an Air Force Informational Bulletin published at Scott Air Force Base; this material later adapted by Mr. Milton to form part of the ATRC Manual *How To Prepare ATRC Training Literature.* Hilary Milton is an Alabama product, with two degrees from and several years' teaching experience at the University of Alabama. He organized and conducted the first airmen-editor's writing training program in the Air Force, and is now Editor, Training Publications Unit, Headquarters Air Training Command, St. Louis. Along with the ATRC Manual mentioned above and other Air Force literature, he produces fiction and poetry as the spirit moves him.

with unity and coherence. We can use easily read sentences; we can choose words that are familiar to the reader; we can eliminate unnecessary adjectives; and we can "write in a conversational style" until the cows come home. But if we do not *plan the way the material should unfold* to the reader, then we cannot expect him to follow the writing.

Actually, an outline is the map that will take you on your writing journey; it is the device that guides you from the first word you write until you have completed the entire manuscript.

Let's think about how we can make a writer's map—how we can organize and outline our writing so the reader is able to follow it. You can establish a good outline by:

- considering the purpose and scope of the writing
- considering the readers
- choosing a specific working title
- selecting a method of approach
- making a preliminary list of major topics
- arranging these according to the method of approach
- putting under each major topic the subtopics which fit the category
- giving *all* topics specific captions.

Purpose and Scope of Writing. The first step an author should take before he begins to organize or write material is to determine the purpose of his manuscript. He may intend for the finished product to teach; he may mean for it to direct a program; he may want it to give advice; or he may simply mean for it to give information. Again, he may want it to motivate readers—students, instructors, or supervisors. Actually, in many cases he will probably intend for it to perform two or more of these services. But whatever the purpose is, the writer should know it so that he can fit his material to it.

Also, the writer should know the scope of the material he intends to write. If he is working within a limited scope, say a piece that should run two to three thousand words, he will know that a brief outline will serve satisfactorily. On the other hand, if he intends to cover a complex area, he should have a detailed outline that reflects careful organization. For example, if an author plans to write a complete manual on a topic such as "The Basic Principles of Aircraft Structure," he knows that he needs a carefully worked-up outline.

Many of us tend to disregard the matter of scope when we organize a piece of writing. We brush the idea aside by saying casually, "Its scope should be limited," or "It should have complete coverage." Such statements *lead you to the scope,* but they do not spell it out. We'd all be better off if we wrote out in specific terms the scope of our material at the same time that we write out the detailed purpose.

Prospective Readers. Once you have identified the purpose and scope of your writing, your next step is to define your audience. Again, you should write out a general description of the people who will likely read the material. Specifically, you should answer such questions as these:

- Who will read this material? Airmen? Officers? Airmen and officers? Students? Operators?

- Have they had previous training? For instance, have they been to a technical school? Have they had certain types of civilian school training?

- What is the approximate education level of these readers?

- How technical can the information be for these people?

- How strongly motivated are the readers?

Of course, this list does not include all the questions you should ask when you define your audience. But these and others like them will help you to know things about the prospective readers—and thus to know how to organize and outline the material you're writing.

Actually, this idea of defining your audience isn't anything new. We've been working at it for a long time. Our curriculum planning, our course scheduling, and our manual writing in the Air Training Command (ATRC) have all been slanted toward the needs and qualifications of the "audience." But here, as with the defined scope and the detailed purpose, we've tended to generalize: "The readers have reached an educational level somewhere near the 8th (or 10th, or 12th) grade." "They don't know anything about this stuff," or "They've been through a basic course." But seldom do we get down to specifics where our readers are concerned. And all too often our writing reflects our vagueness on the audience subject.

Frankly, we'd just as well face the fact here and now as somewhere else and later on: If we don't define our audience, if we don't find out things about our readers, we cannot write to suit their needs or to suit their reading abilities.

When you set out to organize and outline a piece of writing, then, make sure that you learn some definite facts about your audience. Don't rely on guesswork; and whatever you do, don't dismiss the matter with a lot of vague generalities.

Specific Working Title. After you have established your purpose and scope and have identified your audience, you must next choose a clearly worded, definite working title.

"That's simple," someone may say. "I'm writing about engines, so I'll just call the book 'Engines'."

The person who casually gives a title to a long piece of writing will probably give the whole manuscript the same kind of treatment. If he doesn't give his proposed project enough thought to select a clear, definitive title, chances are he'll be just as indefinite with his writing.

Let's just analyze the casual "Engines" statement.

In the first place the man has no intention of writing about engines. If he did, he'd have to deal with automobile engines, aircraft engines, stationary engines, aircooled engines, water cooled engines, jet engines, reciprocal engines, Diesel engines, and a host of others. Furthermore, he'd have to write basic facts, advanced theories, description of *all* working parts, how elements work, and how to repair all the various types. In short, he'd have to write an encyclopedia.

That is, if he's being honest with his readers.

Of course, we know the man who gives his writing a title such as "Engines" or "Aircraft" doesn't mean that he'll cover all the aspects that come under the title. So why would he want to use such a title in the first place? Why not spend a little time and thought and come up with something meaningful?

A good working title does two things: first, it tells you what your writing will include; and, second, it omits those things which you *will not* include. In other words, your working title should completely box you in and put a fence around your considerations. To make this point clearer, let's take "Engines" and develop a working title which the writer can really use.

If we have just the one word, we could illustrate it with a straight line, like this:

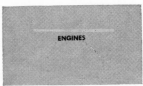

There's no clearly defined point of beginning and no limit at all; like a straight line that runs around the world, the title could run from here to eternity.

Suppose, though, that we add the word *jet* to the title. Our diagram would now look something like this:

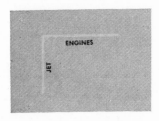

By this simple addition we have excluded many topics which the word *engines* alone might cover. Specifically, we have eliminated Diesels, reciprocating engines, radial engines, and automobile engines (since we do not use jets in automobiles at the present time).

However, the writer might still have a lot of liberty because he could talk about how to repair jet engines, what they consist of, or which principles they employ. Also, he could go from very simple to very complex treatments of the title. So right now he's bound by only two sides of a fence.

Now, suppose we add another word to the title: "Principles." The illustration changes somewhat, and it looks something like this:

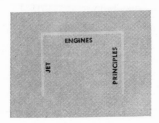

That additional word puts boundaries on three sides of the writer. In other words, by adding *principles* we've eliminated the possibility of the writer's talking about how to repair jet engines and what they consist of. If he stays within these limits he can discuss only the principles that govern the jet engine's operation.

However, one side of the fence will still allow him to "break through." The author can talk about the simple principles, or he can talk about the most advanced theories if he wishes. So we need to "build another wall."

We can do that by adding the word *basic*. Now the fence is complete.

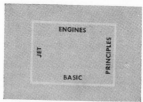

Once a writer has bound himself in, he will stay within the limits if he intends to be honest with his readers.

True enough, the title seems simple in this example; but you can follow the same process when you choose *any* title for *any* piece. Consider this one: "How to Overhaul Reciprocating Engines." The four variables of this title put the four sections of the fence around the writer. Remove *How to, Overhaul, Reciprocating,* or *Engines* and you've changed the title.

Just as an experiment, why not try this business of making a good working title? Take any topic you can think of—aircraft, for instance—and see how you can fence yourself in.

Selecting A Method of Approach. Once you've chosen your title, you should next select the method of approach to use with your particular piece of writing. As you may already know you can present your material according to the time-sequence method, the logical method, or the psychological method.

TIME SEQUENCE. The time-sequence method really needs little explanation here. It simply means that you begin at the beginning and present your information according to the time of occurrence. For example, if you intended to write about the growth of the Air Force, about the history of a particular program's development, or about a man's progress, you'd follow the time-sequence method. If you are writing a manual which should bring reservists up to date on a particular topic, this method of approach would serve you well.

Actually, however, the time-sequence plan has certain limitations. For one thing, it doesn't emphasize any one part of the writing. For another, it does not allow you to apply your data or your information. And often it will not hold your reader unless the style appeals to him.

LOGICAL METHOD. The logical method is similar to the time-sequence method in that it moves from one point to another in a first-second-third-fourth order. However, the logical method does have the advantage of letting you pause along the way and integrate your materials. And it does help you to include details which the time-sequence method doesn't allow.

Many writers find the logical method quite helpful when they wish to give all the details of an experiment, when they want to show every part of an analysis, or when they want to teach readers how to repair equipment.

Once more, however, the logical method doesn't allow room for emphasis nor does it allow you to shift from one part of your explanation to an unrelated section or topic without confusing your reader. You may find it helpful if you know that your audience can follow you or if you are presenting fairly simple information. But if you plan to introduce a lot of new terms—equipment or techniques —you may find that the logical plan won't satisfy your needs.

PSYCHOLOGICAL METHOD. The psychological arrangement, last of the three, leads you to present your information in an order that is neither chronological nor logical (as we defined logical). With this method you may go from the familiar to the unfamiliar, from the simple to the difficult, from basic principles to complex theories. Also, this method allows you more leeway when you want to present material in a reader-appeal manner.

With much of our writing, particularly the training literature side of it, we should follow the psychological method. For example, a piece of writing that teaches a man *how to operate* (not repair) equipment would help the reader if presented according to this method.

Many writers have found that the psychological method helps them present material in various stages. For example, they have used this arrangement when they want to tell their readers how to do a particular thing, what happens when they do it, and why it happens.

We can say, then, that the psychological method becomes quite useful to the man who writes training literature as well as to the one who writes almost any type of motivational material.

Actually, though, when you get down to it, you'll probably find that a combination of two or more methods will help you better than any one of them by itself. That's all right. Nobody's going to pin you down to only one. But if you recognize the various methods, and if you know the purpose of your writing, you can do a better job of organizing.

Preliminary List of Topics. As the fifth step on preparing this writer's map, make a preliminary list of the major topics which you should include. Such a list usually becomes a chapter breakdown; so as you write down the topics, be sure to include all the major areas that need treatment. For example, if you intended to write a training manual on automotive maintenance, you might list such topics as these:

> movable parts
> internal combustion
> lubricating system
> cooling system
> fuel system
> ignition system
> housing assembly

At this point neither the wording nor the arrangement represents the final working approach. You're still a long way from the outline you'll need to guide the actual writing. But this topic list does become the first concrete step in making the outline.

Many writers like to support these major topics with certain important subtopics at the time they make this list. For example they may want to add to the list certain *must* items:

> housing assembly
>   block
>   head
>
> fuel system
>   carburetor
>   fuel tank and lines
>
> movable parts
>   crankshaft
>   rods
>   pistons
>   (etc)

This expanded list still doesn't represent the working outline; but it helps to identify points that the writer means to include in that outline.

Arrange Topics According to Method of Approach. After you've listed *all* the major topics which you need to include in your manual (or report or Training Project Outline), you must next put these into the sequence you've decided to use. As we mentioned earlier, this sequence depends on the purpose of the writing, the audience to which you're addressing the material, and the scope of the work.

When we get to this stage of the game, many of us tend to put topics into almost any order that *seems* reasonable. But often the thing that seems reasonable doesn't satisfy all the needs. So we should give a lot of thought to the plan because the success of the whole thing often depends on the order of presentation.

To make that thought clearer, just consider the topics we've listed. If you began your maintenance book with a section on "movable parts," then followed it with one on "internal combustion," the reader would very likely be confused. However, if you began with a discussion of "internal combustion," explaining the theories and principles, then *rearranged* the other topics to follow a logical order, you'd help the reader.

Let's put these topics in an order that would really lead the average reader through an orderly sequence of thoughts:

Internal combustion
Housing assembly
Movable parts
Fuel system
Ignition system
Lubricating system
Cooling system

The arrangement here will help the reader to understand automotive maintenance practices and procedures. Take a moment to examine the plan and you'll see why.

Subtopics. Once you have the arrangement set up according to the plan that seems most useful, you next want to put under each major topic *all* the subtopics that you intend to discuss, in the order in which you mean to discuss them. At this point you're getting down to details, and you can no longer generalize. In the earlier steps you looked at the "broad picture," but in the final analysis the supporting sections will determine the success or failure of your efforts. So right here you *must* give serious thought to the necessary coverage.

To emphasize this idea, let's just take one of the major topics and subdivide it:

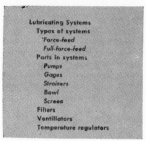

Lubricating Systems
    Types of systems
        Force-feed
        Full-force-feed
    Parts in systems
        Pumps
        Gages
        Strainers
        Bowl
        Screen
    Filters
    Ventillators
    Temperature regulators

These subtopics and sub-subtopics become the supporting sections and subsections within the chapter. Your identifying them in the outline tells you that you must include them in your finished product.

Perhaps you'd like to go farther in your breakdown than our outlined chapter indicates. Fine! Go ahead. The more detailed you make your working outline, the more complete you'll make your manual or long report. After all, that's one of the purposes of a good outline; it identifies the sections you intend to include and gives the order of presentation for those sections.

Your seventh step in organizing and making a good working outline, then, is to list in order *all* the subtopics and sub-subtopics which you'll need to give detail and support to your various chapter divisions.

Give All Topics Specific Captions. The final step is to give specific wording to all the captions, major as well as minor ones. Many of us tend to ignore this step in our outlining; most of us think that if we merely name the point to be discussed, we have satisfied the demands of an outline. So we blithely give a caption such wording as "Generator," "Carburetor," "Oil Pumps," and dismiss the point. We justify such casual treatment by saying, "Oh, I know what I want to say on carburetors," or "There's nothing much to be said about oil pumps, anyway." Such dismissal indicates the lack of real thought on the part of the planner. Furthermore, it may probably lead to some confused thinking later on.

When we get down to the writing job, we tend to forget some of the points we *knew we'd remember* at the time we made the outline. We may have intended to explain *how to repair* a carburetor when we wrote out the topic; but three months later, when we get to that part of our plan, we don't remember whether to talk about how to repair the carburetor, what the carburetor does, or how it works.

We can avoid such confusion by using concrete terms with our topics while we're making the outline. Specifically, we can improve the outlines by giving our topics one of three types of captions: informative, instructive, or directive.

To help you recognize—and use—these captions in the right way, suppose we point out some concrete examples. First, let's look at informative captions:

> Two Systems Are Used in Engines
> Force-feed System Utilizes Splash
> Full-Force-Feed System Does Not Use Splash
> The Systems Have Several Parts
> Oil Pumps Keep Oil Circulating
> Oil Gages Indicate Amount of Lubricant
> Oil Strainers Keep Trash out of Pump
> Oil Filters Clean Oil
> Crankcase Ventillators Help Cool Lubricant
> Oil Temperature Regulator Maintains Even
> Temperature

Lubrication Systems Preserve Parts and Cool Engines.

Informative captions like these do two things for the writer: They synopsize the material which they introduce, and they *tell the writer what approach* to use when he gets to the various parts of the outline. They tell him to describe the work of the particular unit.

Instructive captions, on the other hand, tell the writer he should emphasize "how-to-do" a certain task. For example, notice these captions:

> How to Repair Parts of an Oil System
> How to Fix Oil Pumps
> Repair Gages This Way
> Overhaul Strainers in This Manner
> (etc)

Emphasis in these captions is on *how to fix* equipment, not what the various elements *do*.

The directive type of caption has some similarity to the instructive type, but it goes one step further. It tells the reader *what to do*.

Such captions in an outline should tell the writer what approach to use in his writing.

To get a better understanding of directive captions, suppose we glance at the headings throughout this article. The overall title of the paper tells you to make an outline that will map your writing journey. The subordinate headings support that title and tell you the steps involved in making the outline.

The type of caption you use will depend on the purpose of your writing, the audience, and the slant of the text. But whichever you choose, be sure to give every major heading and all the subheadings specific wording; make certain that they synopsize the material they introduce; and give them the same slant that the writing will have.

Again, Outline Your Writing Project. When you have a writing assignment, then, follow some definite steps to outline the task. Specifically, you should

- consider the purpose
- remember the readers
- get a good title
- choose the method of approach
- make a list of topics
- arrange these in a definite order
- support major topics with subtopics
- and give *all* the topics specifically worded captions.

These steps may not absolutely guarantee unity in the writing because you still have to put words into sentences and sentences into paragraphs. But if you organize your material and make a clear, mapping outline at the very beginning, you'll do much to help your reader follow a clear line of reasoning throughout the text.

Chapter 14

LANGUAGE, SEMANTICS, VOCABULARY: READINGS

Our National Mania for Correctness [*]

by DONALD J. LLOYD

Every now and then the editors of the university presses let out a disgruntled bleat about the miserable writing done by scholars, even those who are expert in literary fields; and from time to time there are letters and editorials in our national reviews bewailing some current academic malpractice with the English language. At present, even *PMLA* (the *Publications of the Modern Language Association*), traditionally the repository of some of the worst writing done by researchers, is trying to herd its authors toward more lucid exposition. And at two recent meetings of the august Mediaeval Academy, one at Boston and one at Dumbarton Oaks, bitter remarks were passed about the failure of specialists in the Middle Ages to present their findings in some form palatable to the general reader, so that he can at least understand what they are writing about.

Even admitting that a really compelling style is the result of years of cultivation, much scholarly writing is certainly worse than it needs to be. But it is not alone in this. Generally speaking, the writing of literate Americans whose primary business is not writing but something else is pretty bad. It is muddy, backward, convoluted and self-strangled; it is only too obviously the product of a task approached unwillingly and accomplished without satisfaction or zeal. Except for the professionals among us, we Americans are hell on the English language. I am not in touch with the general run of British writing by non-professionals, but I suspect that is nothing to make those islanders smug, either.

[*] Reprinted by permission from *The American Scholar*, Summer, 1952. Dr. Lloyd teaches at Wayne University; he has just written an admirable new grammar.

Furthermore, almost any college professor, turning the spotlight with some relief from himself and his colleagues to his students, will agree that their writing stinks to high heaven, too. It is a rare student who can write what he has to write with simplicity, lucidity and euphony, those qualities singled out by Somerset Maugham; far more graduating seniors are candidates for a remedial clinic than can pass a writing test with honors. And freshmen writing is forever the nightmare of the teachers of composition, as it would be of their colleagues if the latter could not escape to the simple inanities of their objective tests.

Yet it was not always so. I have on my desk a little manuscript from the fourteenth century written by an unknown author, which I am in the process of editing. When I read it to one of my classes, as I occasionally do, with no more modernization than my own Great Lakes pronunciation and the substitution of a word for one which has become obsolete, it is a simple, clear and engaging document. "Where is any man nowadays that asketh how I shall love God and my fellow-Christians?" it begins. "How I shall flee sin and serve God truly as a true Christian man should? What man is there that will learn the true law of God, which he biddeth every Christian man to keep upon pain of damnation in hell without end? . . . Unnethe [scarcely] is there any lewd man or lewd woman that can rightly well say his Pater Noster, his Ave Maria, and his Creed, and sound the words out readily as they should. But when they play Christmas games about the fire, therein will they not fail. Those must be said out without stumbling for dread of smiting. But if a lewd man should be smited now for each failing that he maketh in saying of his Pater Noster, his Ave Maria, and his Creed, I trowe he should be smited at the full." And so on, to the beautiful poetic line, "Then think it not heavy to dwell with thy mother in her wide house, thou that laist in the strait chamber of her womb." The spelling in the original is hectic, and the capitalization and punctuation sporadic, to say the least.

Yet there was a man who knew what he had to say and set out about saying it, with no nonsense and no fumbling. He aimed for his audience and, judging by the dog-ears and sweat-marks on the book, which is about the size of one of our pocket books, he hit it. Why cannot we do as well in our time? Indeed, the eighteenth century was about the last age in which almost any man, if he was literate at all, could set down his thoughts—such as they were—so that they did not have to be excavated by the reader. We have an abundance of letters, diaries, pamphlets, and other papers from that period, and they are well written. It was the age, we may recall, not only of Boswell and Johnson, but of Pepys and Franklin as well, and of a host of other men whose main legacy to us was a simple, direct, workmanlike style, sufficient to the man and to the occasion, which said what it had to say and said it well. With the end of that century we go into the foggy, foggy darkness, and God knows whether we shall ever find our way out of it—as a people, that is, as a nation of thinking men and women with something to say.

Nevertheless, there is no question what makes our writing bad, or what we shall have to do to better it. We shall simply have to isolate and root out a monomania which now possesses us, which impedes all language study and inhibits all mastery of our native tongue—all mastery, that is, on paper; for as speakers of English, we Americans are loving and effective cultivators of our expression. I recall the gas station attendant who was filling my car. The gasoline foamed to the top of the tank, and he shut off the pump. "Whew!" I said, "that nearly went over." "When you see white-caps," he replied, "you better stop." "You better had," I said, lost in admiration. But if you had given him a pencil, he would have chewed the end off before he got one word on paper.

The demon which possesses us is our mania for correctness. It dominates our minds from the first grade to the graduate school; it is the first and often the only thing we think of when we think of our language. Our spelling must be "correct"—even if the words are ill-chosen; our "usage" must be "correct"—even though any possible substitute expression, however crude, would be perfectly clear; our punctuation must be "correct"—even though practices surge and change with the passing of years, and differ from book to book, periodical to periodical. Correct! That's what we've got to be, and the idea that we've got to be correct rests like a soggy blanket on our brains and our hands whenever we try to write.

This mania for correctness is another legacy from the eighteenth century, but it did not get a real grip on us until well into the nineteenth. Its power over us today is appalling. Among my other tasks, I teach advanced courses in the English language to students preparing to teach. Most of these are seniors and graduate students, and in the summer especially, there is a sprinkling of older men and women, experienced teachers, who are sweating out a

master's degree. They have had courses in "English" throughout
their schooling. But of the nature and structure of the English
language, the nature of language habits, the relation of speech to
writing, and the differences in usage which arise from dialect and
from differing occupational and educational demands—of all these,
they know nothing at all. Nor do they come to me expecting to
learn about these. They want to know two things: what correct
usage is and how you beat it into the kids' heads. That there are
other considerations important to an English teacher is news to
many of them. What they get from me is a good long look at their
language.

To trace this monolithic concentration on usage is to pursue a
vicious circle, with the linguists on the outside. The literate public
seems to get it from the English teachers, and the teachers get it
from the public. The attitudes and pronouncements on language
of a Jacques Barzun, a Wilson Follett, a Bernard De Voto, or a
Norman Lewis ("How Correct Must Correct English Be?") mean
more to English teachers than anything said by the most distinguished professional students of language—such as Leonard Bloom-
field, Robert Hall or Charles Carpenter Fries. Correct usage is
pursued and discussed, furthermore, without much reference to the
actual writing of literary men. Now and again I amuse myself by
blue-penciling a current magazine such as the *Saturday Review* or
Collier's against the rules. I have to report that error is rampant,
if variation is to be considered error. The boys just don't seem to
pay attention to the rules. Moreover, having seen some of their
first drafts, I am pretty sure that what conformity they do display
is the work of their wives, secretaries, editors, proofreaders and
typesetters, rather than their own. It takes a determined effort to
beat the old Adam out of a readable manuscript.

Thus it is only the determined, consciously creative professional
who can build his work on the actual language of men. In a recent
issue of the *Saturday Review,* I stumbled on a quotation from Wolf-
gang Langewiesche. "Well, it isn't crowned by no castle, that's for
sure," he wrote, "and by no cathedral either." My eyes popped,
and I read it again. I liked it. It looked right; it sounded right;
it had a fine Chaucerian swing to it. But I bet it cost him some
blood and a fifth of Scotch to get it into print. In my own limited
publication, I find "a historical" changed to "an historical," all my
"further's" changed to "farther" and all my "farther's" to 'further,"

"than us" watered down to "than we," and many, many more. How E. M. Forster got by with "the author he thinks," and got it reprinted in a freshman handbook a few pages along from the prohibition of such locutions baffles me. A phony standardization of usage appears in print, the work of editors unconscious of the ultimate meaning of what they do.

The result of all this is that a wet hand of fear rests on the heart of every nonprofessional writer who merely has a lot of important knowledge to communicate. He writes every sentence with a self-conscious horror of doing something wrong. It is always a comfort to him if he can fit himself into some system, such as that of a business or governmental office which provides him with a model. It is thus that gobbledygook comes into being. I once braced a distinguished sociologist, a student of occupational myths and attitudes, about the convoluted, mainly nominal turgidity of his writing. He apparently admitted verbs into his sentences the way we admit DP's into the United States, reluctantly and with pain. In speech he was racy, confident and compelling, a brilliant lecturer. "It's the only way I can get my work into the periodicals," he told me blandly. "If it's clear and simple, they don't think it's scholarly." With what relief the pedagogues subside into pedagese!

If we really want to get good writing from people who know things, so that we can come to learn what they know as easily as we learn from their talk, we can do it in a generation or so. In school and out, in print and out, we can leave usage to its natural nurse, the unforced imitation of the practices which are actually current among educated people. We can use our English courses in school and college, not to give drill on questionable choices among common alternatives, demanding that one be taken as right and the others as wrong, but to give practice in reading and writing. We can learn to read and write for the idea, and for the idea without regard for anything else. Then our young people will come to maturity confidently using their pencils to find out what they think and get it down on paper; then our scholars will come to write simply, clearly and brilliantly what they brilliantly know.

In our speech we have arrived, I think, at a decency of discourse which is conducive to effective expression. We listen, with a grave courteous attention, to massive patterns of speaking different from our own because they come from differences in dialect and social status; we listen without carping and without a mean contempt.

Furthermore, we participate; we go with a speaker through halts and starts, over abysses of construction, filling in the lacunae without hesitation; we discount inadvertencies and disregard wrong words, and we arrive in genial good will with the speaker at his meaning. In this atmosphere, our speech has thrived, and the ordinary American is in conversation a confident, competent expressive being. In writing he is something else again.

No one flourishes in an atmosphere of repression. It is possible, of course, for a person with special aptitudes and a special drive to bull his way past the prohibitions and achieve an individual style. But with the negative attitude that attends all our writing, those whose main interest lies elsewhere are inhibited by fear of "error" and the nagging it stirs up from setting pen to paper, until the sight of a blank white page gives them the shakes. It is no wonder that their expression is halting and ineffective. They cannot fulfill the demands of a prissy propriety and trace the form of an idea at the same time. Thus they arrive at adulthood victims of the steely eye of Mr. Sherwin Cody, whose bearded face stares at them from the countless ads for his correspondence school, demanding, "Do YOU make these mistakes in English?" The locutions he lists are not mistakes, and Mr. Cody knows they are not; but his readers do not know it, and they do not know that they don't matter anyway.

For usage doesn't matter. What matters is that we get done what we have to do, and get said what we have to say. Sufficient conformity is imposed upon us by the patterns of our language and by the general practice of its users so that we do not have to run the idea of conformity into the ground by carping about trivial erratics in expression. Why in this matter of language alone complete conformity should be considered a virtue—except to typists, printers and typesetters—it is difficult to see (unless, perhaps, we are using it as a covert and pusillanimous means of establishing our own superiority). In our other concerns of life, we prize individuality; why in this one matter we should depart from a principle that otherwise serves us well is a puzzle for fools and wise men to ponder, especially since there is no general agreement on what to conform to, and one man's correctness is another's error. Not until we come to our senses—teachers, editors, writers and readers together—and stop riding each other's backs, will the casual, brisk, colorful, amused, ironic and entertaining talk of Americans find its way into print.

We should all be happy to see it there.

Korzybski and Semantics *

by STUART CHASE

Semantics is a department in the overall study of communication, along with linguistics, cybernetics, perception theory, and many other disciplines. Among those who contributed importantly to it are Ogden and Richards, Rudolf Carnap, Bertrand Russell, and various other scientists. But the most colorful, newsworthy, and perhaps original of them all was Alfred Korzybski. Though he created no earth-shaking new philosophy, he dramatized an idea of great import and made it appeal to a wide audience. He helped to place it in the advancing field of social science, the field that Alexander Pope once called the proper study of mankind.

I followed Korzybski's work with interest, excitement, and some frustration for many years, and am grateful for the wholesome shock my nervous system received when I first read his magnum opus, *Science and Sanity*. It forced me to recognize the unconscious assumptions imbedded in the language, which I as a writer had been calmly accepting. Nature, he said, does not work the way our language works, and he proceeded to give shrewd suggestions for a closer relationship. He called his approach "General Semantics."

As I knew him in his later years—he was seventy when he died in 1950—he had the general aspect of an amiable Buddha, bald as a newel post, with kindly, intelligent eyes behind vast, round spectacles, and a rich, rolling Polish accent. He was rude, formidable, oververbalized, and strangely appealing—for all I know an authentic genius.

Piecing together parts of his background, we note that he was a count from a proud and ancient family, with an estate in the country and properties in Warsaw. Trained as a chemical engineer at the Warsaw Polytechnic Institute, he read widely in law, mathematics, and philosophy. He was also, we are told, handsome and a bit

* Reprinted from *The Saturday Review*, June 19, 1954, pp. 11-12; 46-48, by permission of the author and *The Saturday Review*. Stuart Chase, graduate of Massachusetts Institute of Technology and Harvard University and author of more than twenty books, has long been a special student of language. His *The Tyranny of Words* (New York: Harcourt, Brace & Co., 1938) was one of the first "semantics" books to receive wide attention. Now he has returned to word-and-meaning study in his current *Power of Words* (New York: Harcourt, Brace & Co., 1954).

wild, as befitted a young nobleman. In World War I he served on the Grand Duke's staff, was twice wounded, and then came to America as an artillery expert for the Czarist Russian Army. He added English to his five Continental languages, and while he never got his phonemes straight, he acquired great fluency and came to prefer it. He wrote his books and articles in English and thought in this language. He married a talented American portrait painter, Mira Edgerly, and later became an American citizen.

He published two books and a score of papers, none of them easy to read. When he conducted an oral seminar, however, with a full display of gestures and his wonderful accent, the communication line was clear most of the time. I can see him now, reaching stout, muscular arms into the air and wigging two fingers of each hand to make the "quote" sign, somewhat the way Churchill made the "V" sign. In semantics quotation marks around a word mean: "Beware, it's loaded!"

Korzybski's chief claim to fame will rest, I think, on *Science and Sanity*, difficult as it is. His earlier book, *Manhood of Humanity* is shorter and less difficult. Its thesis is that man is distinguished from the rest of earth's creatures by his language and the ability to pass down what he learns from one generation to the next. Even the most intelligent elephant has to begin over with each generation. "The proper life of man *as man*, is not life-in-space like that of the animals, but life-in-time. . . . Bound-up time is literally the core and substance of civilization." This passing-down process, to which Korzybski gives the name "time-binding," runs parallel with the culture concept of the anthropologists.

After publishing *Manhood of Humanity*, Korzybski spent ten years of intensive work preparing for and writing *Science and Sanity*. It was published in 1933 at the bottom of the Depression —hardly an auspicious year to bring out an expensive book. In it Korzybski explored relativity, quantum theory, colloid chemistry, biology, neurology, psychology, psychiatry, mathematical logic, and what was then available by other students of communication theory and semantics. The question he set himself to answer was how the structure of language could be brought closer to the structure of the space-time world. He cited the new talk of scientists, following the Einstein revolution. If physicists could teach themselves to communicate more clearly about atoms and nebulae, would it not be possible for the rest of us to do likewise about politics, economics, and human relations?

The word "semantics" first appeared in dictionaries about fifty years ago, defined as "studies having to do with signification or meaning." The Society for General Semantics in Chicago has issued two short, comprehensive definitions, as follows:

Semantics . . . The systematic study of meaning.

General Semantics . . . The study and improvement of human evaluative processes with special emphasis on the relation to signs and symbols, including language.

Note the accent on "evaluation" in defining General Semantics. Whenever we become conscious about the meaning of a context— "What is the Senator trying to say?" . . . "How can I tell her more clearly?" . . . "What kind of double talk is that?"—we are practising elementary semantics.

The goals of General Semantics are three:

1. To help the individual evaluate his world. As our environment grows more and more complex, greater precision is needed to interpret it.
2. To improve communication between A and B, also within and between groups of all sizes.
3. To aid in clearing up mental illness. General Semantics was used with good results by Dr. Douglas Kelley in the treatment of some 7,000 battle-shock cases in World War II.

Korzybski, together with other semanticists, was shy of "high order terms," the phrase he employed to characterize vague verbal abstractions. He went so far as to construct a little gadget of wood and metal to help the user analyze verbal abstractions. Watching one's step on abstraction ladders is not as academic as it sounds. For example, what do the following words mean? What can A and B both point to so they may find some common ground in discussing them?

American Way	Creeping Socialism
Appeasement	Democracy
Balanced Budget	Fascism
Big Business	Free Enterprise
Bureaucracy	Free World
Communism	Government Interference

Labor Agitators	Spending
Leftist, Rightist	Statism
Loyalty, Security	Subversives
Monopoly	Totalitarianism
New Deal	Wall Street
Socialized Medicine	Welfare State

Two or more citizens can start an argument on any of these terms which may rage for hours without a referent in sight, beyond "Uh, I knew a man whose brother had it straight that . . . ." Yet down the ladder below these words are events and issues of the first importance which Americans must face. Every item in the list belongs in Korzybski's upraised fingers: "Quote—unquote. Beware, it's loaded!" Such terms are in marked contrast to low-order terms like "100° F.," "my cat there," "pure oxygen," "the key of C-sharp minor," "40 M.P.H." When I was writing *The Tyranny of Words,* everybody was talking, if not shouting loudly, about "Fascism." I asked a hundred persons from various walks of life to tell me what they meant by Fascism. They shared a common dislike for the term, but no two agreed what it meant. There were fifteen distinguishable, and contradictory, concepts in the answers submitted. This gave an idea of the chaos involved in the indiscriminate use of high order terms.

Today, Fascism is out of style and everybody is talking, or shouting, about "Communism." Reporters from the *Capital Times* in Madison, Wisconsin, asked 197 persons on the street to answer the question: "What is a Communist?" Here are some of the replies:

> *Farmer:* "They are no good to my notion. I can't figure out what they are."
> *Stenographer:* "If a person didn't have a religion I would be tempted to believe he was a Communist."
> *Housewife:* "I really don't know what a Communist is. I think they should throw them out of the White House."
> *High school student:* "A Communist is a person who wants war."
> *Office worker:* "Anyone that stands for things that democracy does not."

Not only was there no agreement, but 123 out of the 197 frankly admitted *they did not know what a Communist is.* All this came at a time when Congressional investigations were flooding the newspapers with the "Communist Menace" inside America. The danger of drowning we know about; but where shall the wayfaring citizen point to the specific danger of Communism within our borders, in the light of this exhibit?

Here is a typical abstraction ladder, beginning at the top and working downward:

Mountains: What can be said about mountains which applies in all cases? Almost nothing. They are areas raised above other areas on land, under the sea, on the moon. The term is purely relative at this stage; something higher than something.

Snow-capped mountains. Here on a lower rung we can say a little more. The elevations must be considerable, except in polar regions—at least 15,000 feet in the tropics. The snow forms glaciers which wind down their sides. They are cloud factories, producing severe storms, and they require special techniques for climbing.

The Swiss Alps. These are snow-capped mountains about which one can say a good deal. The location can be described, also geology, glacier systems, average elevation, climatic conditions, first ascents, and so on.

The Matterhorn. Here we can be even more specific. It is a snow-capped mountain 14,780 feet above the sea, shaped like a sharp wedge, constantly subject to avalanches of rock and ice. It has four faces, four ridges, three glaciers; was first climbed by the Whymper party in 1865, when four out of seven were killed—and so on. We have dropped down the ladder to a specific space-time event.

To the question whether it is "safe" to climb the Matterhorn, Leslie Stephen, one of the great Alpinists, gave two answers of large semantic importance in 1871, long before the word appeared in the dictionary:

Statement 1. "There is no mountain in the Alps which cannot be climbed by a party of practised mountaineers with guides, in fine weather and under favorable conditions of the snow, with perfect safety."

Statement 2. "There is no mountain in the Alps which may not become excessively dangerous if the climbers are inexperienced, the guides incompetent, the weather bad and the snow unfavorable. . . . There are circumstances under which the Rigi is far more dangerous than the Matterhorn under others. Any mountain may pass from the top to the bottom of the scale of danger . . . in a day or sometimes in an hour."

Stephen gives us an unforgettable example of the perils of generalization. The "Matterhorn" in the morning is not the "Matterhorn" in the afternoon. A is not A. Matterhorn$_1$ is an easy jaunt for a woman climber; Matterhorn$_2$ is certain death for the best climber who ever lived.

Korzybski often used the simile of the map. A map of the territory, he says, useful as it may be to travelers, is not the territory. Similarly, language is not the world around us, but rather an indispensable guide to that world. The map, however, is worthless if it shows the traveler a structure different from the terrain he sets out upon. Structure in this context means order and relations, what comes after what. If the order of cities on our map does not agree with the order on the territory, we may find ourselves driving to Montreal when we hoped to go to Chicago.

However detailed the map may be, it can never tell *all* about the territory. Similarly, language cannot tell "all" about an event; some characteristics will always be omitted. At the end of every verbal definition, if it is pushed far enough, there are undefined terms; we reach the silent level where we can point, but we cannot say. If there is nothing to point to, the communication line may break. This is one reason why physicists were driven to devise operational definitions in contrast with verbal ones. They performed operations with their hands in order to clarify what they meant.

Korzybski places an apple on the table and asks us to describe it. We can say it is round, red, appetizing, with a short stem and one worm hole. But carefully as we may observe it, in the laboratory or out, we can never tell *all* the characteristics of the apple, especially as we approach the submicroscopic level. What all the billions of atoms are up to nobody knows except in the most general, statistical way.

Korzybski sets another apple beside the first, of similar shape and color. Is it identical? We are inclined to think so, but looking more closely we see that the stem is shorter, the red color is less vivid, and there are two worm holes instead of one. Apple$_2$ is not apple$_1$. By the same token, amoeba$_2$ is not amoeba$_1$; Adam$_2$ is not Adam$_1$. Nothing in nature is ever identical with anything else if the observations are carried far enough. Beware of false identifications, says Korzybski; you will only confuse yourself and your hearers. Beware of thinking of "Baptists," "Americans," "businessmen," "workers" as identical. Whatever characteristics they may have in common, they have others which are different.

An object is not even identical with itself. Apple₁ is a *process*, changing its characteristics imperceptibly in a minute, slightly in a day, drastically in a month. Nothing in nature is quite what it was a moment ago. Even the Matterhorn wears slowly away, as rock avalanches come down the couloirs. Diamonds last longer than apples, but not forever. Be careful of thinking of apples, diamonds, people, or nations as unchanging events. Said Korzybski:

> The only possible link between the *objective* world and the verbal world is *structural*. If the two structures are similar, then the empirical world becomes intelligible to us—we "understand," can adjust ourselves. . . . If the two structures are not similar . . . we do not "know," we do not "understand," the given problems are "unintelligible" to us . . . we do not know how to adjust ourselves.

Korzybski, as we have said, was profoundly influenced by the new language of science. Thermodynamics, he observed, could not have been built on such loose terms as "hot" and "cold"; a language showing minute quantitative changes and relations had to be developed—the calculus. Our languages are full of primitive metaphysical concepts, and the effect is like emery dust in a delicate machine. General Semantics seeks to substitute a good lubricant for the emery. "We usually have sense enough to fit our shoes to our feet, but not sense enough to revise older methods of orientation to fit the facts."

From Korzybski's introduction to the second edition of *Science and Sanity*, which summarized the main principles of General Semantics, I have drawn the following twenty-one propositions or statements, trying to make a fair and objective digest.

In any scientific endeavor we borrow foundations from those who have gone before—a part of the process of "time-binding." All the propositions put forth by Korzybski are built on groundwork laid by earlier scientists. Nobody makes completely original inventions nowadays. The first twelve statements now to be recited seem to me to rely heavily on the work of preceding scientists, while the last nine are more Korzybski's own. Certainly he developed them uniquely.

1. *No two events in nature are identical.* This proposition is accepted by modern scientists. It runs counter to the "is of

identity" in Indo-European languages, and to the "A is A" of formal logic.

2. *Nature works in dynamic processes.* Accepted by modern scientists and by some schools of philosophy. It disagrees with the linear, cause-and-effect structure of our language.

3. *Events flow into one another in nature by "insensible grada-tions."* Nature is all of a piece, though our language tends to separate it into classes.

4. *Nature is best understood in terms of structure, order, relation-ships.* Einstein helped to establish this through the principles of relativity. Indo-European languages, with substantives, entities, absolutes, are at odds with the proposition.

5. *Events in nature are four-dimensional.* Modern physicists think in terms of space-time. Indo-European languages are struc-tured for three dimensions, and those who speak them have great difficulty with the concept of time.

6. *Events have unlimited characteristics.* Our languages leave many of them out and thus often distort a judgment.

7. *There is no simultaneity in nature.* Western languages assume it as a matter of course.

8. *There are no abstract entities outside our heads.* But lan-guages may create verbal spooks which seem to be moving out there. My 100 respondents mostly thought of "Fascism" as an entity, a beast moving.

9. *Natural "laws" are at best only high probabilities.* Scientists are now pretty well committed to the probability theory. The structure of English, among other languages, favors absolute laws and eternal principles.

10. *Multi-valued logic is cardinal in understanding and explaining nature.* Indo-European languages tend to force us into two-valued thinking—the traps of either-or, black or white, "those who are not with us are against us."

11. *A word is not a thing but an artificial symbol.* This has long been known, but the language structure still objectifies words and encourages word magic, where the word takes precedence over the physical event.

12. *A fact is not an inference: an inference is not a value judgment.* The distinction is well known to the law, but not to the laity, and vast confusion results. The distinction may be illustrated by three statements:

    (A) This train is going at twenty miles an hour. *A fact.*
    (B) At this rate we'll be an hour late. *An inference.*
    (C) This lousy railroad is never on time! *A value judgment.*

Asked to define an event, most of us jump to the level of value judgment. A proper definition begins at the other end.

Now let me list the nine statements which seem more uniquely Korzybski's.

13. *A map is not the territory.* Our words are not nature, but their structures should correspond if we are to understand our world.

14. *The language of mathematics contains structures which correspond to the structure of nature.* Korzybski expected a crop of young geniuses in physics as a result of the new talk following Einstein—and sure enough, they appeared! Robert Oppenheimer was one of them.

15. *"Reality" is apperceived on three levels: macroscopic, microscopic, sub-microscopic.* This point is not unique with Korzybski, but his emphasis is unique.

16. *The systems of Aristotle, Euclid, and Newton are now special cases, and outmoded as general systems.* Korzybski does not hold that these three great men are wrong, only that their "laws" cover less territory than was formerly supposed.

17. *Extensional, or objective, thinking is clearer and more accurate than intensional, or thinking inside one's skull.* This is another way of saying "look outside," "Find the referent"—the latter a phrase which Korzybski did not like to use.

18. *At the end of all verbal behavior are undefined terms.* This is the point where the senses in eye and ear and skin must pick up the signs from nature. Korzybski has emphasized this "unspoken level" more forcefully than any other student.

19. *Language is self-reflexive.* It is possible to make a statement about a statement about a statement indefinitely. (No apologies to Gertrude Stein.)

20. *Man, alone among earth's creatures, "binds time";* that is, profits by the experience of past generations. Well-known and obvious long before Korzybski, but uniquely phrased by him. (Not included in his appendix directly.)

21. *The nervous system can be consciously reoriented to improve evaluation.* Science can restore sanity. Korzybski deeply believed this, titled his book as a result of it, but his proof is not conclusive. If the proposition turns out to be true it may add considerably to his stature. Delayed response, the use of warning signals, awareness of abstracting, and the rest, do improve evaluation without question. But does the use of General Semantics *retrain the whole nervous system,* so that improved evaluation becomes as automatic as the knee jerk? Psychiatrists are sceptical.

It seems plain that while General Semantics has made important contributions to the study of communication it has not seized the leadership. Compared with cultural anthropology, with linguistics, with the work of Claude Shannon on mathematical theories of communication, it is more a point of view than a rigorous scientific discipline.

Korzybski "brought together a useful way of thinking and talking about human thinking and talking," says Professor Irving J. Lee. "He had devised and explained the principles; he had not established a training-testing program with equal thoroughness." He inaugurated no clinic for practising his methods, no controlled experiments to validate them.

Korzybski was something of a prima donna, and he had a few unfortunate prejudices. He was overcritical of the work of others in his field. I felt the sting of this criticism from time to time, though I had done my best to make his work more widely known. Sometimes it seemed as if the originator of General Semantics were trying to set up a one-man philosophy in the great tradition, which would supersede the system of Aristotle, Aquinas, or Hegel. Yet the scientific method, upon which he mainly relied, is intolerant of one-man philosophies.

Despite the feelings of frustration engendered by parts of "Science and Sanity," the determined reader has in the end a rich reward. Doors which had been closed begin to open; the world takes on a new dimension. Among the semanticists who have been carrying on since Korzybski's death in 1950—Hayakawa, Lee, Rapoport, Chisholm, Kelley, to name a few—are objective scholars, shy of cults and revelations. They will succeed, I believe, in fusing General Semantics into the amalgam of the social sciences where it belongs, linked with all the other disciplines.

Meanwhile, I can testify that twenty years of exposure to General Semantics have demonstrated that the evaluation of men and events can be sharpened by its use, that certain mental blocks can be remedied, that one's writing can be clarified.

Students of General Semantics report a better ability to listen, a reduction in the terrors of stage fright, help in cases of stuttering. General Semantics can aid in teaching children to understand their world, and in bringing "backward" scholars up to mark. It has led to a healthy re-examination of verbal proof.

This is no small contribution for one person to make. We owe

Korzybski a good deal, not only for what he discovered or highlighted, but for the furor created by his personality. He lit fires, started controversies, caused people to examine what lay behind their terms, and so gave a much-needed impetus to the whole subject.

"What is the difference, Count Korzybski, between man and other living creatures?" he was sometimes asked. His eyes would gleam behind the great round spectacles and his deep voice with its rolling accent would reply: "A quar-rter-r- of an inch of cor-rtex."

The Language of Reports *

by S. I. HAYAKAWA

For the purposes of the interchange of information, the basic symbolic act is the *report* of what we have seen, heard, or felt: "There is a ditch on each side of the road." "You can get those at Smith's hardware store for $2.75." "There aren't any fish on that side of the lake, but there are on this side." Then there are reports of reports: "The longest waterfall in the world is Victoria Falls in Rhodesia." "The Battle of Hastings took place in 1066." "The papers say that there was a big smash-up on Highway 41 near Evansville." Reports adhere to the following rules: First, they are *capable of verification;* second, they *exclude,* as far as possible, *inferences* and *judgments.* (These terms will be defined later.)

Verifiability. Reports are verifiable. We may not always be able to verify them ourselves, since we cannot track down the evidence for every piece of history we know, nor can we all go to Evansville to see the remains of the smash-up before they are cleared away. But if we are roughly agreed on the names of things, on what constitutes a "foot," "yard," "bushel," and so on, and on how to measure time, there is relatively little danger of our misunderstanding each other. Even in a world such as we have today, in which everybody seem to be quarreling with everybody else, *we still to a surprising degree trust each other's reports.* We ask directions of total

* This excerpt is quoted by permission from *Language in Thought and Action* (New York: Harcourt, Brace & Co., 1949), pp. 28 ff. Dr. Hayakawa has taught at the University of Chicago and Illinois Tech; he is now Editor, *Etc., a Review of General Semantics,* and a lecturer in much demand on language, art, and jazz.

strangers when we are traveling. We follow directions on road signs without being suspicious of the people who put them up. We read books of information about science, mathematics, automotive engineering, travel, geography, the history of costume, and other such factual matters, and we usually assume that the author is doing his best to tell us as truly as he can what he knows. And we are safe in so assuming most of the time. With the emphasis that is being given today to the discussion of biased newspapers, propagandists, and the general untrustworthiness of many of the communications we receive, we are likely to forget that we still have an enormous amount of reliable information available and that deliberate misinformation, except in warfare, still is more the exception than the rule. The desire for self-preservation that compelled men to evolve means for the exchange of information also compels them to regard the giving of false information as profoundly reprehensible.

At its highest development, the language of reports is the language of science. By "highest development" we mean greatest general usefulness. Presbyterian and Catholic, workingman and capitalist, German and Englishman, *agree* on the meanings of such symbols as $2 \times 2 = 4$, 100° C., HNO_3, 3:35 A.M., 1940 A.D., 5000 r.p.m., 1000 kilowatts, *Pulex irritans,* and so on. But how, it may be asked, can there be agreement about even this much among people who are at each other's throats about practically everything else: political philosophies, ethical ideas, religious beliefs, and the survival of my business *versus* the survival of yours? The answer is that circumstances *compel men to agree,* whether they wish to or not. If, for example, there were a dozen different religious sects in the United States, each insisting on its own way of naming the time of the day and the days of the year, the mere necessity of having a dozen different calendars, a dozen different kinds of watches, and a dozen sets of schedules for business hours, trains, and radio programs, to say nothing of the effort that would be required for translating terms from one nomenclature to another, would make life as we know it impossible.*

* According to information supplied by the Association of American Railroads, "Before 1883 there were nearly 100 different time zones in the United States. It wasn't until November 18 of that year that . . . a system of standard time was adopted here and in Canada. Before then there was nothing but local or 'solar' time. . . . The Pennsylvania Railroad in the East used Philadelphia time, which was five minutes slower than New York time and five minutes faster than Baltimore time. The Baltimore & Ohio used Baltimore time for trains

The language of reports, then, including the more accurate reports of science, is "map" language, and because it gives us reasonably accurate representations of the "territory," it enables us to get work done. Such language may often be what is commonly termed "dull" or "uninteresting" reading: one does not usually read logarithmic tables or telephone directories for entertainment. But we could not get along without it. There are numberless occasions in the talking and writing we do in everyday life that *require that we state things in such a way that everybody will agree with our formulation.*

Inferences. The reader will find that practice in writing reports is a quick means of increasing his linguistic awareness. It is an exercise which will constantly provide him with his own examples of the principles of language and interpretation under discussion. The reports should be about first-hand experience—scenes the reader has witnessed himself, meetings and social events he has taken part in, people he knows well. They should be of such a nature that they can be verified and agreed upon. For the purpose of this exercise, inferences will be excluded.

Not that inferences are not important—we rely in everyday life and in science as much on *inferences* as on reports—in some areas of thought, for example, geology, paleontology, and nuclear physics, reports are the foundations, but inferences (and inferences upon inferences) are the main body of the science. An inference, as we shall use the term, is *a statement about the unknown made on the basis of the known.* We may *infer* from the handsomeness of a woman's clothes her wealth or social position; we may *infer* from the character of the ruins the origin of the fire that destroyed the building; we may *infer* from a man's calloused hands the nature of his occupation; we may *infer* from a senator's vote on an armaments bill his attitude toward Russia; we may *infer* from the structure of the land the path of a prehistoric glacier; we may *infer* from a halo

running out of Baltimore, Columbus time for Ohio, Vincennes (Indiana) time for those going out of Cincinnati. . . . When it was noon in Chicago, it was 12:31 in Pittsburgh; 12:24 in Cleveland; 12:17 in Toledo; 12:13 in Cincinnati; 12:09 in Louisville; 12:07 in Indianapolis; 11:50 in St. Louis; 11:48 in Dubuque; 11:39 in St. Paul, and 11:27 in Omaha. There were 27 local time zones in Michigan alone. . . . A person traveling from Eastport, Maine, to San Francisco, if he wanted always to have the right railroad time and get off at the right place, had to twist the hands of his watch 20 times en route." Chicago *Daily News*, September 29, 1948.

on an unexposed photographic plate that it has been in the vicinity
of radioactive materials; we may *infer* from the noise an engine
makes the condition of its connecting rods. Inferences may be care-
lessly or carefully made. They may be made on the basis of a great
background of previous experience with the subject-matter, or no
experience at all. For example, the inferences a good mechanic
can make about the internal condition of a motor by listening to it
are often startlingly accurate, while the inferences made by an
amateur (if he tries to make any) may be entirely wrong. But the
common characteristic of inferences is that they are statements about
matters which are not directly known, made on the basis of what
has been observed.

The avoidance of inferences in our suggested practice in report-
writing requires that we make no guesses as to what is going on in
other people's minds. When we say, "He was angry," we are not
reporting; we are making an inference from such observable facts
as the following: "He pounded his fist on the table; he swore; he
threw the telephone directory at his stenographer." In this particular example, the inference appears to be fairly safe; nevertheless,
it is important to remember, especially for the purposes of training
oneself, that it is an inference. Such expressions as "He thought a
lot of himself," "He was scared of girls," "He has an inferiority
complex," made on the basis of casual observation, and "What Russia
really wants to do is to establish a world communist dictatorship,"
made on the basis of casual newspaper reading, are highly inferential. One should keep in mind their inferential character and, in
our suggested exercises, should substitute for them such statements
as "He rarely spoke to subordinates in the plant," "I saw him at a
party, and he never danced except with one of the girls who asked
him to," "He wouldn't apply for the scholarship although I believe
he could have won it easily," and "The Russian delegation to the
United Nations has asked for A, B, and C. Last year they voted
against M and N, and voted for X and Y. On the basis of facts such
as these, the newspaper I read makes the inference that what Russia
really wants is to establish a world communist dictatorship. I tend
to agree."

Judgments. In our suggested writing exercise, judgments are also
to be excluded. By judgments, we shall mean *all expressions of
the writer's approval or disapproval of the occurrences, persons, or*

objects he is describing. For example, a report cannot say, "It was a wonderful car," but must say something like this: "It has been driven 50,000 miles and has never required any repairs." Again statements like "Jack lied to us" must be suppressed in favor of the more verifiable statement, "Jack told us he didn't have the keys to his car with him. However, when he pulled a handkerchief out of his pocket a few minutes later, a bunch of car keys fell out." Also a report may not say, "The senator was stubborn, defiant, and unco-operative," or "The senator courageously stood by his principles"; it must say instead, "The senator's vote was the only one against the bill."

Many people regard statements like the following as statements of "fact": "Jack *lied* to us," "Jerry is a *thief*," "Tommy is *clever*." As ordinarily employed, however, the word *"lied"* involves first an inference (that Jack knew otherwise and deliberately misstated the facts) and secondly a judgment (that the speaker disapproves of what he has inferred that Jack did). In the other two instances, we may substitute such expressions as, "Jerry was convicted of theft and served two years at Waupun," and "Tommy plays the violin, leads his class in school, and is captain of the debating team." After all, to say of a man that he is a "thief" is to say in effect, "He has stolen *and will steal again*"—which is more of a prediction than a report. Even to say, "He has stolen," is to make an inference (and simultaneously to pass a judgment) on an act about which there may be difference of opinion among those who have examined the evidence upon which the conviction was obtained. But to say that he was "convicted of theft" is to make a statement capable of being agreed upon through verification in court and prison records.

Scientific verifiability rests upon the external observation of facts, not upon the heaping up of judgments. If one person says, "Peter is a deadbeat," and another says, "I think so too," the statement has not been verified. In court cases, considerable trouble is sometimes caused by witnesses who cannot distinguish their judgments from the facts upon which those judgments are based. Cross-examinations under these circumstances go something like this:

WITNESS: That dirty double-crosser Jacobs ratted on me.

DEFENSE ATTORNEY: Your honor, I object.

JUDGE: Objection sustained. (Witness's remark is stricken from the record.) Now try to tell the court exactly what happened.

WITNESS: He doubled-crossed me, the dirty, lying rat!

DEFENSE ATTORNEY: Your honor, I object.

JUDGE: Objection sustained. (Witness's remark is again stricken from the record.) Will the witness try to stick to the facts.

WITNESS: But I'm telling you the facts, your honor. He did double-cross me.

This can continue indefinitely unless the cross-examiner exercises some ingenuity in order to get at the facts behind the judgment. To the witness it is a "fact" that he was "double-crossed." Often hours of patient questioning are required before the factual bases of the judgment are revealed.

Many words, of course, simultaneously convey a report and a judgment on the facts reported. For the purposes of a report as here defined, these should be avoided. Instead of "sneaked in," one might say "entered quietly"; instead of "politicians," "congress-men," or "aldermen," or "candidates for office"; instead of "bureau-crat," "public official"; instead of "tramp," "homeless unemployed"; instead of "dictatorial set-up," "centralized authority"; instead of "crackpots," "holders of uncommon views." A newspaper reporter, for example, is not permitted to write, "A crowd of suckers came to listen to Senator Smith last evening in that rickety firetrap and ex-dive that disfigures the south edge of town." Instead he says, "Be-tween seventy-five and a hundred people heard an address last evening by Senator Smith at the Evergreen Gardens near the South Side city limits."

Improve Your Vocabulary, But Keep Big Words in Their Place *

by GEORGE SUMMEY, JR.

You already know that without an adequate vocabulary you will miss a good deal of what you hear or read and be unable to put your communications into clear, easy, and vigorous English.

And of course you know that you have three overlapping vo-cabularies—one for speech, a larger one for writing, and a much larger recognition vocabulary for hearing and reading.

* Quoted by permission from C. W. Wilkinson, J. H. Menning, and C. R. Anderson, *Writing for Business* (Chicago: Richard D. Irwin, Inc., 1951), pp. 130 ff. George Summey, Jr., Professor of English at the Agricultural and Mechanical College of Texas, is best known for his significant book *American Punctuation* (New York: The Ronald Press Co., 1949).

Let's get two mistaken notions about personal vocabularies out of the way— (1) that an average college student knows only 5,000 or perhaps 10,000 words, and (2) the widely held but evil notion that by carefully heaping up and showing off a big stock of fine words, so many every day or week, you can make yourself a big man. That's a short way to make yourself look silly.

If you think you know only 5,000 words, you can get some idea of the range of your vocabulary by making a rough inventory of a few kinds of names you know—of persons living or dead, on the campus and elsewhere; of countries, states, cities, streets, and buildings; of foods and drinks; of things you wear; of sports and sports equipment; of birds, beasts, and plants; of articles on hardware counters; of machines and the materials they fabricate. If you write out some of these lists, leave plenty of room for additional names that will pop up in your mind. And of course you know pronouns, connective words, many adjectives and adverbs, and great numbers of verbs.

Popular estimates of personal vocabularies are much too low. The Danish linguist Otto Jespersen cites an estimate of the vocabulary familiar to Swedish peasants—26,000 words or more. And F. M. Gerlach (cited in George Philip Krapp's *Knowledge of English*) estimates that at the time of graduation, a college student should be in command of 100,000 words, more or less, not including names of persons in books or in real life, names of ships, slang expressions and colloquialisms, brands of goods, and other familiar terms. The result, Mr. Gerlach remarks, is "an indefinitely large, truly appalling, vocabulary."

In all probability your recognition vocabulary is astonishingly large. What you need to do is to improve your understanding of words you already know after a fashion and to add words as you need them for exact and lively expression.

Perhaps you have misunderstood what Johnson O'Connor had to say in his article "Vocabulary and Success"—a frequently quoted article that has been misquoted or misinterpreted by many who ought to know better. Mr. O'Connor tried a 150-word test of general reading vocabulary—not speech or writing vocabulary—on various classes of persons. Average numbers of errors were as follows: Major business executives, 7; college professors, 8; one thousand college students, 27; seven hundred college freshmen, 42. Department heads in manufacturing concerns scored about 15 errors, shop foremen about 27.

Mr. O'Connor's conclusions are (1) that "an exact and extensive vocabulary is an important concomitant of success," (2) that such a vocabulary can be acquired, and (3) that vocabulary "increases as long as an individual remains in school or college, but without conscious effort does not change materially thereafter."

What conclusions do you draw from Mr. O'Connor's findings? Is a big vocabulary the key to success? Or is it possible that success is the key to vocabulary? In particular, can you make yourself a big man by transferring unfamiliar words from your reading vocabulary to your speech and writing vocabularies? The test Mr. O'Connor used included *glabrous, polyglot,* and *refulgent.* Can you use any of these to advantage in your next letter or report? And what of the following words from one of the *Reader's Digest* tests ("It Pays to Increase Your Word Power")—*cajoling, auro, apocryphal, au fait, garniture, lucent, insouciance?* If you try some of these in your next business letter or report, you will startle your readers and look silly. The words will be like green patches on a blue suit.

A reasonable conclusion about the known relation between vocabulary and success is (1) that you can build a strong vocabulary only by alert and successful activity, and (2) that a strong vocabulary helps you succeed. Success and vocabulary work together.

If President Allen of the big ABC Manufacturing Corporation reached his high place on merit, the reasonable explanation is that he rose by knowing more than ordinary men about raw materials, machines, assembly lines, markets, and good ways of dealing with his fellow men. By alert attention to what he had to know and do, he learned facts and the big words that stood for these facts. And because he knew the meanings of his words and knew words for what he had to write or talk about, he was able to build up a strong and useful vocabulary. And no doubt he kept learning facts, relations of fact to fact, and words for these facts and relations long after he reached a good position and comfortable salary.

If you have the intelligence and will to master a useful and ready vocabulary, the following ways are open to you. If they are not easy, that is the way of life.

1. Most important: by mastering the facts and words you need to know as students of chemistry, accounting, or whatever

else, and the facts and words you need to know for the purposes of your personal and social life. By keen, vigorous, successful bodily and mental activity you can get firm possession of facts and ideas and of words that stand for them. If you are not willing to pay this price for words, do not expect to find any magical way of learning the words you need to know.

2. You can learn much, especially about the meanings of abstract terms such as *democracy, liberty, free enterprise,* and *Americanism* by paying good attention to well informed persons who talk sense, whether you are in a lecture room or sitting in on a conversation. And don't lose opportunities to ask good questions about words you need to know or know better. After a lecture by Norman Thomas at College Station, a student asked a good question—"Mr. Thomas, what is the difference between socialism and communism?" He got an answer that enlightened him and everyone else in the audience.

3. When you read, read with alert attention, and go to a dictionary for the meaning of key words you do not understand. But remember that the new words you learn in your reading may not be useful in your next letter or class paper. If they are needed, use them. If they are not certain to be clear to your readers, make them clear by definition or illustration.

4. When you write, and especially when you revise your first drafts, take pains to use exact and expressive words. "Use the right word," says Mark Twain, "and not its second cousin." The right word may be abstract or concrete, general or specific, according to circumstances. If you need a word that includes bonds, preferred and common stocks, mortgages, notes, and option warrants, the best word is *securities.* If you need to name only one type or a single issue, the best term may be *investment-grade preferred stocks* or *Union Pacific 4% noncumulative preferred.* The same principle applies to abstract and concrete words. *Market value* is a useful abstract term; but there are times when it is best to be concrete—"the price a bidder is willing to pay and an owner to take."

A glance at a list of synonyms in your dictionary may
help you find a better word when you are not satisfied with
a word you have written down. In the article *courage*, one
dictionary lists the synonyms *fearlessness, dauntlessness, in-
trepidity, fortitude, pluck, heroism, daring, hardihood, brav-
ery, valor*. The same dictionary lists under *inexorable* the
synonyms *relentless, unrelenting, implacable*, and refers the
reader to *inflexible*, under which the four synonyms are
explained.

5. Actively observe the ways of words in actual use—their
   meanings, their connotations, and their tone. Be especially
   careful of words that are often confused. *Official* and *officious* differ in denotation; an official notice is not officious,
   and the remarks of an officious person are not official. A
   three-ton truck is an *effective* carrier of a half-ton load but
   not *efficient*. *Negligent* homicide is not *negligible*, as you
   will learn if you run a red light tomorrow morning and
   kill somebody. *Essential* means more than *important*. *Residence* and *amity*—useful words in their place—are colder
   than *home* and *friendliness*. *Valor* is less likely to be useful
   in everyday speech or writing than *courage*, though *valor*
   is a useful word in an army commission.

6. Though meanings of words are determined by actual use
   and not by derivation, a study of word formation—in dictionary entries or elsewhere—will give you a better understanding of derivative words such as *atrophy, synthesis* and
   synthetic, antipathy, entomology, thermodynamics. And
   derivation will help you grasp the standard meanings of
   certain words that keep their derivative meanings—*entomology*, for example, *annihilate, decimate, literally*. (A
   person who is *literally frozen to death* should be buried.
   When you hear a woman use *literally* that way, just remember that it's a woman's privilege.)

By all means increase the range and improve the quality of your
vocabulary. But don't be fooled into dressing up your speech and
writing with bookish, unusual words. If an unusual word is required for accuracy, use it—with whatever explanation you need to
give your reader. But do not assume that a word you have learned

to recognize in reading—*legerdemain, hegemony, refulgent, verve, nuance, tenuous,* or *factitious*—will be useful in your writing.

Here are some reasons why you need to use plain wording—and sometimes to put your darling big word on the shelf:

1. Plain wording makes easy reading. A style overloaded with technical terms and strange derivatives will make heavy reading. A safe rule: Make your wording clear and simple. So far as you can without loss of accuracy, use familiar words. Plain writing can be strong and beautiful, as Shakespeare and Defoe well knew.

2. Plain wording lets the light through; fancy wording is often a camouflage for empty or silly matter. When you put thought into plain, familiar words, you will know whether you are talking sense or nonsense. Don't use stuffed-shirt language.

3. Plain wording, if accurate and expressive, is in good taste; fancy, pompous wording makes it appear that the writer is a big-wordy showoff—a Mr. Vocabulary Builder like foolish Sir Andrew Aguecheek in Shakespeare's *Twelfth Night.*

4. If you go in for unfamiliar words, you are in danger of making yourself ridiculous by confusing words you have only half learned. You cannot afford to say *flaunt* when you mean *flout, decimate* when you mean *annihilate* or *wipe out, cooperation* when you mean *corporation,* or *calvary* when you mean *cavalry.* Don't be a Mrs. Malaprop. If you don't know what she did with big words, skim through Sheridan's comedy *The Rivals.*

In order to make your wording clear and idiomatic and at the same time vigorous and lively, do not fail to make good use of three classes of words:

1. Lively verbs and adverbs such as *break, pull, strike, blow, apart, through, under,* and idiomatic verb-adverb combinations such as *hold on, hold off, hold out; blot out; wipe out; take off, take down, take after; put about, put aside, put away, put by, put down, put in, put off, put on, put out, put up.*

2. Self-explaining compounds. (Don't look for these in vocabulary tests. They are too easy on the reader.) Compare

the derivatives in the first column with the compounds in
the second column. The compounds are easier English.

premeditated killing	*cold-blooded* killing
exterminate, annihilate	*wipe out*
extinguish the fire	*put out* the fire
resuscitate	*bring to*
impetuous haste	*headlong* haste
natal day	*birthday*
intrepid fighters	*stouthearted* fighters
mellifluous orators	*honey-tongued* orators
pusillanimous	*weak-souled*

3. Nouns as modifiers of nouns, except when adjective forms
are customary, as in *Cuban cigars, Italian olive oil*. The
expressions in the second column are more idiomatic than
those in the first column.

original members	charter members
ecclesiastical property	church property
labial consonants	lip consonants
industrial sites	factory sites
pecuniary income	cash income
monetary value	cash value
piscatorial stories	fish stories
commercial loans	business loans
urban lots	city lots
literary words	book words
nocturnal predators	night prowlers

In your enterprise of improving your vocabularies for reading
and hearing, speech, and writing, keep the following facts in mind:
(1) That you already have a large vocabulary, which you can improve by learning better the facts represented by the symbols you
already know. (2) That words are worth adding to your writing
and speech vocabularies when they meet real needs—saying clearly
and accurately what you either cannot now say or cannot say well.
(3) That many of the words you need to recognize in reading are
not useful in your speech or writing, because they might leave your
readers puzzled. (4) That plain wording is honest and in good
taste, and much more readable than pompous, bookish, pretentious
wording. (5) Most important: that you learn words naturally and
put yourself in firm possession of them by alert, intelligent, success-

ful activity in reading and hearing, learning the facts you need to know, thinking out what you need to understand, talking sense in the clearest English you can command, and writing good sense in easy and accurate English that will be clear at sight—not to readers in general but to the readers for whom you are writing.

Chapter 15

STYLE: READINGS

People in Quandaries *

by WENDELL JOHNSON

The Basic Features of Science as Method. [We shall here] examine briefly some of the more "obvious"—but very important and not at all commonly employed—features of scientific method.

We may say, in briefest summary, that the method of science consists in (*a*) asking clear answerable questions in order to direct one's (*b*) observations, which are made in a calm and unprejudiced manner, and which are then (*c*) reported as accurately as possible and in such a way as to answer the questions that were asked to begin with, after which (*d*) any pertinent beliefs or assumptions that were held before the observations were made are revised in the light of the observations made and the answers obtained. Then more questions are asked in accordance with the newly revised notions, further observations made, new answers are arrived at, beliefs and assumptions are again revised, after which the whole process starts over again. In fact, it never stops. Science as method is continuous. All its conclusions are held subject to the further revision that new observations may require. It is a method of keeping one's information, beliefs, and theories up to date. It is, above all, a method of "changing one's mind"—sufficiently often.

Four main steps are indicated in this brief sketch of the scientific method. *Three of them are concerned primarily with the use of language:* the asking of the questions that guide the observations, the reporting of the observations so as to answer the questions, and

---

* By permission from *People in Quandaries* (New York: Harper & Bros., 1946). Dr. Johnson received his three degrees and has spent his teaching career at the State University of Iowa. His book from which this excerpt is taken is one of the classics of semantics.

the revising of beliefs or assumptions relevant to the answers obtained. The things which we seem most commonly to associate with scientific work, namely, the apparatus and the observational techniques, these make up but one of the steps—and this is one part of the whole procedure that can be managed more or less entirely by technicians or laboratory assistants, provided there is a scientist to tell them what techniques and what apparatus to use. The recording, tabulating, and writing up of the observations can also be done in many instances and for the most part by assistants capable of following fairly simple instructions. But nobody else can take the place of the scientist when it comes to framing the questions and the theoretical conclusions. That, above everything else, is his work as a scientist, and that is work that requires the ability to use language in a particularly effective way. *The language of science is the better part of the method of science.* Just so, *the language of sanity is the better part of sanity.*

Of this language there are two chief things to be said. It must be clear and it must be accurate or valid. Whether or not it is grammatically "correct" is of secondary importance; certainly one can write with grammatical "correctness" and yet fail to achieve either clarity or validity. Scientific language need not, but may, embody what the literary circle would call good style. At least, it is generally agreed that there are many fascinating scientific books. Incidentally, at least the first fifty pages or so of Einstein's little book entitled *Relativity* might well be recommended to high school and college students as a model of English composition.

The Language of Science and of Sanity. There is a cardinal principle in terms of which language is used scientifically: *It must be used meaningfully.* The statements made must refer directly or indirectly (by means of interrelated definitions) to something in the realm of experience. It is not enough that they refer to something for the speaker and that they also refer to something for the listener. What is required is that they refer to approximately the same thing for both the speaker and the listener. In speaking meaningfully one does not just communicate, one communicates something to someone. And the something communicated is not the words that are used, but whatever those words represent. The degree to which communication occurs depends precisely upon the degree to which the words represent the same thing for the listener that they do for the speaker. And the degree to which they do is an index of the clarity of the language employed—the clarity that is such a basic feature of scientific language. (It is to be understood, of course, that what is here being said holds for both spoken and written language.)

Clarity is so important in the language of science—which is to say, in the language of sanity—because clarity is a prerequisite to validity. It is to be considered that statements that "flow beautifully" and are grammatically superb may be also devoid of factual meaning, or meaningful but vague, or precise but invalid. Now, scientific statements—that is to say, statements that serve to make adequate adjustment probable—must be both clear and valid. They can be clear without having validity, but if they are unclear their validity cannot well be determined. They must then, first of all, be clear or factually meaningful; they must be that before the question of their validity can ever be raised. We ask "What do you mean?" before we ask, "How do you know?" Until we reach agreement as to precisely what a person is talking about, we cannot possibly reach agreement as to whether or in what degree his statements are true.

Only to the extent that those who hear a statement agree as to the specific conditions or observations required for ascertaining its validity can the question of its validity have meaning. And the extent to which they do agree in this sense is, of course, an indication of the extent to which the statement is clear or meaningful. If a statement is such that those who hear it do not agree at all as to how it might be verified or refuted, the statement may be "beautiful" or "eloquent," or grammatically irreproachable, but it is also, and above all, nonsense. It cannot be demonstrated to be valid or invalid, and is meaningful therefore, if at all, only to its author and to his psychiatrist. Otherwise it is mere noise, melodious and rhythmical, made up of more or less familiar words, perhaps, but taken altogether it is no more factually meaningful than the noise of a rattling steam radiator.

An example of such noise may be seen in the statement made by Dr. Pangloss in Voltaire's *Candide* that "this is the best of all possible worlds." Coming upon it as it stands, one would certainly have to do a considerable amount of inquiring in order to discover just what it is about. What, for example, does Voltaire's good Doctor represent by *this* world? Does he mean the world as he knows it, or "everybody's" world, or only as it is experienced by certain persons; or does he mean only part of the world as anyone might experience it? With the little word *is*, does he refer to the world as one finds it, or to its ultimate possibilities? Then, too, there are the spell-marks *best* and *possible* and *worlds*, to say nothing of *all*. It does not take much examination to see that the famous statement of Dr. Pangloss is hardly less noisy than Lewis Carroll's " 'Twas brillig and the slithy toves did gyre and gimble in the wabe." One may be pardoned for recalling, in this connection, the following which appeared in a 1939 Associated Press dispatch from Washington, D.C.: "Asked to interpret a statement in the President's message that the United States had no political involvements in Europe, Early [Secretary Stephen Early] replied that it meant exactly what it said."

Questions Without Answers. What has been said above concerning statements holds also, and with particular emphasis, for questions. In the meaningful use of language it is a cardinal rule that the *terminology of the question determines the terminology of the answer.* One cannot get a clear answer to a vague question. The language of science is particularly distinguished by the fact that it centers around well-stated questions. If there is one part of a scientific experiment that is more important than any other part, it is the framing of the question that the experiment is to answer. If it is stated vaguely, no experiment can answer it precisely. If the question is stated precisely, the means of answering it are clearly indicated. The specific observations needed, and the conditions under which they are to be made, are implied in the question itself. As someone has very aptly put it, a fool is one who knows all the answers but none of the questions.

Individuals who suffer from personality maladjustments are especially well characterized by the fuzziness of the question which they persistently ask themselves. What these individuals want, above everything else, are answers. What keeps them awake nights, what puts furrows in their brows and ulcers in their stomachs, is the fact that they cannot satisfactorily answer their own questions. They persistently stump themselves. Their failure to find the answers that would serve to relax them is not due primarily to their "stupidity," or to the general impenetrability of nature, as they commonly suppose. It is mainly due, instead, to the fact that they frame their questions in such a way that no amount of genius would enable them, or anyone else, to answer the questions. When maladjusted persons state their problems in the form of highly answerable—that is, clear and precise—questions, they frequently discover that their tensions are quickly and materially relieved. What they discover is simply that they knew the answers all the time; what they hadn't known was that those were the answers they were seeking. Their vague questions had obscured that fact.

On Absolute Measurement *

by N. ERNEST DORSEY and CHURCHILL EISENHART

Report. The work should be fully reported, so that the reader may know what was done, may have the means for forming an independent judgment of the work and for checking possible errors and omissions, and may have the worker's experience to build upon in case he himself should undertake a similar piece of work. The last is certainly a very important function of such a report, and should never be ignored.

The report should, of course, give a clear indication of the care with which search was made for sources of error, and of the thought that was given to it. Otherwise, one has no choice but to conclude either that no search was made, or that the author attached no special importance to it. In either case, the work is of little, if any, objective value; its acceptance can rest only on authority, on subjective grounds.

Data should be reported as fully as may be. But in every series of observations some are erratic, especially at the start. How should they be treated? Those that occur in the body of the work should certainly be reported as fully as if they were not erratic, and if the cause of the trouble is known, that should be explained.

Those that occur peculiarly at the beginning of the series, arising mainly from maladjustment and inexperience, furnish very valuable information regarding details of adjustment and manipulation that had escaped the foresight of the worker, and that might, therefore, readily escape the attention of the reader and of subsequent workers. In certain cases they give valuable information about unsuspected

* Excerpts quoted by permission from Dr. Eisenhart's selection (in *Scientific Monthly*, August, 1953) of material from Dr. Dorsey's classic "The Velocity of Light," *Transactions of the American Philosophical Society*, Vol. 34, pt. 1 (1944). Dr. Eisenhart is associated with the National Bureau of Standards.

sources of error. For such reasons, they should never be completely omitted. They need not always be given in full, but they should be given to such an extent and in such detail as will show the reader what they were like and how they were related to the pertinent conditions, and should be accompanied by such explanatory text as will show him how they were regarded by the worker, and how he contrived to remove the disturbing conditions.

In brief, the report should give the reader a perfectly candid account of the work, with such descriptions and explanations as may be necessary to convey the worker's own understanding and interpretation of it. Anything short of that is unfair to the writer as well as to the reader. Every indication that significant information has been omitted reduces the reader's confidence in the work.

It is the unquestioned privilege of the worker to say where the boundary lies between preliminary or trial determinations, made primarily for studying and adjusting the apparatus and procedures, and those that were expected to be correct. But he should give good reasons for placing that boundary where he does; and those preliminary determinations should be reported to the extent already indicated.

Furthermore, it is scarcely fair, to anyone concerned, to describe a series of determinations as "preliminary," thus implying, in accordance with common usage, that they are open to question, that they are merely preparatory for something better, and then, later on, to include that same series in the list of good, acceptable determinations. To do so, both confuses the reader and suggests to him that the use of the adjective "preliminary" may have been merely a face-saving device intended to justify the ignoring of that series in case it should be found to disagree uncomfortably with later ones.

Miscellaneous. To say that an observer's results are influenced by his preconceived opinion does not in the least imply that those results were not obtained and published in entire good faith. It is merely a recognition of the fact that it seems more profitable to seek for error when a result seems to be erroneous, than when it seems to be approximately correct. Thus reasons are found for discarding or modifying results that do violence to the preconceived opinion, while those that accord with it go untested. An observer who thinks that he knows approximately what he should find labors under a severe handicap. His result is almost certain to err in such a direction as to approach the expected value.

The size of this unconsciously introduced error is, obviously, severely limited by the experimenter's data, by the spread of his values. The smaller the spread, the smaller, in general, will be this error. The size will be much affected also by the circumstances of the work, and by the strength of the bias. If the work is strictly exploratory, its primary purpose being to find whether the procedure followed is at all workable, then only a low accuracy will be expected, and there will be no serious attempt to explain departures from the expected, even though the departures be great. Consequently, this error of bias may be entirely absent from such results. But if the worker is striving for accuracy, then departures from the expected will appear to him serious; and the stronger the bias, the more serious will they seem. He will seek to explain them; and that seeking will tend, in the manner already stated, to introduce an error. An error arising in this way will seldom be negligible, but in no case should one expect it to be great, the work being done in good faith.

❊   ❊   ❊

. . . published definitive values, with their accompanying limits of uncertainty, are not experimental data, but merely the author's inferences from such data. Inferences are always subject to question; they may be criticized, reexamined, and revised at any time.

❊   ❊   ❊

. . . it is every author's duty to publish amply sufficient primary data and information to enable a reader to form a just and independent estimate of the confidence that may be placed in the inferences that the author has drawn therefrom. If he does not, he is false to both his reader and himself, and his inferences should carry little weight, no matter how great his reputation may be. . . .

Indeed, values reported without such satisfactory supporting evidence have no objective value whatever, no matter how accurate they may happen to be. They rest solely on the authority of the reporter, who is never infallible.

Chapter 16

VISUAL AIDS: READINGS

Meaning in Space *

by LORING M. THOMPSON

Even though a picture is worth a thousand words, the invention
of printing gave a tremendous impetus to the use of written language. With the development of modern techniques for repro-
ducing illustrations and charts, the graphic language of pictures,
charts, and diagrams is now assuming greater prominence, as shown
by its current use both in popular literature and in scholarly publications. A full understanding of the graphic language and its
grammar should give us a greatly expanded capacity for expression,
insight, and reasoning.

Although charts and graphs are being used increasingly today,
the simple fundamentals which underlie their preparation and interpretation remain to be elucidated. Although these fundamentals
have very broad applications, they are so simple that they might
easily be taught in elementary schools.

The Graphic Context of Space. In spoken and written language
the meaning of words is determined by (*a*) their general definition
which is made more specific by (*b*) the context in which the words
are employed. The word "girl," for example, has different meanings
in "I'm going to take my girl to the movie," and "Our first girl was
born last month." The meaning of any particular word is modified
by the words which come before it and after it. In this respect the

* Quoted by permission from *Etc.: A Review of General Semantics*, Spring,
1951, pp. 193 ff. Loring M. Thompson wrote "Meaning in Space" while he was
a graduate student in the program of Education and Research in Planning,
University of Chicago. He was formerly a member of the department of engineering drawing, Northeastern University.

context of verbal language is "one-dimensional." The context of any word must come before or after it. It cannot be above or below as well as before or after, as is the case in the two-dimensional graphic language. Herein lies a distinction between verbal and graphic language.

By its very nature, the graphic language has a tremendous potential usefulness for dealing with both physical objects and abstract ideas. No one will contest the attractiveness and accuracy of a picture compared with a verbal description of a house, a horse, or a pretty girl. What remains to be recognized is that the same language is just as useful for communicating abstract relationships. It gives the thinker increased capacity for fruitful thinking in abstract realms. For example, the familiar organization chart of a business (Fig. 50) elucidates relationships that are not readily described in words. These relationships are not physical. They could not be photographed. Yet they are easily depicted in the graphic language.

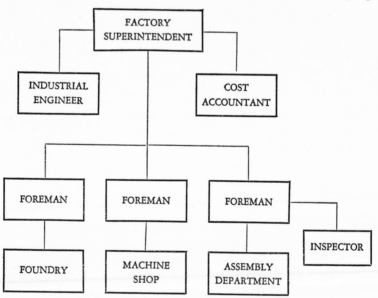

FIGURE 50. Typical Organization Chart. The relationships or structure of the organization in a manufacturing establishment are depicted by the spatial position of the boxes and the lines between them.

Significance of Spatial Positions. Although words are an important part of graphic charts, the words appear in a context of space rather than in a context of sentences. While most charts contain practically no verbs, the absence of verbs does not prevent charts from conveying ideas of existence and action. The verbs are replaced by the spatial relationships of the symbols on the chart. In the case of an organization chart these are the lines which indicate the flow of authority and information between the persons or departments named in the boxes.

The outstanding feature of the graphic language is that its context of two-dimensional space gives significance to the *position* of the symbols. Symbols appearing on a chart are interpreted according to the context that appears on all sides—above and below as well as before and after. On the organization chart in Fig. 50, the superintendent is placed above the foreman because he is responsible for supervising the foremen. Horizontally, the chart is arranged according to the flow of work through the shop, starting with the foundry and ending in the assembly department. The reason for placing the foundry foreman to the left is distinctly different from the reason for placing him in the lower part of the chart.

The utilization of the two dimensions of the graphic language may also be illustrated by the listing of people according to two

Technical Ability			
	Excellent	Good	Fair
Excellent		Green Hollingson	Talker Slapper
Good	Stanpipe Brooks Drury	Jones Collins Reed Taber	White
Fair	Hale Jenkins	Lowell	

FIGURE 51. Analysis of a Group of Persons from Two Different Viewpoints or Bases of Classification.

different bases of classification. Let us suppose that the salesmen of an engineering firm are classified in one list according to technical knowledge and in another list according to sociability. On the basis of technical ability, the members of the sales force rank as follows:

excellent—Brooks, Drury, Hale, Jenkins, and Stanpipe; good—Collins, Green, Jones, Hollingson, Lowell, Taber; fair—Slapper, Talker, and White. On the basis of sociability they rank as follows: excellent— Green, Hollingson, Slapper, and Talker; good—Brooks, Collins, Drury, Jones, Stanpipe, Reed, Taber, and White; fair—Hale, Jenkins, and Lowell.

In Fig. 51, the two "one-dimensional" lists are combined into a two-dimensional chart. One axis of the chart is the basis of classification used for the first list. The second axis of the chart is the basis of classification used for the second list. The chart makes it easier to select men for particular jobs requiring varying degrees of sociability and technical knowledge. The chart also presents a much clearer picture of these two characteristics of the sales force and the relations between these two characteristics.

The Grammar of Graphic Communication. What is the fundamental grammar of the graphic language? What rules should be followed for clarity and conciseness? Fortunately the important fundamentals of the graphic language are much more simple than the grammar of English and other verbal languages. The essential point in the grammar of charts is that on each chart the same consistent pattern for locating symbols be employed over the entire chart.

The fundamental graphic grammar is illustrated by Fig. 52 in which the caption, "Receipts," at the top of the second column applies to all the figures beneath it in the column. No number which describes receipts appears anywhere else on the table but in this column. Similarly, the year 1940 applies to all items on the first line of the table. Nothing occurring in 1940 appears anywhere else on the table except this first line.

Two bases of classification may be used on all two-dimensional tables and charts. On Fig. 52 the years listed on the left make up one basis of classification, a chronological basis. The two column headings make up the other basis of classification, the nature of the transaction—whether a receipt or expenditure. One basis of classification is set up horizontally and each of its designations applies to everything above or below it. The other basis is set up vertically and each of its designations applies to everything on the same level.

The scales on a numerical chart, such as Fig. 53, serve essentially the same function as the captions and stubs on a table. On Fig. 53, all points representing 1948 are placed directly above their number on the horizontal scale. Readers who are familiar with mathematical coordinate systems will recognize that these systems may be applied to charts with many types of symbols, giving symbols distinct meanings according to their location with respect to the coordinate system of a particular chart.

PER CAPITA RECEIPTS AND EXPENDITURES
Treasury Department
United States of America

Year	Receipts	Expenditures
1940	$ 41	$ 71
1941	57	104
1942	95	255
1943	162	584
1944	320	692
1945	333	719
1946	305	451
1947	300	295
1948	305	268

Source: Treasury Dept. Annual Statements

FIGURE 52. Numerical Table. The meaning of the numbers is interpreted according to their position in space rather than in the context of sentences.

Following the rules of their grammar outline above, all properly constructed charts and tables have a consistency of meaning for the positions of the component symbols. Sometimes this is defined by verbal or numerical scales as in Figs. 52 and 53. In other cases the scales are inferred by the reader. On the typical organization chart, as in Fig. 50, it is apparent that the chart was drawn in conformity with a theoretical vertical scale of authority running from top to bottom. If such a theoretical scale were not followed, an organization chart could become very confusing, as shown in Fig. 54.

We see then that the fundamental principle of graphic language is concerned with the significance of each part of the graphic area. This significance may be explicitly defined by numerical or verbal scales, or it may be apparent from the nature of the chart. In any event, the defined graphic area provides a context that gives each symbol greater meaning than it would have if used in a context of writing or conversation.

Increased Capacity of Language. With an understanding of graphic fundamentals we have greatly increased the capacity of our language. If there is any question about this point, translate into sentences all of the information contained in Figs. 50 and 52. Compare the sentences with the graphic representation from the standpoint of attractiveness, clarity, speed of comprehension, and ease of retention.

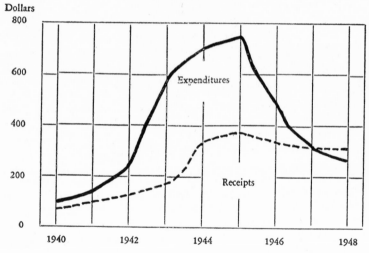

PER CAPITA RECEIPTS AND EXPENDITURES
Treasury Department
United States of America

FIGURE 53. Line Chart. As in organization charts and numerical tables, the spatial position of the symbols, lines in this instance, determines their significance.

In a world torn apart by conflicting relationships and viewpoints, graphic language should be a useful tool for dealing intelligently with current problems. By using the two dimensions of a chart we may consider simultaneously two different viewpoints or bases of classification. In both physical and social sciences we are becoming increasingly aware that the relations between things are more important than the things "in themselves." Indeed, Korzybski has said that relations and structure are the only content of knowledge.

Graphic language aids immensely in thinking about problems in structural terms.

Perhaps more important than the capacity of graphic language to facilitate communication is its capacity to facilitate insight and reasoning. Man visualized long before he verbalized. In comparison with visualization, verbalization is a more laborious process of translating ideas and relationships into a code of words and sentences. According to psychologists, a great deal of man's thinking is visual rather than verbal or at least a combination of the two.

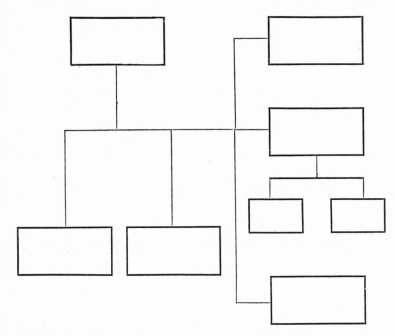

FIGURE 54. Confusing Pattern for an Organization Chart. Are the boxes on the right intended to be subordinate to the box in the upper left?

With an understanding of graphic language, the path is opened for more natural and direct thinking, even about the structure and relationships of abstract ideas. With the increased capacity of graphic language as a part of one's thinking, it naturally becomes the medium for personal understanding of complex matters and also the medium for initial insight leading to new fields of scientific knowledge.

EXPRESSION

Graphic	Oral	Written
Space	Pause	Paragraph
Size	Volume	Weight of type
Refinement of line	Enunciation	Italics

FIGURE 55. Verbal Table of a Comparison of Techniques of Communication. Are the various techniques simply applications of all-inclusive fundamental principles?

Figure 55 shows that three important forms of expression— graphic, oral and written—have certain elements in common. If this were not true, it would be just as sensible to place "enunciation" in the first line opposite "pause," for example. More rigorous proof of the common elements would be difficult to establish, but an

COMMUNICATION

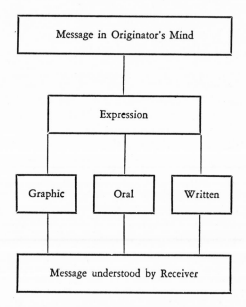

FIGURE 56. A Graphic Definition of Communication. Effectiveness of communication may be increased by the coordination of graphic, oral, and written expression.

initial insight of their possible existence is worth following up to see if any useful ideas may be associated with it.

If there are several different forms of expression which involve common elements, then the chances for effective communication of a message would be increased by the coordinated use of all channels of expression. Some persons may respond more readily to the graphic form of the message and others to the oral form. If the common elements in each form of expression have been applied successfully, then the different forms should be mutually reinforcing. In the cinema, for example, the tempo of the music reinforces the emotional climax of the plot. In an ordinary conversation, a person's gestures should be in keeping with his words. If they are not, then a personality disturbance may be indicated. Although some artists scorn the use of words to elucidate and reinforce the message of their paintings, teachers find they must provide both verbal and graphic explanation so that students may achieve a greater appreciation of the artist and comprehend his message. The concept of coordinated expression for effective communication is expressed graphically in Fig. 56.

The Problem of Language. Of course, graphic language, like all others, has its limitations. At best, language is only a link between the reality of the outside world and the concepts or thoughts in people's minds. Students of semantics have pointed out that strong emotional reactions are often caused by words alone. In many cases an emotional blockage may be minimized by greater use of graphic language. For the representation of physical objects, the structure of the picture-symbol bears some resemblance to the object being portrayed—the shape and proportions of the picture are similar to those of the object—whereas verbal representation is entirely abstract and symbolic. To a lesser degree, the use of spatial axes clarifies abstract relationships and avoids some of the dangers and difficulties in bridging the gap between symbols and reality.

For improved understanding, there should be an alignment between (*a*) outside things and events, (*b*) the language used, and (*c*) a person's evaluations of things and events. To insure understanding and rapport between two people, both of them should have the same alignment, as indicated in Fig. 57. Absence of this double alignment readily leads to confusion. People often regret

that they have said one thing when they meant another. Current
diplomatic negotiations have indicated that words of agreement
do not necessarily mean agreement on basic definitions or action.
Witness the various interpretations placed on "democracy." There

THING OR EVENT		?
SYMBOL	TREE	DEMOCRACY
THOUGHT OR CONCEPT		?

FIGURE 57. A Graphic Portrayal of the Problem of Language of Bridging
the Gap Between Things and Thoughts. It is difficult enough to achieve this
rapport with respect to simple physical objects, let alone abstract ideas such as
democracy, justice, and so forth.

is no magic language that can bridge the gap between things,
symbols, and thoughts. This paragraph has attempted to define
the problem more clearly by coordinated use of graphic and written language.

One of the limitations of graphic language is the difficulty of
using more than the two-dimensional context of a flat page in order
to include a greater number of viewpoints on the same chart. This
difficulty is not insurmountable from a technical standpoint since
there is no theoretical limit to the number of axes which may be
conceived mathematically. Techniques have been devised for showing on flat pages maps of three-dimensional mountains. Similar
techniques may be employed for the graphic portrayal of the rela-

tionship and structure of abstract ideas but with some sacrifice of popular appeal and clarity. Nevertheless, the joint study of mathematics and graphic representation promises to increase the effectiveness of everyday language for both thinking and communication.

Illustrating the Technical Presentation *

by Thomas S. Michener, Jr.

Although most scientific reports are not primarily planned to produce attractive pages in a publication, some well illustrated reports approach this result.

Usually this effectiveness does not occur by chance, but is produced by carefully prepared, adequate illustrations. This paper is intended to assist authors who wish to improve their reports by learning to plan and produce better technical illustrations.

The achievement of a coordinated, illustrated report requires more than haphazardly tracing curves from the experimenter's notebook. Each chart or illustration that is to serve as an interesting focus in the text, as well as an aid to understanding, must receive ample consideration. To be most useful, the illustration must show data in ways that give the reader an instant comprehension of the subject.

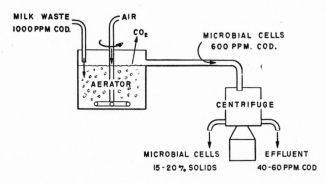

FIGURE 58. Good Diagram of a Process.

* Quoted by permission from *Journal of Chemical Education*, June, 1954, p. 318. Thomas S. Michener, Jr., is associated with Eastern Regional Research Laboratory, Philadelphia, Pa., one of the laboratories of the Bureau of Agricultural and Industrial Chemistry, Agricultural Research Administration, U.S. Dept. of Agriculture.

Since illustrations are usually conceived when the author is concentrating on writing his manuscript, they may easily fail to receive proper attention. Therefore it is suggested that as the first step toward good charts and graphs the author give more thought to their selection, content, and form.

Selection. How can the data be illustrated to best advantage? The answer to this question depends entirely on the subject of the report. The author should examine his data carefully and make a preliminary selection of items for possible illustration. He should then review this list to eliminate repetition but still be sure the subject is covered. An attempt should be made to provide the most interesting illustration for the most important part of the topic. Since each illustration is placed close to its reference in the text, the sequence of the illustrations will follow the progress of the work being reported. In some cases, the effort to provide good continuity in the illustrations may suggest changes in the arrangement of the text. If a change will produce a clearer exposition or greater emphasis, it should be made. Illustrations and text should combine to give a clear, unified statement.

Form and Content. Careful consideration should be given to the form and content of each drawing. To select the best form, the author needs to be familiar with the different types of drawings and their proper usage. The type of illustration most frequently used is the graph with a continuous curve showing the relationship of variables. This type of illustration is easily understood by the reader and when properly prepared is generally pictorially satisfying.

The continuous curve should not be used to illustrate periodic data. It gives the reader an erroneous idea of continuity of relationship that does not exist. The proper form of illustration for showing static values is the bar graph. Bar graphs may show more than one set of values, each series being identified by its particular cross-hatching. The bars may also consist of rows of symbols, such as silhouette drawings or dollar marks, which identify them.

It is suggested that some form of "pie" chart be used when the data show the relative parts of a whole. This easily constructed diagram does not appear as frequently as it might. Because the eye is able to compare both the area and central angle of one sector with any of the others in the chart, the reader easily grasps and retains the relative proportion of the parts demonstrated this way.

Drawings of apparatus and equipment also require considerable thought. There is a distinct difference between working drawings and illustrations. Working drawings should never be published with reports, since the many details required for correct manufacture of the equipment are not needed by the reader. The drawing that illustrates equipment or apparatus for a report must be made as simple as possible; all details except those to which the text refers should be eliminated. Illustrations of technical apparatus should be clear, well proportioned, and labeled with the names or functions of the parts. There should be no crowded or confusing areas on the drawing.

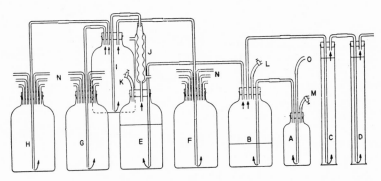

Figure 59. Confusing Diagram.

Figure 58 illustrates a good diagram of a process; it is simple, direct, and easy to understand. Figure 59 gives an example of the confusion caused by including too many details.

In attempting to work out the details of any illustration, it should always be borne in mind that there is a limit to the material that may be included in one drawing. This limit may be understood if the author assumes that some of his readers or audience are unfamiliar with the data. This unfamiliarity requires that complicated ideas should be explained in small, easily understood steps. If the author fails to recognize and stay within the bounds of assimilable illustrations, his readers or listeners will miss important points and lose interest. Crowded drawings may easily confuse the subject rather than clarify it. Furthermore, the author will find that limiting the quantity of data will simplify making the drawing.

Lantern Slides. When a lantern slide is to be made, it is recommended that the drawing be made to fit the size and shape of a slide opening. Fortunately, prepared commercial slide masks are made with openings of many shapes and sizes, so that this is not difficult. It should be pointed out, however, that only the large openings having a greater width than height use the screen space efficiently when projected. The table gives dimensions of the openings in some of the more frequently used slide sizes.

SUGGESTED SIZES OF DRAWINGS FOR LANTERN SLIDE OPENINGS

Lantern Slide Opening		Drawing	
Width, inches	Height, inches	Width, inches	Height, inches
2¾	2¼	9¾	8
3	2¾	8¾	8
3	1¾	10½	6⅛
2¾	2⅞	8	8⅜
2¼	2¾	8	9¾

Instead of allowing the photographer who makes the slide to choose the mask opening to fit the drawing, it would be better for the author to plan the drawing proportion to fit a definite slide opening. The most satisfactory arrangement is for the author to select a slide opening and make the drawing three to four times larger. If the drawing is made larger than this, it will be more difficult to gage the proper thickness of lines and size of the lettering. If it is smaller, the inevitable imperfections in drafting will be greatly magnified when the slide is shown on the screen. Another advantage to be found in using a drawing three to four times the size of the slide is that it fits a standard letter-size sheet of paper. The drawing sizes in the table, which are between three and four times the size of the slide, all fit the standard letter-size paper. All numbers, captions and clear space for a border should be included within these dimensions.

SELECTING SCALES FOR GRAPHS. When the drawing for a slide is to consist of a graph containing one or more curves, the scale for the ordinate and abscissa should be carefully selected to make the size of the significant data as large as possible. It would be good practice to plot the data first as a rough draft on any graph paper available. If the first plotting does not produce a satisfactory graph, a larger or smaller scale may be tried for one or both of the coordinates to improve the appearance, increase the legibility, and produce proportions that will fit the slide opening. It almost invariably helps at this stage to consult the draftsman who is to make the finished drawing. When the graph seems to be suitable for the final drawing, it would be well to ask a few questions about the appearance of the sketch. For instance, will the data fill the available space effectively? Will there be ample space for proper line thickness and lettering? Will the slide be too crowded for instant comprehension by an audience whose attention may be diverted by normal auditorium noises?

In "Aids to Technical Writing," Jordan and Edwards (1) state: "It is recommended that a single slide contain not more than 20 words, including the title, and present only one idea." They also make the following statement about this type of chart: "If curves presented on charts are not of the same slope and family, it is recommended that, for clarity, not more than three curves be shown on a single slide."

Figure 60 demonstrates the effects of overcrowding. The different angles of slope and the crossing of the curves cause confusion. Figure 61 shows the maximum number of curves that should be drawn on one chart, even though they all be similar.

In regard to the use of tabular data for slides, Jordan and Edwards state: "The use of tables should be avoided wherever possible in oral presentation of scientific data. . . . Detailed tables are impossible to comprehend when flashed on the screen for a short period of time. Furthermore, it is generally found that only a few of the values presented in the tables are actually discussed by the speaker, and little, if any, reference is made to the remaining material." If the author is inclined to use several tables for slides, he should suspect that he has not given enough thought to the audience's reception of his material. He may be trying to give too many data without proper predigestion and selection. If the information can be converted to a graphic illustration, the audience will be able to understand it more quickly and more thoroughly. Tables should be used only if there is no way to illustrate the material by means of a graph or chart. If tables are necessary, no more than 16 items should be included, each word or three-digit number being counted as an item.

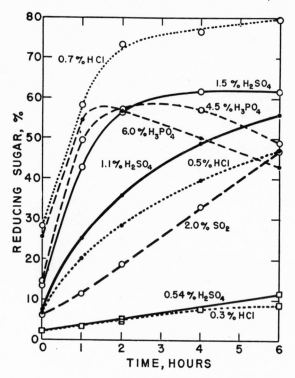

FIGURE 60. Overcrowded Chart.

LINES FOR LETTERING. Another difficulty often encountered by
the technical author—selecting the size of the lettering and thickness of lines—can easily be overcome by planning slide drawings
for the sheet sizes recommended in the table. Jordan and Edwards
(1) show that if the drawing is made approximately three times the
size of a proposed slide, the minimum size of the lettering should
be that produced by No. 140 lettering guide (Wrico or Leroy) and
the minimum line thickness on the drawing should be 0.008 inch
(or 0.2 mm.) for background grid, guide, and dimension lines.
When an open-background chart is used, the scale-division marks
along the border should be approximately twice this thickness.
Border lines and letter strokes should be heavier still, and the curves,
which are the most important feature of the chart, should be thick-
est of all (not less than 0.03 inch or 0.75 mm.). Uniformity of
thickness of the lines throughout their length is important in work

that is to be reproduced photographically; thin spots may fail altogether.

MAKING THE FINISHED DRAWING. If the author is making his own finished drawings, he would do well to observe the precautions listed below. He may also find them useful when checking the work of others.

(*a*) Restrict the number of scale division marks or background grid lines to the few needed for approximate readings only. Interested persons will no doubt request copies of the numerical data.

(*b*) Grid rulings should not run through lettering or data symbols, but may cross curves without interruption.

(*c*) Use simple, easy-to-reproduce data points. The simplest is an open circle having an outside diameter three to four times the thickness of the curve. Its line thickness should be one-third to one-half the thickness of the curve. Use, in the following order, the solid round dot (two and one-half times the curve thickness), the open square, and the open triangle. The square and triangle should fit in a circle five to six times the thickness of the curve, and their lines should have the same thickness as the open circle.

(*d*) When curves represent experimental results, it is good practice to include the points on the drawing.

(*e*) When data points cause crowding or confusion, omit some of them. The important feature of the drawing from the reader's point of view is the curve, not the points.

(*f*) In general, use solid lines for curves. However, variations in the type of line used for curves on the same chart give more positive differentiation than do varied data points. If lines are varied, use, in the following order, the solid line, then lines consisting of long dashes, short dashes, dots, and alternating dots and dashes.

(*g*) Maintain uniformity of symbols and lines throughout the series of drawings.

(*h*) Identify all curves, parts of apparatus, processes, and materials by adjacent horizontal labels, placed so that there can be no mistake about the label that applies to the item. If necessary, use arrows to tie the label to the item. Labels should be brief, not more than two long words or three short ones.

(*i*) Mark coordinates at the left and along the bottom. The American Standards Association (*2*) recommends that the dependent variable be placed vertically along the ordinate, and the independent data across the abscissa, from left to right. The captions for these numerical values should be given in plain vertical letters and should state what is measured or represented, followed by the unit of measurement (for example: TIME, HOURS). A simple system of numbering, consisting of multiples of 5 or 10, should be used.

(*j*) On drawings of apparatus or equipment, include dimensions or other means of establishing the scale.

(*k*) In lettering the drawing, leave a space between the letters at least twice the thickness of the letter stroke. Between words and between lines use a space equal to or greater than the height of the letters. It is the white, open space around the letters or symbols that makes them legible.

Some of these suggestions were taken from the American Standards Association (2); others are the result of personal experience. The list could be amplified with many more "do's" and "don't's," but the items omitted will be taken care of by good drafting practice and common sense. It should be emphasized that the author is always responsible for accuracy regardless of who prepares the drawing.

TYPEWRITER SLIDES. A typewriter may be used for lettering drawings for slides when other means are unavailable, if the size of the drawing is proportioned to fit the smaller lettering. "Radio-Mats" can also be used. These devices, made of cardboard and cellophane, produce legible slides when used for typewritten material. The space available for typing limits the words and numbers that can be included. Typed lettering on "Radio-Mats" will usually project legibly, but graphs or other drawings are beyond their limitations. It is better to draw directly on the window with India ink, although this cannot be expected to adhere very long.

When prepared devices are not available and slides are required urgently, it is also possible to use cellophane or other clear sheeting in the same way that "Radio-Mats" are used. Typing can be made to adhere if carbon paper is placed in the typewriter so that both sides of the slide will receive the impression. J. L. Wilson (3) also suggests cardboard stiffening masks for this type of work.

When the minimum sizes of lettering recommended by Jordan and Edwards (1) are used, the maximum drawing size should be

2.1 times the slide opening for pica type and 1.9 times for elite type (the usual large and small typewriter types). These measurements will give rectangles within which to work, including all drawings, typing, and borders.

When the lettering is done by typewriter, sharp results can be obtained by using a new ribbon and a good grade of glossy, white paper. Do not try to erase mistakes; it cannot be done easily and is rarely successful. Alterations should be made by typing the correction on a separate piece of paper and cementing it in place with rubber cement.

CHECKING THE SLIDE. A simple way to determine whether a slide will project well is to inspect it from a distance of 20 inches. If all parts can be distinguished easily when it is held toward a well-lighted, light-colored surface, it will project satisfactorily. Similarly, if a drawing three times the size of the finished slide can be read easily at three times 20 inches, a well made slide from this drawing will also be satisfactory.

Drawings for Publication. When an author is planning to publish an illustrated manuscript in a technical publication, he should first examine several copies of the periodical. He should notice the details of the illustrations, keeping in mind that the drawings have been photographically reduced to conserve space and make the cut fit the width of the column. In technical periodicals the column may be from 2⅛ to 6 inches wide. The difference between the width of the proposed drawing and the column width will determine the amount of reduction the drawing will require. Unlike drawings for slides, drawings for publication may have an elastic vertical dimension. The vertical size of illustrations may be expanded or compressed to emphasize some aspect of the data or reduce its importance with respect to horizontal components. Careful consideration and consultation at this time with the draftsman or other authors often result in changes that improve the visual impact of the data or make rapid comprehension easier for the reader.

Another difference between drawings for publication and those for slides is the amount of reduction required for good results. Drawings for slides should allow enough reduction to reduce imperfections so that they will not be noticeable when greatly enlarged on a screen. Drawings for publication, however, need only moderate reduction. If it were not for the difficulty of drawing thin lines and microscopic lettering, these drawings could be prepared for exact-size reproduction.

To avoid some of the difficulties in drafting, it is recommended that drawings for publication be planned to allow a reduction in width of one-third to two-thirds. This reduction requires that the

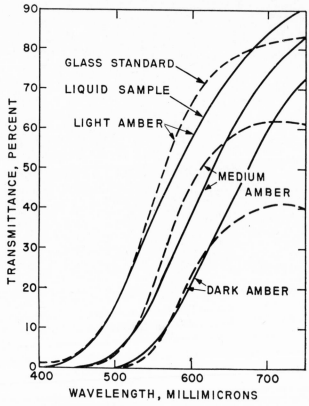

FIGURE 61. Maximum Material for a Chart.

width of the drawing be one and one-half to three times the width of the finished cut. The height of the drawing should then be planned to show the data to advantage but not waste space. It would be well at this time to consider the proportions of rectangular drawings. To avoid awkward rectangles, Hambidge (4) suggested the use of one of the following ratios: 1.414 to 1.0, 1.732 to 1.0, 1.0 to 1.0, 2.0 to 1.0, and 2.236 to 1.0. These ratios are based on measurements of many buildings and art objects.

Lines and lettering should next receive attention. Since in a finished cut lines thinner than 0.006 inch may fail to reproduce properly in spots, it would appear advisable to use this as a minimum and determine the thickness of lines on the drawing by means

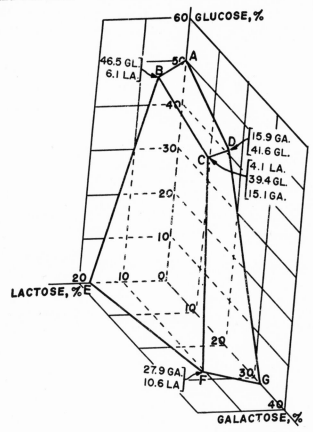

Figure 62. Dimetric Illustration of Three-Dimensional Data.

of the ratio of width of drawing to width of cut. Other lines should be proportionately thicker as described under drawings for slides.

To be legible, lettering on a finished cut should never be less than $\frac{1}{16}$ inch high. The minimum size of lettering on the drawing can be determined by using the ratio indicated above. Lettering should be plain and neatly spaced. In general, to provide interest and contrast with the grey body of text, the lines and lettering should be larger and heavier than the minimum recommended.

SHEET SIZE. It cannot be too strongly emphasized that drawings both for slides and publication should be made on letter-size sheets. Drawings smaller than the standard 8 by 10½ inches or 8½ by 11 inches may be easily lost, because envelopes and filing cabinets are made for this size sheet. Drawings larger than letter size cause great inconvenience, because they require folding or rolling to be mailed or stored. If larger drawings are necessary, they should be in multiples of this size.

Reader Interest. At some point in the process of illustrating his manuscript, the author might well think about the effect his drawings will have on the reader or audience. A report may be remembered for either of two reasons—because of interest in the subject or because it is presented in an unusual way. Compare the average scientific report with articles in technical periodicals intended for the general public. Much of the effectiveness of the latter is a result of dramatic illustrations.

Has anyone tried publishing a technical report that contains nothing but illustrations, their captions, the summary, and the bibliography? Possibly a time may come when words will be accessory to illustrations in the technical field, as in today's pictorial newsmagazines. Many readers will recall attending excellent seminar lectures that consisted entirely of slides with a brief discourse about each. Usually, however, this proportion of words to illustrations is not retained when the report is published.

For an exposition of a way to reduce statistics to a striking image-language story on a chart, the reader is referred to "How to Use Pictorial Statistics," by Rudolf Modley (5). Basic rules are given for the production of striking charts. The author emphasizes that considerable study is needed to present statistics with the strongest graphic effect, but states that it is well worth the effort.

The type of drawing can of itself stimulate the reader's interest. The drawings easiest to comprehend are the isometric, dimetric, and perspective projections with parts "exploded" or cut away to show the hidden details. Plastic drawing guides and special, perspective sketch books are now available for making these drawings, including the ellipses of many shapes and sizes needed for this work. These systems can be extremely effective when used for flow diagrams and equipment illustrations. Figure 62 shows an unusual dimetric chart that illustrates data with three variables.

Color can be used on lantern slides to make them attractive and to help distinguish the parts. An easy method is to have the chart reproduced as a negative of the correct size for a slide, and then color the separate curves or bars with photographer's transparent water colors. This kind of work will probably be confined to slides, because few journals are equipped for profuse color printing.

Eye-catching devices such as these can make a scientific report stand out from the average hard-to-read treatise. Many authors will no doubt conceive still other methods of enriching their reports.

Literature Cited.

(1) JORDAN, R. C., and M. J. EDWARDS, "Aids to Technical Writing," Minn. Engin. Expt. Sta. Bul. 21, 1944.

(2) AMERICAN STANDARDS ASSOCIATION, "Engineering and Scientific Charts for Lantern Slides," Standard No. Z15.1, New York, 1932.

(3) WILSON, J. L., J. Chem. Educ., 8, 2212 (1931).

(4) HAMBIDGE, J., *Elements of Dynamic Symmetry*, Brentano's, New York, 1926, pp. 17 ff.

(5) MODLEY, R., *How to Use Pictorial Statistics*, Harper & Bros., New York, 1937.

Top-Level Sales Communications *

by JAMES K. BLAKE

A truism that has come to mean more and more to sales executives is that the primary function of a report is to communicate something. A second truism that haunts the sales vice-president with an overloaded brief case is that an executive is only as good as his sources of information. To those, add a third. A man can only absorb and act upon a limited quantity of facts in a given time. Then, balance all three against the undeniable fact that effective sales management *must* work with more tools and more company departments (as well as outside consultants) than ever before and you end up with some of the reasons why companies are streamlining their reporting procedures. Their objective: more information in more usable form—faster!

For some general idea of the changes that are taking place and the tightening up processes that are going on, take a look at the Lukens Steel Company. Says Market Development Manager

* Abridged by permission from *Dun's Review and Modern Industry*, January, 1954. James K. Blake is Marketing Editor of the magazine.

Faunce, "If we are to influence the flow of goods, we must know all the factors of competition, the bases of product acceptance, the channels of distribution, the alignment of promotion effort and services that accompany these services."

Commercial Research Manager Aires points out it's not enough to know your own costs and methods. He explains, "By analysis of our customer's industry we can help the fabricator aim his sales activities. We can show him where *his* markets are going. We're spending roughly 50 per cent of our commercial research time helping customers find and develop their markets. The key to our part of the steel business is better service and this means that, somehow, we've got to put money in the customer's pocket."

For Sales Vice-President Wiese, the progressive shift in marketing approach meant a heavier stream of factual reports and a new flood of purely qualitative information that had to be evaluated and acted upon. It was apparent that some type of reporting method would have to be developed to bring the dozens of separate, though interrelated, facts together to give them perspective and focus.

The first job was to streamline the commercial research department and to open up the chain of communications so that all market facts would flow to one source. One of the first discoveries was that their fund of external marketing data was incomplete for some industries. Another was that, and this is not unusual, many facts that should have been flowing to sales management were compactly stored in the heads and files of other management personnel. And, again a typical experience, many of the management repositories were unaware that other executives were in need of the facts they, themselves, took for granted.

An important offshoot of this development is the recent creation of what Lukens calls its "Market Facts Board." The board is a large panel about eight by eleven feet which will hold up to 60 charts. On it, plotted for trends, is most of the operating information that sales management needs to know. The significance of the board is reflected in its heavy use by the top sales team. Actually, little information is charted that was not available somewhere in some form in the company before, but the fact that it is now collected and presented clearly in one place makes it seem, as one executive said, "as though I'm looking at different facts."

In a sense he is, because the addition of visual aids here results in clearer communication of shifting, complex relationships. Backstopping the faster communication of facts to sales and other Lukens' executives is the commercial research department which schedules thirteen meetings a year to brief management and interpret trends in terms of external (national) as well as internal (company) movements.

Aside from these periodic briefings, the Market Facts Board is always available for all executives. Lukens keeps it in Marketman Faunce's office for refresher purposes and the pipe-line to commercial research for additional views is kept open. As the significance of speed in the transmission of fact becomes more evident —as it has already in sales management's improved grasp of the total picture—new ways are being found to hurry up the evaluation of raw data. Recently, for example, most of Lukens' major customers were recoded on IBM cards in terms of their major markets, total sales, and so on. As a result, Lukens' sales management now get a quicker, better picture of its markets and also saw a solid promotional tool in the making. Result: A quarterly letter now goes to Lukens' customers discussing market trends in the customer's industry and in the *customer's* markets!

In Chicago a similar problem resulted recently in a somewhat similar solution. The Admiral Corporation last summer developed a centralized report room to service its sales executives. Admiral's basic dilemma is typical of many firms. Every month and every week literally tens of thousands of market facts come flooding in ("Distributor A moved fourteen units of Model X during such and such a period"). No executive can review and analyze them all. He'd have no time to be an executive. And if he did study them all, he'd have wasted most of his time anyway because he would not have enough time left to do anything about most of them.

Admiral's answer is a "Sales Intelligence Room" which shows carefully summarized results on wall charts arranged at eye level. They're easy to prepare and easy to read and they leave the center of the room free for action-planning conferences. They are instantly available for reference.

With a system of tabular reports (the conventional type), there would be a choice between a delayed final report and a series of incomplete interim reports. Now charts begin to change as soon as the first statistics are received and analysis and planning can start without delay.

Eastman Kodak's vice-president in charge of sales and advertising, James E. McGhee, says of the written reports he reads: "What

I see is a part of a steady flow." As the reports move into McGhee's office from the accounting and treasurer's office, many of them via the chief statistician's branch, any break in an orderly trend is easily spotted and the telephone usually brings the answers. Vice-President McGhee points out that he can hardly be out of touch with production and inventory developments because two or three times each day he runs into or has lunch (only once per day) with executives responsible for those areas.

Beyond the daily reports, however, EK has developed a system designed to take many of the headaches out of its sensitively seasonal business. Once each month Mr. McGhee attends a series of meetings. The purpose of these sessions is to put meat on the bones of the daily and weekly reports, through additional interpretation and group discussion, and to facilitate coordination of production and sales planning. Whereas the weekly reports show sales by products, branches, and distributors in almost traditional fashion with the usual breakdowns and comparisons with past periods, the monthly seminars are patterned to help sales and production management plan for the immediate and long-range future.

The reports as presented in these meetings all originate in widely separated company departments. But, before top sales management sees them, they have been culled by Chief Statistician King's department and adapted to bring out the facts that the key men need to know. Early in the evolution of the seminars there was naturally a considerable amount of experimenting with different types of presentations. Management knew, of course, what major items should be included, but it took some living with the figures before the supporting data included became standardized. And even now, the reporting departments check up periodically to see how important sales considers the various studies that flow across their desks.

The central thought that emerges from a study of reporting procedures in these and other firms is that it is a rare executive who is able to grasp both the details and the broad picture of company operations and act on the information. In order for the top sales staff to function efficiently in an administrative and a creative sense, they must get an assist from one or more of the staff departments. Normally, the key supporting department is commercial research, sometimes billed as the statistical department.

Because sales management is a relative newcomer to the administrative field, there are frequently organizational roadblocks to break through before efficient communications with the major supporting department or section can be set up. This is particularly true in companies where a long-established commercial research department has been functioning under the budget of another group, the treasurer's department, for example. The problem then, naturally, is the one of disturbing old work-patterns during the creation of new ones, as the research people design the new type of analytic summary reports the sales department requires.

Occasionally this means that market specialists attached to the sales department must be reassigned to the research department in order to integrate the entire technical reporting procedures. In some firms the fairly generalized commercial research group—in terms of specialized functions—has been split up and the smaller group servicing both the advertising and sales departments assigned to their budget.

Visual aids, which are becoming extremely important in communication of technical information, are no better than the amount of information they transmit in a given time. The companies studied in this article find that to get fast understanding, the techniques themselves must be easy to understand. In other words, the medium must not stand in the way of the matter. Logarithmic scales, for example, are a waste of effort because the typical sales executive is not familiar with them.

But the heavier emphasis on visual aids is part of a definite reporting trend. Another part of the same trend is the summary report, a reflection of the fact that top sales management is being forced to delegate authority as functions become more specialized. Some sales executives still insist on full reports with supporting data —but it's a moot point whether they read them *in toto*.

Periodic seminars or briefing of the top sales team serves the same end as the summary report and the use of visual aids. They bring together all of the myriad facts that facilitate analysis of operations. Some companies with a tightly knit policy and planning team are able to by-pass most of these techniques because they communicate informally and daily. These, however, are the exceptions to a growing trend toward delegation of responsibility and reliance on facts and conclusions gathered by others. In a real sense, it suggests that sales *management* is coming into bloom.

Chapter 17

SPECIAL APPLICATIONS TO BUSINESS AND ENGINEERING: READINGS

Internal Reports—Too Much Paper Work? *

In order to maintain and improve their business health during the next 12 months or so, most firms will have to know exactly where they stand—in terms of costs, margins, quality, and efficiency. Fortunately, it is possible, by following a few ground rules, to minimize the irritations and frustrations connected with internal controls.

First, *don't ask for data you don't use.* Executives operating with a limited staff tend to insist on more daily or weekly reports than they can possibly digest; and this attitude often filters down to the lower levels, with the result that operating personnel spend almost as much time collecting figures as doing their main job. Current reports should be reviewed with the idea of eliminating all those which haven't been put to any practical use in three months or more. Facts still being compiled in a form that no longer meets current needs, and "temporary" reports that turned out to be permanent because management never set cut-off dates, are other things to watch for.

Second, *let clerks collect the figures.* Though operating executives should carry final responsibility and should maintain interest in the figures, they ought not to carry the clerical burden. On the other hand, assigning the whole chore to the main office in order to minimize interference with the operating jobs increases chances for error in transmission and complicates checking or verification. If someone on the spot maintains the necessary records, the depart-

---

* Quoted by permission from the *Management Review,* December, 1952. The full article originally appeared as *Operations Report,* Research Institute of America, Inc., September 9, 1952.

ment in question will be more "figure-minded" and have fewer errors.

Third, *don't send reports to people who aren't concerned.* Important reports should be prepared with the receiving department or executive in mind; chief shipping clerks, for example, don't need a full detailed copy of next week's production schedule. A wise idea is to circulate a list of current reports periodically, so that executives can check those they wish to receive.

Fourth, *see to it that reports come in early enough to be of use.* Reports with no immediate operating application are often turned out long before others that could be used immediately. Too, the bookkeeping department must be made to recognize that absolute accuracy or completeness is not always required in these internal reports and that it is senseless to hold up budgets or cash and cost projections for a few minor entries.

Fifth, *make sure that the significance of each report is clear to the reader.* Where executives insist on receiving fully detailed reports, each report should be preceded by a half-page summary of the few exceptional occurrences, so that the reader can spot the points that require his attention. A top sheet that summarizes the week-to-week or month-to-month trend and reflects its effect on the company's costs, margins, and cash position will increase the utility of the report.

$E = MC^2$ *

by ALBERT EINSTEIN

In order to understand the law of the equivalence of mass and energy, we must go back to two conservation or "balance" principles which, independent of each other, held a high place in pre-relativity physics. These were the principle of the conservation of energy and the principle of the conservation of mass. The first of these, advanced by Leibnitz as long ago as the seventeenth century, was developed in the nineteenth century essentially as a corollary of a principle of mechanics.

* Quoted by permission from *Out of My Later Years* (New York: Philosophical Library, 1950). Dr. Einstein is, as everyone knows, one of the foremost scientists of this or any generation. He won the Nobel Peace Prize in 1922. This article is reprinted to show his method of preparing a scientific article of a comparatively non-technical nature.

Consider, for example, a pendulum whose mass swings back and forth between the points A and B. At these points the mass m is higher by the amount h than it is at C, the lowest point of the path (see drawing). At C, on the other hand, the lifting height has

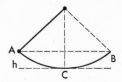

disappeared and instead of it the mass has a velocity v. It is as though the lifting height could be converted entirely into velocity, and vice versa. The exact relation would be expressed as $mgh = \frac{m}{2} v^2$, with g representing the acceleration of gravity. What is interesting here is that this relation is independent of both the length of the pendulum and the form of the path through which the mass moves.

The significance is that something remains constant throughout the process, and that something is energy. At A and at B it is an energy of position, or "potential" energy; at C it is an energy of motion, or "kinetic" energy. If this concept is correct, then the sum $mgh + m\frac{v^2}{2}$ must have the same value for any position of the pendulum, if h is understood to represent the height above C, and v the velocity at that point in the pendulum's path. And such is found to be actually the case. The generalization of this principle gives us the law of the conservation of mechanical energy. But what happens when friction stops the pendulum?

The answer to that was found in the study of heat phenomena. This study, based on the assumption that heat is an indestructible substance which flows from a warmer to a colder object, seemed to give us a principle of the "conservation of heat." On the other hand, from time immemorial it has been known that heat could be produced by friction, as in the fire-making drills of the Indians. The physicists were for long unable to account for this kind of heat "production." Their difficulties were overcome only when it was successfully established that, for any given amount of heat produced by friction, an exactly proportional amount of energy had to be expended. Thus did we arrive at a principle of the "equivalence of work and heat." With our pendulum, for example, mechanical energy is gradually converted by friction into heat.

In such fashion the principles of the conservation of mechanical and thermal energies were merged into one. The physicists were thereupon persuaded that the conservation principle could be further extended to take in chemical and electromagnetic processes —in short, could be applied to all fields. It appeared that in our physical system there was a sum total of energies that remained constant through all changes that might occur.

Now for the principle of the conservation of mass. Mass is defined by the resistance that a body opposes to its acceleration (inert mass). It is also measured by the weight of the body (heavy mass). That these two radically different definitions lead to the same value for the mass of a body is, in itself, an astonishing fact. According to the principle—namely, that masses remain unchanged under any physical or chemical changes—the mass appeared to be the essential (because unvarying) quality of matter. Heating, melting, vaporization, or combining into chemical compounds would not change the total mass.

Physicists accepted this principle up to a few decades ago. But it proved inadequate in the face of the special theory of relativity. It was therefore merged with the energy principles—just as, about 60 years before, the principle of the conservation of mechanical energy had been combined with the principle of the conservation of heat. We might say that the principle of the conservation of energy, having previously swallowed up that of the conservation of heat, now proceeded to swallow that of the conservation of mass —and holds the field alone.

It is customary to express the equivalence of mass and energy (though somewhat inexactly) by the formula $E = mc^2$, in which c represents the velocity of light, about 186,000 miles per second. E is the energy that is contained in a stationary body; m is its mass. The energy that belongs to the mass m is equal to this mass, multiplied by the square of the enormous speed of light—which is to say, a vast amount of energy for every unit of mass.

But if every gram of material contains this tremendous energy, why did it go so long unnoticed? The answer is simple enough: so long as none of the energy is given off externally, it cannot be observed. It is as though a man who is fabulously rich should never spend or give away a cent; no one could tell how rich he was.

Now we can reverse the relation and say that an increase of E in the amount of energy must be accompanied by an increase of $\dfrac{E}{c^2}$ in the mass. I can easily supply energy to the mass—for instance, if I heat it by 10 degrees. So why not measure the mass increase, or weight increase, connected with this change? The trouble here is that in the mass increase the enormous fact c^2 occurs in the denominator of the fraction. In such a case the increase is too small to be measured directly, even with the most sensitive balance.

For a mass increase to be measurable, the change of energy per mass unit must be enormously large. We know of only one sphere in which such amounts of energy per mass unit are released: namely, radioactive disintegration. Schematically, the process goes like this: An atom of the mass M splits into two atoms of the mass M′ and M″, which separate with tremendous kinetic energy. If we imagine these two masses as brought to rest—that is, if we take this energy of motion from them—then, considered together, they are essentially poorer in energy than was the original atom. According to the equivalence principle, the mass sum M′ + M″ of the disintegration products must also be somewhat smaller than the original mass M of the disintegrating atom—in contradiction to the old principle of the conservation of mass. The relative difference of the two is on the order of 1/10 of one percent.

Now, we cannot actually weigh the atoms individually. However, there are indirect methods for measuring their weights exactly. We can likewise determine the kinetic energies that are transferred to the disintegration products M′ and M″. Thus it has become possible to test and confirm the equivalence formula. Also, the law permits us to calculate in advance, from precisely determined atom weights, just how much energy will be released with any atom disintegration we have in mind. The law says nothing, of course, as to whether—or how—the disintegration reaction can be brought about.

What takes place can be illustrated with the help of our rich man. The atom M is a rich miser who, during his life, gives away no money (*energy*). But in his will he bequeaths his fortune to his sons M′ and M″, on condition that they give to the community a small amount, less than one thousandth of the whole estate (*energy or mass*). The sons together have somewhat less than the father had (*the mass sum M' + M" is somewhat smaller than the mass M of the radioactive atom*). But the part given to the community, though relatively small, is still so enormously large (*considered as kinetic energy*) that it brings with it a great threat of evil. Averting that threat has become the most urgent problem of our time.

A New Sales Control System Hits the Business Horizon *

by John M. Gilliam

In any business employing a large field force of salesmen to sell their products, there are at least three basic objectives to be desired:

1. To have the salesmen so routed that they will at all times perform their selling tasks most efficiently.
2. To get the most business out of the available customers from each territory covered by a company salesman.
3. To have harmonious relations between the salesmen and the home office so that there is a mutual trust and honor.

To satisfy these and other objectives, a new control system has made its appearance on the business horizon. It is so revolutionary and effective that all persons connected with its use are full of enthusiasm and praise.

To present the new system to you properly, let us first look at the typical sales force in operation. The salesman is required to make a daily sales report, a various number of other reports, either daily or otherwise, and do certain other details—in addition to doing the actual work of selling the product of the company he is representing. The very fact that he is *required* to do these administrative details, puts him on the defensive. It makes him feel as if the home office is making him do work that is really not necessary, and actually not used by anyone. The company whose new system I am going to describe was no exception to this old method. The salesman was made to fill out a daily sales call report covering each of the 8 to 20 daily calls he was expected to make. On this

---

* Prepared especially for *Report Writing;* scheduled to be published also in *Sales Management*. John Gilliam is Purchasing Agent for Lumber, The Vulcan Corporation, Cincinnati. He has been associated with the Andrew Jergens Company, the Dwight Hinckley Lumber Company, and the M. B. Farrin Lumber Company, Cincinnati.

report he was to record sales, results of interviews, promotions set up or serviced, and any other information that might come to light.

This company is a manufacturer of a complete line of beauty soaps, cosmetics, and allied products. Its products are sold in almost every grocery, drug, variety and department store throughout America and Canada. To sell them, it employs a force of over 200 salesmen and some 10 or 12 Division Managers. Each salesman used to send in a daily call report, plus various other reports, such as promotional reports, credit reports on new customers, reports of complaints from customers, and still others. This took an average of from one to three hours' time after his regular day's work of calling on the customer was finished. It actually meant that the salesman was sometimes spending as many as eleven hours daily working, and receiving pay for eight!

The salesman's resentment of this overload of work was well justified in the case of our company. Who could do justice to receiving and tabulating information from 200 salesmen's reports daily? It would have taken quite a force of expert analysts to do the job thoroughly. Then who would have used the information, once it was compiled? This company, too, had the very real problem of territory coverage by the salesmen, and the problem of territory changes and their justification. These changes used to come rather frequently, and were a severe headache to all of the home office sales department, the credit department, the order department, and everyone in general.

The result of all this seeming confusion was an earnest searching for some method or manner of dealing with the overall problems of territory coverage, salesmen's efficiency, and sales promotion that would culminate in a smoothly working organization where efficiency would be rewarded with everyone able to concentrate on the task of selling more and more of their products in all outlets. From this earnest research, much of which was actually trial and error, the new method took shape and grew to the present efficient system which has salesmen, division managers, and home office sales personnel enthusiastic and happy. No, the system was not devised overnight, nor by any stroke of genius on anyone's part, but as a result of four years of hard and continuous effort on the part of everyone in the Sales Department, including salesmen and their Division Managers.

The new system is very simple in operation, especially to anyone familiar with IBM reporting and tabulating systems. It is very similar in almost all respects to the newer control systems now in effect in accounting, finance, production control, research, and many other branches of general business—this is, however, the first I have heard of its being used to control a field sales force. And it is adaptable to every business or industry that uses a large force of salesmen in the field to sell their products—the farther from the home office the salesmen, the more profitable its benefits become. It involves the use of the small check-sized IBM cards with which everyone is familiar. One of these small cards is made up for each customer of the company throughout the United States and Canada. At first the card contains the very minimum of information—customer's name, address, size of business and class of trade (whether retail, chain or wholesale grocery or drug). These cards were then sent to the Division Managers who, together with the salesman who was going to call upon the particular account, decided how often it should be contacted in order to obtain maximum business from it during the year. They also inserted any other useful information peculiar to that customer, and then returned the card to the home office for punching, sorting and filing. When returned the first time from the salesmen and Division Managers, the cards were punched, sorted according to territory, and placed in files. During the last week of each month the cards are all run through the key sort machine, and cards for all those customers who are to be contacted during the following month are pulled out according to sales territories. These cards are then bundled and sent to the salesmen. *When the salesmen receive these individual cards, their complete routing of their territory for an entire month in advance is complete!* One of the major problems of the Sales Executive has been accomplished—the salesman knows where he must go during the month, whom he must see, how many daily calls he will have to average, and, in fact, just about everything it is possible to convey to him.

When the salesman starts over his territory, he makes his calls just as before, but instead of presenting each customer with an assortment of 5 to 20 or more items, he makes a presentation of his promotional item, and only those other items which he has advance information the customer will and can profitably handle. He carries the small IBM card with him for each of his customers he calls upon, and as he completes each call he records on the card all his sales (space has been provided on the cards for all products, and special promotions offered by the company) and at the end of the day drops all the cards covering his calls for that day in the mail. He then can either plan his next day's calls, or do whatever he wishes, *for all the reporting he now has to do was accomplished with the filling out of the little card,* as he talked to his customer. The cards come back to the company, and all new information is coded and set up in print on the card, which then goes back in file until it is time for that particular customer to be called upon again. Each time the salesman gets that card back, *a complete story of the sales to that customer for the entire current year is readily available to him* for guidance in presenting his sales talk to secure additional business.

The other revolutionary part of the system is the sending of reports to the salesman from the home office, instead of asking the salesman to send in the reports. The salesman used to be required to send in special reports regarding promotions, reports of sales, displays established, etc., ad infinitum. Now the home office sends the salesman reports showing information about his particular customers, their purchases by class of trade and by item, the results of promotional campaigns, the rise or fall of the customers in his territory according to past volume of business, and numerous other facts that are invaluable to the salesman in appraising his territory and his customers. In addition, they convey this same information to the Division Managers, who in turn make comparison reports to each of their salesmen showing their standing among the members of the division, and within the entire company. This serves as a barometer of how well the particular salesman is doing, and also serves as the basis for building a spirit of friendly competition among salesmen to see who can come in with top honors—the accomplishment of this means a bonus from the company, and also from Division Managers. These reports from the company enable the Division Manager to supervise his division more efficiently, with less control from the home office, and relieve the Sales Department of countless minor details that are now handled by the Division Manager, *if not corrected by the salesmen themselves beforehand.* It eliminates, almost entirely, the duplication of effort of the home office and the Division Manager in supervising the salesmen—a task that was of no small degree of importance under the old system. It enables the Division Manager to hold his own sales meetings on the spot and in the territories where they are most needed, with complete information available to himself, the same as if the meetings were held at the home office. In a company where some of the salesmen and Division Managers are three thousand miles from the home office, this is a considerable saving in time and money, both for the salesman and the company.

To get these reports out to the salesmen and the Division Managers, the home office routes all orders from their salesmen through the control point. From here all the information is taken from the orders, coded and tabulated with the information sent in by the salesman on his IBM cards, and grouped according to the specific category in which it falls. To bring to a minimum the chance for error, the company revised their promotional sales program during this period also. Now, instead of having promotions running haphazardly all over the United States, they have established the policy of starting one new promotion each month. Each promotion runs at least one month, and no promotion can ever run more than 90 days. This means that almost every time a salesman calls upon a customer he has at least one new item to present, but at no time does he have more than one or two such items. Production quotas are established for each territory according to past experience, and those quotas will not be exceeded for any reason. This, too, eliminates a very sore spot with salesmen, for under the old system there was the chance that one salesman could obtain more than his rightful share of a "hot" promotion, while some other poor fellow was not even in a position to offer that promotion to his customers.

The experience of this company has been that the rather high dollar cost of the system is minor compared to the benefits that can come from it. The company is most enthusiastic about the new system, and so are the salesmen and Division Managers I have had occasion to talk to. I am of the opinion that any company using a large sales force could gain much by considering the adoption of the same or a similar system for their own use.

The Presidents' Round Table *

A Panel Session

The Panel:

> JAMES D. WISE, President, Bigelow-Sanford Carpet Company, Inc., New York (Chairman)
>
> CHARLES S. CRAIGMILE, President, Belden Manufacturing Company, Chicago
>
> GEORGE S. DIVELY, President and General Manager, Harris-Seybold Company, Cleveland
>
> EDMUND FITZGERALD, President, The Northwestern Mutual Life Insurance Company, Milwaukee
>
> STANLEY C. HOPE, President, Esso Standard Oil Company, New York
>
> CHARLES LUKENS HUSTON, JR., President, Lukens Steel Company, Coatesville

Chairman James D. Wise: The purpose of this panel discussion is to try to explore the question: What is a president supposed to do? How does he keep in close touch with what is going on? How can he measure the effectiveness of various departmental activities?

Keeping Informed of Departmental Activities. The first question we come to is: How do you keep yourself informed about the activities of the various departments of your company? Then there is a very closely related question which I think we might cover at the same time: How do you know whether a good job is being done by the individual departments?

Mr. Hope: The old saying that the owner's foot in the plant is the best thing for the plant, still applies. I think perhaps my best means of finding out what is going on is by field visits to our sales divisions, to our refineries, and, when occasion permits, to our various departments at headquarters. That is still, in my opinion, the best way for a president of a company to know what is going on. However, that is not the scientific solution, which in our case is accomplished by a system of contact directors.

---

* Abridged by permission of the American Management Association from AMA General Management Series Number 150, *The Job of the Company President.* The papers contained in the article were presented at a round table discussion at the 27th Annual General Management Conference of the AMA, held at the Waldorf-Astoria Hotel, New York, June 1-2, 1950.

Each operational and functional department of the company reports to a director. The director does not operate the department in most cases. He is merely there for advice and counsel. This serves as a means of directing action outward through the company, provides channels for bringing to the board problems and ideas of importance. We consider that setup a very important one. And our organizational chart shows the initials of contact directors, so that there is no question as to how the setup should work.

Then we have periodic reviews of departmental progress. We have a special committee which reports on the personnel, base requirements, and housekeeping factors. Those reports are circulated to the board, and on occasions of perhaps a year are reviewed and discussed.

That, in brief, is how I keep in touch with my various departments.

Chairman Wise: Mr. Fitzgerald, will you tell us how you keep yourself informed about the kind of job being done by your individual departments?

Meetings and Reports.

Mr. Fitzgerald: We have a great quantity of records, of course, in the life insurance business. We have daily and monthly reports. In the last five years we have adopted the practice of having a very complete annual report made by each department head, in which he outlines the problems that he has encountered, the steps that he has taken to solve them, and the major objectives of the year ahead.

I go over these reports with each department head in some detail. I find that a very effective control.

Another way of keeping track of what our departments are doing is through a monthly meeting of our executive committee. The executive committee is, of course, a committee of the board of trustees of the company. Each department head—we have 11— attends the meeting, makes a written report which is sent to the executive committee before the meeting, and then personally presents the most important features in those reports.

We also have a check-up through an examining committee of policyholders that comes in each year and looks us over.

My problem is much simpler than that of many other company presidents because of the fact that we are all operating in the same building. We lunch together every day. My chief purpose is to try to keep myself available—not to be involved in a great many things which make it difficult for the departmental head to reach me. I think the position of the president is that of a consultant rather than a doer.

Now, as to how we check up on the kind of a job these departments are doing: Again, I know no business that has the records that the life insurance business keeps. For years we have been dealing with these reports that many of you are now confronted with, and must file very voluminous reports with every state in which we do business. In order to save time, the life insurance companies mail these reports to one another, so that we do not have to go to the state capitols to see what our competitors are doing. This gives us a check on how our people are doing as compared with our competitors.

I find, too, that the president very rapidly gets the reaction of the policyholders to our standards of service. Complaints all seem to flow to the desk of the chief officer.

Then, of course, with our usual group of staff people, such as the controller on costs, a planning department, the personnel department, and management consultants that we may bring in, we do get a good idea of what our people are doing.

We have also adopted a device of placing a representative, a junior officer from each one of our departments, on the policyholders' service committee. These are young fellows who do not believe that what we have been doing is necessarily the correct thing to do. They check up on one another and come up with some very good suggestions, and also point up weaknesses.

Frankly, I find it less difficult to get the facts than to do something about the facts once I have them.

Chairman Wise: Mr. Huston, will you tackle these two questions?

Mr. Huston: With respect to the question: How do I keep informed about the activities of the various departments of my company? By use of virtually all the mediums—word of mouth, the written word, charts and other visual aids, and so on.

Specifically, we have each division report to the president once each year on the job that it has done in meeting the goals set for it during the preceding year. Anything unusual that has been accomplished outside of the goals is reported. In addition, goals are set for the coming year. That is followed up every half-year by a progress report.

The report not only goes to me, but it goes to each member of the management committee, which committee comprises the principal officers and the division heads of the company. They make a critical review of the contents of every progress report, and particularly the annual divisional report. After the criticism, the report may be changed and improved before it is consolidated and goes to the board of directors.

In addition to these annual and progress reports, there are regular and special reports on individual programs, problems and projects. Each day at noon those who are in town lunch together, and while the discussion is by no means confined to business, we do often transact inter-division matters at the table.

Then there is at least one meeting a week of the management committee, devoted to policy questions and current problems. And once a month, not only the division heads and the management committee, but their immediate subordinates, get together for a general information session. A subordinate supervisor from each division comments on his particular activity, the business prospects, and what has been happening, for the information of the rest of the group. There are about 50 in that particular group.

In addition, there are individual and group conferences with executives on special matters. And there are personal visits to the plants, to customers, financial institutions, and to competitors' plants. I agree with Mr. Hope that it is certainly helpful to check what is going on by discussions here and there in the plant, by visits with customers, and by personal contacts with financial institutions and others.

How do I know whether a good job is being done by individual departments? The annual reports and the definite goals established by the departments of each division provide a standard against which to check results. We feel that the setting of that standard is important. And in recognition of the fact that each member of the management committee has a chance to criticize and question the initial report when it comes up, and that each man represents 20 to 40 years of experience with the company, the resulting final standard and goal set for each department has considerable weight separate and apart from the weight of the experience of that department in setting such goals.

Then, of course, there is constant follow-up and checking of current performance against the established goals, both formally and informally in the course of daily contacts. All these things are help-ful to us in knowing whether a good job is being done by individual departments.

Chairman Wise: Mr. Craigmile, will you tell us how you keep yourself informed of departmental progress?

Mr. Craigmile: We hear a great deal about the delegation of authority and responsibility. I think generally we do a pretty good job of that. But I think the danger is that top management may delegate it too far and lose touch with what may be going on.

Interdepartmental Coordination. As a practical matter, in our company we instituted a program which I think is quite common now. Every Monday morning the officers of the company meet in executive session to discuss anything about the business. I found that the problem was not so much keeping the president informed about what was going on as to keep each individual department head informed about what the others were doing.

I have come to the conclusion that there are no unrelated parts of the business. I feel that one of the president's most important jobs is to be sure that all his division heads have an opportunity to confer with each other in making decisions.

How do I know whether a good job is being done? Again, I think that the fundamental answer is our contact with the men who head the divisions of our business.

The second means, of course, is the ordinary operating report. In our case, we have a daily report which is very instructive. It shows our orders and billing, unfilled orders, accounts receivable, how much money we have in the bank, and how much we owe. This daily report to some degree acts as an immediate warning of a change.

Contact with Second-Line Supervision. Once a month, at our divisional meetings, we bring in the second line of supervision—department heads, including the purchasing agent, the head of pro-duction planning, the heads of the various sales units, plant super-intendents, chief industrial engineer and comptroller.

I believe that if you sit down and talk to your people about business, you will learn more than you can even from reports. Cer-tainly our most valuable source of information as to what is actually going to come from the discussions we have is in these meetings. And second to that, of course, are the normal operating reports.

Use of Special Reports.

Chairman Wise: Now I would like to call on Mr. Dively on the same two questions.

Mr. Dively: We came out of the war virtually out of business insofar as our normal products were concerned. Our industry was one of the most completely converted to specific war products. So we had to begin almost from scratch in a business where specialized experience is highly important, with an expanding program and a shortage of experienced help. This intensified the need for effective exchange of information and a well-oiled internal communication system.

I agree with the other panel members that informal personal contacts, group meetings and written reports are the best means of keeping posted.

In view of the need and desire to keep our organization informed, considerable attention is given to the design of reports so that they not only give the necessary factual information but also reflect performance and provide a degree of self-measurement. Let me try to illustrate with a few words about one of these reports—our industrial relations summary.

The development of this monthly summary report resulted from the consolidation and elimination of a dozen or more individual reports from our personnel department which had accumulated throughout the years. This over-all report is built around our particular problems, our particular personalities, and our particular jobs. Among other items, it shows, by manufacturing and field divisions, the average number of hourly and salary employees for the month, compared with last month and the average for last year; labor rates by divisions of employment, with premium and overtime shown separately; labor turnover, accidents and grievances with comparative last-month and last-year data; and various comparative direct and indirect labor data which can be used to exercise control in line with previously established industry ratios.

As another illustration there is a series that I call project reports. They reflect our industrial engineering, market study and development and research activities. These reports are issued bi-monthly. They show the activity, measure progress and reflect the forward programs for individual projects.

Reporting in a Control Group Organization [*]

by THOMAS J. McGINNIS

Reporting is more than the keeping of a business diary which merely records for posterity the historical data of today. Indeed, it is Koppers' philosophy that reports should instead be looked upon as management's means of measuring the effectiveness of all its other means of control and of doing something about the future.

Reports are fundamentally a means of determining whether or not the company is succeeding and, if not, why not. Consequently, there needs to be some definition of what constitutes success. This is a basic concept on which our use of reports is founded, for in Koppers management provides itself with a clear definition of its goals and reports evaluate results in terms of these goals.

The Koppers Program. To amplify this statement, it must be understood that Koppers each year draws up a program that defines in considerable detail the ambitions and goals of the company, as well as the specific results which, if attained, will mean the fulfillment of these ambitions and goals. The program is a carefully constructed plan for the operation of the company. It spells out the various new undertakings, projects, expansions, and improvements which we will pursue during the year. It states the advances which we hope to make in the fields of research, development, transportation, public relations, sales, production, industrial relations, and the other functions which are the responsibility of our staff departments. It programs in detail the operations of our divisions in terms of their production, sales, manufacturing costs, overhead expenses, and profits. Within these divisions, the corresponding data for indi-

[*] Quoted by permission of the American Management Association from the AMA booklet *Reports to Top Management for Effective Planning and Control*, New York, 1953. After receiving his BSME degree from Purdue University, Thomas J. McGinnis served variously as design and test engineer, Norge Division, Borg Warner Corporation; design engineer, Link Belt Company; and Major, U. S. Army Ordnance Department, in the Chicago Ordnance District (later as Assistant Chief, Industrial Division). Mr. McGinnis began his association with Koppers Company, Pittsburgh, Pennsylvania, in 1946 as organization administrator in the Control Section and afterwards was named Assistant Manager of the Control Section. Mr. McGinnis was appointed to his present position as Manager, Control Section, in 1951. He is the author of "The Control Section as an Aid to Management."

vidual plants, groups of plants, products, and sales districts are projected.

On the financial side, the program sets forth all the sources and requirements of cash which correspond to the projected operations. The elements of working capital are programmed from the grass roots up, resulting in the determination of the amounts that will be required for inventories, receivables, payables, free cash balance, payment of income taxes, and other current items. A detailed schedule for the year's capital expenditures is provided, including a schedule of new appropriations to be authorized. If new financing or the retirement of debt is indicated, the program is specific in setting forth the nature and the timing of such transactions. These matters are summarized in detailed and consolidated balance sheets and cash statements.

The program is, in other words, a sort of progress report in perspective. It is prepared in light of the very best forecasts of the general economy that are available to us and is an expression of where we want to be, and should be, at the end of each month of the coming year. If we are able to control each of the multitudinous factors which affect over-all performance, we should find ourselves just where we wanted to be at month's end, and when the year has passed we shall have accomplished the things we started out to do.

It can be seen how the existence of Koppers' program influences the nature of the reporting system by which management is kept aware of progress. In the first place, the entire emphasis is placed upon the relationship of current operating results of the program, thereby focusing attention on today's problems and their influence on tomorrow's business. The time-honored but nonetheless impractical comparison of today's results with those of last month, last year, and five years ago is eliminated to a large extent, because it is not believed that looking backward contributes very much to moving forward.

Organization of the Company. Koppers is a highly diversified company, producing a wide variety of products and services, mostly for use by other industries. Figure 63 shows the over-all organization plan, indicating the manner in which the operating portion of our business is divided into six operating divisions. Each of these is an integrated unit, producing and selling its own products or services.

The divisions differ widely in terms of their physical and geo-graphical characteristics. The Engineering and Construction Division is a service organization, a designer and builder of coke ovens, steel plants, chemical plants, and other industrial installations; it carries out its engineering work in Pittsburgh and Chicago and its construction activities at many locations both here in the United States and abroad. In contrast, the Tar Products and Wood Preserving Divisions, which are product-manufacturing businesses, each operate more than 20 small to medium-sized plants, well dispersed over the country. The Metal Products Division, on the other hand, operates only two plants, both of which are quite large and are located in Baltimore. All in all, Koppers has 55 plants plus a large number of sales offices, distribution centers, and construction sites.

Supporting the operating divisions and the company in general are the staff departments, each of which operates in a specific functional field, providing assistance, advice, and in some cases operating service to the divisions. They are located at company headquarters in Pittsburgh but are responsible for over-all coordination of their particular function, irrespective of where or by which unit it is performed.

Note that the Control Section, reporting directly to the President, is the only unit whose title does not give an immediate clue to its function or scope. Perhaps this is significant, for in reality the Control Section covers all functions and its scope is as broad as the company itself. It is a management control group, whose purpose is to establish and operate the broad management controls by which the company's top management can direct its business. The Control Section's duties extend into the fields of organization planning, procedures and methods, and a wide variety of special studies and analyses of company affairs. But it is with this group's work on reports that we are particularly concerned in this discussion.

The Reporting Activity. It is the Control Section that designs, coordinates, and produces the company's program. In the process of programming, the Control Section employs channels of communication and information that reach directly into each of the divisions and staff departments and, through them, indirectly to every operating unit and location of the company. Through these channels come the plans, forecasts, standards, and goals, which, as

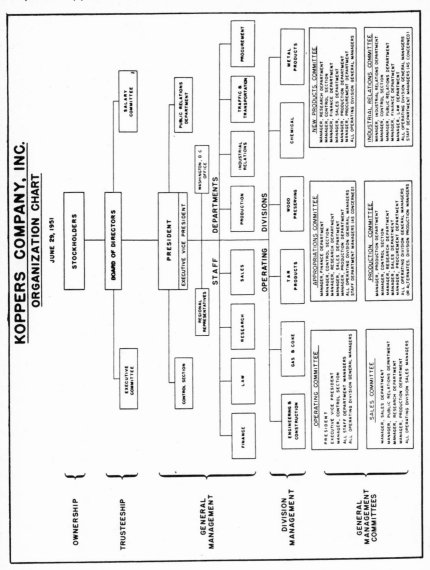

FIGURE 63.

they reach the Control Section, are analyzed and appraised prior to being accepted for consolidation into the final program.

It is the Control Section, using these same channels of communication and information, that plans, coordinates, and produces Koppers' Monthly Progress Report. This is generally referred to as *the* report, and the singular connotation is significant, for it is *the* report which top management uses to inform itself on the company's progress and to plan management action.

The Control Section's wide scope of interest and broad coverage of functions serve it well in carrying out the reporting activity. This is so because the Progress Report, in order to achieve maximum usefulness to management, must be completely factual, must present information in a completely impartial and analytical manner, and must be objective always and critical where necessary. Since the Control Section has no predominant interest in any one function or type of operation, it is in a position to be objective about all phases of the business and to coordinate and resolve differing points of view held by various other units on a particular subject.

Collecting the Statistics. Two major sources of information are used, one to obtain the statistical data and the other to obtain the explanatory, narrative material. The source of the statistical data is largely the Finance Department and, more specifically, its Treasury and Accounting Section, wherein is performed the actual detail and general accounting for four of our six divisions. The other two divisions carry on their accounting on a completely decentralized basis, in finance units which are an integral part of their divisional organizations. In the case of these two divisions, the statistical data come directly from them.

In order to obtain all the information that is required, to obtain it in the form in which it is most useful, and to facilitate its adaptation to the finished report, the Control Section prepares in advance the forms on which the data will be supplied to it. A set of these forms, including all the tabulations required to present the monthly results of a particular division, is furnished to the appropriate accounting group shortly in advance of the monthly closing. On these tabulations the Control Section has entered the data representing the programmed performance for the month or for the year to date as the case may be. In the accounting groups, the corresponding actual figures are entered on these work sheets as the various accounts are closed, the percentage of the actual to the program is calculated and entered, and the completed forms are returned to the Control Section. To give some idea of the size of this job, the

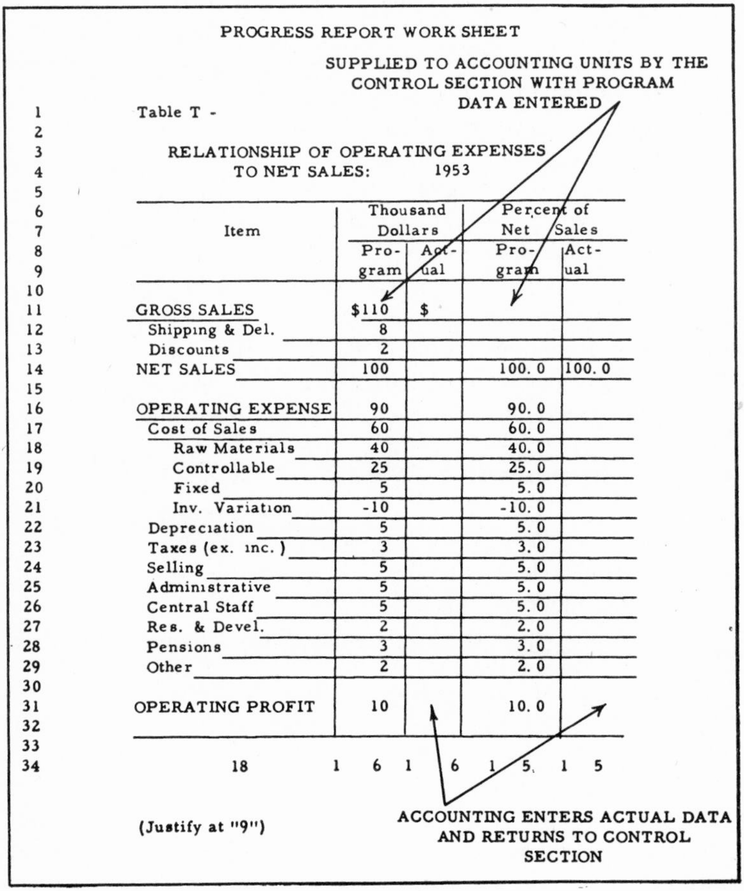

PROGRESS REPORT WORK SHEET

SUPPLIED TO ACCOUNTING UNITS BY THE
CONTROL SECTION WITH PROGRAM
DATA ENTERED

Table T -

RELATIONSHIP OF OPERATING EXPENSES
TO NET SALES: 1953

| | Thousand Dollars | | Percent of Net Sales | |
Item	Pro-gram	Act-ual	Pro-gram	Act-ual
GROSS SALES	$110	$		
Shipping & Del.	8			
Discounts	2			
NET SALES	100		100.0	100.0
OPERATING EXPENSE	90		90.0	
Cost of Sales	60		60.0	
Raw Materials	40		40.0	
Controllable	25		25.0	
Fixed	5		5.0	
Inv. Variation	-10		-10.0	
Depreciation	5		5.0	
Taxes (ex. inc.)	3		3.0	
Selling	5		5.0	
Administrative	5		5.0	
Central Staff	5		5.0	
Res. & Devel.	2		2.0	
Pensions	3		3.0	
Other	2		2.0	
OPERATING PROFIT	10		10.0	

18   1   6 1   6   1   5   1   5

(Justify at "9")

ACCOUNTING ENTERS ACTUAL DATA
AND RETURNS TO CONTROL
SECTION

FIGURE 64.

number of such work sheets sent to and returned by the accounting units averages about 325 per month. Figure 64 is an example of a typical Progress Report work sheet.

Narrative Material. The sources of the explanatory, narrative material are the operating divisions and the staff departments. Although this type of material does not lend itself to the use of prepared forms as in the statistical phase, the Control Section has established with the divisions and departments, as a result of repetitive and constantly improved practice, an effective and well-understood method of covering all the pertinent phases of the month's operations.

The staff departments report to us their activities of the month, indicating the progress they have made on the special projects in which they are engaged; they also submit some statistical data measuring the volume of the routine service work they perform, as well as general comments on current developments in their functional fields. To the extent that the progress of these units has been programmed, their actual performance is measured against the program—for example, by relating the actual starting and completion dates of projects to those programmed, measuring the actual against the programmed cost of such projects, and relating the results to those that were anticipated.

From the headquarters of each of the six operating divisions we obtain a narrative report commenting on the month's business. Since virtually every phase of the division's operation has been programmed, we expect to receive the appropriate explanations wherever actual performance has varied significantly from the program. Comments deal with sales, sales prices, market developments, production, production difficulties, production costs, overhead and general expenses, profits, investment, the elements of working capital, capital expenditures, progress on new projects, new orders, backlog of orders, business outlook, and such other subjects as are applicable to the individual division reporting.

The Data Analyzed. With these channels of information supplying the raw material for a portrayal of the company's progress, the Control Section goes about the business of producing a progress report which will show this progress—or lack of it—in as complete and objective a manner as possible. In doing so we are possessed by the curiosity of the proverbial cat and guided by the determination that the finished report will leave no room for an unanswered "why" in the minds of its readers.

The information received from the operating divisions and staff departments is thoroughly analyzed and related to the statistical data which it is supposed to explain. Because it is simply not human nature for an operating or staff official to write an extensive criticism of his own failures, we often must amplify these reports, adding pertinent comments that are reflected but unsaid in the data. Very frequently we must contact units to request more information on matters which have not been covered in the reports, or on which the reports were inadequate.

The analysis to which these reports are subjected is extremely thorough. Explanations of variations from programmed performance are in all cases tested against the statistical facts, very often with the result that some factor other than the one explained is found to have been the real cause of especially good or bad performance. The Control Section adds its own observations and comments to these reports, until we have, to the best of our ability, answered each "why" that might arise in management's mind.

Every phase of the business receives comment in the final report. Production efficiencies, yields from raw materials, scrap rates, unit manufacturing costs, raw materials supply, production difficulties and bottlenecks, maintenance and repair, usage of fuel and utilities, and many other down-to-earth matters are analyzed and then portrayed in the report in the most practical manner.

Careful Interpretation Needed. It must be kept in mind that the thoroughness and care with which this report is compiled, and the wide scope of the report itself, are justified not only because it is the report that will go to top management (including the Board of Directors) but by the fact that it is the *only* report this level of management will receive and therefore serves in lieu of the many individual reports which are common in some companies.

Our objective in preparing the report is to include in it a complete interpretation of the monthly results, thereby freeing management from the time-consuming task of interpretation and allowing its full concentration on necessary action. The complete checking and cross-checking of data results in the elimination of confusion and consequent mistrust in the minds of management, since it is never exposed to conflicting information on a particular subject— as may frequently be the case where many individual reports are received from different sources. It also eliminates the possibility of buck-passing, since the spotlight is turned on the true source of trouble as the result of the analyses made prior to using the data.

The work of analysis and editing connected with this report is performed by men who know the company well, know the accounting system well, have an intimate knowledge of how the program was prepared, and know where and how to look for the real truths that lie in the statistics and other information they work with.

The Finished Report. The cover of the Koppers Monthly Progress Report carries the notation "Secret." That means what it says, for the report contains complete financial, profit, sales, and technical information and therefore is intended for use only by authorized members of management. The distribution is carefully recorded by copy number, and the copies are recalled and destroyed when they have served their purpose. Consequently, the material shown on pp. 342-49 has had the significant figures and statements deleted from it. It is highly important that the use of such a report, in whatever company, be governed with great care.

The Monthly Progress Report is divided into four main sections. Section 1 covers "Koppers Company, Inc., and Subsidiaries"; in other words, it provides a consolidated picture of the over-all company's progress and results. The Control Section prepares this part of the report by summarizing the most important factors which have a bearing on our success or failure to attain our over-all goals. Section 1 is particularly useful to our Board of Directors, for in it the directors can find the over-all picture of the company's progress and status, free of the detail with which this level of management is not usually concerned.

Section 2 contains six individual reports, one for each of the operating divisions. These are the end product of the statistical and narrative information we receive from our correspondents, augmented and purified by our own efforts. Section 3 contains the reports of our staff departments, 11 in all, which are in the main narrative reports, supported by charts and tables where applicable. Section 4 is a monthly economic review, prepared from information submitted by the Market Research and Economics Section of the Staff Sales Department, in which the nation's economy, its trends, and the effect of these trends on Koppers' business are discussed. It is the report's sole departure from actual facts—our own private "crystal gazing" in print.

From month to month, the content of this report is varied as necessary in order to emphasize certain phases of operations which have become particularly important or critical. Also, in selected issues we include as a fifth section an exhaustive treatment of some special subject, such as general and administrative expense, maintenance and repair cost, actual versus estimated earnings from new capital projects, and others.

The accompanying outline of a typical Koppers Monthly Progress Report, with selected excerpts (pp. 333-41), will indicate the general content and the manner in which it is handled.

Mechanics of Preparation. The report has a pleasant, finished appearance. The narrative is blended with the appropriate tables and charts, so as to present in one general area all the information on a particular subject. We find that some people like to read a story about the business, some prefer tables which show the results, and some are proponents of graphs or charts. We try to please them all by providing enough of each. Actually, of course, each form supplements the others, with the text providing the analysis and the conclusions that a chart or table cannot alone provide.

The typical table used provides a column for the program, one for the corresponding actual figure, and one for the percentage of the actual to the program. The chart shows both the monthly and the year-to-date program and actual data and, as a slight concession to comparison with past history, the actual results of the preceding year. Throughout this report, dollar amounts are generally shown to the nearest thousand dollars.

All the textual and tabular material is typed in the Control Section, using electric typewriters equipped with carbon paper ribbons and a justifying attachment which permits the even righthand margin and the two-column style. A draftsman, also a member of the Control Section, prepares all the charts, which are used over again each month by merely adding the current month's bar and extending the shaded areas. All checking and proofreading are done in the Control Section, and the finished work is reproduced on the company's own equipment in a central reproduction service unit which is administered by the Staff Finance Department.

Distribution and Use. When is such a report issued? How long does it take to prepare it? How many copies are issued and to whom? Finally, how is the report used? All these points are important to a discussion of the Koppers Monthly Progress Report.

This finished report is distributed between the 12th and the 20th of the month following the month being reported. The exact date is dependent on the dates of the Operating Committee and Board of Directors meetings, which vary depending on the calendar (Fig. 65).

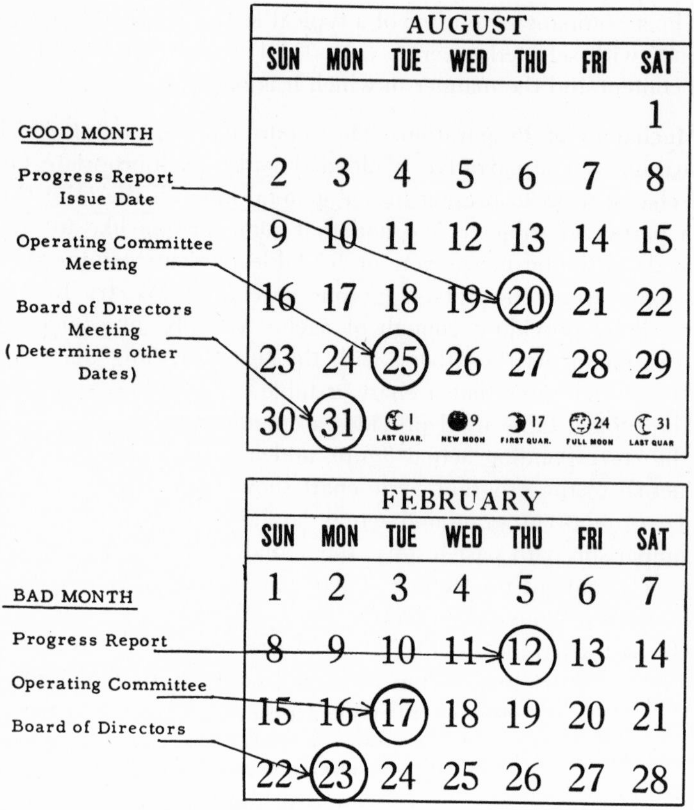

GOOD MONTH

Progress Report
Issue Date

Operating Committee
Meeting

Board of Directors
Meeting
(Determines other
Dates)

BAD MONTH

Progress Report

Operating Committee

Board of Directors

FIGURE 65. Schedule for Monthly Progress Report—A Good Month and a Bad Month.

From 5 to 12 days before the report is issued, the management has been advised of the final profit for the month, by divisions and in total. This schedule is fairly good, considering that Koppers must draw together the results at 55 different plants and about 30 or more construction sites. Incidentally, our monthly closings are as of the last calendar day of the month. The schedule is made possible by a well-documented and supervised procedure for transmitting information from the field to headquarters and thence to the Control Section.

APPENDIX: KOPPERS MONTHLY PROGRESS REPORT

A. Outline of a Typical Report

Section 1

SUBJECT	NATURE OF MATERIAL	NAME OF MATERIAL	REMARKS
Summary of activities	Table	"Summary of Activities—November 19—"	A quick summary of monthly and year-to-date earnings to common, sales, and profit, as well as total investment and inventories
Earnings to common stock	Text	——	Narrative material, which, as in the case of all text, recites the pertinent reasons and factors for actual results and variations from program and gives other explanatory information
"	Chart	"Earnings per Share of Common Stock"	Graphic portrayal of monthly and year-to-date actual results, also showing the program and, for comparison, the previous year's actual results
Sales	Text	——	Narrative treatment of sales results
"	Table	"Net Sales During November 19—"	Tabulations of sales (in thousands of dollars, as is the case in almost all tables), showing program, actual, and percent of program for total company sales and for each of the company's divisions
"	"	"Net Sales—January-November 19—"	Tabulations of year-to-date sales in same form as for the month
"	Chart	"Net Sales of Koppers Co, Inc., & Subs."	Bar chart for monthly sales (program, actual, and last year) and area chart for same results on a year-to-date basis
Profit	Text	——	Narrative treatment of profit results, including costs and expenses that influenced profits
"	Table	"Profit During November 19—"	Tabulation of program, actual, and percent of program. Shows division profits and deductions therefrom for general expenses, interest, taxes, etc., ending with profit after taxes
"	"	"Profit During January-November 19—"	Tabulation of year-to-date profit in same form as for the month
"	Chart	"Net Profit Before Income Taxes"	Monthly and year-to-date program, actual, and last year

Outline of a Typical Report (cont'd)

Section 1 (cont'd)

SUBJECT	NATURE OF MATERIAL	NAME OF MATERIAL	REMARKS
Profit	Chart	"Operating Profit as Percent of Net Sales"	Bars for annual average for the past five years. Line chart showing last year's and current year's monthly percentages
"	Table	"Net Profit Before Taxes as a Percent of Sales and Investment—January-November 19—"	Program and actual percentages for the company as a whole and for each division
"	"	"Koppers General Net Expense—November 19—"	Unallocated costs and expenses, less miscellaneous revenue and "other income"; program, actual, and percent of program
Investment	Text	——	Narrative treatment of investment, stockholders' equity, and factors causing investment changes
"	Table	"Investment (Common Stock and Surplus)—November 30, 19—,"	Detail of investment showing property, working capital, debt, etc., leading up to total common stockholders' equity; program, actual, percent of program
Capital authorizations and expenditures	Text	——	Narrative treatment of the month's new authorizations, expenditures, and status of major projects
"	Chart	"Property Additions—Cumulative"	Area charts showing program and actual authorizations, expenditures, and unexpended balance for year to date. Unexpended balance divided into "committed" and "uncommitted" funds
"	Table	"Total Open Capital Appropriations—November 30, 19—"	Tabulation of each project with an unexpended balance of more than $100,000, showing amount authorized, amount expended (for the month and project to date), and the unexpended balance (total and portion committed). Smaller projects are grouped in one entry
"	"	"Capital Authorizations and Expenditures—January-November 19—";	Tabulation of unexpended balance at start of year, authorizations to date, expenditures to date, and unexpended balance at November 30, 19—; program, actual, and percent of program
Cash and U. S. Governments	Text	——	Narrative treatment of cash movement for the period, principal sources, and requirements

Subject	Nature of Material	Name of Material	Remarks
Cash and U. S. Governments	Chart	"Cash and U. S. Governments"	Bar chart showing end-of-month program, actual, last year's actual. Current month's actual divided between cash and government securities
"	Table	"Cash Transfers to Koppers General"	Tabulation of cash transferred from general accounts to division accounts (or vice versa) by divisions and in total; month and year to date; program and actual
"	"	"Cash Source and Application—January-November 19—"	Tabulation of cash balance at start of year, various sources and requirements for the year to date, and balance at November 30, 19—; program and actual
"	Chart	"Cash Source and Application—November 19—"	Two divided bars of equal height, one showing sources for the month, by major sources, and the other showing requirements, by major requirement
Accounts receivable	Text		Narrative treatment of status of accounts receivable and analysis of collection experience
"	Chart	"Ratio of Accounts Receivable to Net Sales"	Bar chart, showing monthly ratio for current year and last year
"	Table	"Accounts and Advances Receivable—November 30, 19—"	Tabulation of program, actual, and percent of program, by division and in total. Actual is also expressed in terms of "months of sales"
Inventories	Text		Narrative treatment of inventory status, critical shortages, oversupply, market availability of critical items, etc.
"	Table	"Inventory Values as of November 30, 19—"	Inventory values by division and in total; actual, program, and percent of program. Also shown is change during the month (in percent)
"	Chart	"Inventories"	Bar chart of program and actual total inventories. Actual divided between "raw material and supplies" and "finished and in process"
Central staff expense	Text		Narrative treatment of expenses of all staff units, explaining unusual changes or trends
"	Table	"Central Staff and Office Management Expense—By Department"	Tabulation of program and actual, for each unit and in total, month and year to date
"	"	"Central Staff and Office Management Expense—By Charge"	Tabulation of program and actual, by type of expense (salaries, rent, travel, etc.), month and year to date

Outline of a Typical Report (cont'd)

Section 1 (cont'd)

Subject	Nature of Material	Name of Material	Remarks
Central staff expense	Chart	"Central Staff and Office Management Expense as a Percent of Net Sales"	Bar chart showing monthly program, actual, and last year's actual percentages
"	"	"Central Staff and Office Management Expenses"	Bar chart showing monthly program, actual, and last year's actual dollar totals
Business outlook	Text	————	Narrative treatment of new orders, backlog, and statement of short-term prospect for sales and profits
"	Chart	"New Orders"	Bar chart showing monthly total of new orders for current year and last year
"	Table	"New Orders Received"	Tabulation of new orders for month, by division and in total, showing comparable figure for same month last year and percent changes from last year
"	"	"	Same as previous table, but on a year-to-date basis
"	Chart	"Backlog of Orders"	Bar chart showing end-of-month backlog total for current year and last year
"	Table	"Unbilled Orders as of November 30, 19—"	End-of-month backlog, by divisions and in total. Shows orders in terms of months of sales and also percent change from same date one year ago
"	"	"19— Compared with 19—"	Summary of highlights compared with last year, including percent change. Includes total sales, profits before and after taxes, earnings per share, investment, inventories, and backlog
Consolidated earnings statement	"	"Consolidated Earnings Statement"	Conventional earnings statement, beginning with net sales and ending with earnings per share. Includes program and actual for month and year to date; also program for current full year and actual for last full year
Statement of financial condition	"	"Statement of Financial Condition"	Conventional balance sheet, but arranged so as to lead to common stockholders' equity. Includes program and actual for November 30, 19—, program for December 31, 19—, and actual for December 31 of last year

Subject	Nature of Material	Name of Material	Remarks
Koppers Company, Inc., and Subsidiaries	Table	"Koppers Co, Inc., and Subsidiaries"	A form of "financial organization chart," showing all subsidiaries, percentage of interest held, and, for all non-consolidated subsidiaries or investments, the market and book values as of November 30, 19—

Section 2

NOTE: This section contains reports for each of six divisions. Only one (Tar Products) is outlined below, but it is fairly typical of all

Subject	Nature of Material	Name of Material	Remarks
Summary of activities	Table	"Summary of Activities—November 19—"	Summary of program, actual, and percent of program for division sales, profits, investment, inventories
Sales	Text		Narrative treatment of division sales, highlighting sales of various products, plants, and groups of plants; treats volume, prices, market conditions, etc.
"	Chart	"Net Sales"	Graphic portrayal of total division sales; bar chart for month showing program, actual, and last year's actual; area chart for same data on a year-to-date basis
"	Table	"Gross Sales of Major Products—November 19—"	Tabulation of program, actual, and percent of program for each major product (23 in this case). Includes both volume (gallons, pounds, units, etc.) and value
"	Chart	"Net Sales by Group"	Bar charts showing program, actual, and last year's actual sales for each of division's five groups, on a monthly basis
"	Table	"Net Sales by Group—November 19—"	Tabulation of month's sales by group and in total; program, actual, and percent of program
"	"	"Net Sales by Tar and Coating Plant"	Tabulation of sales by individual plants (30 in this case) showing monthly program, actual, and percent of program for year to date
"	"	"Net Sales by Group—January-November 19—"	Tabulation of year-to-date sales by group and in total; program, actual, and percent of program
Profit	Text		Narrative treatment of profit results and discussion of costs and expenses influencing results
"	Chart	"Tar Plants—Tar Cost and Average Sales Price of Tar and Tar Derivatives"	Chart of monthly programmed and actual average raw material cost (crude tar) and sales price of products (on a per gallon basis)
"	Table	"Net Profit by Group"	Tabulation of program, actual, and percent of program, by groups and in total; month and year to date
"	"	"Net Profit as Percent of Net Sales and Investment"	Program and actual percentages (for over-all division), showing month and year-to-date results. Return on investment is annualized

Outline of a Typical Report (cont'd)
Section 2 (cont'd)

Subject	Nature of Material	Name of Material	Remarks
Profit	Chart	"Net Profit"	Bar chart for division monthly profit, program, actual, and last year's actual. Area chart for same data on year-to-date basis
"	Table	"Relationship of Operating Expenses to Net Sales—November 19—"	Tabulation of sales, all direct and overhead costs, and resulting profit, in dollars and as a percent of sales; program and actual
"	Chart	"Net Profit by Group"	Bar charts showing program, actual, and last year's actual profits for each of the division's five groups, on a monthly basis
"	Table	"Net Profit by Group—November 19—"	Tabulation of month's profits by group and in total; program, actual, and percent of program
"	"	"Net Profit by Group—January-November 19—"	Same as previous table, but on a year-to-date basis
"	"	"Net Profit by Tar and Coating Plant"	Tabulation of profits by individual plants (30) showing monthly program, actual, and percent of program; also shows percent of program for year to date
"	Chart	"Overhead Expense"	Monthly area chart showing selling, administrative, and other overhead costs, total overhead, and program for total overhead
"	"	"Maintenance and Repair Expenses"	Monthly bar chart showing cost of maintenance labor, material, total maintenance cost, and program for total maintenance cost
Direct production expenses	Text	——	Analysis of individual plant variations from standard or allowable direct costs of production
"	Table	"Direct Production Expense of Plants Having Variances of 10 Percent or More"	Tabulation of standard cost, actual cost and variance for the month in dollars, and actual as percent of standard for month and year to date. Data are weighted for month's actual operations performed. Only plants varying 10 percent or more are shown separately, but all-plant total also is shown
Investment	Text	——	Narrative treatment of all factors contributing to investment level and changes therein. As applicable, it mentions receivable, payable, capital expenditures, new capital projects, etc.

Subject	Nature of Material	Name of Material	Remarks
Investment	Table	"Capital Authorizations and Expenditures—January-November 19—"	Table of unexpended balance at beginning of year, authorizations and expenditures for year to date, and new unexpended balance; program and actual
"	"	"Investment as of November 30, 19—"	Tabulation of total investment and elements thereof; program, actual, percent of program
"	Text		Although part of investment, is important enough to warrant separate analysis. Shows levels, shortages, oversupply, availability of raw materials in the market
"	Table	"Tar Plants—Inventories of Selected Products—November 30, 19—"	Tabulation of a few products comprising largest volume. Shows program, actual, percent of program, and percent change during month, all on a volume basis
"	"	"Inventory Values—November 30, 19—"	Tabulation of dollar value, by plant groups, by major classes of inventory; program, actual, percent of program, and change during month in percent
"	Chart	"Inventories"	Monthly bar chart showing actual and programmed value of total inventory. Actual is divided between "raw materials and supplies" and "finished and in process"
Business outlook	Text		Narrative treatment of new orders, backlog, and short-term outlook for sales and profits
"	Chart	"New Orders"	Monthly bar chart of new orders for current and last years
"	"	"Backlog of Orders"	Monthly bar chart of order backlog for current and last years
"	Table	"New and Unbilled Orders by Plant Group"	For each group and total, shows month's new orders, backlog at end of month, and percent change in backlog since last month

Section 3

NOTE: This section contains reports for each of 11 staff units. Only one (Finance Department) is outlined below, but it is fairly typical of all

Finance Administration Section	Text		Summarizes month's general financial administration activities, such as tax payments, purchase or sales of government or other securities, new financing or debt retirement, renegotiation proceedings, special project studies, etc.
Real Estate Section	"		Summarizes month's activities in real estate sales or purchases, lease transactions, property appraisals, assessments and taxes, property zoning problems, etc.

Outline of a Typical Report (cont'd)

Section 3 (cont'd)

SUBJECT	NATURE OF MATERIAL	NAME OF MATERIAL	REMARKS
Insurance Section	Text	——	Summarizes month's activities in new insurance purchases or changes in coverage, insured losses and collection of claims on such losses, self-insurance experience, etc.
"	Table	"Property Losses Reported During November"	Tabulation of location, date of loss, cause of loss, and amount
"	"	"Insurable Losses Adjusted During November"	Tabulation of location, date of loss, cause of loss, and settlement made
Treasury and Accounting Section	Text	——	Narrative report of progress in improving, simplifying, and scheduling accounting operations
Procedures and Auditing Section	"	——	Summary of procedures and audit projects and results
Credit and Collection Section	"	——	Review of month's collection experience and analysis of status of past due receivables
"	Chart	"Percent of Total Receivables Past Due Over 30 Days"	Monthly area chart showing percentage of past due receivables to total receivables. Area is divided into 21-60-day, 61-90-day, and over-90-day classes. Company total only
"	Table	"Collections During November 19—"	Tabulation, by divisions and for company total, of receivables at beginning of month, collections during month, and collections as a percent of receivables at beginning of month
"	"	"Percentage of Total Accounts Receivable Past Due Over 30 Days"	Tabulation by divisions and company total of percent of past due receivables to total receivables in the 31-60-, 61-90-, and over-90-day classes
Building Section	Text	——	The Building Section is a unit which operates the 33-story Koppers Building in Pittsburgh (renting also to outside tenants) and the office services for the Koppers headquarters. This text is a summary of the financial results of the building operation and of activities in office management work, including communication facilities, etc.
	Chart	"Koppers Building—Net Sales"	Monthly bar chart showing sales; program, actual, last year's actual

SUBJECT	NATURE OF MATERIAL	NAME OF MATERIAL	REMARKS
Building Section	Chart	"Koppers Building—Net Profit"	Monthly bar chart showing profit; program, actual, last year's actual
"	Table	"Sales and Profits of Koppers Building"	Tabulations of the monthly and year-to-date sales and profits; program, actual, percent of program

Section 4

NOTE: This section is a monthly review of economic trends, government actions, industrial activities, and economic forecasts. Its contents vary from month to month to suit the current situation. Hence the following outline is given only as a typical month's coverage

SUBJECT	NATURE OF MATERIAL	NAME OF MATERIAL	REMARKS
General	Text	—	Narrative treatment of important economic developments in government, industry, and commerce which should affect over-all business conditions
Bank loans	"	—	An analysis of bank-loan trends and how government and bank interest rates may change trends and affect business. A chart on bank loans is included
Natural gas	"	—	Summary of latest developments in natural gas production, transmission and use, government and industry action, etc. As this is very important to a number of Koppers divisions, this subject is covered each month
Factors affecting Koppers Company divisions	"	—	A narrowing-down to specific factors which may affect the business of Koppers divisions, including predictions of the results. An analysis is included for each division, including special charts where applicable. This subject is covered each month
"	Table	"Weekly Statistics of Business Activity"	A tabulation of the generally used indicia of business activity (FRB, BLS, *N. Y. Times*, etc.)
"	"	"Monthly Statistics of Business Activity"	"

Section 5

At scheduled intervals a Section 5 is included in this report in which some special subject is treated in considerable detail, using text, charts, and tables to show trends and progress, historical data, and other applicable material. Examples of subjects are:

Inventories	Maintenance and repair
Administrative expenses	Training and personnel
Cost controls	Organization and procedures
Appropriations review	Selling expense and sales

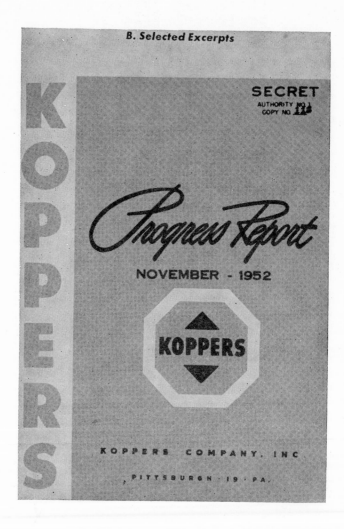

KOPPERS CO., INC. & SUBS.

EARNINGS TO COMMON STOCK

Earnings per share of common stock exceeded the program by a wide margin in November. Although profit before taxes was substantially below program, profit after taxes was considerably above. This resulted from an excess profit credit of $ thousand additional, in November, to   that programmed. In addition, tax adjustments applicable to Chilean income amounted to a reduction in taxable income of $ thousand. These factors tended to reduce the tax for the month; however, an additional amount $ thousand over program was provided in the reserve for tax contingencies, as was also done last month, and partly offsets these reductions. For the year to date, earnings to common are above those programmed by   per share outstanding.

SALES

Company sales dropped approximately   percent from the previous month but were, nevertheless, $ million in excess of the

Table K1

SUMMARY OF ACTIVITIES-NOVEMBER 1952

Item	Program	Actual Amount	Percent of Program
	(In thousands of dollars)		
NET SALES			
November	$	$	
January-November			
NET PROFIT a/			
November			
January-November			
COMMON & SURPLUS			
INVENTORIES			
	(In dollars)		
EARNED PER SHARE OF COMMON STOCK b/			
Bef.Spec.Items			
November	$	$	
January-November			

a/ Before taxes and special items.
b/ Based on 1,867,125 shares.

CHART-K1

EARNINGS PER SHARE OF COMMON STOCK (BEFORE SPECIAL ITEMS)*

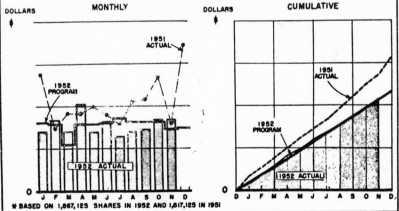

※ BASED ON 1,867,125 SHARES IN 1952 AND 1,817,125 IN 1951

EXHIBIT 2
PAGE 1, SECTION 1, SHOWING TEXT, CHART, AND TABLE

KOPPERS CO., INC. & SUBS.

the first part of the month, lower yields and a greater proportion of furnace coke shipments than anticipated. The loss programmed for Brooklyn was reduced to $ thousand in spite of the change in operations at this plant since the original program was prepared.

The Tar Products Division incurred a net loss during the month whereas a sizable profit had been programmed. Settlement of the use and occupancy insurance claim in connection with the Follansbee naphthalene still fire contributed $ thousand to the month's income. Low sales volume was the main reason for the division's loss. All plant groups, except Brokered, were below program.

INVESTMENT

Common stockholders' equity in the company was $ at November 30, an increase of $ during the month, and $ over program.

Table K8

INVESTMENT (COMMON STOCK AND SURPLUS)
NOVEMBER 30, 1952

(In thousands of dollars)

Item	Program	Actual	% of Program
TOTAL	$	$	
NET PROPERTY			
WORKING CAPITAL			
Cash			
U. S. Gov'ts			
Receivables			
Inventories			
Prepaid Items			
Less: Cur. Liab.			
INVESTMENTS			
OTHER ASSETS			
LESS: DEBT			
PREF. STOCK			
RESERVES			

CHART - K5

PROPERTY ADDITIONS
CUMULATIVE

MILLION   AUTHORIZATIONS
$

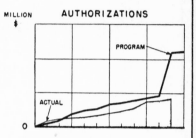

EXPENDITURES

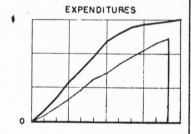

UNEXPENDED BALANCE

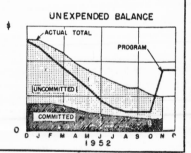

EXHIBIT 3
ANOTHER PAGE FROM SECTION 1

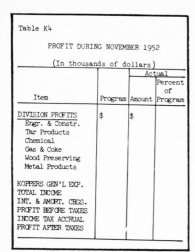

Table K4

PROFIT DURING NOVEMBER 1952

(In thousands of dollars)

Item	Program	Actual Amount	Percent of Program
DIVISION PROFITS	$	$	
Engr. & Constr.			
Tar Products			
Chemical			
Gas & Coke			
Wood Preserving			
Metal Products			
KOPPERS GEN'L EXP.			
TOTAL INCOME			
INT. & AMORT. CHGS.			
PROFIT BEFORE TAXES			
INCOME TAX ACCRUAL			
PROFIT AFTER TAXES			

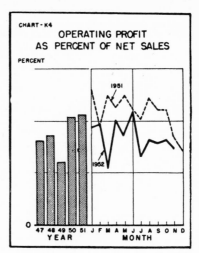

CHART-K4

OPERATING PROFIT
AS PERCENT OF NET SALES

PERCENT

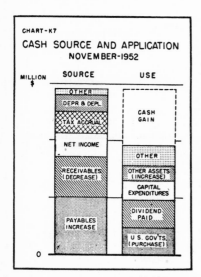

CHART-K7

CASH SOURCE AND APPLICATION
NOVEMBER-1952

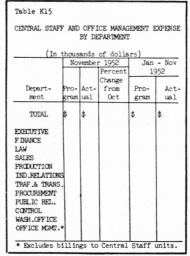

Table K15

CENTRAL STAFF AND OFFICE MANAGEMENT EXPENSE
BY DEPARTMENT

(In thousands of dollars)

Department	November 1952 Program	Actual	Percent Change from Oct	Jan - Nov 1952 Program	Actual
TOTAL	$	$		$	$
EXECUTIVE					
FINANCE					
LAW					
SALES					
PRODUCTION					
IND.RELATIONS					
TRAF.& TRANS.					
PROCUREMENT					
PUBLIC REL.					
CONTROL					
WASH.OFFICE					
OFFICE MGMT.*					

* Excludes billings to Central Staff units.

EXHIBIT 4

TYPICAL TABLES AND CHARTS, SECTION 1

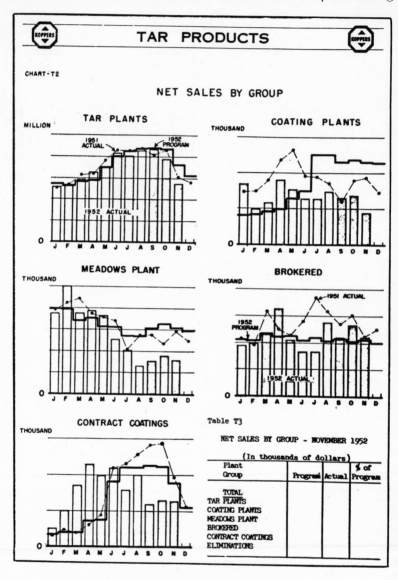

CHART-T2

TAR PRODUCTS

NET SALES BY GROUP

EXHIBIT 5

A Page from Section 2

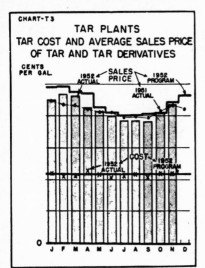

CHART-T3

TAR PLANTS
TAR COST AND AVERAGE SALES PRICE OF TAR AND TAR DERIVATIVES

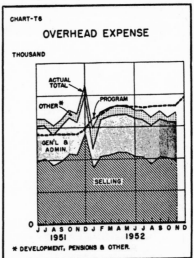

CHART-T6

OVERHEAD EXPENSE

* DEVELOPMENT, PENSIONS & OTHER

Table T8

RELATIONSHIP OF OPERATING EXPENSES TO NET SALES - NOVEMBER 1952

Item	Thousand Dollars		Percent of Net Sales	
	Pro-gram	Act-ual	Pro-gram	Act-ual
NET SALES	$	$		
OPERATING EXP.				
Cost of Sales				
Raw Materials				
Contr.Pl.Costs				
Fixed Expense				
Inventory Var.				
Depreciation				
Taxes (Excl.Inc.)				
Selling Expense				
Gen'l.& Admin.				
Central Staff				
Research & Devel.				
Pension				
Other				
OPERATING PROFIT				

Table T11

DIRECT PRODUCTION EXPENSE OF PLANTS HAVING VARIANCES OF 10 PERCENT OR MORE OCTOBER 1952

(In thousands of dollars)

Plant	October 1952 Expense		Var-iance	Actual as % of Std.	
	Std.	Actual		Oct	Jan-Oct
TOT.(ALL PLTS.)	$	$	$		
TAR PLANTS					
Berkshire					
St.Paul					
Everett					
Warren					
Utica					
Youngstown					
COATING PLANTS					
Garwood					
Houston					
Follansbee					
Port Arthur					
Illinois Ave.					

EXHIBIT 6
TYPICAL TABLES AND CHARTS, SECTION 2

FINANCE

FINANCE ADMINISTRATION SECTION

During the month $ million par value of U. S. Treasury Bills matured and the proceeds were reinvested in new Bills. An additional $ million par value 91-day Bills were purchased so that at November 30 a total of $ million par value of these Bills were held, of which $ million will mature in December. The program for November 30 calls for $ million of Bills to be held in order to cover the programmed tax accrual at that date; however the tax accrual is more than $ million below program. The most recent purchase was made on the basis of a 1.87 yield, very close to the highest rate the company has obtained.

Pursuant to arrangements made by the Law Department with the Securities and Exchange Commission, an order was placed with a Pittsburgh brokerage firm for the sale of   shares of common stock of Of this amount,   shares had been sold at November 30 at prices of   and The proceeds from this portion were approximately $ thousand. The book value of the shares is $ thousand (per share) and the tax base is about $· thousand (per share). The complete sale of these shares will be sufficient to offset the estimated $ thousand of capital gains for   and to provide a margin of about $ thousand of tax loss for unforeseen further capital gains. Since the book value of this stock was written down to   per share in this sale will provide an estimated book gain of about $ thousand.

A rather comprehensive credit report was prepared on the major steel company in   , which has asked Koppers through Freyn to assist it in financing the purchase of certain blast furnace equipment. A report on the subject was forwarded to Freyn for discussion purposes.

The 1953 Program of Koppers General was consolidated with the operating divisions and turned over to the Control Section for printing.

REAL ESTATE SECTION

The Chicago sales office lease in the   expires May 1, 1953. The management of the building requests an increase of   percent in rent (from $ per year to $ per year) on a three year renewal with a two year option basis.

A study of the entire Freyn Engineering Department office rental situation in the (square feet) and (25,355 square feet) Buildings was made. The rental agent of the   Building had suggested an increase from $ per sq. ft., the average rental for the entire space occupied in that building, to $ per sq. ft. per floor for the three floors proposed to be leased under present plans. After further negotiations this was reduced to $ per sq. ft. or a total of $ thousand per floor for the three floors proposed to be leased for three years with option for two more years, from September 30, 1953 (lease expiration date). As for the   Building, the space averages $ per sq. ft., but Koppers will probably relinquish all this space. If present plans materialize, the overall result would be a reduction in rent of about $ thousand, based on total rental of $ per square foot.

The conveyancing papers covering the sale of part of the Clifton Yard idle real estate were approved and arrangements have been made by the Law Department for the consummation of this transaction prior to the end of the year. Arrangements were made to sell under option three acres of the company's undeveloped land at the   to   Corporation for a consideration of $ thousand, considerably in excess of the book value of this property. The   will take over one of the piston ring leaseholds in San Francisco, releasing Koppers from any obligation thereunder. A further study was made of the Independence County, Arkansas idle real estate and a revised list with location, acreage and sales price was submitted to Koppers' real estate representative at Batesville, Arkansas to develop prospects for the sale of this

EXHIBIT 7

PAGE 1, SECTION 3

ECONOMICS

GENERAL

There has been no change in the business picture over the past month. Industrial activity continues at peak rates and the demand for steel and other basic materials remains high. Retail trade has not picked up as much as hoped for but Christmas buying is barely underway and it may yet reach the record levels anticipated earlier.

While the immediate business picture is excellent, a downturn still appears inevitable after years of over-stimulation to the economy. No severe depression is foreseen, for it would require only a modest recession to provide the overdue correction to our business system.

The economy as a whole is basically strong. A growing population needs more and more goods. Geographical shifts in population multiply the demand for many kinds of goods and services even beyond that which a rising population alone would exert. There is no evidence that these trends will halt. In addition, the standard of living is rising and will continue to rise. Per capita income available for spending has increased faster than the cost of living, and people generally have been taking advantage of their increased leisure time and improved incomes to enjoy the better living conditions open to them. The banking system is sound. Our natural resources are large, our inventive genius is active, and our initiative is still alive.

These factors cannot prevent cyclical changes in the level of business but they give promise of a dynamic future and provide a cushion against a severe readjustment. In addition to these, there are a number of more specific cushions that will operate to prevent a spiral of deflation of the sort that cumulates as it progresses:

1. Even though military expenditures will shortly flatten out and then decline somewhat, a minimum estimated at $30 billion annually for national security will probably be maintained indefinitely. This contributes to the demand for goods and constitutes a stabilizing influence never previously experienced.

2. Business and individuals have strong financial positions generally. Even though corporate and personal indebtedness seems high, working capital positions are comfortable, farm debt is small, and individuals' savings are very large.

3. Deposit insurance should prevent any fears for the safety of depositors' money. The banking system is strong and liquid, with little apparent danger of trouble.

4. Wage rates are likely to be relatively steady, creating the incentive for labor saving and cost reducing devices.

5. Unemployment is unlikely to be severe. The labor force now includes a growing proportion of older workers who would first be retired.

6. Unemployment insurance offers a means of income and a sense of greater security for those who may lose their jobs.

7. Social security programs will similarly provide a steady amount of funds to eligible persons, adding thereby a further degree of stability to national income.

8. The farm price support program will prevent crop prices from collapsing and will help to maintain farm income. Severe liquidation of farm commodities or real estate will not be forced.

These are all elements of strength that should provide a floor to any dip in business activity at levels not too far down. Even though they cannot completely prevent a correction, they can help to eliminate the unwarranted pessimism that can make recovery more difficult. Many of these cushions involve government expenditures and because of their size, it will be difficult to reduce the federal budget enough to provide for extensive tax reduction. The twin objectives of national security and prosperity are not entirely consistent with the urge toward lower federal budgets and tax relief, except on a

EXHIBIT 8

PAGE 1, SECTION 4

About 160 copies of the report are issued, although only about 100 are complete. The rest contain only certain sections and go to lower management levels within certain divisions. Each member of the Board of Directors receives a complete copy.

At the monthly meeting of the Operating Committee, composed of all six division general managers and the managers of all staff departments, this report is gone over in great detail. The President of Koppers, who also is Chairman of the Operating Committee, makes full use of this report as a means of conducting the business. He has read every word in it prior to the meeting, and with his red pencil has noted the matters he intends to emphasize. Here in this committee meeting many matters of policy and courses of action are indicated to correct the weak points in our progress and in general to strengthen the company's progress toward its goals. Following the meeting, the Committee's secretary prepares and issues minutes which remind the members of these decisions.

This Monthly Progress Report has been well received and put to good use at Koppers. It has proved to be an excellent means of taking much of the bother and annoyance out of the reporting job and providing management with the kind of report it needs and wants. (See pp. 332-48 for outline and sample pages.)

Technical Writing Grows into New Profession: Publications Engineering [*]

by ROBERT T. HAMLETT

Summary—Engineering-level technical writing is described as requiring, foremost, the skills and knowledge of an engineer and, secondly, the ability to write well. For this combination of work the term "Publications Engineer" is proposed. The writer's participation in an engineering project is outlined on a time basis, starting with the sources of information and completed with delivery of the printed work. Satisfying aspects of the field are discussed and the future is predicted as of growing value to the engineering profession as a whole.

Introduction. The tremendous expansion in the size and productiveness of the engineering profession has been due, in a large measure, to the ability of research and development engineers to

[*] Quoted by permission from the *Proceedings of the I.R.E.*, Vol. 40, No. 10, October, 1952. Robert T. Hamlett, Senior Member, I.R.E., is Engineering Department Head for Publications, Sperry Gyroscope Company.

enlist other engineers for special tasks or services related to their basic problems. It was not so many years ago that an *engineer* was *the engineer*—he was charged with responsibility for all *engineering* work on a project. This was possible because the end result of his engineering work was usually a single unit or instrument which operated without "tie-in" or reference to other equipment. He found time somehow to solve all of the engineering problems that arose in connection with his "brain child."

But the modern era of "systems" rather than "instruments" has changed the engineering approach to a very marked degree. One hears now about systems engineers, product engineers, project engineers, standards engineers, administrative engineers, test engineers, field engineers, production engineers, packaging engineers, industrial engineers, and so on. What has happened? Simply that the individual engineer cannot any longer carry all the burdens of the job of "engineering" of a system or even of a single instrument which ties into a system. While a very gifted engineer, possessing high skill in many branches of engineering, may still be able to visualize and guide the work on his project, he is no longer able to carry on the many individual investigations, attend the frequent engineering conferences, plan the fiscal and field-testing programs, solve the production and packaging problems, or create the publications which are necessary.

This ability of the engineer to pass on responsibility to other engineers has given rise to still another field of specialization within the engineering profession—that of TECHNICAL WRITING. (See Fig. 66.) The products of this new field are instruction books, training manuals, engineering reports, technical data sheets, and many other types of technical information, a sampling of which appears in Fig. 67. The workers in this field are referred to as "Technical Writers," "Engineering Writers," "Specification Writers," "Technical Report Writers," and the like. This author prefers to call the workers in this field "Publications Engineers," in keeping with other well-established titles such as "Standards Engineer," "Test Engineer," and "Field Service Engineer." This new title will be used throughout the article.

What Is a Publications Engineer? The principal reason why this author prefers the new title "Publications Engineer" to that of "Technical Writer" is that it more clearly designates the duties of

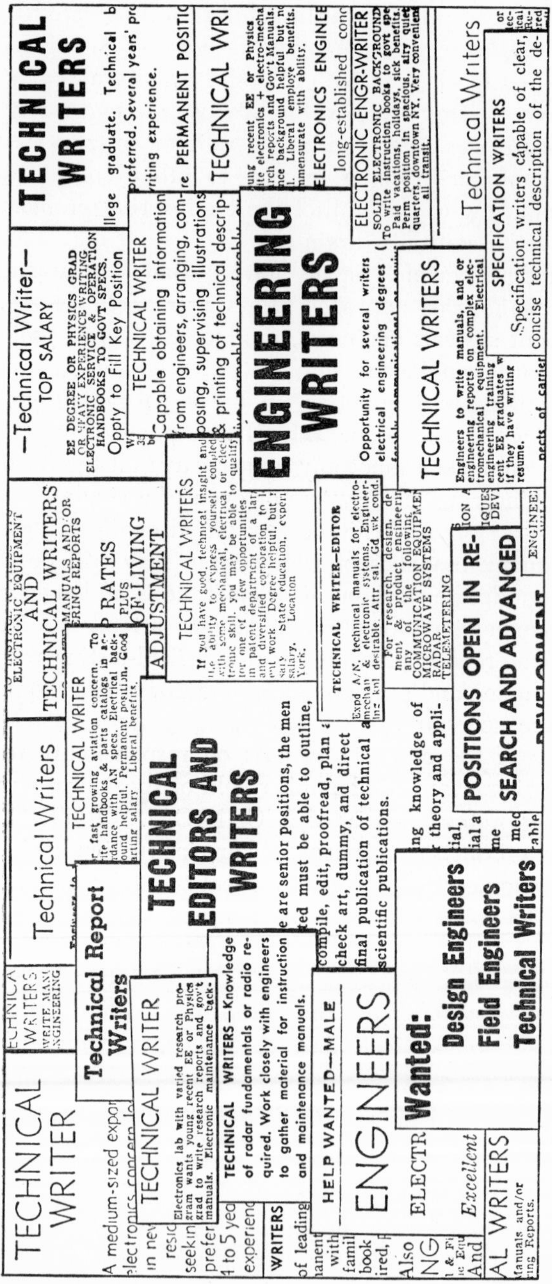

Figure 66. Demand for Engineer-Writers, Identified Herein as "Publications Engineers," Is Evidenced by These Classified Advertisements Selected at Random from Newspaper and Magazine Employment Sections.

FIGURE 67. Publications Engineers Produce a Variety of Printed Matter Requiring the Combined Skills of the Engineer and the Writer.

such a worker, and also places him in a proper professional status with fellow engineers, where he rightly belongs. For he is an engineer first, and secondly a writer. The term "Technical Writer," as commonly accepted, refers to a writer who writes material on technical subjects to various levels of intelligence but who is not usually concerned with the actual publication processes and problems.

The Publications Engineer is an engineering specialist who relieves other engineers of the major portion of the responsibility for production of all publications required as a result of the engineers' work. The Publications Engineer writes technical material, plans and directs preparation of copy, and carries through on all details concerned with actual production of the publication. It is necessary to repeat that he is first an engineer, then a writer, and finally, a publication man.

Engineers have always labored under the stigma that they cannot write well. It is a common attitude, even in precollege education, to assume that because the student is superior in mathematics he must be inferior in English. This affects the student's attitude and he very naturally uses it as an excuse for not seriously studying the subject in which he is prejudged to be inferior. When the "superior" math student goes to engineering school, it is a foregone conclusion that there is very little that can be done to help him there. However, he is given one or possibly two courses in English (especially "arranged" for engineers) early in his college work. No further attempts are made to help him overcome a deficiency which will handicap him throughout his entire career.

There is no doubt that some engineers cannot write—but some lawyers, some accountants, and some doctors cannot write well! Some doctors do not develop a pleasing "bedside" manner, so they become fine surgeons or specialists. So some engineers do not take time to write well, and because of this other engineers now find an interesting and well-paid profession.

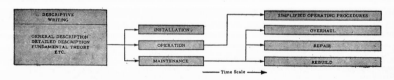

FIGURE 68. Typical Writing Assignments on a System.

The Publications Engineer must be an engineer who has writing aptitude. This aptitude may have never become very obvious because of the misguidance and lack of encouragement received during his education. The author has seen many engineers who felt certain that they were below average in writing aptitude develop into excellent writers of technical material. No one can doubt that the engineering profession would be in a much better position if there were more effective writers among us. (The same might be said for speakers.)

The Publications Engineer must be an engineer with unquenchable thirst for learning. If he is a mechanical engineer, he must be learning more about electronics; if he is an electrical engineer, he must be learning about aerodynamics, hydraulics, and the like. He is constantly challenged to describe something about which he knows practically nothing. But with his basic engineering education under his hat, he tackles each unknown with some confidence that he can understand and interpret it for others who may know more or less about it than he does. Many fine technical descriptions result when engineers who are educated in one field begin to write on subjects in other engineering fields; they use analogies which help the reader in applying the description to his own experience.

The Publications Engineer must have a working knowledge of the advantages and disadvantages of many types of reproduction processes, such as spirit duplication, mimeograph, Photostat, blueline, and blueprint, Ozalid, and offset printing and letterpress printing. He is familiar with type faces, paper stock, cover materials, binding methods, and the like. He understands the problems involved in production of copy by typewriters, Varitypers, typesetting, and phototype. He has a practical knowledge of the arts of photography and retouching, and he guides technical illustrators in visualizing and rendering special illustrations for use with his written words.

All of his talents and acquired knowledge are combined in the process of preparing a publication that must meet government or commercial specifications covering content, format, practicability, and literary standards. He is at the same time an engineer, a writing specialist, a publications expert, and a student of psychology!

Variety of Work. When the young Publications Engineer has overcome his inferiority complex in tackling new writing projects, he finds the variety of writing assignments to be one of the most attractive features of his job. It is a familiar complaint among engineers that they become too specialized and know too little of what is taking place in the scientific world around them. While no scientist can hope to keep abreast of the tremendous evolution of technical achievements now taking place, the Publications Engineer finds real satisfaction in testing and adding to his knowledge in many different fields. As an example, in the author's company

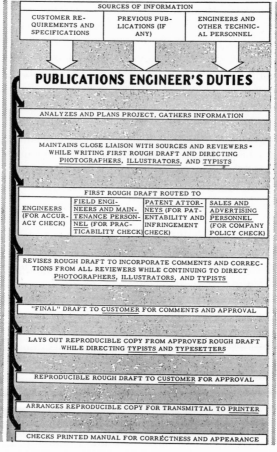

FIGURE 69. Publications Engineer Participates in Every Phase of Manual's "Life Cycle"; He Must Gain Broad Knowledge of Product's Engineering, Manufacture, and Customer's Application. Persons with whom he deals directly are underscored.

the skilled Publications Engineer develops a descriptive knowledge in such varied fields as radar, hydraulics, servomechanisms, gyroscopics, computing mechanisms, ballistics, optics, navigation, and aerodynamics. When the occasion demands, he becomes, for a time, a writing specialist in one or more of these fields.

In addition to the variety of writing from the product standpoint, there is also much variation in the material to be gathered on any one product or system. Fig. 68 illustrates some of the writing assignments on a single system. Some of the assignments require the Publications Engineer to work intimately with the equipment; in some cases he completely disassembles and reassembles the units. In other cases, he accompanies the equipment on trial runs or field tests. These experiences give a "practical" satisfaction to those who like to feel that they are not just "theoretical" writers.

Another attractive feature of the Publications Engineer's work lies in the variety of contacts which he makes in the course of the development and approval of a publication. Fig. 69 shows a typical "life story" of an instruction book prepared for the Armed Services. The underlining in the diagram gives an indication of the many individuals concerned in the preparation or approval of the publication prior to its final printing; the Publications Engineer works constantly with all of those shown.

The Future for Publications Engineers. Young engineers often raise the question as to the future of Technical Writing or Publications Engineering. There are several factors which appear to be of importance in attempting to predict the future—but to the author they all look favorable toward increasing opportunity for this new profession. First, the complexity of equipment and systems certainly will continue to increase; automatic control is the ultimate goal of nearly all future instrumentation, and with such control always comes increased technical complexity. With increasing complexity there is greater need for more complete instructional material. As one associate put it, "the equipment becomes more complex but the intelligence of the average user remains the same." Second, granted that complexity will increase, there is the immediate following condition that the equipment will be much more costly and must be repaired rather than replaced. This adds again to the need for publications which will be adequate for the purpose. The funds allocated for publications will necessarily increase, but will still be a very small portion of the total cost of the equipment. Third, if the caliber of engineering graduates coming into Publications Engineering is maintained or raised, there will be a broadening in the scope of their work since they themselves will develop opportunities for using their special skill to supplement the work of other engineers. This is a very important responsibility in any new profession—to develop and broaden the particular skills and to offer them to others.

Conclusion. Publications Engineering is a new profession which has grown rapidly in the past few years because of the increasing complexity of equipment and the inability of the research and development engineers to undertake the extensive writing projects which became necessary.

The Publications Engineer must have a sound engineering education and must possess writing aptitude—although it is pointed out that the possession of this aptitude may not be realized by many young engineers.

The Publications Engineer develops a knowledge of the reproduction and printing processes, and can guide the publication through all of its stages from rough draft to its printed form.

The variety of work assignments and personal contacts appeal greatly to certain engineering graduates. Some of the writing arrangements cover theoretical aspects, others are along practical lines where the writer works closely with the equipment in the factory or in the field.

The "personal-satisfaction" factor is quite high for the Publications Engineer since his assignments are usually of short duration, compared to those of the engineer, and he "sees" the final results of his labors at more frequent intervals.

Finally, the future of this new profession looks promising because of the trend towards more complex equipment and the accompanying requirements for more complete handbook and engineering report coverage. The future also depends upon the efforts which Publications Engineers make to find new areas of service to the engineering profession.

PART IV

Work Materials

Chapter 18

CASE STUDIES

Case Study I

On April 1, 1952, Milton Mishler (a Miami University senior) sent a questionnaire to 144 business and professional men in Troy, Ohio, to determine some customer preferences and prejudices in their eating out at restaurants. He received a 52 per cent reply. Here are his covering letter and questionnaire tally sheet; you may make whatever use of them your professor suggests.

> May I have ten minutes of your time?
>
> I am trying to find out why people choose one restaurant instead of another. After I graduate from college I plan to open a restaurant of the type which serves complete meals rather than short orders and sandwiches. I would like to attract people like you as customers, and I am getting an early start in making my plans.
>
> You can help me plan my restaurant if you will fill out the enclosed questionnaire and return it to me in the envelope provided. I would certainly appreciate it if you would share with me the advantage of your experience.

"Pet Peeves" Mentioned in Replies.

Steaks spoiled by the use of rancid cooking utensils or greases. Coffee that is not good, especially because it was left over or because the urns were not kept scrupulously clean. Coffee should never be over six hours old.

1. How often do you dine at a restaurant?
   _15%_ Almost every day.
   _50%_ Usually at least once a week.
   _26%_ Usually at least once a month.
   _7%_ Usually at least once a year.
   _2%_ Never.

2. Which type of restaurant do you patronize most often?
   _7%_ Cafeteria.
   _5%_ Buffet Style (Smorgasbord).
   _85%_ Table Service.
   _3%_ All about the same.

3. How far do you usually travel to go to a restaurant of your
   choice? 50%: _10-20_ Miles. 37%: under 10 miles. 13%: over 20 miles.

4. Are these factors important in influencing your choice of a
   restaurant?
       Parking facilities.   Yes _84_ No _8_
       Special exhibits or displays, quaint or
       unusual decor.   Yes _25_ No _54_
       Personality of the waiters or waitresses.   Yes _83_ No _9_
       A "speciality of the house" such as unusual
       side dishes or salads.   Yes _49_ No _48_
       If your answer to the last question is yes,   (some did not
       please name or describe the specialty.   answer)
       Good steaks, seafood, corn fritters, good coffee, salad tray.

5. Which of the following do you feel is most important in
   restaurant food?
   _72%_ Quality of the food.
   _16%_ Attractiveness of the serving.
   _0%_ Size of the serving.
       _12%_ All are equally important.
   _____ None are of any real importance.

6. Which do you prefer?
   _18%_ Ala carte menus; that is, where each course is priced.
   _60%_ Table de hote service; that is, where the price quoted on
       the menu includes everything from the cocktail to the
       dessert.
   _22%_ No preference.

7. Do you like to have reservations if the party is small?
   _24%_ Yes.   _36%_ No.   _40%_ It does not make any difference.

8. What do you feel would be a fair price for the following dinner?

	Fruit Juice	$1 - $1.49 14%
Salad	Rolls	$1.50 - $1.99 46%
	Fried Chicken	$2.00 - $2.49 23%
Mashed Potatoes Green Vegetable		$2.50 - $2.99 19%
$ _____ Coffee	Dessert	over $3 3%

9. Please describe any "pet peeve" that you have in connection
   with a restaurant.

("Pet Peeves" *continued*)

Poor ventilation—air permeated with frying foods.

Indifference of the service and cold food.

A slow or careless waitress—regardless of how good the food is—we *won't* go back.

Poor service. Over-cooked vegetables. Greasy foods.

Failure of waiter to leave the check when the meal is over.

No warm breads or rolls and insufficient butter. There should at least be an inquiry to determine whether or not more butter is desired. Too many restaurants provide a lot of bread or rolls together with a dab of butter which can hardly be seen. If more butter is out of the question, provide jelly or jam as a substitute.

Food that is cold. People apparently known to the restaurant personnel being served ahead of strangers.

Cold food—including *cold rolls*.

Orders delivered to the table at variance with original order given; *e.g.*, (1) Coffee with cream instead of "black"; (2) salad with dressing after ordered "plain."

Too often coffee isn't good.

Poor food or tough steak. Lack of butter.

Cold food, too long a wait to be served, spotty silverware and glasses.

Sloppily dressed help, poor service—makes me very angry, poor food, untidy surroundings.

Sloppy waitress with chiding manner of service and speech. Forgetfulness. Table service not clean. Menus spotted and dirty.

Poor and "messy" service. Cold soup.

Poor service.

Poor service. Being made to feel that you must hurry through a meal so as to make room for other customers.

Smoky air. Unkept floors, table service and furnishings.

No paper napkins—I *don't* want paper napkins.

Put water bottle on table. *Never enough* water.

Slow service. Steam table vegetables. Lack of enough butter to complete your meal. Poor chef. If the cook is poor the food will also be bad and no matter if you only charge fifty cents, the meal will not be worth it.

Noise. Advertisements, calendars, etc. posted, hung or tacked on walls.

To walk into a restaurant and not be able to find a convenient place to hang a coat and crutches.

Smart acting or sloppy waitress. The boss bossing the help in public.

Sweeping of floors while customers are eating. Flies. Cold food, coffee or tea. Loud juke boxes. Slow service.

Delay in getting check when finished with meal.

Cold food supposed to be served hot.

Serving another party first even though you arrived first.

Offensive odors from any source.

Taking a given meal, with few trimmings added and jacking the evening price over the noon price. Pseudo-courtesy.

Not serving food hot. Not giving a choice of green vegetable in place of potato.

Waitress spilling coffee into saucer and doing nothing about it. Not bringing bill when finished serving, often necessitating a long wait.

Juke boxes. Poor ventilation. Booze—unless notice is given *outside*.

Cold food. A menu for soft diet customers should be included.

Indifferent and untidy waitress.

Waiting too long to be served, such as half an hour.

Failure to have facilities to serve small children of high-chair age, together with the seemingly lack of knowledge upon the part of the restaurant people as to what is a satisfactory small child's portion.

Waiting too long to be served. Mashed potatoes almost never good. Waitresses gabbing too much with themselves and customers.

Poor service.

Using poor grade canned vegetables on an otherwise good meal.

Cold food.

We don't patronize a restaurant that is not neat and clean.

Poor service. Loud music. No accommodations for children such as special rates for small servings.

Case Study II

Robert J. Weber (a Miami University senior) interviewed four successful accountants; he asked each one to discuss the most important qualities (in order of their importance) that a college graduate should possess to be hired by his firm. Mr. Weber took careful notes and wrote the following summaries of his interviews. Make whatever use of them that your professor assigns.

ABNER J. STARR (Lybrand, Ross Bros., & Montgomery, Cincinnati, Ohio).

Mr. Abner J. Starr is a Certified Public Accountant and resident partner of the Cincinnati office of Lybrand, Ross Bros., & Montgomery, a national public accounting firm. He has been in the public accounting profession for a great many years, working himself up from the bottom to his present position without the aid of a college education.

Mr. Starr gives accounting grades the first consideration on a student's job application form. The accounting grades should be high but need not be extremely high, for it was his opinion that the student with the very high grades did not have to work so hard since he probably achieved them by superior intelligence. The man who had to work hard for his grades was a better risk, in his opinion, since that man had developed good work habits.

Nevertheless a good average in accounting is an important factor in selection, more important than the over-all average. If the accounting grades are acceptable it is not necessary for the over-all average to be high. Also, the courses outside the accounting curriculum need not be in any particular field; a well-diversified selection of courses is most desirable.

The next important requirement is enough college activities to display to the firm that the applicant has experience in meeting and working with people and that he has a personality that is acceptable to others. The activities do not have to be numerous, but they should be sufficient to give an indication that the applicant gets along with people.

The next most desirable quality is a good appearance. The man should be dressed neatly and make a good all-around appearance.

The applicant should be able to carry on a good conversation and have the ability to express himself clearly. Mr. Starr states that this quality is essential when the accountant is working for a large number of clients each with a different personality. He also states that it is essential for the accountant to have the ability to sell himself and his suggestions and recommendations to the client. All the qualities just mentioned point to one thing—personality. Success in the profession of public accounting requires a good personality.

The applicant must have at least a normal physical strength and build. This is essential when taking inventories where the count is not an easy task.

The man must not use intoxicants to an excess. Mr. Starr states that a drinker has no place in the public accounting field.

The applicant should show skill in the use of language. He must be able to make himself understood without impressing the client as being pedantic. Mr. Starr states that many of the clients are hostile to the accountant and that it takes a great deal of tact to satisfy them.

Draft status has little bearing on the applicant's chances of being hired by the firm. If he is a good man he will be hired regardless of his draft status, unless of course he has received notice to report for duty.

The marital status of the college graduate has no bearing on his opportunity of being selected. Mr. Starr reports that his firm hires both married and single men.

The aptitude of the graduate is judged from his performance in college and the way he presents himself in the interview.

BERL G. GRAHAM, C.P.A. (Gano & Cherrington, Cincinnati, Ohio).

Mr. Berl G. Graham is a Certified Public Accountant and a partner in the firm of Gano & Cherrington in Cincinnati. Mr. Graham has been engaged in numerous responsible positions in the accounting field; he is a member of the Ohio Society of Certified Public Accountants, The American Institute of Accountants, The Certified Public Accounting Examination Board, and former member of the teaching staff at the University of Cincinnati.

Mr. Graham's major emphasis is placed upon the applicant's character. Honesty, he stated, is essential in a man entering the accounting profession. By "honesty" he means upholding the basic principles of accounting, that is, not permitting the client to use in his accounting statements methods which are not consistent with generally accepted accounting principles and which lead to a misstatement of fact. Mr. Graham said that many accounting students come out of college with the opinion that what they learned is not what is done in practice. He said that students should not doubt the principles learned in college but should uphold those principles.

Educational requirements for a position with Gano & Cherrington include a good understanding of accounting principles. An applicant must prove, by grades or otherwise, that he has this basic understanding before he can be accepted. Graduate work is not necessary; experience helps more than advanced study in reaching the goal of passing the Certified Public Accountant examination.

Personality is an important factor to Mr. Graham in considering a man for public accounting work. A good appearance is essential since the accountant represents the firm when away from the office. He said that the client does not think of his men as individuals but as Gano & Cherrington, the public accounting firm. Manners are also important in this respect, for if the client judges the man as uncouth it is probable that the client will likewise judge the entire firm as uncouth.

Linguistic ability has its importance, according to Mr. Graham. It is necessary for the applicant to express himself in good English, for bad English has a definite tendency to cause loss of respect for the firm for which he is working.

College activities were given little or no weight in his decision upon a man's acceptability.

The draft status of an individual is of major importance because of the conditions which exist today. Mr. Graham remembers all too vividly losing eighteen men at the outbreak of World War II and also the caliber of men he had to accept to replace them.

Although the marital status is not as important as the draft status, single men were preferred by Gano & Cherrington.

Previous accounting experience in a recent college graduate, Mr. Graham stated, would probably be looked upon as desirable to his other partners, but for himself he prefers a man with no experience. He said that a man without experience presents no problem of unlearning what he may have originally learned wrong. A man with previous experience (unless it was diversified, which is unlikely) seems to relate existing situations back to his previous job, and the two situations are usually not comparable. For instance, if the accountant encounters a problem while working on a department store and he tries to solve this problem by analyzing it from the standpoint of a manufacturing concern, he may easily arrive at a faulty conclusion.

Aptitude for accounting work is not judged in a scientific manner. The interview and application blank are used to judge this point in a subjective manner.

H. W. CUTHBERTSON, C.P.A. (Cuthbertson, Hawk & Arnold, Dayton, Ohio).

Mr. H. W. Cuthbertson is a Certified Public Accountant and partner in the firm of Cuthbertson, Hawk & Arnold in Dayton, Ohio. Mr. Cuthbertson is a veteran in the public accounting profession, and is well qualified to comment on the subject of this report.

He rated on an almost equal basis ability and personality with ability having a slight edge. He stated that a person must be able to sell himself and also have something to sell. The accountant must be able to talk to a client; gain his confidence and then have the client state his problem. The accountant must then give him a solution that will send him away well satisfied. He must talk to the client on his plane and stay away from technical terminology that may leave him unimpressed.

Mr. Cuthbertson felt that ability is important, but he did not want the man with the highest grades. He felt that a man with high grades in accounting had to neglect other portions of his education to attain them or else he was a person who could read something once and have it. He felt that the man with exceptionally high intellectual ability is not necessarily the most desirable to hire in the public accounting profession.

His third requirement and a very important quality is a desire to serve. The man in a profession to serve his client will be the man who will be successful. A man entering the profession with the idea of making money might make money for awhile but it will not last. He says a man who has but one motive, that of giving service, will be the man to gain real success. If he has that attitude he will automatically make money.

Character is the next quality a man in the public accounting profession must possess in order to succeed. Without good character he cannot be respected in his profession and will soon be on the outside.

Although honesty and integrity are components of good character, Mr. Cuthbertson gave them separate consideration to emphasize their importance. He could not remotely consider any applicant whose honesty and integrity were questionable.

Mr. Cuthbertson says that the ability and service attitude could be developed, as could personality (to a certain extent); but character, integrity, and honesty could not be developed. A man's character relates back to his childhood, and if he did not acquire it then he will never possess it. Therefore, good character is a requisite for anybody planning to enter the accounting profession.

A man's education for public accounting must be broad, according to Mr. Cuthbertson. A man with a broad education as opposed to a specialized education is far better equipped to handle people and to learn. He says the accountant can pick up the specialized phases by experience, but a broad diversified background is desired for working with the public.

Graduate work is not recommended by him. He thinks that the best thing a man graduating from college can do is to get experience. He does not mean by this that education is not good, but he thinks that the experience is far more important to the man just graduating.

Mr. Cuthbertson states that his firm is using tests for selecting personnel. This is the only firm in the survey that is using a testing program for personnel selection. The testing program consists of an intelligence test, a Strong Interest Test, and selected accounting problems. He says his firm adheres to these tests quite religiously since no one in the firm has the qualifications to judge a man without these aids.

Linguistic ability, he thinks, is of great importance to a person entering any profession. He thinks that one year of speech should be required by colleges for anybody entering a profession. He feels that the accounting profession in general is weak on this point and that it should be stressed far more than it is. Writing ability also is important; he thinks that there is too much stilted phraseology and ambiguity in accounting reporting.

Mr. Cuthbertson also stressed the fact that clear oral expression is needed by business persons such as public accountants who have personal contacts with the general public.

College activities are also considered important by Mr. Cuthbertson since they teach a man how to mix with different groups and broaden his personality. He says that his firm have a place on their job application blank for the applicant to list his college activities.

A man with limited accounting experience (everything else being equal) would have preference over a man with no experience, according to Mr. Cuthbertson.

The draft status of a man is considered very carefully when hiring. Mr. Cuthbertson says this is due to the fact that four of their key men are in the reserves and are subject to call at any time. The tendency right now is to hire draft-exempt men.

THOMAS A. CARNEY, C.P.A. (Trout & Barstow, Dayton, Ohio).

Mr. Thomas A. Carney is a Certified Public Accountant and partner in the firm of Trout & Barstow in Dayton, Ohio.

Mr. Carney states that the first thing he looks for in an individual applying for a position is his general appearance. It is not necessary that he be handsome, but his dress should be neat and pleasing to the eye. The reason he places appearance first is the fact that this is the first thing that makes contact with him in an interview. However, the most important requirement is that the applicant have a basic understanding of accounting principles. It is not necessary for him to have outstanding grades in accounting, but there must be evidence that he has a basic knowledge of the subject. Mr. Carney expresses the opinion that outstanding grades are not necessary. It is his opinion that the very intelligent individual memorizes much of his material and does not remember it as well as the person who pores over the books.

Another attribute that Mr. Carney rates high in an applicant is the ability to express himself effectively. He states that expression is one of the most powerful weapons in the world and that not enough people possess this ability. He thought the educational institutions, particularly the grade schools, did not stress this phase of education adequately.

Mr. Carney states that an applicant's character should be unquestionable if he is to succeed in public accounting. Accounting work is highly confidential and should not be discussed outside the line of duty. The temptation to talk often presents itself, but the character of the accountant should be such that he is not swayed by temptation.

Speed is another characteristic that is desired. Mr. Carney states that the only thing the accountant has to sell is his time and that a man who does not possess a reasonable amount of speed is not going to make money for his employer.

College activities are desirable in a man applying for a position because they are a sign of being able to meet and get along with people. This characteristic is much desired in a small public accounting firm, for this is the manner in which many new accounts are acquired.

An analytical mind is one of the more essential attributes that Mr. Carney thinks an applicant should possess. He defined an analytical mind as the ability to tackle a problem with an open mind; to help the client find his difficulty when something appears to be going wrong.

Case Study III

In May, 1954, Pat Morris (a Miami University sophomore) made a comparative study of Cincinnati, Hamilton, and Dayton, Ohio, as prospective locations for the Auto-Stoker Company. She gathered her information from many sources: Chambers of Commerce, U.S. Department of Commerce, industry, reference books. Reprinted here is her introduction, her analysis of one of the cities (Hamilton), her summary of comparisons, and a weighted rating chart which she used in making her final decision.

1. Write the *Conclusions and Recommendations* section to accompany the report.
2. Write an introductory summary for the report. Write the letter of transmittal.
3. Using Miss Morris' information about the Auto-Stoker Company's requirements and her evaluation of Hamilton, prepare a comparative analysis of Hamilton and a city in your area as possible sites for the company. You will need to secure the same kind of information about the city you choose, from much the same sources.
4. Using Miss Morris' information about the Auto-Stoker Company's requirements, prepare a comparative analysis of three cities in your area as possible sites for the company.
5. Prepare charts to accompany Miss Morris' report, based on the following information from the 1950 U.S. Census.

	POPULATION		EMPLOYMENT, 1950 (METROPOLITAN AREAS)		
	1940	1950	Total Civilian Working Force	Employed	Un-employed
Hamilton ..	50,592	57,951	23,724	22,683	1,041
Dayton	210,718	243,872	109,973	105,654	4,319
Cincinnati ..	455,610	503,998	214,209	201,825	12,384

INTRODUCTION

This plant-location study has been prepared at the request of the Board of Directors of the Auto-Stoker Company to serve as a guide in their choice of a city in which to locate a new plant as a branch of the main plant in Portland, Oregon.

On the basis of a previous market analysis it has been found that southern Ohio is centrally located in the midwestern market for both home and industrial stokers and is also in a favorable position to serve the southern states. Therefore, Cincinnati, Hamilton, and Dayton have been chosen as possible cities in which to locate.

In order to effectively evaluate the importance of the various plant location factors for this particular industry, it is first necessary to analyze the product and the method of manufacture.

"The Auto-Stoker is made up in three units: a sheet-metal hopper with air blower attached, a patented driving-gear mechanism enclosed in a gearbox, and a cast-iron burner with feed pipe and spiral feed screw attached. The whole mechanism is electrically driven. . . . The hopper can be readily produced at any sheet-metal works. The burner, feed pipe, and screw, which are heavy castings requiring little finishing, can be easily produced in almost any foundry." * The important unit is the driving mechanism which accounts for approximately 50 per cent of the entire cost of manufacturing the stoker. Its production requires a well-equipped machine shop; heat-treating ovens; dies, jigs, and tools of special design; and a skilled labor force.

According to the plan previously established by the Board of Directors, the branch plant is to be equipped to produce the driving mechanism, while the castings and sheet metal parts are to be purchased from merchant foundries and sheet metal works. The branch plant is to finish the rough castings and assemble the component parts.

Governed by this manufacturing plan, the basic factors to be evaluated in surveying tentative locations for this plant are·

1. General nature of the city.
2. Location and availability of production material—that is, foundries and sheet metal works for producing the hoppers

---

* Franklin E. Folts, *Introduction to Industrial Management* (New York: McGraw-Hill Book Co., 1949), pp. 289, 290.

and castings and a source of supply for the specially designed manufacturing equipment needed.

3. Availability, skill, and conditions of the labor force.
4. Industrial fuel, water, and power.
5. Transportation and distribution facilities.
6. Laws and regulations; general attitude toward industry.
7. Tax structure.
8. Living conditions.

Of the three cities mentioned, in the light of these factors, Cincinnati appears to be the most desirable location for the new branch plant.

The report is divided into five parts. In the first three sections each city—Cincinnati, Hamilton, and Dayton—is examined and analyzed separately. In the fourth section the three cities are grouped together for comparison of advantages and disadvantages. The last section presents the conclusions and reasons for arriving at them.

HAMILTON

GENERAL INFORMATION.

Location. Hamilton is located 24 miles north of Cincinnati and about 16 miles east of the Indiana state line. It is the county seat of Butler County.

Area. City of Hamilton . . . . 7.94 square miles

Population.

Corporate City Limits
1950 census	57,951
1953 est., Hamilton Chamber of Commerce	62,000
City Zone (Audit Bureau of Circulation)	64,436
Butler County (1950 census)	147,203
Retail Trading Area (Audit Bureau of Circulation)	147,478

The Bureau of the Census has broken down this population as follows:

Native white	58,659
Negro	3,219
Foreign-born white	1,332
Other	60

Hamilton is a manufacturing boom town. The rapid expansion of its industry has swelled the population with a huge influx of laborers from Indiana and particularly from Kentucky, attracted there by the ready availability of jobs. The people here are considered to be of a conservative nature, and community relations are generally good.

Layout of City. Hamilton's average altitude is about 609 feet. The city is built on the banks of the Great Miami River, which bisects the downtown area. Shopping and manufacturing areas are centered on both sides of the river, with the outlying districts constituting the residential sections.

Climate. The temperature averages 75 degrees in the summer and 34 degrees in the winter. Precipitation does not vary widely throughout the year. March has the heaviest rainfall, with an average of 3.9 inches. October has the lightest, with an average of 2.4 inches.

Government. Hamilton has a seven-man council, one of whom serves as mayor, and a hired city manager to administer the city.

It might be said that industry governs Hamilton rather than Hamilton governing industry. Consequently, industrial restrictions are practically nonexistent.

Hamilton's police department is equipped with twelve cruisers, six motorcycles, one ambulance, and adequate personnel for the city's traffic and protection needs. The fire department consists of six fully equipped and manned fire stations.

Hamilton's municipal planning program includes improvement of traffic facilities, establishment of off-street parking areas, construction of a modern sewage disposal plant, and redevelopment of the city's several blighted slum areas. Many of these projects are already under way.

Banks. There are three banks in Hamilton.

Total assets	$73,360,062
Total deposits	$66,914,092

Housing. (Total dwelling units)

City of Hamilton	17,578
Butler County	42,343

PRODUCTION MATERIALS.

Hamilton has 17 sheet metal works, which are capable of satisfactorily supplying the sheet metal parts needed for the stoker. There are also four foundries for supplying the rough castings. These foundries would easily be able to absorb the additional work, since the period of the Auto-Stoker Company's largest demand for castings comes at a time which is the natural slack period for most foundries.

There are only two firms in Hamilton that could possibly furnish the specially designed tools, dies, and jigs needed. This, however, presents no difficulty, since the Cincinnati machine tool industry is so near. Consequently, Hamilton's supply of the needed production materials is quite adequate.

LABOR FORCE.

Availability. The 1950 Census lists the following figures:

Total civilian labor force 23,724
Employed 22,683
Unemployed 1,041

These figures are not for the number of people *employed* in Hamilton, but only for the number of workers who *live* within the city limits. The number of people employed in manufacturing in Hamilton in 1953 was 19,094. Many of these workers commute from surrounding areas in Ohio, Indiana, and Kentucky.

The largest industries, with the number of their employees, is as follows:

Paper manufacturing 3,867
Automobile bodies 2,157
Machinery 3,926
Safes 1,524

Skill. One of Hamilton's greatest drawbacks is its scarcity of skilled labor. Although the labor supply is plentiful, it is mostly constituted of unskilled workers.

Wages. The prevailing wages in Hamilton are approximately the same as in Cincinnati. The largest industrial pay days are the first and second Tuesdays of the month.

Type of Industry	Av. Wkly. Wage
Food	$52
Printing, publishing	56
Machinery (except electrical)	61
Fabricated metal products	54

Tractability. Labor relations in Hamilton have been exceptionally good. However, one disadvantage is the relatively high percentage of labor turnover.

UTILITIES.

Fuel. The municipally owned gas distribution system provides an adequate supply of gas at very reasonable rates. It has been their practice to offer special rates for industrial consumption.

Power. Hamilton also operates its own power plant and distribution system, which supplies most of the city. The Cincinnati Gas & Electric Company provides the rest. Of the 31 municipally owned power plants in the United States, Hamilton's has the lowest average rates.

Water. Hamilton gets its water supply from deep artesian wells. The water softening and filtration plant is city-owned. This plant, which softens the water to 5 grains of hardness, has a pumping capacity of 6,000,000 gallons per day. However, this has proved inadequate for Hamilton's expanding needs. During the last two summers water has had to be restricted. This situation is now being corrected by the drilling of a new well field and the construction of additional softening equipment.

TRANSPORTATION AND DISTRIBUTION FACILITIES.

Rail. Hamilton is served by two railroads—the Baltimore & Ohio and the Pennsylvania.

Truck. Hamilton is on U.S. Highway 127 and State Highways 4, 177, 128, 129, and 130. Fifteen major truck lines are available, seven with their headquarters in Hamilton.

Airports. Hamilton has one Class II Commercial airport.

Bus Lines. Ohio Bus Lines provides inter-city service, while a Hamilton line provides service within the city.

LAWS AND REGULATIONS.

There are no important industrial restrictions, leaving industry pretty much unhampered. The general attitude toward industry is very favorable.

TAX STRUCTURE.

The city's tax rate is $22.89 per $1,000 of assessed valuation. This is one of the lowest tax rates in the country.

LIVING CONDITIONS.

Hamilton is a typical middle-sized manufacturing town. Its living conditions are good. The public school system consists of twelve elementary schools, two junior high schools, and one senior high school. Plans for another junior high and a senior high school are now under way. In addition, there are nine parochial schools, and two business colleges. Both Miami University and Western College for Women are located just 14 miles away in Oxford, Ohio.

Hamilton has 105 churches of 64 different denominations to serve the religious needs of its people. Other community facilities include three hospitals, radio station WMOH, the Lane Public Library with two branches, and a daily evening newspaper, *The Hamilton Journal-News*.

Hamilton's outdoor recreational facilities are excellent. There are 47 parks and playgrounds, including swimming pools, tennis courts, ball fields, and other play activities. Millikin Woods and Crawford's Woods provide popular picnic areas and Potters Park golf course furnishes an excellent eighteen-hole course. This, though, is about the extent of Hamilton's recreational facilities. However, for those who want more elaborate or different entertainment, Cincinnati is only about 45 minutes away.

This holds true for the shopping situation as well. Although Hamilton has a fair-sized shopping section for a city of its size, those who want a wider selection must find it in Cincinnati.

SUMMARY OF COMPARISONS OF THE FACTORS
IN CINCINNATI, DAYTON, AND HAMILTON

PRODUCTION MATERIALS.

The supply of the three production essentials is quite adequate in all three cities. Therefore, it need no longer be considered as a determining factor.

LABOR.

Availability. The size of the labor force within the actual city is proportionate in these three cases to the size of the city, with Cincinnati ranking first, Dayton second, and Hamilton third. However, all three draw laborers from a large surrounding area, so the size of the labor force is equally adequate in all three cities.

Skill. More important to the Auto-Stoker Company than the size of the labor force is the number of skilled workers it can draw from. Here Dayton ranks first, with an extremely high percentage of skilled workers among her labor force, and Cincinnati second. Herein lies Hamilton's greatest weakness—her scarcity of skilled laborers.

Wages. Dayton, partly because of the highly skilled quality of her working force, has a considerably higher prevailing wage than does Cincinnati or Hamilton. The average wage rates in Cincinnati and Hamilton are about on a par.

Tractability. Labor relations are relatively good in all three cities, with Dayton perhaps ranking a little ahead of the other two.

Labor turnover seems to be inseparably related to the degree of skill of the labor force. Therefore, it is no surprise to find labor turnover unusually low in Dayton; about average in Cincinnati; and rather high in Hamilton.

UTILITIES.

Fuel. Cincinnati has a slight advantage over Dayton and Hamilton in the fuel situation because of her abundance of cheap coal. The availability and rates for gas are about the same for all three.

Power. The conditions and availability of power are equally satisfactory in the three cities. Hamilton ranks first in the power situation, however, because of lower rates.

Water. Dayton's water supply is one of her most valuable assets. There is an ever-abundant source in the underground reservoir that lies beneath the entire city. Most industries take advantage of this most desirable situation and sink their own wells.

The Cincinnati waterworks draws the city's supply of water from the Ohio River. The pumping capacity of this plant is quite adequate for the normal needs of the city.

In Hamilton, the water shortage that existed during the last two summers is being solved by the drilling of a new well field and construction of additional waterworks equipment.

TRANSPORTATION AND DISTRIBUTION FACILITIES.

Cincinnati ranks first, Dayton second, and Hamilton third in the availability of rail and truck transportation. Cincinnati has an unusually favorable rail rate situation due to the fact that it is located in both the Official and the Southern freight territories.

Its location on the Ohio River gives Cincinnati a second valuable advantage over the other two cities—cheap river transportation to the markets in the South.

LAWS AND REGULATIONS.

The attitude toward industry is equally favorable in Cincinnati, Dayton, and Hamilton, with bothersome restrictions being at a minimum.

TAX STRUCTURE.

Taxes are lowest in Hamilton, which has a rate of $22.89 per $1,000. Next comes Dayton with a rate of $26.80 and also a half of one per cent city income tax. Cincinnati's taxes are highest, with a regular rate of $27.80.

LIVING CONDITIONS.

Naturally, the larger a city is, the more resources it will have to serve its populace. Therefore, Cincinnati ranks first, with Dayton and Hamilton second and third, respectively, in the number of cultural opportunities available. However, Dayton and Hamilton have other advantages. Dayton is known as being an unusually clean and beautiful city, while Hamilton has many attributes for those who prefer a small-town life.

WEIGHTED RATING CHART

Below is a weighted rating chart evaluating the relative importance of the various factors in each of the three cities.

Each factor has been weighted according to its importance to the business.

Each city has then been assigned points of 1, 2, or 3 for each factor according to how it compared with the other two cities.

Next, the weight assigned each factor was multiplied by the ranking points (1, 2, or 3) of each city for that factor to determine its weighted value.

Example: Dayton is the best of the three cities for water, so is given three points. These three points are multiplied by the assigned weighting of three to find its weighted value of nine points.

Weighting Factor	Conditions	Cincinnati	Dayton	Hamilton
	Production Materials			
9	Foundries	9	9	9
9	Sheet Metal Works	9	9	9
5	Manufacturing Equipment	5	5	5
	Labor			
8	Tractability	16	24	8
7	Wage Costs	14	7	14
10	Availability of Skilled Workers	20	30	10
	Utilities			
5	Fuel	10	5	5
6	Power	6	6	12
3	Water	6	9	3
	Transportation and Distribution Facilities			
9	Water	27	9	18
9	Rail	27	18	9
9	Truck	27	18	9
1	Laws, Regulations, Attitude Toward Industry	1	1	1
4	Tax Structure	4	8	12
2	Living Conditions	6	4	2
	TOTAL WEIGHTS	187	162	126

Case Study IV

Joe Jones, 35, ordinary guy, got back from a vacation in mid-June. It was a hot day, on the dusty side, and Joe pulled his car into the garage with a sigh of relief. Driving in weather like this was no picnic, vacation or no vacation. The family piled out of the car, and Joe started after them, but before he could make it to the house Tom, his neighbor on the right, hailed him from down the road.

"Congratulations," Tom said. "How was the trip?"

"For what?" Joe said. "The trip was fine. Caught my limit in an hour and a half yesterday morning."

"We elected you Road Commissioner," Tom said.

"You what? The heck you did." Joe's voice went up a notch, and he set down the suitcase he'd been pulling out of the trunk.

"Yeah, we did. We had that meeting anyway, even if three of the guys couldn't come. My company is transferring me to the home office in Jersey, and I'll be out and gone inside a month. So I won't be much good as Road Commissioner. Besides, I'd had it for three years. And honest, Joe, we weren't trying to put it over on you; we all thought you'd do a good job. You want to improve the road, and you know everybody back here."

"Yeah, but—" Joe was thinking of the work, and the phone calls, and making up the assessment letters to buy more gravel to put on the road, and the job it was to get the property-owners to help keep the road in repair. "We'll sure miss you, Tom."

"We'll hate to leave—. We talked about your idea of black-topping," Tom went on. "We decided to have another meeting a week from Saturday to talk about it again. I think we can put it over if we can get the job financed through the bank so that we won't have to pay for it all at once. I know the couple that were looking at my house—Sniders, new at the college next year—would want the road paved some way; they were worrying about the dust and mud. Of the twelve families, the only ones I'd say were doubt-ful are Hackers and that other new family, what's their name? Holmann. All you'd have to do is get the figures together and send them around before the meeting so that we'd all know what we're talking about."

"Well, I'll try," Joe said. "I still think it was a lowdown trick to elect me when I wasn't there to defend myself."

"All very democratic," said Tom. "Say, Joe—"

"Yeah?"

"I still think concrete would be better, and so does Paul."

"It might be better, but it sure would cost more," said Joe.

"Not so much more that it wouldn't be worth it. Why don't you get the figures on concrete too?"

"Well, OK—" and Joe finished unpacking the car, listened to the news, ate his dinner, and then got on the phone. He called several more times the next morning, and made two trips uptown; when he pulled up a chair at his old portable typewriter the pad he had used was full of figures. The lane that twisted through the little subdivision just outside the corporation limits of Newton was 845 feet long; Joe had measured it. The grading required was estimated by the Frank Crane Company of Newton: four days, roughly $320. The charge for moving in a grading crew from the city Joe had estimated at $80, and so he had not bothered to call any of the grading companies there; the local lumber dealer had told him the rates were the same anyway after the company had brought in its equipment. $320 plus $80 was too much for grading; Joe ruled the Crane Company's competitors out. Besides, he hated to spend money on long-distance calls, and the information was needed quickly.

Blacktop surface was quoted by the Hall-King Road Company of nearby South Newton at $2.80 a running foot of 18-foot roadway. The Hall-King Company promised the same professional blacktop job that it supplied the county and the state on road contracts, except that the surface would not be so thick. Joe assumed that since the lane was a dead end, there would be little heavy truck traffic. The same type of blacktop surface was quoted by the Frank Crane Company at $2.95 a running foot of 18-foot roadway.

The man Joe talked to at the Frank Crane Company was Robert Sandefur, whose sons had organized a construction company during the past month. Sandefur had been directing some minor contracts to them, supposedly jobs Crane had not wanted, though Joe had heard rumors that Crane had given Sandefur notice. Sandefur had quoted Joe the $2.95 figure, and then said that Ajax Construction (run by his sons) had a new blacktop method that would cost less than half as much. This new method required no rolling, no heavy equipment, gave a long-lasting and smooth job, was unconditionally guaranteed by Sandefur himself, and could be had at an introductory price (just so the community could see how good it was) of $1.25 a running foot of 18-foot road. Sandefur suggested a further saving: reducing the road width to 14½ feet. Such a road he felt sure he could talk his sons into building for a flat $1 a running foot.

The Hall-King Road Company seemed reluctant to quote on concrete roadway; they had built so few that they were not sure how to make the estimate. They said it would take at least 375 yards of concrete at $13 a yard, a steel center strip at $54 per thousand feet, 36 contraction joints at $1.10 each, and forms, labor—they couldn't be sure, but the whole job would run anyway $6000, maybe $7000. The Frank Crane Company preferred not to bid on concrete; Joe saw Frank at the bank and checked with him directly so that he would not have to talk with Sandefur about it. Frank suggested that Joe and his neighbors buy the ready-mix concrete and lay the road themselves on Saturday and Sunday afternoons. Joe called the Home Gravel Company and learned that concrete was $13 a yard, as Hall-King had said, and that an 845-foot road would take between 350 and 400 yards, depending on how thick a roadway was wanted. Mr. Jackson at the gravel company said that forms could be rented for $250-$300 and that he had heard of some men in a nearby town who had made their own concrete road at a saving of one fourth over the contractor's estimate.

Joe called the Hackers and the Holmanns to find out how they felt about the road so that he would know their objections, if any, and how to get information to answer them. The Hackers said they were broke and just couldn't afford it at all; they weren't taking any kind of vacation this year and were about to sell their car. Besides, they lived at the end of the road and weren't bothered by dust. The Holmanns were suspicious of Joe; they felt that he was trying to put something over on them just because they were new. They had been told, they said, that when they bought their property they gained access to all improvements, water lines, phone lines, etc., and they felt this should include all future improvements. They had heard about the "assessment racket" that was tried on newcomers, and they wanted Joe to know they weren't going to be taken in.

From the President of the bank Joe learned that the total bill for the road would be paid by the bank, which would then divide up the sum into twelve equal shares. Any property-owner could pay this sum in a lump, without interest of course, or pay it quarterly for ten years at an average interest of 2½ per cent a year, the interest to be figured each year on the original sum borrowed rather than on the unpaid balance.

Joe decided he was as ready as he would ever be to write his report to the property-holders; he put plenty of carbon paper in his typewriter and started to work.

. . . Let's assume you're Joe; write his report.

SUPPLEMENTARY LIST OF TITLES, INFORMAL REPORTS

Export Sales Organization of Ford Motor Co.

Direct Mail Program for Van Wert Fire Insurance Co.

Personnel Program for Washington Hotel Dining Room and Coffee Shop.

Sales Presentation: Lewyt Vacuum Cleaners.

Sales Analysis: Posture Foundation Shoes.

A Public Relations Program for the Miami University Student Union Committee.

Reducing Fatigue and Waste Motion in the Stenographic Department.

Shall Ajax Distributing Corp. Subscribe to Dun and Bradstreet Services?

Procedure of the Contract Department, Ralph H. Jones Co.

Employee Deaths and Injuries, Transportation Department, New York Central System, Big Four District, June, 1955.

Proposed New Layout for Finishing Department, A-1 Dry Cleaners, Inc.

Insurance Rating Survey on the Great Atlantic and Pacific Tea Co. Building at 3250 Fredonia Avenue, Cincinnati, Ohio.

Shall Tom Collins, Jr., Co. purchase the Pitney-Bowes Model PS Postage Meter Machine?

The Necessity of an Accident Prevention Program at Philips Manufacturing Co.

Outline of an Accident Prevention Program.

Report of the Effectiveness of Three Typewriters Used in the Preparing of Master Plates for the Multigraph Machine at The Diem and Wing Paper Co.

Improvement Resulting from Installation of Monorail System for Materials Handling.

Proposed Rearrangement of the Inventory File at the Alvey-Ferguson Co.

Union Bonnet Rings Made from Continuous Castings.

A Plan for More Economical Purchasing of Meat by Institutions.

Need for a Personnel Department at Ajax Distributing Co.

Proposed Method of Moving Urgent Material Through G. E. Lockland Plant.

Study of Method of Tabulating Inquiries from Magazine Advertising of the Alvey-Ferguson Co.

Report on Fire at Terrace Park Country Club: Terrace Park Fire Department.

Report on Operation of New Check-Out System, Dean Grocery Co.

Report on the Proof-Box Method in Proofing Doughnuts.

Suggested Changes in Initial Distribution Methods for Dairy Products.

Six-Months Report of the Service Department, Walker Motor Co.

Construction Estimate Report: a Three-Car Garage.

Report on New Billing Form D-1680.

Report on Containers Used for Shipping Tomatoes from Florida Points.

Effect of Unvented Gas Consuming Equipment in Prefabricated Homes.

Report on the Operation of the Proof Department, First National Bank.

The Advisability of Establishing a Garage in Yorkville.

Report on the Elimination of the White Shoe Bottleneck in the Packing Room.

Statistical Hazard Facts and Suggestions for Elimination of Hazards.

How to Improve Production Quality and Eliminate Excessive Waste of Molded Products.

Proposed New Warehouse for Albert Door Co.

Proposed Method of Reporting Production in the Candy Department, Kroger Grocery and Baking Co.

Test and Inspection Report, Distribution Cabinet #531.

Report on a Proposed Subsidiary Plant at Memphis, Tennessee.

Survey: Salesmen's Opinions of the Bold Venture Sales Contract.

Report on False Alarms at Pease Co. and Suggestions for Readjustment of Automatic Fire Alarms.

Report on Management Conference Attended as Delegate of Hamilton Foundry Co.

Proposed Order Handling and Shipping Procedure.

Shall the Andrews Co. Install an IBM Accounting System?

Unimelt Welding in Steel Mills.

Labor Report on the New Model 10 One-Floor Six-Room Ranch House.

Deodorization with Chlorine Dioxide.

INDUSTRIAL ENGINEERING REPORT SUBJECTS (INFORMAL)

Suggested by JAMES H. BATCHELOR, *Industrial Engineering Consultant*

A Wage Incentive System.
Machine Rearrangement.
Preferred Numbers.
Two Alternative Plans for Expansion of Manufacturing Capacity.
Plant Layout for a Department.
Use of Smaller Balls in Ball Mill.
A Quality Content System for Pharmaceuticals.
Problems Confronting a New Farm Implement Dealer.
Project for Improving Patterns.
Product Classification.
Preferred Voltage Ratings for Alternating Current Systems and Equipment.
Procedure for Physical Inventory.
Addition of Two-Phase Test Facilities.
Production Control in a Pipe Fabrication Shop.
Introduction of Methods Charts.
Scheduling Problems.
Carton Survey.
Graphic Method of Preparing Wage Schedules.
Purchased and Fabricated Parts Inventory Control.
Banner Welding Machine Operation.
Deficient Output of a Tool and Die Shop and Some Corrective Suggestions.
Soy Bean Processing.
History and Establishment of a Farm Supply Inventory Control System.
Method Study of Chemical Analysis of Carotene and Xanthophyll in Grains and Feeds.
Supervisory Training in Personnel Management.
Incentive Standard Set up Applied to the Corner Wheel Operation.
Method of Incentive Checking.
Group Incentive in Herculite Department.
Diking Storage Tanks.
Factors in Setting Up a Casting Production Schedule.

Some Major Considerations in Plant Location.
Duties of a Plant Superintendent.
A Plan to Gain Production Space.
The Establishment of an Incentive System—and Some Results Obtained.
Analysis of Organizational Functions of a Clerical Department.
Application of Scientific Management to the Production of Alcohol.
Scientific Management Approach to Small Structural Engineering Office.
Product Process Chart.
Process Charts Applied to a Laundry Industry.
Getting the Job Evaluation Program Going in the Office.
A Labor Recruiting Program.
Method of Trimming Helmet Ears.
Morale of Employees and Quality of Work.
A New Plant Layout Plan.
Absentee Record of Stitching Department of a Shoe Factory.
Recording Scale for Weighing Wire Bundles.
The Layout and Operating Methods of an Employment Department.
Advisability of Installing Chip Screw Feed on Asplund Defiltrator.
Equipment Survey of Manufacturing Plant for Automotive Clutches.
Business Management Service for Distributorship Operations.
Centralized Purchasing Procedure.
Scheduling Operations of a Garment Company.
Proposed Sewing Room Layout of Proposed New Plant (Garment).
Receiving Raw Materials by Rail versus Water (Barge Line).
Promoting Personnel from the Ranks.
Moving Empty Drums from Storage to Packing Area.
Foreman Training.
Production Efficiency Curves.
Installation of Lubricating Devices.
Shop Rearrangement to Conserve Space and Time.
Reduction of Scrap Parts and Materials.
Assignment of Duties and Responsibilities of Engineering Personnel.
Use of Trucks for Storage to Eliminate Handling.
Scaffolding Casts.
Processing Retirement Deductions of Overseas Civilian Employees.
Stepping Telephone Poles.
Methods Improvement.
Cost Reduction Through Time Studies and Methods Changes.
Part Numbering Plan for Drafting Department.
Authority Responsibilities and Duties of the General Superintendent.
Production Scheduling Plan.
Foreman Training.
Procedure in Setting Up an Inventory Control.

Production Control.

Application and Control of Carbide Tools.

Color Dynamics.

Study of Permanent Type Concrete Ring Tank Foundation Forms Compared to Wooden Forms.

Cost Reductions in Export Packing.

Installation of Trim Rack for Painting and Transporting Trims.

Increased Production and Cost Reduction Through Application of Methods.

Advantages of Installing New Pickling Tank.

Scaling Plank Lumber before Processing for the Blocking Operation.

Scheduling in a Pipe Fabrication Shop.

Qualification Requirements for Promotional and Recruiting Purposes for A-N Branch USAF Aeronautical Chart Plant.

Operation Job Changes and Intercommunication Equipment.

Lighting System in a Cutting Die Shop.

Investigation of Customer Complaints on Appliance Functioning and Corrective Measures.

Factors Involved in Submitting a Quotation for a Low Production Run in a Job Shop.

Equipment for Grog Handling and Plant Clean-Up.

Procedure for Preparation of a Spare Parts Engineering Breakdown.

Plant Layout of Screw Machine Department.

Control of Tubular Equipment Gasket Stocks.

To Improve Efficiency in the Inspection Department.

Conveyor System Tie-In Between Metal Finishing Department and Assembly Line.

Beginning of a Quality Control Department.

Method for Adapting Stores and Maintenance Accounting to Mechanical Tabulation.

Pressing and Folding Shirts on a Conveyor.

Machine Finishing Problem.

Analysis of Organizational Functions of a Clerical Department.

Material Requisition System.

Studies and Analysis for a Budgetary Control in Assembly Section.

Development of a Critical Shipping Weight Table.

SUPPLEMENTARY LIST OF TITLES, FORMAL REPORTS

Motion Picture Film Distribution System in Southern Illinois.
Use of Photo-engraving and Duplicate Plates in Advertising.
The Rate-Bureau System and the Reed-Bullwinkle Act.
Encephalitis in the Skunk.
F. & R. Lazarus Co. Executive Training Program.
Accounting Internship Program at Miami University.
Investment Analysis of Investment Trusts.
Financial Analysis of Chesapeake & Ohio Railroad.

Sorg Paper Co.
Aeronca.
Atlantic Coast Line Railroad.
Electric Auto-Lite Corp.
Anheuser-Busch.
Dayton Rubber Co.
Pennsylvania Railroad Co.
Baldwin Locomotive Works.

Security Analysis of Seven Selected Stocks.

Four Oil Stocks.
Four Grocery Chains.
Four Natural Gas Stocks.
Big Steel.
Oil Firms Operating in the Williston Basin.

Current Automobile Market Trends.
Municipal Income Tax of Springfield, Ohio.

Toledo, Ohio.

Effects of Television on Children's Play Habits.
Juvenile Delinquency Among Children from Broken Homes.
Social Work in Finland.
Social Problems Current Among the Navaho.
Proposed Cost Accounting System for Marion Forge Co.
Reserves on the Balance Sheet.
Capital Gains and Losses on the Balance Sheet.
Four Plant Expansion Alternatives for the Timken Roller Bearing Co.
A Technical Facilities Plan for a College FM Station.

Market Research Report: Alba Tube Starch Co.

Consumer Lipstick Pilot Survey.

Consumer Preference in Restaurant Design and Operation.

The CIO's Attempted Organization of Marvel Schebler Carburetor Co.

Attributes Desired by Public Accounting Firms When Hiring a College Graduate.

Insurance as a Protection for Business Partnership.

Psychological Testing: Current Trends in Industry.

Application Letters: Survey of the Qualities Desired by Personnel Directors.

Corporate Structure and Tax Position of the Miami Foundation.

Organization of the Ben Franklin Department Stores System.

Effects of American Economic Trade Barriers on the Watch Industry of Switzerland Since 1900.

Choice of a Plant Site: Geneva Castings Co.

Survey of Personnel Directors' Opinions on the Possibilities of Advancement for the Salesgirl.

Handling of Grievances at the Acme Motors Co.

Product Development Research Trends.

Recent History of Federal Control of Cosmetic Advertising.

A Credit and Analysis Program.

Testing Advertising Copy.

Tumey vs. Ohio: the Authority of Mayor's Court.

Organized Crime and the American Culture.

Current Problems in Education in Alabama.

Some Aspects of the 19__ Individual Income Tax.

Survey: Taste in Popular Music and Trends in Record-Buying Among College Students.

Foreign Trade of Taiwan Since 1950.

Choice of a Camera to Be Used for Photomicography.

History of Labor Unions in the United States, 1660-1940.

Two Specific Applications of Industrial Television.

Geology of the Area Around Dubois, Wyoming.

Modernization Program of Chicago & Great Western Railway.

Impurities in Marine Boiler Feed Water and Their Effect on Efficiency and Maintenance.

Future Granite Resources in the Barre, Vermont, Area.

Establishing a Greenhouse in Enid, Oklahoma.

A Five-Year Fashion Analysis: Women's Coats.

Should Richmond, Indiana, Have a Better Business Bureau?

Effects of Soil Bacteria: Report of a Controlled Experiment.

Reforestation of the Bachelor Estate.

Predator Habits of the North American Wolf.

Compensation of Salesmen as Influenced by Inflation and Deflation.

Housing Problems in Lafayette, Indiana, 1955.

Analysis of Current Trends in the Paper-Converting Industry in the Chicago Area.

Social Influences on Advertising Policy.

The Nature of Sound.

Mathematical Inversion.

Methods of Measuring Selling Effectiveness on TV.

Changes in the Psychology and Philosophy of Advertising Since 1925.

An Analysis of the Current Condition of Retail Selling in the Shoe Industry.

An Executive Testing Program.

A Business Indicator for the Chrysler Corporation.

SELECTED BIBLIOGRAPHY

Books on Writing

Composition and Rhetoric

DAVIDSON, DONALD. *American Composition and Rhetoric.* 3d ed. New York: Charles Scribner's Sons, 1953.

THOMAS, JOSEPH M., FREDERIC A. MANCHESTER, and FRANKLIN W. SCOTT. *Composition for College Students.* 5th ed. New York: Macmillan Co., 1948.

WARFEL, HARRY R., ERNST G. MATHEWS, and JOHN C. BUSHMAN. *American College English.* New York: American Book Co., 1949.

Handbooks of Composition

FOERSTER, NORMAN, J. M. STEADMAN, and JAMES B. MCMILLAN. *Writing and Thinking.* 5th ed. Boston: Houghton Mifflin Co., 1952.

HODGES, JOHN C. *Harbrace College Handbook.* 3d ed. New York: Harcourt, Brace & Co., 1951.

KIERZEK, JOHN M. *The Macmillan Handbook of English.* 3d ed. New York: Macmillan Co., 1954.

PERRIN, PORTER G. *Writer's Guide and Index to English.* Rev. ed. Chicago: Scott, Foresman & Co., 1950.

Manuals for Term Papers, Theses, and Reports

ALBAUGH, RALPH M. *Thesis Writing.* Ames, Iowa: Littlefield, Adams & Co., 1951.

CAMPBELL, WILLIAM G. *Form and Style in Thesis Writing.* Boston: Houghton Mifflin Co., 1954.

Government Printing Office Style Manual. Rev. ed. Washington: Government Printing Office, 1953.

LUTZ, R. R. *Graphic Presentation Simplified.* New York: Funk & Wagnalls Co., 1949.

A Manual of Style. 11th ed. Chicago: University of Chicago Press, 1949.

PARKER, WILLIAM R. *The MLA Style Sheet.* New York: Modern Language Association, 1951.

TRELEASE, SAM F. *The Scientific Paper: How to Prepare It, How to Write It.* Baltimore: Williams & Wilkins Co., 1947.

TURABIAN, KATE L. *A Manual for Writers of Dissertations.* Chicago: University of Chicago Press, 1949.

WILLIAMS, CECIL B., and ALLAN H. STEVENSON. *A Research Manual.* Rev. ed. New York: Harper & Bros., 1951.

General

CHASE, STUART. *Power of Words.* New York: Harcourt, Brace & Co., 1954.

FLESCH, RUDOLF. *The Art of Readable Writing.* New York: Harper & Bros., 1949.

FLESCH, RUDOLF. *How to Make Sense.* New York: Harper & Bros., 1954.

HAYAKAWA, S. I. *Language in Thought and Action.* New York: Harcourt, Brace & Co., 1949.

LARSON, SPENCER A. *Better Business Communications.* Detroit: Wayne University Press, 1952.

SAUNDERS, A. G., and C. R. ANDERSON. *Business Reports.* New York: McGraw-Hill Book Co., Inc., 1940.

SHIDLE, NORMAN G. *Clear Writing for Easy Reading.* New York: McGraw-Hill Book Co., Inc., 1951.

WHYTE, WILLIAM H. *Is Anybody Listening?* New York: Simon & Schuster, Inc., 1952.

WILKINSON, C. W., J. H. MENNING, and C. R. ANDERSON, eds. *Writing for Business.* Chicago: Richard D. Irwin, Inc., 1951.

Reference Books

Guides and Bibliographies

ALEXANDER, CARTER, and A. J. BURKE. *How to Locate Educational Information and Data.* New York: Teachers College, Columbia University, 1950.

Bibliographic Index: A Cumulative Bibliography of Bibliographies. New York: H. W. Wilson Co., 1938 and later.

COMAN, EDWIN T. *Sources of Business Information.* New York: Prentice-Hall, Inc., 1949.

DALTON, BLANCHE H. *Sources of Engineering Information.* Berkeley: University of California Press, 1948.

Handbook of Latin American Studies, 1935. Cambridge: Harvard University Press, 1936 and later.

WILLIAMS, CECIL B., and ALLAN H. STEVENSON. *A Research Manual.* New York: Harper & Bros., 1951.

WINCHELL, CONSTANCE M. *Guide to Reference Books.* 6th ed. Chicago: American Library Association, 1951.

Encyclopedias: General

Columbia Encyclopedia. 2d ed. New York: Columbia University Press, 1950.

Encyclopedia Americana. New York: Americana Corp. 30 vols. 1952.

Encyclopaedia Britannica. Chicago: Encyclopaedia Britannica, Inc., 1953. 24 vols. Published in cooperation with the University of Chicago.

Encyclopedias: Specialized

Encyclopedia of Chemical Technology. New York: Interscience Encyclopedia. In process, 1947 and later.

Encyclopaedia of the Social Sciences. New York: Macmillan Co., 1930-35. 15 vols. Reissue in 8 vols., 1948.

Hutchinson's Technical and Scientific Encyclopedia. New York: Macmillan Co., 1936. 4 vols.

MONROE, W. S. *Encyclopedia of Educational Research.* Rev. ed. New York: Macmillan Co., 1950.

Yearbooks

American Year Book, 1910-1919; 1925. New York: American Yearbook Corp., 1911 and later.

Americana Annual. New York: Americana Corp., 1923 and later.

Book of the States. Chicago: Council of State Governments, 1935 and later. Biennial.

Britannica Book of the Year. Chicago: Encyclopaedia Britannica, Inc., 1938 and later.

Commodity Year Book. New York: Commodity Research Bureau, 1939 and later.

Municipal Year Book. Chicago: International City Managers Association, 1934 and later.

Social Work Year Book. New York: Russell Sage Foundation, 1929 and later. Biennial.

Statistical Abstract of the United States, 1878 and later. Washington: Government Printing Office, 1879 and later.

World Almanac and Book of Facts. New York: World-Telegram, 1868 and later.

Dictionaries: Word

The American College Dictionary. New York: Harper & Bros., 1947.

New Standard Dictionary. New York: Funk & Wagnalls Co., 1913. Plate revisions, 1938 and later.

Webster's New Collegiate Dictionary. Springfield, Mass.: G. & C. Merriam Co., 1949.

Webster's New International Dictionary. Springfield, Mass.: G. & C. Merriam Co., 1950.

Dictionaries: Biographical

Current Biography, Who's Who in the News and Why. New York: H. W. Wilson Co., 1941 and later.

Dictionary of American Biography. New York: Charles Scribner's Sons, 1928-37. 20 vols. and index. Supplements.

Webster's Biographical Dictionary. Springfield, Mass.: G. & C. Merriam Co., 1943.

Who's Who in America, 1899, 1900 (and later). Chicago: A. N. Marquis, 1899 and later.

Who's Who in Commerce and Industry. Chicago: A. N. Marquis Co., 1953.

Who's Who in Engineering. New York: Lewis Historical Publishing Co., 1948.

Who Knows—and What. Chicago: A. N. Marquis Co., 1954.

Dictionaries: Miscellaneous

Dictionary of American History. New York: Charles Scribner's Sons, 1940.

SCHWARTZ, ROBERT. *Dictionary of Business and Industry.* New York: B. C. Forbes & Sons Co., 1954.

Webster's Geographical Dictionary. Springfield, Mass.: G. & C. Merriam, 1949.

Atlases:

Encyclopaedia Britannica World Atlas. Chicago: Encyclopaedia Britannica, Inc., 1952.

Hammond's Standard World Atlas. New York: C. S. Hammond & Co., Inc., 1953.

Rand, McNally Commercial Atlas and Marketing Guide. 84th ed. Chicago: Rand, McNally & Co., 1954.

Catalogues

LEIDY, W. PHILIP. *A Popular Guide to Government Publications.* New York: Columbia University Press, 1953.

Publishers' Trade List Annual. New York: R. R. Bowker Co., 1872 and later. 2 vols. plus index vol.

United States Catalog: Books in Print. New York: H. W. Wilson Co., 1928. Supplements, called *Cumulative Book Index,* 1928 and later.

United States Government Publications: Monthly Catalog. Washington: Government Printing Office, 1895 and later.

U.S. BUREAU OF THE CENSUS. *Census Publications, Catalog and Subject Guide.* Washington: Government Printing Office, 1947 and later. Quarterly.

U.S. DEPARTMENT OF COMMERCE. *List of Selected Publications of the Bureau of Foreign and Domestic Commerce.* Washington: Government Printing Office. Annually.

Periodical Indexes

AYER, N. W., & SON. *Directory of Newspapers and Periodicals.* Philadelphia: N. W. Ayer & Son, 1880 and later.

Book Review Digest, 1905. New York: H. W. Wilson Co., 1906.

BOWERMAN, ELIZABETH G. *Union List of Technical Periodicals.* 3d ed. New York: Special Libraries Association, 1947.

Canadian Index: A Guide to Canadian Periodicals and Films, 1948 and later. Ottawa: Canadian Library Association, 1948 and later.

Engineering Index, 1884 and later. New York: Engineering Magazine, 1892-1919; American Society of Mechanical Engineers, 1920 and later.

GREGORY, WINIFRED. *American Newspapers, 1821-1936: A Union List.* New York: H. W. Wilson Co., 1937.

———. *Union List of Serials in Libraries of the United States and Canada.* New York: H. W. Wilson Co., 1943. Supplements.

Industrial Arts Index, 1913 and later. New York: H. W. Wilson Co., 1913 and later.

International Index to Periodicals, 1907 and later. New York: H. W. Wilson Co., 1916 and later.

New York Times Index, 1913 and later. New York: New York Times, 1913 and later.

Nineteenth Century Readers' Guide, 1890-1899. New York: H. W. Wilson Co., 1945.

Poole's Index to Periodical Literature, 1802-1906. Boston: Houghton Mifflin Co., 1882-1908.

Public Affairs Information Service (PAIS), 1915 and later. New York: Public Affairs Information Service, 1915 and later. Includes books, pamphlets, documents.

Readers' Guide to Periodical Literature, 1900 and later. New York: H. W. Wilson Co., 1905 and later.

Technical Book Review Index. New York: Special Libraries Association, 1935 and later. Also published 1917-28. Pittsburgh: Carnegie Library, 1917-29.

Library Resources: Miscellaneous

Special Library Resources. New York: Special Libraries Association, 1941-47. 3 vols.

Union List of Microfilms. Philadelphia: University of Pennsylvania, 1942. Supplements.

Vertical File Service Catalog: An Annotated Subject Catalog of Pamphlets, 1900-33. New York: H. W. Wilson Co., 1934. Supplements.

Business Directories and Services

American Business Directories. Washington: U.S. Domestic Commerce Office, 1947.

BROWN, STANLEY M., *et al.*, eds. *Business Executive's Handbook.* New York: Prentice-Hall, Inc., 1953.

Business Literature. Newark, N. J.: Newark Public Library. Monthly, 1928 and later.

Daily Report for Executives. Washington: Bureau of National Affairs.

DAVIS, MARJORIE V. *Guide to American Business Directories.* Washington: Public Affairs Press, 1948.

Dun & Bradstreet's Reference Book. New York: Dun & Bradstreet, Inc. Annually.

Kiplinger Washington Letter. Washington: Kiplinger Washington Agency. Weekly.

Poor's Register of Directors and Executives. New York: Standard and Poor's Publishing Co. Annually, 1928 and later. Quarterly supplements.

The United States News and World Report. Washington: United States News Publishing Corp. Weekly.

Whaley-Eaton American Letter. Washington: Whaley-Eaton Service. Weekly. Whaley-Eaton also publish a *Foreign Letter.*

See also such magazines as *Business Week, Fortune, Harvard Business Review, Journal of Business, Nation's Business, Newsweek,* and *Time.*

Report Writing Fields

Accounting and Statistics

FINNEY, HARRY A. *Principles of Accounting.* 4th ed. New York: Prentice-Hall, Inc., 1951-52. Vol. I, Intermediate; Vol. II, Advanced. Introductory, 4th ed., 1953.

LANG, THEODORE, ed. *Cost Accountants' Handbook.* New York: The Ronald Press Co., 1944.

PATON, WILLIAM A., ed. *Accountants' Handbook.* 3d ed. New York: The Ronald Press Co., 1943.

See also *Journal of Accountancy,* monthly; *Accounting Review,* quarterly.

GOVERNMENT STATISTICS BUREAU. *The Handbook of Basic Economic Statistics.* Washington: Government Statistics Bureau. Annually, 1947 and later.

HAUSER, PHILIP M., and WILLIAM L. LEONARD, eds. *Government Statistics for Business Use.* New York: John Wiley & Sons, Inc., 1946.

SMITH, J. G., and A. J. DUNCAN. *Fundamentals of the Theory of Statistics.* New York: McGraw-Hill Book Co., Inc., 1945. 2 vols.

U.S. BUREAU OF THE CENSUS. *Statistical Abstract of the United States.* Washington: Government Printing Office. Annually, 1879 and later.

Periodicals: *Dun's Statistical Review, Journal of the American Statistical Association, Review of Economic Statistics, Survey of Current Business.*

Advertising and Marketing

ASPLEY, JOHN C., ed. *The Sales Manager's Handbook.* 6th ed. Chicago: Dartnell Corp., 1949.

FREY, A. W. *Advertising.* 2d ed. New York: The Ronald Press Co., 1953.

KLEPPNER, OTTO. *Advertising Procedure.* 4th ed. New York: Prentice-Hall, Inc., 1950.

MAYNARD, H. A., and T. N. BECKMAN. *Principles of Marketing.* 5th ed. New York: The Ronald Press Co., 1952.

Standard Rate and Data Service. Chicago: Standard Rate and Data Service, Inc. Monthly.

U.S. Bureau of the Census. *Census of Business.* Washington: Government Printing Office, 1951-52. 7 vols.

U.S. Department of Commerce. *Market Research Sources.* Washington: Government Printing Office, 1950.

WINGATE, M. W., and N. A. BRISCO. *Buying for Retail Stores.* 3d ed. New York: Prentice-Hall, Inc., 1953.

Periodicals: *Advertising Age, Advertising and Selling, Chain Store Age, Dun's Review and Modern Industry, Journal of Marketing, Journal of Retailing, Printers' Ink, Sales Management, Tide.*

Finance

BOGEN, JULES I., *et al.*, eds. *Financial Handbook.* 3d ed. New York: The Ronald Press Co., 1948.

DAUTEN, CARL A. *Business Finance.* New York: Prentice-Hall, Inc., 1948.

MUNN, GLENN G. *Encyclopedia of Banking and Finance.* 5th ed. New York: The Bankers Publishing Co., 1949.

Periodicals: *American Banker, Banking Journal of the American Bankers Association, Barron's National Business and Financial Weekly, Journal of Commerce, Wall Street Journal.*

Foreign Trade

Exporters' Encyclopedia. New York: Thomas Ashwell and Co. Annual.

HENIUS, FRANK. *Dictionary of Foreign Trade.* New York: Prentice-Hall, Inc., 1947.

PAN AMERICAN ASSOCIATES. *Pan-American Yearbook.* New York: Macmillan Co. Annually.

PRATT, E. E. *The Foreign Trade Handbook.* Chicago: Dartnell Corp., 1952.

U.S. BUREAU OF FOREIGN AND DOMESTIC COMMERCE. *Summary of Foreign Trade of the United States.* Washington: Government Printing Office. Annually and Monthly.

VAN CLEEF, EUGENE. *Getting into Foreign Trade.* New York: The Ronald Press Co., 1946.

Periodicals: *American Exporter, Commercial America, Foreign Commerce Weekly.*

Industry and Industrial Relations

ASPLEY, JOHN C., and EUGENE WHITMORE. *Handbook of Industrial Relations.* Chicago: Dartnell Corp., 1952.

DICKERMAN, MARIAN, and RUTH TAYLOR. *Who's Who in Labor.* New York: Dryden Press, Inc., 1946.

Industrial Marketing: Market Data Book Number. Chicago: Advertising Publications. Annually.

INSTITUTE OF LABOR STUDIES. *Yearbook of American Labor.* Northampton, Mass.: Institute of Labor Studies. Biennial.

INTERNATIONAL LABOUR OFFICE. *Yearbook of Labour Statistics.* Geneva: International Labour Office, 1953. Brought up to date monthly in *International Labour Review.*

NATIONAL INDUSTRIAL CONFERENCE BOARD. *The Management Almanac.* New York: National Industrial Conference Board, 1946. Brought up to date monthly in *The Conference Board Management Record.*

Thomas' Register of American Manufacturers. New York: Thomas Publishing Co. Annually.

YODER, DALE. *Personnel Management and Industrial Relations.* 3d ed. New York: Prentice-Hall, Inc., 1948.

———. *Personnel Principles and Policies.* New York: Prentice-Hall, Inc., 1952.

Periodicals: *Advanced Management, Ceramic Age, Chemical Engineering, Factory Management and Maintenance, Industrial Relations Magazine, Personnel, Personnel Journal, Progressive Architecture, The Rubber Age.*

For divisions of industry, such as Building, Electrical Equipment Industries, Petroleum, Textiles, etc., see Coman, *Sources of Business Information.*

Management

NATIONAL OFFICE MANAGEMENT ASSOCIATION: RESEARCH COMMITTEE. *Bibliography for Office Managers.* Philadelphia: National Office Management Association, 1945.

ALFORD, LEON P., and H. RUSSELL BEATTY. *Principles of Industrial Management.* Rev. ed. New York: The Ronald Press Co., 1951.

ALFORD, LEON P., and JOHN R. BANGS, eds. *Production Handbook.* New York: The Ronald Press Co., 1944.

BONN, A. E. *The Management Dictionary.* New York: Exposition Press, 1952.

HALSEY, GEORGE D. *Handbook of Personnel Management.* Rev. ed. New York: Harper & Bros., 1953.

TERRY, GEORGE. *Office Management and Control.* Rev. ed. Homewood, Illinois: Richard D. Irwin, 1953.

Periodicals: *Advanced Management, Factory Management and Maintenance, Management Review.*

Real Estate and Insurance

CROBAUGH, CLYDE J. *Handbook on Insurance.* 2d ed. New York: Prentice-Hall, Inc., 1949.

HOLMES, L. G., and CARRIE M. JONES. *The Real Estate Handbook.* New York: Prentice-Hall, Inc., 1949.

The Insurance Almanac. New York: The Underwriter Printing and Publishing Co., 1912 and later. Annually.

MAGEE, JOHN H. *Property Insurance.* 2d ed. Chicago: Richard D. Irwin, 1946.

Unique Manual of Insurance. Cincinnati: National Underwriter Co., 1954. Annually.

Periodicals: *American Builder, Architectural Forum, Building Reporter and Realty News, Buildings, Journal of Real Estate Management, Operative Builder and Contractor. Best's Insurance News, Journal of Commerce, National Underwriter.*

Science: Biological and Physical

DENNIS, W. K. *Recent Aeronautical Literature.* Wichita, Kansas: Beech Aircraft Corp., 1947.

HAWKINS, R. R. *Scientific, Medical, and Technical Books.* New York: R. R. Bowker Co., 1946.

An International Bibliography on Atomic Energy. Lake Success, New York: Atomic Energy Commission Group, United Nations, 1949. Supplements.

LIGHT, ISRAEL. *Annotated Bibliography on Atomic Energy.* New York: Teachers College, Columbia University, 1947.

PARKE, N. G. *Guide to the Literature of Mathematics and Physics.* New York: McGraw-Hill Book Co., Inc., 1947.

SOULE, BYRON A. *Library Guide for the Chemist.* New York: McGraw-Hill Book Co., Inc., 1938.

Van Nostrand's Scientific Encyclopedia. New York: D. Van Nostrand Co., Inc., 1947.

WRIGHT, JOHN K., and ELIZABETH T. PRATT. *Aids to Geographical Research.* New York: Columbia University Press, 1947.

Periodicals: *Aeronautical Engineering Review, Chemical Abstracts, Industrial and Engineering Chemistry, Science News Letter, Science Abstracts.*

Science: Social

BALDWIN, J. M., ed. *Dictionary of Philosophy and Psychology.* New York: Peter Smith, 1949. 3 vols. in 4.

BEERS, HENRY P. *Bibliographies in American History.* New York: H. W. Wilson Co., 1942.

BURCHFIELD, LAVERNE. *Our Rural Communities.* Chicago: Public Administration Service, 1947.

GOOD, CARTER V., and DOUGLAS E. SCATES. *Methods of Research, Educational, Psychological, Sociological.* New York: Appleton-Century-Crofts, Inc., 1954.

HIRSHBERG, H. S., and C. H. MELINAT. *Subject Guide to United States Government Publications.* Chicago: American Library Association, 1947.

INTERNATIONAL COUNCIL ON RELIGIOUS EDUCATION. *Classified Bibliography of Youth Publications.* Chicago: United Christian Youth Movement, 1948.

SECKLER-HUDSON, CATHERYN. *Bibliography on Public Administration.* Washington: American University Press, 1949.

Periodicals: *American Journal of Sociology, American Political Science Review, Economic Journal, Mississippi Valley Historical Review, Sociology and Social Research.*

Transportation

AIRCRAFT ASSOCIATION OF AMERICA. *Aircraft Year Book.* Washington: Lincoln Press, 1953.

American Aviation Directory. Washington: American Aviation Publications, 1939 and later. Semi-annually.

ASSOCIATION OF AMERICAN RAILROADS. *Railway Literature:* A Bibliography. Washington: Association of American Railroads, 1942.

————. *Transportation in America.* Washington: Association of American Railroads, 1947.

Automobile Facts and Figures. Detroit: Automobile Manufacturers Association. Annually.

FREDERICK, JOHN H. *Commercial Air Transportation.* Chicago: Richard D. Irwin, 1951.

Who's Who in Railroading in North America. New York: Boardman Publishing Corp., 1949.

Periodicals: *Aero Digest, Air Transportation, American Aviation, Aviation Week, Railway Age, Railway Mechanical Engineer, Transportation Supply News. Automotive Digest, Bus Transportation, Transport Topics.*

Selected Articles in Periodicals

ALLEN, L. A. "Five Keys to Better Report Writing." *Mill and Factory.* 50 (April, 1952), 85-87.

BELLO, FRANCIS. "The Information Theory." *Fortune,* 48 (December, 1953), 136-58.

BUSCHMANN, A. D. "Management Needs Good Maintenance Reports." *Factory Management,* 112 (April, 1954), 130-31.

CHASE, STUART. "How Language Shapes Our Thoughts." *Harper's Magazine,* 208 (April, 1954), 76-82.

COLLINS, JAMES H. "The Ordeal of the Annual Report." *Public Utilities Fortnightly,* 52 (November 19, 1953), 772-79.

DORIS, LILLIAN. "How to Prepare Written Material for General Use or Publication." *The ABWA Bulletin,* 17 (March, 1953), 4-16.

HAYAKAWA, S. I. "Semantics." *Etc.: A Review of General Semantics,* 9 (Summer, 1952), 243-57.

KNOWLTON, DON. "The Semantics of Annual Reports." *Accountancy Review,* 22 (October, 1947), 360-66.

MATTILL, JOHN I. "Writing as Communication: The Engineer Must Learn How to Reach His Constituents." *The Journal of Engineering Education,* 44 (April, 1954), 476-79.

MERRILL, PAUL W. "The Principles of Poor Writing." *The Scientific Monthly,* 64 (January, 1947), 72-74.

MILES, STEPHEN B. "Report Writing." *The ABWA Bulletin,* 16 (December, 1951), 3-9.

NEIKIRK, W. W. "Organizing the Business Report." *N.A.C.A. Bulletin,* 30 (October 15, 1948), 193-204.

RAPOPORT, ANATOL. "What Is Information?" *Etc.: A Review of General Semantics,* 10 (Summer, 1953), 247-60.

ROLPH, S. W. "Strong Case for Standardization of Modern Business Reports." *Advertising Management,* 19 (March, 1954), 9-11.

SLATE, F. O. "Organization of the Technical Report." *Journal of Chemical Education,* 23 (September, 1946), 439-40.

SOUTHER, J. W. "Applying the Engineering Method to Report Writing." *Machine Design,* 24 (December, 1952), 114-18.

STRUCK, HERMAN R. "Recommended Diet for Padded Writing." *Science,* 119 (April 23, 1954), 522-25.

SUHR, D. C. "Increasing Foreman Effectiveness with Management Reports." *Management Review,* 42 (March, 1953), 153-54.

TONG, KIN NEE. "Helping the Student Master the Art of Thinking." *The Journal of Engineering Education,* 44 (November, 1953), 169-72.

WHORF, BENJAMIN LEE. "Language, Mind, and Reality." *Etc.: A Review of General Semantics,* 9 (Spring, 1952), 167-88.

INDEX